THE NAVAL AVIATION GUIDE

THE NAVAL AVIATION GUIDE

FIFTH EDITION

Edited by
Lt. Cdr. Richard R. Burgess, USN (Ret.)

Naval Institute Press
Annapolis, Maryland

© 1996 by the United States Naval Institute
Annapolis, Maryland

Portions of this book were originally published as *The Naval Aviator's Guide*, copyright © 1963 by the United States Naval Institute.

All rights reserved. No part of this book may be reproduced without written permission from the publisher.

Library of Congress Cataloging-in-Publication Data
The naval aviation guide. — 5th ed. / edited by Richard R. Burgess.
    p.   cm.
  Includes bibliographical references and index.
  ISBN 1-55750-611-6 (alk. paper)
  1. United States. Navy—Aviation.   2. United States. Navy—Officers' handbooks.
I. Burgess, Richard R., 1953–
VG93.N34   1996
359.9'4'00973—dc20   96-12124

Printed in the United States of America on acid-free paper ∞
03 02 01 00 99 98 97 96   9 8 7 6 5 4 3 2
First printing

*Dedicated to
Robert L. Lawson
who has inspired so many in the appreciation and
preservation of naval aviation heritage*

Contents

	Preface	ix
	Acknowledgments	xi
1	Naval Aviation: The Legacy	1
2	Wings: The Challenge	55
3	The Squadron	83
4	A Naval Aviation Career	107
5	Naval Aviation Organization	137
6	The Aircraft Carrier	158
7	Aviation Enlisted Ratings	187
8	Acquisition and Support: The Naval Aviation Systems Team	214
9	Safety and NATOPS	230
10	Aerospace Medicine	240
11	The Naval Air Reserve	259

| 12 | Marine Corps Aviation | 275 |
| 13 | Coast Guard Aviation | 296 |

Appendixes

A	Navy Wings	311
B	Naval Aircraft	316
C	Naval Aviation Ships	327
D	Naval Aircraft Squadrons	331
E	Marine Corps Aircraft Squadrons	339
F	Squadron Aircraft Markings	343
G	Navy and Marine Corps Air Stations and Facilities	346
H	Coast Guard Air Stations and Facilities	351
I	The Blue Angels	353
J	Naval Aviation in Space	356
K	Naval Aviation Hall of Honor	359
L	Medal of Honor Winners	369
M	Aces and MiG Killers	374
N	Naval Aviation Associations and Museums	386
O	Naval Aviation Periodicals	395
P	Suggested Reading and Reference	398
Q	Naval Aviation Acronyms, Abbreviations, and Terms	402

Index 423

PREFACE

The fifth edition of *The Naval Aviation Guide* comes into print over a decade after the advent of the fourth edition. Naval aviation has undergone tremendous change in the interim, with the end of the Cold War, a war in southwest Asia, and considerable organizational change and downsizing. Readers of the previous edition will recognize a continuation of the style of that edition, and even elements included in the first edition, written by Capt. Malcolm W. Cagle and published in 1963 as *The Naval Aviator's Guide*.

This edition of *The Naval Aviation Guide*, like the previous one, is designed to be an informative, concise, and useful tool for the naval aviation profession. It amasses a large amount of information which is, for the most part, available in a variety of other sources but which is more accessible under one cover. Every major facet of naval aviation is treated in this volume, from its origins and development to its organizational relationships and working parts. Seventeen appendixes provide additional ready-reference material to help answer day-to-day questions or simply to satisfy the reader's curiosity.

The Naval Aviation Guide is an introduction for those considering that first step into the exciting world of naval aviation as well as for those already earning their wings of gold. The guide should prove helpful to naval aviators, naval flight officers, and other naval aviation personnel beginning their careers, and it should serve as a handy reference source for old hands. And for anyone, military or civilian, professional aviator or armchair pilot, who wants to learn more about the profession, this guide is designed to present a clear picture of an important aspect of naval warfare as it approaches its second century.

All of the chapters and appendixes are revisions—in most cases substantial revisions—of those of the previous edition. Information in each has been carefully edited and updated to reflect recent developments.

Acknowledgments

A reference work such as *The Naval Aviation Guide* contains thousands of facts, impossible for one author to have at his fingertips. Hence, this edition is the fruit of many individuals who provided facts, photographs, and drawings, and, of course, it still reflects the efforts of the contributors acknowledged in previous editions.

All chapters and appendixes from the previous edition have been revised extensively by the editor or revisers, but still retain text from their original authors or revisers: Cdr. Jess Barrow, USCGR (Ret.); Capt. Paolo Coletta, USNR (Ret.); Capt. J. J. Coonan, USN; Maj. John Elliott, USMC (Ret.); CWO J. Emmert, USN; JOCS Kirby Harrison, USN; Capt. Richard Knott, USN; Cdr. Peter Mersky, USNR; Capt. John Noll, MC, USN; Capt. Albert Raithel, USN (Ret.); Capt. Rosario Rausa, USNR (Ret.); Lt. Peter Reynierse, USNR; Cdr. Van N. Stewart, USN; Rear Adm. Jeremy Taylor, USN; and Mr. Robert H. Thompson.

The following individuals graciously made major revisions to chapters within their expertise. Dr. William J. Armstrong, Naval Air Systems Command Historian, made a complete revision of his chapter on the Naval Aviation Systems Team. Cdr. John W. Mills, MC, USN, revised the chapter on aerospace medicine.

Special thanks are due to Norman Polmar, who gave useful guidance and detailed suggestions in revisions for this edition.

The following individuals provided research assistance, references, and leads in answering the hundreds of questions necessary for a revision of such scale: Roy Grossnick, Judith Walters, Gwendolyn Rich, and Steven Hill of the Naval Aviation History Office of the Naval Historical Center; Sandy Russell, Charles Cooney, Joan Frasher, Hal Andrews, JOC Jim Richeson, JO1 Eric Sesit, and JO1 Milinda Jensen of *Naval Aviation News* magazine; Capt. Steven U. Ramsdell, USN, and Cdr. Steven Silverio, USN, of the Naval Aviation History and Publication Division, Naval Historical Center; John C. Reilly of the Ships History Branch, Naval Historical Center; Robert L. Lawson; Robert F. Dorr; Capt. Richard C. Knott, USN (Ret.); Capt. Al Raithel, USN (Ret.); Capt. Rosario Rausa, USNR (Ret.), editor of the Association of Naval Aviation's *Wings of Gold* magazine; Capt. Earl Rogers of the Naval Aviation Museum Foundation; Cdr. Peter B. Mersky, USNR (Ret.), of *Approach/Mech* magazine; Maj. John Elliott, USMC (Ret.); Capt. Steve Millikin, USN (Ret.), Cdr. Jan C. Jacobs, USNR (Ret.), and Michael Weeks of *The Hook* magazine; John Gresham; Bud Joyce; Lee Saegesser of the National Aeronautical and Space Administration's historian office; Lt.(jg) Michael Schneider of the navy's Chief of Information office; Capt. Marty Reagan, USN (Ret.); Capt. Marion "Gus" Shrode, USCG (Ret.); Cdr. Mark Johnson, USNR, Cdr. Vic Ristvedt, USNR, Lt. Cdr. T. B. Floyd, USN, Lt. Cdr. Steve Smith, USN, and Linda Crawford of the office of Director, Air Warfare, Office of the Chief of Naval Operations; and Maj. Paula Bogdewich, USMC, of Headquarters, Marine Corps.

Photographic and art support was provided by Russell D. Egnor and JOC Rick Toppings of the News Photo Division, Chief of Information; Wayne Paugh and PA1 Telfair Brown, USCG, of Headquarters, U.S. Coast Guard; Sandy Russell; Charles Cooney; Robert L. Lawson; Robert F. Dorr; Bob Harper, editor of *Airborne Log*; Cdr. Peter B. Mersky, USNR (Ret.); and Valerie McCann of the Emil Buehler Naval Aviation Library of the National Museum of Naval Aviation.

Many periodicals and newspapers proved to be excellent sources of reference for information on naval aviation: *Naval Aviation News*; *Wings of Gold*; *The Hook*; *Foundation*; *Flyby*; *Navy Times*; *U.S. Naval Institute Proceedings*; *Aviation Week and Space Technology*; *Approach/Mech*; the

Yellow Sheet; *Marine Corps Gazette*; *Flightlines*; *World Air Power Journal*; *Airborne Log*; *Maritime Patrol*; *Sea Power*; *Soundings*; the *Virginian Pilot*; the *Washington Times*; and *British Aviation Review*.

Excellent support was provided by the Naval Institute staff and copy editor Melissa McNitt.

Last but not least, I express my appreciation to my wife, Eleanor, and to my children for their unlimited patience while this work was in progress.

THE NAVAL AVIATION GUIDE

ONE

NAVAL AVIATION: THE LEGACY

Revised from an original chapter written by
Capt. Albert L. Raithel, USN (Ret.)

The Pioneers

At its inception, naval aviation, the projection of naval warfare into the air, was a revolutionary idea with far-reaching effects. With all the advantages of hindsight, we today can appreciate the impact naval aviation has had on our national defense and the wisdom of those who spurred its development. But this was not always the prevailing view; naval officers who championed the idea of naval aviation did so at considerable risk to their careers and their credibility. Yet they persisted, and it was only through their foresight and determination that naval aviation eventually came into its own.

Five years after the Wright brothers flew their aeroplane at Kitty Hawk, North Carolina, in 1903, a joint board was convened at Fort Myers, Virginia, to evaluate the Wright aircraft for possible military use. Lt. George C. Sweet, the navy member, and Naval Constructor William McEntee observed the demonstration flights, which ended in tragedy when the army pilot was killed in a crash. Despite this sobering turn of events, Lieutenant Sweet was impressed with the potential of the aeroplane and recommended the purchase of four aircraft for adaptation for naval use. However, the secretary of the navy, who had also observed the trials, was more impressed by the crash, and no further action was taken.

In 1910, the navy appointed Capt. Washington Irving Chambers to keep himself informed on the progress of aviation. That fall he met inventor-aviator Glenn Curtiss and Eugene Ely, an associate of Curtiss. Curtiss and Chambers soon embarked on a series of dramatic demonstrations to show the adaptability of the aeroplane to the navy.

On 14 November 1910, Ely successfully flew from a platform hastily erected on the cruiser *Birmingham* (CL 2) at Norfolk, Virginia, becoming the first man to fly an aircraft from a ship. This flight generated enormous interest in the United States and abroad, but it did not prompt the navy to provide funds for the purchase of aircraft. Curtiss, moving his aviation camp to California for the winter, teamed up again with Chambers and offered to instruct a naval officer to fly a Curtiss plane at no cost to the government. Lt. T. G. "Spuds" Ellyson, a submariner, was ordered to the Curtiss camp at North Island, California, to become the first U.S. naval aviator.

Ely made the first shipboard landing of an aircraft on 18 January 1911, touching down on a platform installed on the armored cruiser *Pennsylvania* (ACR 4). Ely launched and returned to the beach the same morning. A month later, Curtiss landed the world's first practical seaplane (one that he had designed with Ellyson's assistance) alongside the *Pennsylvania,* and crew members hoisted the plane on board with the ship's boat crane. Following the success of these demonstrations, Chambers prepared the requisition to purchase two Curtiss biplanes, the navy's first aircraft. That day, 8 May 1911, is considered the official birthday of naval aviation.

The first of the two Curtiss aircraft was called the Triad, because it could operate from the land, from the sea, and in the air. Later, an aircraft was purchased from the Wrights. These two manufacturers each agreed to train a pilot and a mechanic to fly the aircraft that they sold to the navy. Lts. John Rodgers and John H. Towers thus became the navy's second and third aviators, respectively.

Captain Chambers established the first naval air station at Greenbury Point near the Naval Academy at Annapolis, Maryland, on 27 June 1911. Much valuable experience was gained there, including the first night operations. The fliers moved back to North Island for the winter of 1911–12, returning to Annapolis in the spring. In May 1912, 1st Lt. Alfred A.

Cunningham reported for training to become the marine corps's first aviator.

The aeroplane had yet to prove itself an asset in the conduct of naval warfare, so Captain Chambers arranged to move the aviation camp to Guantanamo Bay, Cuba, for the first practical tests with the fleet. Five planes and all of the navy's aviators and student aviators deployed there, with the objective of proving the value of aircraft for scouting, to test the ability of the aircraft to detect submerged submarines and mines, and to indoctrinate as many fleet officers as possible on the fleet potential of the aircraft.

First Call to Action

The aviation camp, now under Lieutenant Towers, moved to Pensacola, Florida, where an aeronautical station was established under the command of Lt. Cdr. H. C. Mustin. Not long after arrival, the majority of aviation personnel and equipment deployed in April 1914 to Mexico under Mustin's overall command. A detachment under Towers sailed to Tampico on board the *Birmingham,* while Lt. Patrick N. L. Bellinger and his detachment on board the *Mississippi* (BB 23) went to Veracruz, where they hunted for mines and flew scouting missions for troops ashore. On one mission, Bellinger's aircraft sustained damage from rifle fire, naval aviation's first combat damage.

Aviation was formally recognized by the navy on 1 July 1914 with the establishment of the Office of Naval Aeronautics in the Division of Operations under the secretary of the navy. Between 1914 and 1917, the navy concentrated on the problem of taking planes to sea on existing warships. The *North Carolina* (ACR 12) was fitted with a catapult, and on 5 November 1915, Lieutenant Commander Mustin was successfully launched with the ship under way in Pensacola Bay.

Following his return from the Mexican expedition, Lieutenant Towers assisted with the testing of the Curtiss flying boat *America* at the Curtiss facility in Hammondsport, New York. The *America,* designed to attempt the world's first flight across the Atlantic, was canceled with the outbreak of World War I but served as a prototype of the flying boats that dominated maritime patrol activities of the U.S. and British navies during and immediately after World War I.

World War I

Events in August 1916 laid the foundation for the rapid expansion of naval aviation when the United States entered World War I. The Appropriations Act of 29 August 1916 provided 3.5 million dollars for aeronautics, authorized the formation of a naval flying corps and a naval reserve counterpart, and provided for a commission to make recommendations for expansion of naval aviation shore facilities. Soon the navy had its first large-scale production contract, for thirty Curtiss N-9 training seaplanes. With the approval of the secretary of the navy, the private National Aerial Coast Patrol Commission was formed, organizing aerial coast patrol units at Yale, Princeton, Harvard, and Columbia universities; these units supplemented the small cadre of regular officers and provided the bulk of leadership when naval aviation commenced war operations.

The United States entered the war in April 1917. It is an understatement to say that naval aviation was ill-prepared for its wartime role. Including the marine corps component, it was comprised of 48 officers, 239 enlisted men, 54 airplanes, 3 balloons, 1 blimp, and 1 air station. German submarine warfare posed the greatest threat to Allied success, so top priority was given to neutralizing the U-boats to maintain the flow of supplies to Europe. For naval aviation, this meant the production and deployment of antisubmarine patrol aircraft. Curtiss had contracts with the Royal Navy for the Large America (H-12) model flying boat, but the problem remained of how to produce a reliable high-powered engine to power it. The solution came later in 1917 in the form of the reliable Liberty engine, which powered all of the navy's wartime patrol and bombing models (H-16, HS-1/2, F-5-L, DH-4, and Capronis).

The buildup for war included increased institutionalization of naval aviation training. A preflight school was established at the Massachusetts Institute of Technology, followed later by others at the University of Washington and the Dunwoody Institute in Minneapolis, Minnesota. Aviation schools for enlisted personnel were established at Great Lakes, Illinois, with technical training conducted at various private industrial facilities and at the navy gas-engine school at Columbia University. Primary lighter-than-air (LTA) training shifted to a Goodyear facility in Akron, Ohio.

Given wartime demand, the navy even established its own aircraft factory. Completed in late 1917, the Naval Aircraft Factory at the Philadelphia Navy Yard was producing aircraft by early 1918. The facility assured part of the navy's aircraft production, served as a source of production cost data, and provided an in-house capability for producing experimental designs.

Over There

The navy's First Aeronautical Detachment, commanded by Lt. Kenneth Whiting, was the first organized unit of the U.S. armed forces to deploy overseas after the declaration of war. Arriving in France on 5 June 1917, the unit trained at French facilities and provided the nucleus of trained personnel for four naval air stations established in France. Italy provided training facilities at Lake Bolsena, which also became a naval air station.

Patrol operations were inaugurated on both sides of the Atlantic after the declaration of war. An antisubmarine patrol station at Punta Delgado in the Azores was established by the First Marine Aeronautic Company, and a naval air station was established at Coco Solo in the Panama Canal Zone to defend the canal.

In Europe, strategic bombing operations were conducted against German industrial and naval targets. The Northern Bombing Group commenced operations several months before the war's end. British squadrons that included some American pilots had concentrated their early efforts against German submarine bases in Belgium. Later operations, particularly those of the Marine Day Wing, supported the Allied land offensives in October and November 1918.

Two additional strategic bombing programs failed to develop fully. One involved towing seaplane bombers on lighters within range of German bases. Some lighter stunts, as they were called, were carried out successfully by the British. Another innovative program involved the use of self-propelled sea sleds, each of which would carry and launch one aircraft to bomb German targets. The sled's shallow draft permitted it to operate over and inside the German defensive minefields. Successful tests were conducted, but the war ended before operations could be carried out.

Other plans for 1919 that were never carried out called for the construction of six aircraft carriers and the formation of a southern bombing group in Italy to operate against the Austrian navy.

By the end of the war the Royal Navy was way ahead of the U.S. Navy in aircraft carrier development. The Royal Navy carrier *Furious* had seen combat action against German targets. In addition, the British had completed two more carriers.

A New Confidence

World War I did much to establish an early role for naval aviation in bombing and antisubmarine warfare. Navy and marine corps aircraft logged over 2,000,000 nautical miles on patrols from bases in the United States and almost 800,000 nautical miles on overseas patrols and bombing missions. More than one hundred thousand pounds of bombs were dropped on German bases and naval targets. Twenty-five attacks were made on German submarines, twelve of which were reported damaged. The airplane had more impact on the course of the war in antisubmarine patrol than in any other type of operations.

A new confidence emerged from the wartime feats of naval aviation. Ens. Charles H. Hammann was awarded the Medal of Honor for his spectacular rescue of a fellow aviator from the Adriatic Sea in the face of fierce enemy opposition. Second Lt. Ralph Talbot and GSgt. Robert G. Robinson were each awarded the Medal of Honor for extraordinary heroism in their running fight with twelve enemy aircraft. Lt. (jg) David S. Ingalls became the navy's first "ace," destroying four enemy airplanes and at least one enemy balloon.

Table 1-1 shows the explosive growth of naval aviation during the nineteen months of U.S. involvement in World War I.

First Flight Across the Atlantic

During World War I, Adm. David W. Taylor had initiated work on long-range flying boats capable of crossing the Atlantic nonstop and possessing excellent sea-keeping capability. Designed by three naval constructors (H. C. Richardson, J. C. Hunsaker, and G. C. Westervelt) in collaboration with Glenn Curtiss, the Navy Curtiss (NC) plane had a 126-foot wingspan, a 45-foot hull, and three Liberty engines. Development continued after the war ended, and a fourth engine was added. During tests, NC-1 carried fifty-one persons aloft, setting a world record.

Table 1-1. Navy and Marine Corps Aviation, World War I

	6 April 1917	11 November 1918
Personnel		
Officers	48	6,998
Enlisted Men	239	32,873
Air Stations		
Continental U.S.	1	12
Overseas	-	31
Aircraft		
Seaplanes/flying boats	51	1,865
Landplanes	3	242
Dirigibles	1	15

The decision to attempt a transatlantic crossing was made. On 8 May 1919, three NCs, led by Cdr. John Towers, departed the naval air station at Rockaway Beach, New York, bound for Plymouth, England, via Halifax, Nova Scotia; Trepassy Bay, Newfoundland; the Azores; and Lisbon, Portugal. All three aircraft left Trepassy Bay as planned, but navigation difficulties forced two of them to land at sea. Towers sailed NC-3 into the Azores, but extensive damage prevented further flight. NC-1 turned over and sank when taken in tow.

NC-4, commanded by Lt. Cdr. A. C. Read and flown by Lt. (jg) Walter Hinton and coast guard lieutenant Elmer Stone, made it safely to Lisbon on 27 May. NC-1 continued on to Plymouth, and the feat won much public acclaim from both sides of the Atlantic.

Years of Growth

The armistice ending World War I was accompanied by a rapid demobilization of the armed forces. Despite this, the navy continued to work on integrating aviation into the fleet, an effort that had been put aside during the massive wartime antisubmarine and bombing effort. In addition to the success of NC-4, 1919 was a decisively successful year for naval aviation.

In January 1919, a squadron of flying boats conducted exercises off

The Navy Curtiss NC-4 was the first aircraft to fly across the Atlantic Ocean. (U.S. Navy)

Guantanamo Bay, Cuba. These aircraft joined a detachment of Sopwith Camels, flying from a platform over a turret of the battleship *Texas* (BB 35), and six kite balloons and their crews based ashore. The flying boats, supported by the minelayer *Shawmut* (CM 4) operating as a seaplane tender, demonstrated that they could travel with the fleet and provide long-range services as required. The success of the Sopwith Camel detachment led to the formation of the Atlantic Fleet Ship Plane Division, which operated aircraft from turret platforms on four battleships.

The Early Carriers

During the spring of 1919, the navy's General Board recommended the establishment of a naval air service and the fullest development of fleet aviation. The board also recommended that the collier *Jupiter* be converted to an aircraft carrier for temporary use and experiments. The USS *Langley* (CV 1) was commissioned on 20 March 1922; later that year, Lt. Cdr. Godfrey deC. Chevalier made the first arrested landing on board the *Langley*, and American carrier aviation was born.

The Washington disarmament treaties of 1922 had an important impact on naval aviation. U.S. battle cruisers then under construction were in excess of treaty limitations and had to be disposed of; however, the treaties allowed the United States two aircraft carriers of not more than 36,000 tons each. Two of the battle cruisers were converted into the carriers

The USS *Saratoga* (CV 3), shown here, and her sister ship, the USS *Lexington* (CV 2), were converted into aircraft carriers from partially built battle cruisers. (U.S. Navy)

Lexington (CV 2) and *Saratoga* (CV 3), both commissioned in late 1927.

The 1920s stand out in the history of naval aviation as a period of phenomenal growth. Although the decade was characterized by declining appropriations, the navy devoted a steadily increasing share to aviation. By 1929, three carriers were in commission; patrol squadrons supported by seaplane tenders performed scouting operations for the fleet; aircraft were based on board battleships and cruisers for scouting and gunfire spotting; and the marine corps had learned many valuable lessons about providing close-air support for expeditionary forces.

Aircraft flew higher, faster, farther, carrying heavier and heavier loads. Naval aviators set many world aviation records. Accurate dive-bombing became an accepted tactic that was to prove decisive in future naval battles. Torpedo attack doctrine, patrol and scouting techniques, and advanced base operations were also developed effectively.

Naval aircraft were instrumental in many exploration and survey efforts during the 1920s. In 1926 amphibious aircraft supported by the tender *Gannet* (AVP 8) made a highly successful aerial survey of Alaska. Cdr. Richard E. Byrd gained international fame for his aerial exploration of Greenland, for the first flight over the geographic North Pole (with naval aviation pilot Floyd Bennett), and for his major expedition to Antarctica in 1929, where he made the first flight over the South Pole. (This latter expedition became the forerunner of a series of U.S. expeditions to Antarctica supported by naval aviation to this day.) In the process he developed many of the cold-weather techniques later used in high-altitude operations in wartime.

A significant organizational change, which had a lasting effect on the development of naval aviation, was the creation of the Bureau of Aeronautics on 10 August 1921. Prior to that time, the various command and material requirements of naval aviation had been accommodated by extensive and at times exhaustive coordination between the Office of the Director of Naval Aviation and the material bureaus of the navy. The Bureau of Construction provided the airframes, the Bureau of Engineering the engines and radios, the Bureau of Navigation the instruments and navigation equipment, and the Bureau of Ordnance the weapons.

The new organization brought the majority of aeronautical material under the cognizance of the Bureau of Aeronautics. Spurred by the energetic leadership of its first chief, Rear Adm. William Moffett, soon to qualify as the navy's first naval aviation observer, and his deputy, Capt. Henry C. Mustin, the navy's senior aviator, rapid progress was made integrating aviation into the navy.

Long-range patrol aviation continued its slow, steady record of achievement. Metal hulls and more reliable engines were incorporated in models that were, to a large extent, improvements on the basic F-5-L design. In 1925, Cdr. John Rodgers and a crew of four in a PN-9 flying boat attempted a nonstop flight from San Francisco, California, to Hawaii. After flying more than three quarters of the way across, they were forced down by lack of fuel. Fashioning a sail from wing fabric and using the flooring for leeboards, they sailed the aircraft tail-first for the remaining 450 miles to the island of Kuaui in ten days. The object of an extensive search, they had almost been given up for lost. (The flight of 1,841 miles was accepted as an international distance record for Class C seaplanes that remained unbeaten for almost five years.)

The Airship Era

The success in World War I of Allied nonrigid airships and the German zeppelins supported the arguments of LTA proponents for a rigid airship program. The availability of inert helium as a substitute for the highly flammable hydrogen greatly reduced the risk of such operations. Encouraged by Adm. William S. Sims, wartime commander of U.S. Naval Forces in Europe, Congress agreed and appropriated funds in fiscal year 1920 for building one rigid airship in the United States and buying one abroad.

The first U.S. rigid airship, the *Shenandoah* (ZR 1), was fabricated at the Naval Aircraft Factory and assembled at the naval air station at Lakehurst, New Jersey. The second, the *R-38*, to be purchased from Britain, was destroyed in a crash in England before acceptance.

Under the Versailles Treaty, the United States was entitled to two German zeppelins as a war reparation. These and other ships scheduled for delivery to the Allies were destroyed by their crews. Subsequently, the Germans built one new zeppelin, the small but highly successful *Los Angeles* (ZR 3).

The *Akron* (ZRS 4), the first of the giant dirigibles, was commissioned on Navy Day in 1931. To overcome a recognized defensive weakness, it was equipped with a hangar and the ability to carry four fighters. The fighters were supplied with overhead hooks and were recovered on board through use of a trapeze. Unfortunately, in April 1933 while on its sev-

The airship *Macon* (ZR 5), seen here over New York City during the early 1930s, carried fighter planes inside a hangar for self-defense and reconnaissance. (U.S. Navy)

enty-fourth flight, the *Akron* crashed during a violent storm off New Jersey; seventy-six of the seventy-nine crewmen died, including Adm. William Moffett, the first chief of the Bureau of Aeronautics.

Not long afterward, in June 1933, the sister ship *Macon* (ZRS 5) was commissioned and based at Sunnyvale, California. It, too, was lost at sea during a storm in February 1935. The day of the giant dirigible in the navy had passed, though nonrigid airships would play an important part in the antisubmarine campaigns of World War II.

Austerity and Exercises

The Great Depression of the 1930s took its toll on naval aviation. Operating tempos and support funds were significantly reduced. Air stations at the low end of the funding priority list fell far behind in their capability to support authorized programs. The USS *Ranger* (CV 4), the first U.S. Navy ship to be designed and built as a carrier, was authorized and her keel laid in 1931, but subsequent appropriations were insufficient to procure planes for her air group. Patrol aircraft assigned to the Panama Canal Zone, Hawaii, and the Asiatic Fleet were reduced to provide funds for the *Ranger*'s planes.

Two reserve air stations established during the 1930s were largely financed by local rather than federal funds. Only construction of the major LTA base at Sunnyvale, California, made progress during this period; it was built on a thousand acres sold to the federal government by local interests for one dollar!

As more carriers joined the fleet and exercises more nearly approached conditions that the navy would encounter during war, it became apparent that the navy would have to develop carrier planes with increased performance capabilities. Some of the great aircraft of World War II began to evolve during the late 1930s. The need for more capable seaplane tenders also became apparent, and the navy began to consider the idea of building small carriers for use in support roles.

Personnel shortages continued to plague the fleet. The Naval Academy was unable to provide sufficient officer graduates as student aviators, and the training of enlisted naval aviation pilots (NAPs), suspended in 1934 as an economy measure, was reinstated in 1936. The Aviation Cadet Act of 1935 once more established a naval reserve program that would provide the experienced cadre on which naval aviation's wartime expansion would draw.

Fleet exercises during the 1930s provided extensive experience in planning and execution of fast carrier strikes against shore installations and in the development of circular screens for antiaircraft defense of carrier formations. The navy and marine corps recognized the vital role of aviation in the support of Fleet Marine Force landing operations and developed a high degree of cooperation. A healthy spirit of competition among naval aviation units further enhanced combat skills.

World War II

War Clouds

Days after the start of World War II in Europe, the Atlantic Squadron was directed to establish "neutrality patrols" over areas as far east as the sixty-fifth meridian and as far south as Trinidad. The objective of these patrols was to make the anti-shipping efforts of the German U-boats as difficult as possible. (Later, the Asiatic Fleet's patrol planes would fly similar patrols in the Far East to track Japanese movements.)

Providing aircraft for the patrols became an immediate concern. In addition to the air groups training for the *Ranger* and *Wasp* (CV 7) and a few planes in the Canal Zone, the Atlantic Squadron had only twenty-five scout planes on battleships and cruisers and fifty-four patrol planes. The rest of naval aviation's combat aircraft were in the Pacific. On 16 May 1940, President Franklin Roosevelt issued his famous call for fifty thousand planes, and a year later declared that an unlimited state of national emergency existed.

In July 1941, the United States took over the garrisoning of Iceland from the British and instituted regular patrol flights from Reykjavík over the Atlantic convoy routes. In October, the navy received its first land-based patrol planes (PBO Hudsons), and in November, operational control of the coast guard passed to the navy.

On the eve of U.S. entry into World War II, naval aviation could muster 6,750 navy, marine corps, and coast guard pilots; 1,874 ground officers; 21,678 enlisted men; 5,260 aircraft of all types (including trainers); 7 large and 1 small aircraft carriers; 5 patrol wings; 2 marine air wings; and a few advanced air bases.

In the Thick of It

The Japanese attack on Pearl Harbor on 7 December 1941 left most of the Pacific Fleet's battleships sunk or damaged, and many navy and marine corps aircraft destroyed; World War II was on for the United States. However, the events hastened a transition that had been slowly taking place in naval thinking. The Pacific Fleet's carriers were all at sea during the attack, and only hours after the Japanese struck, the carriers became the capital ships of the fleet, a cause for hope in the desperate months ahead.

The situation in early 1942 was grim. Wake and Guam had fallen, and American forces in the Philippines were overwhelmed by a sustained Japanese assault. The naval forces that survived the initial assault fought a series of delaying actions as they fell back through the Netherlands East Indies to Australia, New Guinea, and New Hebrides. The PBY Catalinas

Naval Aviation: The Legacy 15

Patrol planes such as this PBY Catalina tracked Japanese fleet movements and conducted antishipping strikes. (U.S. Navy/Robert L. Lawson collection)

of Patrol Wing 10 performed courageously in the face of great odds to provide scouting and patrol reports and to attack whenever possible, but nothing stopped the Japanese advance. The navy's first carrier, the USS *Langley* (AV 3), converted to a seaplane tender, was sunk while ferrying a load of army fighters to defenders in the Netherlands East Indies.

The handful of U.S. carriers spent the first half of 1942 conducting a series of raids that kept the Japanese off balance. With the *Saratoga* temporarily out of action from a submarine torpedo hit, task forces built around the USS *Lexington*, *Yorktown* (CV 5), and *Enterprise* (CV 6) carried the war to enemy bases in New Guinea, the Gilberts, the Marshalls, and Marcus Island. One of these raids produced the navy's first ace of the war, Lt. Edward "Butch" O'Hare, who shot down five Japanese planes in a single action in defense of his carrier, an action for which he was awarded the Medal of Honor. In April, Adm. William "Bull" Halsey led a task force with the *Hornet* (CV 8), escorted by the *Enterprise*, that launched sixteen army B-25 bombers led by Lt. Col. James H. (Jimmy) Doolittle on raids against Tokyo and three other Japanese cities. These raids did little damage but gave the navy and the nation tremendous boosts in morale, and undermined the confidence of the Japanese.

The Battles of Coral Sea and Midway

Partially spurred on by the Halsey-Doolittle Raid, the Japanese commenced a series of operations to secure a defensive outer perimeter of their Pacific expanse. Now came the first real test of U.S. carrier aviation.

In a series of engagements in May 1942 that later became known as the Battle of the Coral Sea, the U.S. Navy foiled the Japanese thrust to capture Port Moresby in New Guinea. SBD dive-bombers and TBD torpedo planes from the *Lexington* and *Yorktown* sank the Japanese light carrier *Shoho* and severely damaged their carrier *Shokaku*. Japanese aircraft inflicted damage on the *Lexington*, which had to be abandoned and sunk. The *Yorktown* was also damaged, but the Americans had turned back the Japanese. It was an especially significant event in the history of naval warfare because the outcome was decided solely by airpower. Opposing surface forces were never within visual or firing range of one another.

Less than a month later, the Japanese put into gear their plan to capture Midway in the Hawaiian chain and several islands in the Aleutian chain. From these bases, Japanese airpower could extend thirteen hundred miles, a radius that included Hawaii. Aware of the strong U.S. effort to secure the sea-lanes to Australia, the Japanese did not anticipate strong opposition to their move on Midway. However, cryptanalysis permitted the United States to read Japanese message traffic, and, armed with this intelligence, Pacific Fleet commander Adm. Chester W. Nimitz ordered all available forces to Midway, including 120 navy, marine corps, and army aircraft. Task Forces 16 (the *Enterprise* and *Hornet*) and 17 (the hastily repaired *Yorktown*) rendezvoused northeast of Midway. Bearing down on Midway were a Japanese carrier strike force with four veteran carriers, a main battle force, and an occupation force.

On 3 June, a PBY from Midway spotted ships of the Occupation Force, and on the following day another PBY spotted Japanese carrier planes inbound to strike Midway. Marine corps fighters put up a valiant defense of the island, and the bombers based at Midway made daring but mostly ineffective torpedo and bombing attacks on the Japanese ships. Diverted by these attacks, however, the Japanese were not prepared to meet the full weight of the American carrier strike that followed. The fighters and ships of the Japanese carrier strike force almost annihilated three U.S. TBD torpedo squadrons, but their sacrifice occupied Japanese defenses long enough to allow four squadrons of SBDs to dive on the Japanese carriers, severely damaging three of them. The *Akagi, Kaga,* and *Soryu* would all sink that day.

The remaining Japanese carrier, the *Hiryu,* was able to launch two counterattacks, severely damaging and forcing abandonment of the *Yorktown,* before succumbing to an attack by SBDs. The *Yorktown* was reboarded and damage control measures were progressing when she was mortally wounded by a brace of torpedoes from a Japanese submarine. On the final day of the battle, SBDs from the *Enterprise, Hornet,* and from the island of Midway sank a cruiser and severely damaged another cruiser plus a destroyer.

With the loss of 4 carriers, all veterans of the Pearl Harbor raid, 1 cruiser, 256 aircraft, and 466 experienced airmen, Adm. Isoroku Yamamoto ordered the abandonment of the operation. The United States had lost 1 carrier, 1 destroyer, 144 aircraft, and 186 airmen. U.S. naval aviation had halted Japanese eastward expansion in what was the turning point of the war in the Pacific and one of the most decisive naval battles in history.

The Japanese operation in the Aleutians fared better. Following a carrier raid on Dutch Harbor, the Japanese occupied the islands of Attu and Kiska at the western end of the chain. It fell to the PBY Catalinas of Patrol Wing 4 to carry the war to the enemy in the Aleutians. Beginning on 11 June and operating from Dutch Harbor and the tender *Gillis* (AVD 12) at Nazan Bay, the Catalinas conducted an around-the-clock operation that came to be called the Kiska Blitz. PBYs carried out continuous bombing and strafing attacks on ships and installations in Kiska's harbor, refueling, rearming, and returning to battle as rapidly as the limited facilities would allow. At times the lumbering PBYs were used as dive-bombers at speeds up to 250 knots. In four days, they had exhausted the limited supply of bombs, torpedoes, ammunition, and fuel.

The Japanese remained but were badly shaken. Aircraft of Patrol Wing

The fast carrier task force swept the Japanese fleet from the Pacific during World War II. (U.S. Navy)

4 and the army's Eleventh Air Force continued to harass and attack the Japanese until they were forced to abandon the Aleutians in the summer of 1943.

Gearing Up for Victory

At home, training shifted into high gear. With a huge demand for pilots, the navy opened new training bases, including many in the Midwest, a move that permitted increased operational flying at coastal air stations. Two side-wheel excursion steamers were converted into the training carriers *Wolverine* (IX 64) and *Sable* (IX 81), which conducted carrier qualifications on the Great Lakes free from enemy submarine interference.

The demands of war pushed innovations in personnel. Non-pilot navigators were trained and assigned to multiengined aircraft units. The first women to qualify for navy wings—six navigation instructors—became naval aviation observers (navigation) in the women's reserve. Other programs trained NAOs for radar and tactical operations. (Each program had its own distinctive insignia until 1947 when all wore NAO wings.) The Naval Aviation Pilot program resumed (and was not eliminated until 1948), and many NAPs were commissioned during the war.

Ground officers assumed a variety of duties. Starting in 1941, aeronautical engineers received direct commissions. An air combat information school was established at NAS Quonset Point, Rhode Island. WAVES (Women Accepted for Voluntary Emergency Service) began to enter the navy in significant numbers; many filled clerical and professional billets at the Bureau of Aeronautics, while others trained in aeronautical specialties.

Shipbuilding support for wartime expansion began in 1941, when the USS *Essex* (CV 9) was being constructed; she was the first of twenty-four fleet carriers of that class, seventeen of which formed the backbone of the fast carrier task forces from 1943 on. Nine light carriers converted from cruiser hulls during 1942–43 became the *Independence* (CVL-22) class which supplemented the fleet carriers. In 1941, the experimental conversion of a merchant hull resulted in the first U.S. escort carrier, the *Long Island* (AVG 1, later CVE 1). During the war, over one hundred escort carriers were constructed for the U.S. Navy and the Royal Navy. In addition, fifteen large and sixty-two small seaplane tenders served the fleet during the war, as did sixteen types of aviation logistic-support ships.

Atlantic Operations

Naval aviation operations against Axis forces in the Atlantic and Mediterranean took on a different emphasis than in the Pacific. Most of the activity centered around neutralizing the German submarine threat, the Battle of the Atlantic. However, there were three carrier operations against land targets, not counting the two runs that the *Wasp* made in 1942 to Malta to ferry the British fighters that helped save the island from conquest.

In November 1942, an invasion fleet crossed the Atlantic and landed American troops in French Morocco. Because Morocco was out of range of friendly land-based air cover, carrier aviation made it possible for the landings to succeed. The *Ranger* and four escort carriers covered the

Navy patrol planes such as this PB4Y-1 Liberator were instrumental in the defeat of the German U-boats in the Battle of the Atlantic. (U.S. Navy/National Archives)

landings, with their SBDs pounding Vichy French defenses, and their F4Fs tangling with Vichy fighters. One of the escort carriers carried a load of army fighters which were flown ashore when an airfield was secured, a scenario that escort carriers would repeat later in the war.

The *Ranger* operated with the British Home Fleet in 1943 and participated in a raid on German naval targets in Norway in October, during which her SBDs and TBFs sank five ships. In August 1944, two U.S. CVEs supplemented seven British escort carriers in the invasion of southern France, during which navy F6F Hellcat fighters flew missions against German targets deep into France. Earlier, during the June 1944 D-Day invasion at Normandy, navy pilots flying Spitfire and Mustang fighters provided gunfire spotting support for the naval bombardment.

For the most part, however, antisubmarine warfare was the occupation of naval aviation in the Atlantic. Patrol planes were staged from Iceland and Newfoundland, down the Atlantic coast, through the Caribbean

A U-boat comes under attack by a Navy PB4Y; the submarine was sunk during this action. (U.S. Navy/ National Archives)

and West Indies, and from the Canal Zone along the coast of South America to Brazil. Air patrols also covered the approaches to Gibraltar, the west coast of Africa, and the Ascension Island area. Blimps and PBY and PBM flying boats were joined in 1943 by long-range, land-based PV-1 Venturas and PB4Y-1 Liberators, which extended search areas and forced the Germans to move their submarine operations to mid-ocean.

New weapons and equipment were introduced as antisubmarine forces grew stronger. Magnetic anomaly detectors (MAD) provided the localization capability needed for attacks on submerged submarines. Retro-rockets allowed attacks on the on-top mark of a MAD contact, as the rearward thrust of the rockets' path compensated for the forward speed of the aircraft. Sonobuoys, which allowed acoustic tracking of submerged submarines, came into limited use.

Some of the most important antisubmarine innovations were the

X-band radar, the Leigh light, and acoustic torpedoes, as well as high-frequency direction-finders (HFDFs). Submarines were vulnerable at night, because they used night hours to run on the surface to position for attack and recharge batteries for submerged operations. The night was "taken away" by aircraft with these small powerful radars and searchlights, and the U-boats found it increasingly difficult to sink ships and survive.

Because patrol planes did not have the range to cover the mid-ocean areas, carrier aviation filled the gap with the advent of the hunter-killer escort carrier groups in March 1943. Each of these groups consisted of a CVE, normally with a squadron of F4F fighters and rocket-armed TBF torpedo bombers, and several destroyer escorts. Eleven CVEs served with these groups; only one CVE (the *Block Island* [CVE 21]) was lost to a German submarine. These CVEs, along with four British escort carriers, sank or shared credit for sinking fifty-nine U-boats during the war. Navy land-based patrol planes and scout planes sank or shared credit for sinking an additional forty-nine U-boats and Italian submarines. These scores do not even reflect the number of U-boat attacks discouraged or disrupted by air patrols, and the number of merchant ships they saved.

Slugging It Out in the Solomons

The United States took the offensive in the Pacific in August 1942 with the amphibious invasion of Guadalcanal in the Solomon Islands and the capture of its unfinished Japanese airfield. Quickly placed into operation as Henderson Field, it became a hotly contested possession and the focal point of intense air and naval battles in the Solomons for the next six months. Marine corps, navy, and army aviators there formed the "Cactus Air Force," and put up a valiant defense of Guadalcanal in spite of appalling operating conditions.

The Guadalcanal invasion precipitated another showdown between U.S. and Japanese carrier forces as the Japanese attempted to reinforce their troops on the island. In the Battle of the Eastern Solomons (24–25 August 1942), the *Enterprise* and *Saratoga* engaged the Japanese, and planes from the *Saratoga* sank the light carrier *Ryujo*. Japanese bombs heavily damaged the *Enterprise,* and a week later a Japanese submarine torpedo put the *Saratoga* out of action once again. Two weeks after that, while escorting troop reinforcements for Guadalcanal a Japanese submarine mortally damaged the *Wasp*; she had to be abandoned and sunk. Retiring for repairs, the *Enterprise* put many of her planes ashore to join the Cactus Air Force, and for a while, the *Hornet* was the only battle-ready U.S. carrier.

In October, the Japanese assembled their largest naval force since the Midway campaign in a major assault on Henderson Field. Only one plane at the field escaped damage from the ensuing bombardment. Another carrier face-off took place in the Battle of Santa Cruz (26–27 October): in the exchange of raids, the *Enterprise, Hornet,* and the Japanese carriers *Shokaku* and *Zuiho* were damaged, the *Hornet* so heavily that she had to be abandoned and sunk.

The *Enterprise*, as the lone U.S. fleet carrier in the South Pacific, carried on the fight. Her aircraft were instrumental in the decisive defeat of the Japanese fleet in the Naval Battle of Guadalcanal (12–15 November) and, along with two escort carriers, in the Battle of Rennel Island (29–30 January 1943).

Most of the Japanese attempts to reinforce their garrisons in the Solomons were made by ships hiding by day and making high-speed runs at night through the New Georgia Sound ("The Slot"), attempting to put troops ashore during darkness. Navy PBY patrol planes, painted black and equipped with radar, struck Japanese shipping at night, wreaking havoc with their surprise attacks. The aggressive PBY crews came to be known as the "Black Cats."

Unlike the patrol squadrons in the Atlantic theater, the Pacific Fleet did not face an organized submarine threat, and its patrol squadrons were engaged primarily in antishipping, search and rescue, and scouting operations. Seldom operating from fixed bases, patrol planes and their supporting tenders moved across the Pacific with the fleet, operating from sheltered waters and advanced airstrips. They attacked everything from battleships to fishing boats, and PBYs and PBMs excelled in "Dumbo" rescue missions in support of carrier strikes and later in support of the Army Air Force B-29 strikes against Japan. Operating from the Aleutians, PV-1 Venturas and PV-2 Harpoons regularly harassed Japanese garrisons in the northern Kuriles. On four occasions in early 1944, PB2Y Coronados made two-thousand-mile round-trip bombing raids from Midway to Wake Island. PB4Y-1 Liberators and PB4Y-2 Privateers

SBD-5 Dauntless dive bombers from the USS *Enterprise* head for targets in the Pacific. SBDs devastated Japanese shipping during World War II. (U.S. Navy/Robert L. Lawson collection)

raided Japanese shipping and provided vital pre-invasion intelligence for amphibious landings.

With Guadalcanal secure by February 1943, U.S. conquest of the rest of the Solomons proceeded over the next two years, in leapfrog fashion in a series of operations that often bypassed enemy-held islands. Land-based navy and marine corps aircraft, including the veteran SBDs and TBFs, and the new F4U Corsair, PB4Y Liberator, and PBJ Mitchell, operated from the captured airfields and flew strikes against the Japanese bastion at Rabaul on the island of New Britain.

Carriers on the Offensive

Given the heavy losses in the Guadalcanal campaign, it was almost a year before U.S. carrier task forces became available in strength to take the offensive. The new *Essex*-class fleet carriers and *Independence*-class light carriers joined the *Enterprise* and *Saratoga*, along with a stream of new pilots and aircrewmen, and new planes such as the SB2C Helldiver dive-bomber and the superb F6F Hellcat fighter, complementing the TBFs and SBDs. Escort carriers with F4F/FM Wildcats and TBF/TBM Avengers filled out "jeep carrier" task groups to support amphibious landings.

In August 1943, Marcus Island was the first Japanese target to feel the sting of the new carrier task forces, followed by the Gilberts and Wake Island. Two separate raids were conducted on Rabaul in November. That month, carrier planes supported landings at Tarawa and other islands in the Gilberts. One CVE (the *Liscome Bay* [CVE 56]) was lost to a Japanese submarine. This operation also featured the first carrier night interception of an enemy air raid, a feat credited with saving the task group from damage.

Carrier task groups raided Nauru in December, and Kavieng, New Ireland, in January 1944. That month, the invasion of the Marshall Islands was supported by Task Force 58 under Rear Adm. Marc Mitscher. (Task Force 38 was the same group of ships, which alternated task force designations as the Third and Fifth fleets alternated command of the ships.) In February, a major carrier raid on the "impregnable" Japanese base at Truk launched 1,250 combat sorties and dropped 400 tons of bombs and torpedoes, sinking 37 war- and merchant ships. This action also featured the first night carrier strike in U.S. history, carried out from the *Enterprise* with twelve radar-equipped TBF-1Cs scoring direct hits on ships in the harbor. Later, Task Force 58 struck the Marianas and the western Carolines; during the latter operation carrier aircraft performed their first aerial mine-laying. Carriers covered the invasion of Hollandia in New Guinea and struck Truk, Marcus, and Wake again, while the *Saratoga*, operating with the British Eastern Fleet, launched raids against targets in the Netherlands East Indies.

The Greatest Carrier Battle

In June 1944, as U.S. forces invaded the Marianas, only one thousand miles from Japan, the Japanese fleet could no longer forego a reaction, challenging the invasion with a nine-carrier task force. Two Japanese carriers (the *Shokaku* and *Taiho*) fell victim to American submarines, but the Japanese were able to launch a series of raids on 19 June. In what later became known as the Marianas Turkey Shoot, Task Force 58's F6F Hellcats downed 402 Japanese planes for a loss of only 17 fighters in aerial combat. Success was due in part to able fighter direction from the carrier combat information centers and the use of IFF (Identification Friend or Foe) equipment. The next day, Task Force 58 planes sank the carrier *Hiyo* and two oilers, though the Americans lost one hundred aircraft in the strike, most of them to fuel exhaustion while returning from the mission. The two-month Marianas campaign, which included strikes on the Bonins and western Carolines, cost the United States no ships, and the 358 aircraft lost (102 in combat) were easily replaced; the Japanese had lost 110,000 tons of shipping and 1,223 aircraft, and Japanese carrier aviation was finished as a fighting force.

During this period, carrier task groups initiated a practice of retiring to advance bases for rest and replenishment; this became standard during future extended periods of action. These interludes were sorely needed, for soon the carriers were back in action softening up the Palaus, Morotai, Angaur, Ulithi, and the Philippines for invasion. In a month of action, Task Force 38 carrier aircrews sank 67 war- and merchant ships and destroyed 893 enemy aircraft. Airfields in Luzon, Formosa, and Okinawa were hit in preparation for the invasion of the Philippines at Leyte.

The Battle of Leyte Gulf

The invasion of Leyte brought out the Japanese navy for what was to be its last major operation. Three groups of Japanese ships converged on the American landing force from three directions. Task Force 38 aircraft attacked the central and southern groups, sinking the super-battleship *Musashi,* but lost the light carrier *Princeton* (CVL 23). The central force proceeded at night through the San Bernadino Strait and attacked six escort carriers and their screening escorts, sinking one CVE (the *Gambier Bay* [CVE 73]) and three escorts in the face of intrepid opposition, during which carrier aircraft sank three Japanese cruisers. The courage of the destroyer sailors and carrier airmen saved the invasion fleet from destruction.

Meanwhile, off Cape Engano, Task Force 38 engaged the northern group, a force of four Japanese carriers that had decoyed the American carriers away from the invasion area. The Japanese carriers (the *Zuikaku,* the last of the carriers that struck Pearl Harbor; the *Zuiho*; *Chitose*; and *Chiyoda*), with only a handful of planes, were overwhelmed and sent to the bottom by Task Force 38 carrier planes and naval gunfire. It was the last time Japanese carriers sortied to battle.

The Battle of Leyte Gulf, the largest naval battle in history, was also the debut of the Japanese kamikaze (Divine Wind) pilots, who in planned attacks flew their explosive-laden aircraft into ships. They sank the escort carrier *St. Lo* (CVE 63) and damaged six more CVEs. As Task Force 38 struck airfields and shipping in the Philippines in late October and in November, kamikazes damaged seven carriers. During October and November, carrier planes destroyed 1,816 Japanese aircraft in the air and on the ground, and sank many ships.

Task Force 38 (under Vice Adm. John S. McCain) supported amphibious landings in Mindoro in December and in Luzon in January 1945. A three-week-long sweep of targets in the Philippines, Formosa, Okinawa, French Indochina, China, and Hong Kong destroyed over 600 Japanese aircraft and sank over 325,000 tons of shipping, preventing Japanese reinforcement of the Philippines. Enemy aircraft only damaged two fleet carriers. Kamikazes, however, damaged five more CVEs and sank one, the *Ommaney Bay* (CVE 79).

The End in Sight

With the liberation of the Philippines under way, the fast carriers turned their attention toward Iwo Jima. The occupation of the Marianas had given the United States airfields from which Army Air Force B-29 bombers could conduct strategic bombing of Japan and mine Japanese waters. The capture of Iwo Jima would provide a base from which P-51 fighters could escort the bombers and provide an emergency landing site for the aircraft involved.

In February 1945, preparing the way for the invasion, Task Force 58 flew raids against Japan itself, as well as against Iwo Jima, the Bonins, Okinawa, and the Ryukyus, destroying 648 enemy aircraft and many merchant ships. By this time, the makeup of carrier air groups was changing; in response to the kamikaze threat, the number of dive-bombers and

Carrier planes swarmed over Japan in the closing months of World War II. These TBM torpedo bombers and SB2C dive bombers are from the USS *Essex*. (Robert L. Lawson collection)

torpedo planes was reduced in favor of more fighters, which had also proven effective as attack aircraft. F4U Corsairs, including those in marine squadrons, joined the F6F Hellcats on board the fleet carriers. In another innovation, the *Enterprise* and *Independence* formed a task group with air groups specially trained in night operations.

Heavily supported by escort carriers, patrol planes, and marine corps and army aircraft, Iwo Jima was secured on 16 March. Kamikazes sank the escort carrier *Bismarck Sea* (CVE 95), damaged another escort carrier, and seriously damaged the *Saratoga*, putting her out of action for the rest of the war.

With its lifelines under continuous attack from both U.S. submarines and aircraft, its fleet all but destroyed, yet with field armies intact, Japan continued to resist. The Allies needed one last base to support the planned invasion of Japan. Okinawa filled the bill.

The last and most violent amphibious operation of the war was supported by hundreds of carrier planes, tender-based patrol planes, and land-based navy, marine corps, and army aircraft. Task Force 58 hit targets in Kyushu, destroying 526 aircraft in five days. Over the next three months, Task Force 58 operated in an area northeast of Okinawa, intercepting air raids, furnishing close-air support in Okinawa, and occasionally hitting airfields in Kyushu. Escort carriers, including two with marine carrier air groups, also provided close-air support for troops on the islands. A four-carrier British task force operated south of Okinawa and hit targets in Formosa; all four took kamikaze hits but kept on operating, saved by their armored flight decks.

During the campaign, the Japanese fleet made one last sortie. The world's largest battleship, the *Yamato*, escorted by one light cruiser and eight destroyers, steamed toward the invasion fleet off Okinawa. Swarms of U.S. carrier planes from Task Force 58 overwhelmed the force, which lost all but four destroyers. It was a fitting metaphor for the supremacy of naval aviation.

The Japanese expended some fifteen hundred aircraft in kamikaze raids during the savage, three-month campaign, giving the navy its heaviest punishment in its history. Thirty-one ships (none larger than a destroyer) were sunk, and 222 were damaged. Three escort carriers were damaged. Task Force 38/58 lost no ships, but kamikazes and bombs damaged nine of its carriers, three so severely (the *Enterprise, Franklin* [CV 13], and *Bunker Hill* [CV 17]) that they were out of action for the duration of the war. At a cost of 880 aircraft (including those lost to mishaps and 266 lost on damaged carriers), the carriers destroyed 2,259 of the 3,594 Japanese aircraft lost during the campaign. The Divine Wind had failed.

Elsewhere, naval aviation continued to hammer the Japanese. The first combat employment of a homing missile occurred in April 1945 when PB4Y-2 Privateers launched two Bat missiles against ships in Balikpapan Harbor in Borneo. Escort carriers supported the landing of Australian troops at Balikpapan in July and conducted strikes against shipping in Tinghai, China. Wake Island became an occasional target for carriers in transit to the western Pacific.

From 10 July until 15 August, Task Force 38, augmented by four British carriers in Task Force 57, conducted strikes against the Japanese homeland, hitting airfields, naval bases, shipping, and other military targets. In this final campaign, carrier planes destroyed 1,223 aircraft (mostly on the ground) and sank 23 warships and 48 merchant ships. Japan's capitulation came after the atomic bombing of the cities of Hiroshima and Nagasaki. On 15 August, when Adm. "Bull" Halsey announced the end of hostilities to the fleet, one carrier raid had already hit Tokyo; the second was recalled in flight.

The mighty effort to forge the navy's air arm had produced results far beyond the wildest dreams of prewar planners. Between 1 July 1940 and the end of the war, over 83,000 aircraft had been built for naval aviation. Over one hundred aircraft carriers of all types had been constructed. A worldwide airline, the Naval Air Transport Service, had been established. Almost 431,000 trained navy and marine corps personnel were serving in aviation at the end of the war.

In protecting convoys carrying the commerce of war throughout the world and in spearheading the massive drive to reconquer the western Pacific, naval aviation produced an impressive record of success. Naval aviation accounted for 174 Japanese warships (including 13 submarines) and 447 large merchant ships, and assisted in the destruction of many more ships and small craft. U.S. navy and marine corps fliers destroyed 15,401 Japanese aircraft (9,249 in the air) yet lost only 897 planes in aerial combat.

Peace and Progress

In the postwar demobilization, naval aviation was reduced to about one-tenth of its wartime strength. Ships were decommissioned and stations and squadrons were disestablished on a wholesale basis. Some mistakes of the previous world war were avoided, however: ships and planes were "mothballed" for future use should the need arise. A strong naval air reserve was created, supported by reserve air stations throughout the country.

New ships and aircraft were reaching the fleet as the war ended and soon afterward. Three large, armored-deck carriers of the *Midway* (CVB 41) class were commissioned. The F8F Bearcat, AD Skyraider, and newer F4U Corsairs replaced the Hellcats, Helldivers, and Avengers on fleet carriers, and soon the navy's first carrier jet fighters (FH Phantom and FJ Fury) entered limited service. Patrol squadrons saw the introduction of the land-based P2V Neptune and P4M Mercator in the late 1940s. Helicopters, available in small numbers during the war, began to prove their value and soon replaced observation floatplanes on board battleships and cruisers. Helicopters were also stationed on board carriers for rescue duties. Larger gas envelopes were developed for the K- and M-class blimps, and the N class was introduced. Advanced aerial rockets were developed, as were drones for various uses.

The advent of the Atomic Age also brought changes to naval aviation. A series of atomic bomb tests at Bikini Atoll in the Pacific was used to evaluate damage to ships, with lessons being incorporated in later carrier designs. By 1950, the navy also had a nuclear strike capability, first with P2V-3C Neptunes launched from carriers, followed by the carrier-based AJ Savage bomber. The navy's fight to retain carrier aviation, including a nuclear-strike capability in the face of air force advocacy of long-range strategic bombers, produced a bitter controversy at the Pentagon and resulted in the cancellation of a new carrier design. However, it would lead to the development of the *Forrestal* (CVA 59) class of "supercarriers."

Naval aviation was also called upon to support many scientific programs, including Project Skyhook, the launching of weather balloons for research in the upper atmosphere; hurricane and typhoon tracking; and nuclear weapons testing. Operation High Jump, the largest single Antarctic expedition, was supported by shore-based R4D aircraft from the *Philippine Sea* (CV 47) and PBM flying boats from several tenders, photo-mapping 1.5 million square miles of the continent and 5,500 miles of coastline.

Naval aviation was still committed overseas, largely in response to communist expansion efforts in the Cold War. The Sixth Fleet in the Mediterranean and the Seventh Fleet in the western Pacific were established to support U.S. interests and treaty commitments. Over fifty years later, naval aviation is still there, having fought a few hot wars in the interim.

Again the Call—Korea

After North Korean forces invaded South Korea on 25 June 1950, President Harry Truman responded by committing U.S. forces to save South Korea, garnering support for a United Nations resolution calling for a North Korean withdrawal and restoration of South Korea's integrity. On 3 July, U.S. and British carriers went into action against the North Koreans.

During combat operations in Korea, the *Essex*-class attack carriers generally operated under Task Force 77 in the Sea of Japan; the light and escort carriers operated under Task Force 95 in the Yellow Sea. American, British, and Australian carriers rotated duty on the line. The U.S. carrier decks were filled with F4U Corsairs (including night-fighter and photo-reconnaissance versions), AD Skyraiders (including specialized night attack, electronic countermeasures, and early warning versions), and the navy's first successful jet fighters, the F9F Panther and F2H Banshee.

For the most part, attack carrier air groups flew interdiction missions, along with some close-air support. A few special missions, however, broke the monotony. On 1 May 1951, the USS *Princeton* (CV 37) launched eight AD Skyraiders from VA-195, armed with torpedoes, which attacked a dam on the Hwachon Reservoir; six torpedoes ran straight and hot, destroying the center sluice gate and opening a hole in another. The communist forces were no longer able to vary water levels in the rivers to their advantage. It was the last use of air-dropped antishipping torpedoes. Another operation involved F6F Hellcat drone conversions launched from carriers and guided to enemy targets.

In another operation, to give impetus to stalled truce talks, navy and air force aircraft attacked thirteen major North Korean power plants in a two-day series of strikes beginning on 23 June 1951. The major strike was flown against the Suiho plant along the Yalu River. ADs and F9Fs from the USS *Boxer* (CV 21), *Princeton*, and *Philippine Sea* flew a completely successful strike, with air force F-84s pulverizing what remained of the power plant.

Enemy air opposition during the Korean War was generally light to nonexistent in the areas in which most of the naval operations were conducted. U.S. Navy pilots downed seventeen enemy aircraft, including five credited to Lt. Guy B. Bordelon, the navy's first night ace. Marines accounted for thirty-five aircraft, including six MiG-15 jet fighters by Maj.

Bomb-laden AD-4 Skyraiders from the USS *Princeton* en route to close-air support mission in Korea in 1951. (Cdr. H. G. Carlson/Robert L. Lawson collection)

John F. Bolt, who scored his victories as an exchange pilot flying F-86 Sabres with the air force. (Twenty-six of the navy and marine corps victories were scored by pilots on exchange duty.) One MiG-15 fell to the guns of marine Capt. Jesse Folmar while he was flying a propeller-driven F4U. Marine night fighters were particularly successful, being called upon to escort air force B-29s with their F3D Skyknight jet fighters to counter the MiG threat. Only two marine and two navy aircraft fell to enemy pilots during the war.

Patrol squadrons flew routine search, reconnaissance, and mine-spotting missions during the war, and even a few treacherous train-strafing missions. P4Y Privateers were also used to illuminate targets at night with flares to aid attacking aircraft interdicting enemy logistics. For the first time, land-based patrol planes were used in greater numbers

Hook down, an F9F-2 Panther prepares to land on board the USS *Boxer* after a mission over Korea. Navy jets saw action for the first time in Korea. (U.S. Navy/Robert L. Lawson collection)

than flying boats, a trend that would continue until the last flying boats were retired in 1967.

The helicopter came into its own during the Korean War; it was used in a wide variety of missions, including rescue and medical evacuation. Helicopters made it possible for a number of downed aviators to be returned safely.

During the Korean War, navy and marine aircraft flew 276,000 sorties, dropped 177,000 tons of bombs, and fired 272,000 rockets. This sortie count is significant in that it is only seven thousand less than that amassed by naval aviation in all theaters during World War II. The three years of grinding war were costly in terms of planes and aircrews: 564 aircraft were lost to the intense enemy defenses and 684 to operational causes.

The Korean War also set a pattern for carrier employment that the navy has used ever since: instead of conducting lightning raids and battling enemy fleets, carriers were used as floating airfields in relatively confined waters, launching strikes day after day against a land power. It would be repeated in Vietnam and Iraq.

Cold War, Jets, Missiles, and Angled Decks

The decade that followed the Korean War was one of dramatic technological advances and Cold War confrontations for naval aviation. Larger carriers, faster jets, and guided missiles characterized the forging of naval aviation during the 1950s.

To handle the increasing size and speed of naval aircraft, the navy built four *Forrestal*-class attack aircraft carriers, with angled decks, steam catapults, and the mirror landing system. These innovations, pioneered by the British, were retrofitted to the *Midway* class and many of the *Essex* hulls. In the early 1960s, the *Kitty Hawk* (CV 63) class joined the fleet, along with the world's first nuclear-powered carrier, the USS *Enterprise* (CVAN 65).

The navy developed a wide variety of jet fighters, replacing their predecessors in rapid succession. The Korean-era F9Fs, F2Hs, and F3Ds gave way to FJ Furies, swept-wing F9F Cougars, F11F Tigers, F7U Cutlasses, F3H Demons, F4D Skyrays, F8U (F-8) Crusaders, and F4H (F-4) Phantom IIs. Air-to-air missiles, both heat-seeking (Sidewinder) and radar-guided (Sparrow) became the main armament of fighters, and continue in use today in improved models. Fighters exceeded the speed of sound and had nose-mounted radars to aid interceptions.

Jet-powered attack aircraft were common on carrier decks before the end of the 1950s. The highly successful A4D (A-4) Skyhawk light-attack jet made its debut, and the A3D (A-3) Skywarrior replaced the AJ in the nuclear strike role. Propeller-driven Skyraiders were still common, but their days were numbered by the advent of the A2F (A-6) Intruder, a truly all-weather attack jet developed out of the lessons of the Korean War. To extend the range of carrier aircraft, aerial refueling was adopted, becoming a standard practice during carrier operations, and saving countless aircraft from fuel exhaustion.

The Cold War continued to absorb most of the attention of naval aviation. Flare-ups occurred on occasion, with navy patrol and reconnaissance aircraft becoming targets for Soviet and Chinese fighters: six P4Y, P2V, and P4M aircraft were shot down between 1950 and 1959, with several other patrol planes damaged. On one occasion in 1954, however, two Chinese LA-7 fighters fell to the guns of navy AD Skyraiders from the *Philippine Sea* during a search for survivors of an airliner downed near Hainan by Chinese fighters.

Keeping in mind the devastation wreaked by Germany's U-boat fleet during World War II, the navy invested considerable resources in countering the potential of the Soviet submarine fleet. Escort carriers with antisubmarine aircraft were replaced with some *Essex*-class ships converted to antisubmarine carriers (CVSs). These ships carried the S2F (S-2) Tracker, a twin-engine plane that combined search-and-attack capabilities in one aircraft. Helicopters, in the form of the HSS (SH-34) Seabat, also took on the antisubmarine role. Antisubmarine warfare also became the primary mission of patrol squadrons, equipped with P2Vs (SP-2) and P5M (SP-5) Marlin flying boats. Blimps, however, were retired in 1961, when the last two squadrons (ZP-1 and ZP-3) were disestablished at Lakehurst, New Jersey, ending forty-four years of navy LTA operations.

Helicopters entered service with the marine corps in increasing numbers in the amphibious assault role, and several straight-deck *Essex*-class carriers were converted to amphibious assault ships (LPHs) to carry the marine helicopters to beachheads.

Naval aviation also participated in defending the United States against surprise attacks from Soviet bombers. Airborne early warning barriers were established to provide radar coverage of the Atlantic and Pacific approaches to the United States as seaward extensions of the Distant Early Warning (DEW) radar network across North America. WV (EC-121) Warning Star aircraft flew millions of miles on barrier patrols during nine years of operation.

Carriers became the force of choice for the United States in responding to many international crises that arose during the 1950s and early 1960s. Carriers supported a marine landing operation in Lebanon in 1958, and provided a show of force in the Formosa Strait crisis that same year. Carriers were called to the scene whenever U.S. interests and those of its allies were threatened; they also participated in many disaster relief operations.

One confrontation, the Berlin crisis of 1961, resulted in five patrol and thirteen carrier ASW squadrons being called to active duty. The Cuban Missile Crisis of October 1962, however, brought the United States and the Soviet Union to the brink of war. Low-level missions flown by Light Photo Squadron 62's RF-8A Crusaders produced proof that the Soviets were installing ballistic missiles in Cuba. Carriers participated in the naval quarantine of Cuba, and patrol planes, including the new P-3 Orion, monitored Soviet withdrawal of missiles and bombers.

Although Cold War vigilance was the norm, naval aviation also continued its tradition of supporting scientific exploration. In preparation for International Geophysical Year (1957–58), the navy, along with the other services, mounted Operation Deep Freeze, the most extensive Antarctic exploration ever conducted. In October 1956, an R4D Skytrain from Air Development Squadron 6 made the first landing at the geographic South Pole. Ever since, naval aviation has provided logistic and rescue support to Antarctic research stations.

In the "space race" that captured the imagination of the American public in the early 1960s, the National Aeronautics and Space Administration set a goal of putting a man on the moon before the end of the decade. Four of the first seven American astronauts were naval aviators. During the Mercury program, Lt. Cdr. Alan Shepard became America's first man in space with his suborbital flight in May 1961. Marine Lt. Col. John Glenn became the first American to orbit the earth in February 1962. Navy ships and aircraft provided the means of recovery for the astronauts and their spacecraft. The follow-on Apollo program resulted in the first landing on the moon on 20 July 1969, with former naval aviator Neil Armstrong becoming the first man to walk on the moon.

Vietnam

Naval aviation was involved in defending South Vietnam and Laos from communist aggression early in the 1960s. RA-3B Skywarriors conducted photo-mapping missions, and a detachment of EA-1F Skyraiders was dispatched to intercept intruding aircraft. Navy pilots trained the South Vietnamese air force pilots to fly their A-1 Skyraiders. Task Force 77 carriers launched reconnaissance missions over Laos. In June 1964, an RF-8A from the USS *Kitty Hawk* (CVA 63) was shot down over Laos; the pilot was captured but escaped three months later.

The Tonkin Gulf incident of August 1964 precipitated U.S. naval aviation's first strikes since the Korean War. On 2 August, the destroyer *Maddox* (DD 731) came under attack by three North Vietnamese torpedo boats. A flight of F-8 Crusaders from the USS *Ticonderoga* (CVA 14) was diverted to assist and sank one of the retiring torpedo boats. Two days later, a second torpedo boat attack purportedly occurred against two destroyers. President Lyndon Johnson ordered retaliatory strikes: on 5 August, the *Ticonderoga* and the *Constellation* (CVA 64) launched A-1, A-4, and F-8 aircraft against North Vietnamese torpedo boats and destroyed more than half of the boats at a cost of two aircraft. Shortly afterward, on 10 August, Congress passed the Tonkin Gulf Resolution, supporting efforts to prevent further communist aggression in Vietnam. Carriers and patrol planes maintained a presence in the area.

In response to communist attacks in South Vietnam, Task Force 77 carriers sent strikes into North Vietnam in February 1965. Marines were committed ashore at Da Nang in March 1965, and that month a bombing campaign, Operation Rolling Thunder, was started. Navy, air force, and marine corps aircraft bombed targets almost daily. For much of the operation, however, the prime targets near Hanoi and Haiphong were off limits. North Vietnamese air defenses evolved into the deadliest ever used in combat, comprised of radar-directed antiaircraft artillery, surface-to-air missiles, and jet interceptors, and they took an increasingly costly toll in U.S. planes and aircrews. This campaign had limited military objectives; its primary goal was to bring the North Vietnamese government to the negotiating table.

Yankee Station was established in the Tonkin Gulf as the operating area for Task Force 77 carrier operations against North Vietnam. Dixie Station was established off South Vietnam; carriers rotating to the war zone would typically launch combat missions in the relatively benign skies over South Vietnam before operating on Yankee Station. Carriers from both the Atlantic and Pacific fleets rotated to the war zone and spent intensive periods on the line interspersed with port calls at friendly nations. CVSs also operated in the war zone area; their S-2s flew surveillance patrols, and their SH-3 Sea King helicopters flew rescue missions for downed aircrews.

The inherent danger of carrier combat operations was made evident on four occasions. During the war, four carriers (the USS *Oriskany* [CVA

An A-1J Skyraider releases bombs on a target in South Vietnam. The Vietnam War was the last war for navy piston-engined aircraft. (U.S. Navy/Robert L. Lawson collection)

34], the *Franklin D. Roosevelt* [CVA 42], the *Forrestal*, and the *Enterprise*) were seriously damaged by flight deck or hangar deck fires that killed many sailors and destroyed many aircraft. The lessons learned from these disasters improved shipboard fire-fighting techniques.

Naval aviation made significant contributions to the war effort inside South Vietnam as well. The 1st Marine Air Wing flew close-air support and helicopter assault missions in support of marines in the northern part of South Vietnam. Navy UH-1 helicopter gunships and OV-10 Broncos supported the riverine operations in the southern river deltas. AP-2H gunships conducted interdiction with sophisticated sensors, and OP-2E Neptunes dropped remote sensors along infiltration routes. SP-2, P-3, and SP-5 patrol planes supported Operation Market Time, the maritime interdiction effort along the coast. (The year 1967 saw the last mission

Navy aircrews filled unfamiliar roles during the Vietnam War. This UH-1B gunship from Helicopter Light Attack Squadron 3 provides cover for a riverine patrol in the Mekong Delta. (U.S. Navy)

flown by a navy flying boat, an SP-5B, ending over fifty years of waterborne operations.)

Operations in Vietnam were enhanced by a new generation of aircraft developed in the late 1950s and early 1960s. The F-4 supplemented and eventually replaced the F-8. The A-6 gave carriers an all-weather attack capability that proved especially effective in the frequent bad weather over Vietnam. The A-7 Corsair II eventually replaced the A-4 in light-attack squadrons, and the A-1 Skyraider was finally retired from attack duty in 1968 (but not before downing two enemy MiG-17 jet fighters). The EA-6B Prowler, E-2 Hawkeye, RA-5 Vigilante, C-2 Greyhound, and EP-3 Orions brought a new dimension to their specialties. By the end of the war, all patrol squadrons were flying the P-3 Orion.

During the war, the turbine-powered helicopters became standard, with the UH-1 "Huey," AH-1 Sea Cobra, H-2 Seasprite, H-3 Sea King, H-46 Sea Knight, and H-53 Sea Stallion performing a wide variety of missions.

While the Vietnam War kept U.S. carriers busy, carriers still responded to crises elsewhere in the world, including the Six-Day War between Israel and several Arab nations (including the Israeli attack on the U.S. Navy intelligence collection ship *Liberty*); the North Korean seizure of the U.S. Navy intelligence collection ship *Pueblo* in 1968; the North Korean shootdown of a U.S. Navy EC-121M electronic reconnaissance aircraft in 1969; the 1970 Jordanian crisis; and the Indo-Pakistani War of 1971.

In the spring of 1968, the Rolling Thunder campaign was restricted to the area south of 20° north latitude, and on 1 November President Johnson ordered a halt to all bombing in North Vietnam to encourage the peace negotiations. Air operations were concentrated on the interdiction of infiltration routes through Laos, particularly the so-called Ho Chi Minh Trail.

In the skies over Vietnam, enemy air opposition was sporadic, but U.S. pilots had to readjust to dogfighting after a decade of emphasis on bomber interception. U.S. pilots encountered MiG jets right from the start of Rolling Thunder, and U.S. Navy aircrews usually had the upper hand. The institution of the Navy Fighter Weapons School (Topgun) and a renewed emphasis on air combat maneuvering would yield big dividends during the last year of the war. In May 1972 alone, navy jets downed sixteen MiGs; from these battles emerged Lt. Randall Cunningham and his radar intercept officer, Lt. (jg) William Driscoll, as the navy's only Vietnam War aces and its only team aces, downing five MiGs. Navy aircrews downed sixty-two enemy aircraft during the war with a loss of fifteen planes to enemy aircraft.

The war intensified in the spring of 1972 when the North Vietnamese launched a major offensive in South Vietnam. President Richard Nixon ordered the air war against North Vietnam resumed with maximum effort against supply lines. He also ordered the mining of Haiphong Harbor, which navy and marine corps A-6 and A-7 jets carried out. The Linebacker I campaign produced impressive results in hindering North Vietnamese supply efforts.

Ongoing peace negotiations resulted in an October 1972 decision to again halt bombing operations north of 20° north latitude. The North Vietnamese once more took advantage of the bombing halt to resupply

Two A-6A Intruder attack aircraft rain bombs on a target in North Vietnam. Naval airpower carried out much of the aerial effort to prevent the communist takeover of South Vietnam. (U.S. Navy)

their forces and reinforce their fighter and antiaircraft forces with supplies brought in from China and the Soviet Union. Recognizing the futility of the bombing halt, President Nixon ordered the bombing resumed in December.

Operation Linebacker II was the most intensive air assault ever mounted until that time. Navy and marine corps aircraft from six carriers flew strikes against enemy defenses and logistics. The new EA-6B Prowler jammed enemy radars to protect the waves of air force B-52 bombers hitting targets in Hanoi. Negotiations resumed in January 1973, and a cease-fire was announced on 23 January. The last missions were flown over North Vietnam on 27 January. With the cease-fire came the release of 566 American prisoners of war (POWs), many of them navy and marine corps fliers.

Combat operations continued in Laos into February, and in Cambodia until August. Off North Vietnam, however, navy and marine corps H-53 helicopters spent five months in Operation Endsweep clearing mines in North Vietnamese waters.

Fighting in South Vietnam continued into 1975, when the North Vietnamese launched a massive offensive that overran South Vietnam, which fell on 30 April 1975. U.S. carriers evacuated Americans and others and flew cover for the evacuation, Operation Frequent Wind. Cambodia fell in April, with marine helicopters pulling out the last Americans. In May, Cambodian Khmer Rouge rebels seized the U.S. merchant ship

Mayaguez; the crew was rescued in an operation that included aircraft from the USS *Coral Sea* (CVA 43). It was a bitter end to two decades of effort in Vietnam.

The war in Vietnam was costly to naval aviation in terms of aircraft: the navy lost over 544 aircraft in combat and over 347 to operational causes; the numbers for the marine corps totaled over 464 and 236 aircraft, respectively. The fate of many missing flyers was unknown at war's end.

The communist conquest of South Vietnam did not bring stability to the region, however. In the late 1970s, thousands of refugees began to flee the country in small, crowded, often unseaworthy boats, suffering the predations of pirates. Many were lost, but many were saved by ships vectored to their rescue by naval aircraft, mostly P-3s flying "boat people" search missions that began in 1979.

Cold War Victory

The Vietnam War had a debilitating effect on the U.S. military, and by the mid-1970s the navy was suffering from serious material and manpower problems. Carriers were in need of upkeep that was delayed because of war priorities. Retention of skilled personnel dropped, causing manpower shortages in critical areas. While the war occupied the center of attention for a decade, positive developments occurred in other areas. Lessons were learned well.

Carrier aviation underwent continuous upgrading. The CVSs were all retired by 1974, and the remaining *Essex*-class CVAs were gone by 1975, with only the *Lexington* (AVT 16) steaming on as a training carrier. A carrier (the *Midway*) was forward-deployed to Japan in 1973. The USS *America* (CVA 66) and *John F. Kennedy* (CVA 67) joined the fleet during the Vietnam War, as did the *Nimitz* (CVAN 68), the lead ship of nine nuclear-powered carriers in the fleet or scheduled to join the fleet. The *Dwight D. Eisenhower* (CVN 69) was added in 1977. The demise of the CVS led to the "CV Concept," with the USS *Saratoga* (CV 60) as the lead ship, incorporating antisubmarine planes into the attack carrier air wing, a standard concept today.

The F-14 Tomcat joined the fleet in 1972, its long-range Phoenix missile capable of countering the Soviet bomber and cruise missile. The

Captain Bruce McCandless became the first man to walk untethered in space; the feat occurred during Space Shuttle *Challenger's* mission 41-B in February 1984. (NASA)

computerized S-3 replaced the S-2 and helped to make the CV concept a success. The highly sophisticated P-3C version of the Orion patrol plane made its first deployment in 1970, and with upgraded older versions and follow-on update versions, allowed the navy to track the Soviet nuclear submarine threat. By the end of the 1970s, the P-3 and A-6 also had formidable stand-off antiship capabilities with the Harpoon cruise missile. Cruisers, destroyers, and frigates received the SH-2 Seasprite Light Airborne Multipurpose System (LAMPS) as an extension of their combat capability. The AV-8A Harrier vertical/short takeoff and landing (V/STOL) attack aircraft entered marine corps service; although limited in capability, it paved the way for the much-improved AV-8B version that replaced it during the 1980s.

Personnel policy changes in the 1970s also affected naval aviation.

A P-3 Orion on a lonely antisubmarine patrol over the Atlantic typified the cat-and-mouse effort to counter the Soviet submarine threat during the long Cold War. (U.S. Navy/PH1 Steve Uhde)

Women had served as aircrewmen, but in 1974 the first women flight surgeons were qualified, and women naval aviators were designated, with Lt. (jg) Barbara Ann Allen becoming the first.

U.S. forces were placed on a worldwide alert during the 1973 Arab-Israeli War in response to the possibility of Soviet intervention in the conflict. Naval forces, including three carriers and two LPHs in the Mediterranean supported U.S. interests in the region. One carrier, the USS *Franklin D. Roosevelt* (CV 42), served as a refueling stop for fifty A-4 attack aircraft being rushed to Israel. The end of that conflict once again saw the navy's aerial mine-sweeping helicopters (this time the new RH-53D versions) in use, clearing the Suez Canal and its approaches.

These RH-53Ds were later selected to fly a special mission, the attempted rescue of fifty-two hostages in the American Embassy in Tehran, Iran, who were trapped there in November 1979 during the Iranian revolution. In April 1980, flying from the USS *Nimitz* (CVN 68) in the Indian Ocean, eight RH-53Ds participated in the mission, but mechanical difficulties forced cancellation at the staging point inside Iran. Tragically, several lives were lost during the withdrawal when an RH-53D collided on the ground with a C-130, and most of the helicopters had to be abandoned. The hostages were finally released 444 days after they were captured.

The 1980s were years of increased defense budgets, combat readiness, and confidence for naval aviation. Material readiness and personnel retention improved substantially. The USS *Carl Vinson* (CVN 70) and *Theodore Roosevelt* (CVN 71) were added to the carrier fleet. The last F-4 fighters were retired, and the F/A-18 Hornet strike fighter entered service to replace the F-4 and the A-7. F-14s added photo-reconnaissance as one of their missions, phasing out the RF-8 and RA-5 aircraft. The SH-60B Seahawk gave surface warships a much more capable LAMPS helicopter. The P-3, SH-3, and S-3 forces were continually modernized to keep pace with Soviet submarine quieting programs. The AV-8B Harrier and the improved CH-46E, CH-53E, and AH-1T/W helicopters, launched from the new *Tarawa* (LHA 1)-class LHAs and *Wasp* (LHD 1)-class LHDs strengthened marine corps amphibious assault capabilities.

The decade was also interspersed with crises that called naval aviation into seven combat operations. In August 1982, during missile-firing exercises in international waters off the coast of Libya, Libyan fighters harassed U.S. naval aircraft. Two Libyan Su-22 fighters fired on two *Nimitz*-based VF-41 F-14A Tomcat fighters, which quickly downed the Libyans, putting a stop to the harassment.

In October 1983, a Marxist regime on the island of Grenada in the Caribbean seized power and held dozens of American medical students hostage. An amphibious assault supported by marine helicopters from the *Guam* (LPH 9), supported by A-6 and A-7 strikes from the *Independence* (CV 62) and by air force AC-130 gunships, quickly liberated the island. Weeks later in the eastern Mediterranean, the *Independence* joined the *John F. Kennedy* (CV 67) in launching strikes against Syrian antiaircraft defenses in Lebanon in retaliation for their shooting at U.S. reconnaissance aircraft. The U.S. Navy lost two planes, an A-6 and an A-7, to ground fire.

Terrorist action supported by Libya and other nations brought naval aviation to bear against the terrorists and their sponsors during the mid-

1980s. In October 1985, guided by an E-2C, F-14s from the *Saratoga* intercepted a Boeing 737 airliner carrying the terrorists who hijacked the cruise liner *Achille Lauro* and forced it down in Sicily, where the terrorists were apprehended. Later, when FBI agents captured a terrorist in the Mediterranean, he was spirited away to the United States tied up in the back of one of the *Saratoga*'s S-3s.

In March and April 1986, carriers conducted strikes against Libya. Operation Prairie Fire in March was launched after Libya declared a "Line of Death" across the Gulf of Sidra and fired a surface-to-air missile at U.S. Navy F-14s. Retaliatory strikes (A-6Es and A-7Es) from the *Saratoga* and the *America* (CV 66) destroyed Libyan missile site radars, as well as three patrol boats at sea. A month later, after a terrorist bombing in Berlin, Germany, had been linked to Libya, President Ronald Reagan ordered Operation El Dorado Canyon; strikes from the *America* and the *Coral Sea* (CV 43)—A-6Es, A-7Es, F/A-18As and EA-6Bs, combined with a long-range Air Force F-111 strike from England—hit Libyan airfields, barracks, and command centers. The U.S. Navy lost no planes in these operations.

The long Iran-Iraq War set the stage for U.S. Navy involvement in combat in the Persian Gulf. In order to curb Iranian and Iraqi strikes on oil tankers steaming in the gulf, the U.S. Navy was called upon to escort the tankers to and from Kuwaiti ports starting in July 1987 (Operation Earnest Will). RH-53D helicopters were dispatched to the gulf on board the *Guadalcanal* (LPH 7) to sweep the tanker lanes for Iranian mines. In September, an Iranian ship was caught laying mines and was captured; the following month U.S. Marine Corps AH-1T helicopter gunships sank three Iranian patrol boats after they fired on an army helicopter. The following April, after the frigate *Samuel B. Roberts* (FFG 58) struck an Iranian mine, U.S. Navy ships, covered by aircraft from the *Enterprise* (CVN 65), retaliated by striking Iranian oil platforms that served as bases for Iranian attacks on shipping. When Iranian naval units sortied to oppose the American ships, intense action followed as U.S. Navy surface warships and A-6Es from the *Enterprise* sank an Iranian frigate, a missile attack boat, and a patrol boat, and damaged another frigate and several patrol boats. The only U.S. loss was a marine corps AH-1T helicopter gunship and its crew. The Iranian navy was severely chastened.

Naval aviation would experience one more encounter with Libya before the decade was over. In January 1989, two Libyan MiG-23 fighters made a threatening approach to two U.S. Navy F-14s from the *John F. Kennedy*-based VF-32 and fell to missiles from the Tomcats.

During the buildup of the 1980s, with increased expenditures on ships, aircraft, and personnel, naval aviation grew to a post-Vietnam War peak in 1986–88, with fifteen carriers and fourteen active carrier air wings. The *Abraham Lincoln* (CVN 72) was commissioned in 1989. The improved F-14B Tomcat, the new E-6A Mercury, MH-53E Sea Dragon, and the P-3C Update III joined the fleet at the end of the decade, and the SH-60F had begun replacing the old SH-3. Various programs to increase the numbers of pilots had been instituted, including the Aviation Duty Officer, Flying Limited Duty Officer (LDO), and the re-instituted Naval Aviation Cadet (NAVCAD) programs. That level, however, proved unsustainable in budget considerations, and Carrier Air Wing 10 was disestablished in 1988 after a short time before it could even deploy.

Navy, marine corps, and coast guard aircrews were committed in substantial numbers during the 1980s to the national drug-interdiction campaign along the southern U.S. coasts and the Caribbean. Patrol, early warning, and observation planes, along with a variety of helicopters, operated together to stem the flow of illegal drugs from some Latin American countries.

Political developments overseas, with the fall of communist dictatorships in Eastern Europe and the Soviet Union, symbolized by the tearing down of the Berlin Wall in 1989, at last brought about the end of the Cold War. Naval aviation had played an important part in that favorable outcome.

The Gulf War and the Drawdown

The breakup of the Soviet Union left the United States as the world's only superpower, able to afford a drawdown from Cold War force levels. Naval aviation began taking its share of force-level reductions. The *Coral Sea* was decommissioned in 1990, and her air wing disestablished. Several patrol squadrons were also cut, the first in over 20 years. In addition, aircraft procurement declined, and replacements for the P-3 and A-6 (the P-7 and A-12) were canceled in view of costly design problems. Planners became concerned that the viability of carrier aviation as a strike force would be weakened by aircraft design and procurement problems. The final variant of the Tomcat, the F-14D, was accepted into fleet service, and production would soon end.

The drawdown was interrupted in August 1990 when Iraq invaded and conquered Kuwait and threatened the supply of oil to western nations and Japan. President George Bush ordered U.S. forces into the breach and soon fashioned a remarkable, broad multi-national coalition to counter Iraq. Navy P-3 patrol planes were the first aircraft to reinforce the small Middle Eastern Force, and the carriers *Independence* and *Dwight D. Eisenhower* rushed to the scene to bring tactical airpower to bear in Operation Desert Shield. Soon augmented by the *Saratoga, John F. Kennedy,* and several amphibious assault ships, these forces were credited with discouraging further Iraqi advances. As these forces flew patrols and assisted in the naval blockade of Iraq, the coalition steadily built up its forces in the region over the next five months.

In November 1990, with Iraq intransigent, President Bush ordered the carrier force doubled. The *Midway* (CV 41) had arrived, the *Independence* and *Dwight D. Eisenhower* had been relieved, and the *Ranger* (CV 61), *America,* and *Theodore Roosevelt* arrived by mid-January 1991. The majority of marine corps aviation was deployed in Saudi Arabia and on ships in the Persian Gulf.

On 17 January 1991, the coalition launched Operation Desert Storm, with massive air strikes against Iraqi forces and installations spearheading the offensive to liberate Kuwait from Iraqi occupation. Navy and marine corps aircraft comprised a large part of the offensive. The carrier strikes marked the first time that navy carriers had conducted strikes from the confined waters of the Red Sea and Persian Gulf, and it was the largest sustained gathering of carriers since World War II. The navy accomplished the impossible by operating four carriers among the oil rigs, islands, and shipping in the Persian Gulf.

The forty-four-day war included the most intense aerial offensive in history. Navy FA-18s, A-6Es, and A-7s pounded Iraqi targets, with EA-6Bs suppressing enemy defenses. Precision guided munitions, including the Stand-off Land-Attack Missile (SLAM), were employed to great effect. Tactical air-launched decoys (TALDs) confused enemy defenses. The Iraqi navy was destroyed mostly by carrier planes vectored by P-3s and S-3s in the Persian Gulf. Helicopters swept mines, inserted special operations forces, and placed boarding teams on merchant shipping. VC-6's

A bomb-laden A-7E Corsair II attack aircraft is flung off the deck of USS *John F. Kennedy* (CV 67), bound for an Iraqi target in the 1991 Persian Gulf War. (U.S. Navy/PH3 Paul Hawthorne)

two remotely piloted vehicle (RPV) detachments provided gunfire-spotting for the two battleships in the gulf. When the ground liberation of Kuwait began on 24 February, marine aviators engaged in classic close-air support.

The navy achieved few aerial victories. On the first day of the war, navy F/A-18s from the *Saratoga*'s VFA-81, while inbound to their targets, downed two Iraqi MiG-21 fighters. The only other U.S. Navy aerial victory was scored by a VF-1 F-14 against an Iraqi helicopter.

Navy and marine aircrews flew about thirty thousand sorties during the Persian Gulf War. Only thirteen aircraft and eight crewmen were lost to enemy action, a tribute to the superb suppression of enemy defenses. Aircrews from all services operated in closer cooperation than at any time

An F/A-18C Hornet strike fighter patrols the Persian Gulf, enforcing the "no-fly zone" over southern Iraq in 1993. Carrier aircraft are one of the nation's primary means of deterrence and projecting power in crises around the world. (U.S. Navy/Cdr. T. B. Surbridge)

since the World War II Solomons campaign. Flaws in joint operational planning and communications architecture made strike coordination difficult, but these problems were recognized and have been attacked vigorously since the war.

The pace has not slackened for naval aviation since the Gulf War, with near nonstop international crises. The evacuations of personnel from Liberia and Somalia; protection of Kurdish minorities in Iraq; disaster relief in Bangladesh, Somalia, the Philippines, Florida, Hawaii, and Guam; no-fly zones over Iraq and Bosnia; all of these were accomplished employing naval aviation. Navy flyers returned to combat in January 1993 when Iraqi violations of the no-fly zone over parts of Iraq were punished with strikes from the *Kitty Hawk*'s air wing. In 1994, two carriers

The 1990s saw increased flexibility in the use of aircraft carriers, particularly for joint operations. Here, troops board an army UH-60 helicopter for an operation on shore. (U.S. Navy)

supported the lift of army helicopters to Haiti in order to restore an elected president there.

The drawdown of naval aviation continued apace into the mid-1990s. The carriers *Lexington, Midway, Forrestal* (AVT 59), *Saratoga*, and *Ranger* were decommissioned, replaced only by the *George Washington* (CVN 73) and *John C. Stennis* (CVN 74), with the *Harry S Truman* (CVN 75) and *Ronald Reagan* (CVN 76) scheduled to replace the *America* and *Independence*. The *John F. Kennedy* remains in service as a deployable training carrier in the Naval Reserve Force. Two active and one reserve air wings were disestablished, as were dozens of aircraft squadrons. Many types of aircraft, such as the A-7 (and soon the A-6) were eliminated from the inventory entirely, some prematurely, in order to reduce costs. In terms of numbers, aircraft procurement dipped to levels below pre-World War II

Naval Aviation: The Legacy   53

The F/A-18E on its first flight. (U.S. Navy)

levels. Many air stations in the United States and overseas were closed or consolidated to reduce the infrastructure overhead costs.

Changes in the carrier wing, however, led to greater multi-mission and offensive capabilities in the 1990s. F-14s and S-3Bs were given significant antisurface strike capability. Carrier air wings with fewer planes than before ended up with greater offensive capability.

Painful personnel adjustments also occurred. Many faced early retirement. Pilot and NFO training was cut dramatically; the Naval Aviation Cadet (NAVCAD) program was again terminated. In 1993, Congress opened all aviation billets to women and flight training was made gender-neutral. Joint flight training became more of a reality by the mid-1990s.

In terms of aircraft, development is pushing ahead on the improved F/A-18E and F/A-18F versions of the Hornet strike fighter, and the Joint Attack Strike Technology program is paving the way for the carrier jet of the next century. The V-22 is under development as the future marine corps assault aircraft. The T-45 and the Beech Joint Primary Air Training System design are bringing new technologies to flight training. Upgrades of many existing aircraft designs are ongoing or planned.

Naval aviation personnel continue to staff the U.S. space program. The space shuttle program inaugurated in 1981 continues on a regular basis to carry valuable scientific payloads into space.

One of the indicators of the maturity of naval aviation during the 1980s and 1990s is the number of senior leaders in government and the private sector who started out in naval aviation. The list of government officials includes President George Bush (World War II torpedo bomber pilot); Senator John Glenn (D-Ohio) (Korean War fighter pilot and the first American to orbit the earth), Senator Jeremiah Denton (R-Alabama) (rear admiral, Vietnam War attack pilot, and POW); Senator Jake Garn (R-Utah) (patrol seaplane pilot); Senator Tom Harkin (D-Iowa) (ferry pilot); Senator John McCain (R-Arizona) (captain, Vietnam attack pilot, and POW); and Representative Randall Cunningham (R-California) (Vietnam War fighter ace). Two naval flight officers served as secretary of the navy (John Lehman and H. Lawrence Garrett), and one naval aviator became secretary of defense (Donald Rumsfeld). Another Vietnam War fighter pilot, Medal of Honor winner, and POW, Vice Adm. James Stockdale, was a candidate for vice president.

As this is written (September 1995), the carrier deployed to the Mediterranean is flying strikes in support of NATO operations in war-torn Bosnia. Patrol and reconnaissance planes and helicopters enforce the maritime sanctions of the region.

Today, naval aviation personnel, ships, and aircraft are deployed around the world, maintaining their solemn vigil in support of U.S. interests. Though the challenges constantly change, naval aviation has built a solid tradition of meeting them and prevailing. The legacy continues.

TWO

WINGS: THE CHALLENGE

Naval aviation is renowned for the demands it places upon its flyers. The skills and concentration required to land a high-performance jet on board an aircraft carrier deck pitching in the black of night, or to track a submarine while flying only a few feet above stormy seas, are not only linked to a solid academic background or to top physical conditioning. There is much more to it than that; it requires a combination of talents and dedication that many people possess, but few are challenged to use to full measure. Some spend their lives avoiding challenge and never know the extent of their real capabilities. Others choose a goal, take a deep breath, and pursue it.

The key to success in naval aviation, as in all high-powered professions, is personal commitment, and each individual must decide if he or she is willing to make that commitment. Navy wings are not for everyone. In the final analysis, they are for those who will accept the challenge—those who will settle for nothing less. The flight training process accepts only the best applicants, and only the best of the best will receive their wings of gold.

Becoming a Student

The Naval Air Training Command conducts naval undergraduate flight training which leads to a designation as a naval aviator (pilot) or naval flight officer (NFO). With the end of the Cold War and associated force-level reductions in the early 1990s, the demand for aviators and NFOs has declined, making competition for the remaining cockpit slots stiffer than it ever has been. The higher standards result in a graduate of consistent high quality never before achieved.

The trademark achievement of a naval aviator has long been the carrier landing. In decades past, every naval aviator became carrier-qualified; not so in these days of increased austerity and specialization. Only those pilots destined for carrier-capable squadrons will be carrier-qualified; those destined to fly with the two other large communities, patrol planes or helicopters, will not be trained in carrier landings. (One out of three naval aviators is a helicopter pilot.) Although there are exceptions, generally pilots will complete their careers in the community in which they began. The paths to undergraduate naval flight training are the same that lead to a commission in the navy, marine corps, or coast guard:

Navy and marine corps:
    The U.S. Naval Academy, Annapolis, Maryland
    Naval Reserve Officer Training Corps (various colleges)
Navy only:
    Officer Candidate School, Pensacola, Florida
Marine Corps only:
    Officer Candidate School, Quantico, Virginia
Coast Guard only:
    The Coast Guard Academy, New London, Connecticut
    Officer Candidate School, Yorktown, Virginia

Some coast guard aviators receive direct commissions from other services; many are former army aviators.

Anyone entering training to become a naval aviator or an NFO must possess a bachelor's degree from an accredited college. The navy terminated the Naval Aviation Cadet (NAVCAD) and the Flying Limited Duty

Officer (FLDO) programs, the only programs that did not require a college degree for entry. In 1994, the navy merged the Aviation Officer Candidate (AOC) program at the Aviation Officer Candidate School in Pensacola, Florida, with the Officer Candidate School (OCS), which moved from Newport, Rhode Island.

Candidates for flight training must also pass a stringent physical examination and meet established physical fitness standards. The requirements for pilots and NFOs differ only in the visual acuity standard, which is stricter for pilots. For the most current details concerning entry requirements, the interested civilian candidate should consult a local recruiting station.

Graduates of the Naval Academy, the Coast Guard Academy, and the Naval Reserve Officer Training Corps (NROTC) are selected for flight training during their final year of school. All are volunteers. They arrive at Pensacola ready to begin the Aviation Preflight Indoctrination (API) program. Civilian college graduates who desire a career in naval aviation may attend OCS (navy, marine corps, or coast guard), where they will receive training standard for all officers of their service.

At the navy OCS in Pensacola, which emphasizes the "one navy" concept without the aviation-specific curriculum, officer candidates receive ten formal courses in thirteen weeks. These courses include naval warfare, damage control, and engineering. Practical navigation, shiphandling, and piloting are taught using 100-foot yard patrol craft (YPs). As ever, physical fitness, swimming skills, and military drill are also emphasized. Of the approximately three hundred OCS students per year, about 40 percent proceed to API as student naval aviators (SNAs) or student NFOs (SNFOs).

Aviation Preflight Indoctrination

Once commissioned, all SNAs and SNFOs begin their formal aviation training by attending six weeks of Aviation Preflight Indoctrination (API) conducted in Pensacola by the Naval Aviation Schools Command. This course involves academic training in aerodynamics, engineering, air navigation, aviation physiology, and water survival, as well as physically challenging practical application of physiology and water survival training. Once they are grounded in these basics, graduates are ready for their

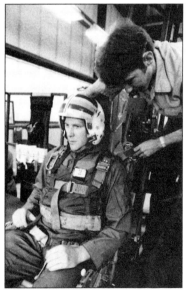

Aviation Preflight Indoctrination at Pensacola includes water survival training (*top*), including disengaging from a parachute harness (*bottom, left*). A simulator (*bottom, right*) is used to provide ejection seat orientation. (U.S. Navy)

primary training "pipelines." At this point, the training tracks for SNAs and SNFOs separate, and they will not fly together until they are designated and learning to fly their particular fleet aircraft in the Fleet Readiness Squadron.

Primary Flight Training

In the primary flight training phase, students continue academics but also begin flying. They start to develop their skills, including the cockpit awareness and "headwork" that will someday make them proficient airmen and efficient warriors.

Flight training in the 1990s is characterized by two broad trends: the increase of computer interactive simulation and the merging of primary training with that of the air force. Merging training, an initiative by the Congress to encourage budget efficiencies, began in earnest in 1994, initially through instructor and student exchanges, and now through integration of training pipelines.

Upon completion of API, a student pilot is assigned to one of five navy training squadrons (VT) flying the T-34C Turbomentor, a single-engine turboprop aircraft, or to an air force flying training squadron (FTS) at the 35th FTS at Reese Air Force Base in Lubbock, Texas, which trains students in the T-37B "Tweet" jet trainer. Primary squadrons training in the T-34C include VT-2, VT-3, and VT-6 at NAS Whiting Field, Florida; and VT-27 and VT-28 at NAS Corpus Christi, Texas. Command of VT-3 and the 35th FTS alternate between navy and air force officers; command of VT-6 alternates between navy and marine corps officers.

Table 2-1. Naval Aviation Training Squadrons

Squadron	Aircraft	Type Training
Commander, Naval Air Training Command		
Commander, Training Air Wing 1		NAS Meridian, Mississippi
VT-19	T-2C	Intermediate Strike
VT-23	T-2C	Intermediate Strike
VT-7	TA-4J	Advanced Strike

Table 2-1. *(continued)*

Squadron	Aircraft	Type Training
Commander, Training Air Wing 2		NAS Kingsville, Texas
VT-21	T-45A	Intermediate/Advanced Strike
VT-22	T-45A	Intermediate/Advanced Strike
Commander, Training Air Wing 4		NAS Corpus Christi, Texas
VT-27	T-34C	Primary
		Intermediate Maritime/Helo
VT-28	T-34C	Primary
		Intermediate Maritime/Helo
VT-31	T-44A	Intermediate E-2/C-2; Advanced Maritime
Commander, Training Air Wing 5		NAS Whiting Field, Florida
VT-2	T-34C	Primary
		Intermediate Maritime/Helo
VT-3	T-34C	Primary
		Intermediate Maritime/Helo
VT-6	T-34C	Primary
		Intermediate Maritime/Helo
HT-8	TH-57B/C	Helicopter
HT-18	TH-57B/C	Helicopter
Commander, Training Air Wing 6		NAS Pensacola, Florida
VT-4	T-2C	Advanced E-2/C-2
VT-10	T-34C, T-39N,	Primary NFO
	T-1A	Intermediate Tactical Navigation
VT-86	T-2C, T-39N	Advanced Strike NFO
	T-1A	Advanced Strike/Fighter NFO
Commander Carrier Airborne Early Warning Wing, U.S. Atlantic Fleet		
NAS Norfolk, Virginia		
VAW-120	E-2C	Advanced ATDS NFO
Air Education & Training Command (USAF)		
Reese AFB, Lubbock, Texas		
35th FTS	T-37B	Primary
		Intermediate Maritime
		Intermediate E-6, E-2/C-2
52nd FTS	T-1A	Advanced E-6
Randolph AFB, San Antonio, Texas		
562nd FTS	T-43A	Maritime Navigator NFO

Student naval aviators preflight a T-34C. Students are indoctrinated in safety right from the start of training. (U.S. Navy/JOC Kirby Harrison)

Primary flight training includes the basics of contact, instrument, formation, and aerobatic flying. Students in primary VT squadrons receive sixty-six hours in the T-34C, before moving on to the selected pipeline intermediate training phase. Students at the 35th FTS receive sixty-six hours in the T-37B, at which point those destined for the strike syllabus or those selected to fly the E-2 Hawkeye or C-2 Greyhound will move on to intermediate training at their respective sites. SNAs at the 35th TFS destined for the maritime, E-6, or helicopter pipelines will remain at Reese AFB for their intermediate phase.

Students are assigned a flight instructor who will train them through the primary phase, giving encouragement, advice, and criticism as necessary. The instructor has a large stake in the success of the student; the progress of the student reflects the competence and effort of the instructor, who takes understandable pride in the student's achievements.

After many hours of instruction and several flights, the student is ready to solo. This is the first big test, the moment when students lift the

A T-34C taxis for the runway at NAS Whiting Field as others await the student and instructor pilots. (U.S. Navy/JOC Kirby Harrison)

plane off the ground all by themselves—and bring it back safely. They will have many memorable experiences after this moment, but none will equal the thrill of that first solo. After more solo flights, the student receives instruction in formation flight, basic instrument flight, and aerobatics.

Upon successful completion of primary training, student aviators are selected for their community pipeline and move on to the intermediate phase. Selection is based on personal preference, individual flight performance, and the needs of the service at that point in time. Student pilots select one of five pipelines: strike (tactical jets); E-2/C-2; maritime; E-6; or rotary-wing (helicopter).

The introduction of joint primary training in the 1990s is paving the way for a proven joint syllabus that will accommodate the Joint Primary Aircraft Training System (JPATS). The Mark II version of the Pilatus

Wings: The Challenge 63

Top: Most student naval aviators and naval flight officers receive their primary flight training in the T-34C. (U.S. Navy/Robert L. Lawson) *Bottom:* With the advent of joint primary flight training in the mid-1990s, some students start flight training in the U.S. Air Force's T-37B jet trainer. (Robert F. Dorr collection)

PC-9, to be manufactured by Beech Aircraft, was selected in June 1995 to replace the T-34C and T-37B and is scheduled to be in service by the year 2000. Like the T-45, the new trainer will be part of a complete training system, including interactive computers for academic instruction and sophisticated simulators.

The Beech PC-9 Mark II was selected in 1995 to eventually replace the navy T-34C and the air force T-37 as the Joint Primary Aircraft Training System (JPATS). (Beech)

Strike Pipeline

Strike students receive their intermediate training at the same base where they will receive their advanced training. These students will complete intermediate training in the T-2C Buckeye or T-45A Goshawk, depending on the base to which they are sent: NAS Meridian, Mississippi, to fly the T-2C with VT-19 or VT-23; or to NAS Kingsville, Texas, to fly the T-45A with VT-21 and VT-22.

Intermediate strike training includes classroom instruction in meteorology, communications, aerodynamics, engineering, and navigation. Flight training includes visual and instrument flight; high- and low-altitude flying; high-speed formation flight; precision aerobatics; and aerial gunnery. Students receive considerable time in simulators to practice flight procedures and prepare for flights.

Strike syllabus student pilots at NAS Meridian obtain their intermediate training in the T-2C jet trainer. (U.S. Navy)

Carrier qualification is the special rite of passage for the strike student. After receiving ground instruction on the optical landing system and practicing carrier landings with an instructor at an airfield, the student makes several more practice landings solo. After demonstrating proficiency, students are ready for the "boat."

Carrier qualification detachments, or "CQ dets," are scheduled during times when the navy's training/reserve carrier, the USS *John F. Kennedy* (CV 67), or another fleet carrier is available. Students are required to complete two touch-and-go landings, four arrested landings, and four catapult launches. With increased confidence, students move on to the advanced phase.

For their advanced phase, students from VT-19 and VT-23 at NAS Meridian move on to VT-7 to train for 104 flight hours and to carrier-

Many strike students meet the aircraft carrier in the T-2C, shown here readying for a catapult launch. (U.S. Navy/Lt. Doug Stevens)

qualify in the TA-4J Skyhawk before graduating sixty-nine weeks after beginning flight training. Students from VT-21 and VT-22 at NAS Kingsville remain with those squadrons through their advanced phase, flying eighty-seven hours and carrier-qualifying in the T-45A before winning their wings after sixty-two weeks of flight training. (VT-21 also conducts a temporary, six-month advanced syllabus for some T-2C intermediate phase graduates, a program that will end when enough T-45As are available and the T-2C is phased out.)

The advanced phase includes more instrument flight, night flight, formation flight, air combat maneuver, weapons delivery, and more carrier qualification.

Flying picks up again with more instrument training, developing the student's confidence in his or her ability to fly an aircraft in all weather conditions. Here, the student will refine and build on instrument techniques learned earlier in the syllabus. Upon completion of an instrument exam and check flight, the student will be qualified to fly under instru-

Strike students at NAS Meridian receive their advanced training in the TA-4J Skyhawk, scheduled to be replaced by the new T-45A. (U.S. Navy)

ment flight rules (IFR) and will have demonstrated competence in airways navigation as well as in instrument departures and approaches to landing, including ground-controlled approaches by radar. During night-flight training, the student will adapt his or her instrument skills to the night environment and become proficient in formation, navigation, approaches, and landings at night.

Formation flying, in which military pilots and their aircraft combine their skills to become mutually supporting, offers a different kind of challenge: it facilitates better coordination of assets and permits concentration of firepower on a target. Student pilots learn to rendezvous with other aircraft; cruise in formation; lead the formation; conduct high-altitude maneuvers; and perform the "break" used to enter the traffic pattern at the carrier.

A TA-4J rolls back to release the wire from its tailhook after an arrested landing. (U.S. Navy/PHAN Charles L. Withrow)

One of the most strenuous, demanding, and stimulating portions of the course is air combat maneuver. The student is taught about relative motion and learns to deal with evasive hard turns and breaks; high rates of closure between aircraft; attack and defensive maneuvers; team tactics; and some of the tricks of the trade, such as forcing an opponent to overshoot an approach.

In weapons training, the students are introduced to conventional air-to-ground ordnance delivery techniques. They learn to consider the parameters of dive angle for bombing, along with the line of flight, release points, target motion, and ballistics. Students also master close-air support using rockets and gunfire. Weapons training is usually conducted with detachments at NAF El Centro in southern California.

Students are taught the essentials of mission planning. Here students grasp the importance of precision navigation at high altitudes and high speeds as well as the criticality of high fuel consumption. They learn cruise control for maximum range or endurance, chart reading, and cross-country and tactical planning based on weather, load, and fuel factors. Emergency procedures, check-off lists, en-route check points, and approach at destination are all part of mission planning.

Final carrier qualification comes with a return to the "boat." The technique of landing an aircraft on a carrier has changed considerably since World War II. The introduction of the optical landing system puts a greater share of the responsibility for a well-executed recovery on the aircrew. The man with the paddles is gone and today's navy pilot relies on the "meatball," an amber spot of light that gives him or her precision glide path information all the way down to the deck. The landing signal officer (LSO) can still be of considerable assistance on a pitching deck, but the aircraft's line-up, angle of attack, and airspeed are largely up to the pilot, who flies the aircraft to keep the "meatball" centered between two rows of green lights.

Strike graduates are assigned to fly F-14, F/A-18, AV-8, EA-6, S-3, and ES-3 aircraft in the fleet.

The T-45 Training System

One of the factors revolutionizing naval aviator training is the adoption of the T-45 Training System (T45TS). The centerpiece of the system is the T-45A Goshawk, a navalized version of the British Hawk trainer. The T-45A will replace the TA-4J Skyhawk advanced trainer by October 1997, and later the T-2C Buckeye intermediate trainer. Consolidating training in a single aircraft will gain considerable cost savings. The T-45A is also much more fuel efficient than its predecessors.

Training students since January 1994, the T-45A incorporates modern features to enhance pilot transition to high-performance fighters, such as the F/A-18 Hornet. The cockpit features modern avionics, including a heads-up display (HUD). A recording system in the aircraft enhances mission debrief by providing video and audio feedback to the student. Later production T-45As will have their conventional "round dial" instrument panels replaced with a state-of-the-art "glass cockpit."

The T-45A is only one part of the T45TS, however. The system contains computerized instruction in the classroom, and sophisticated simulators that cover formation flight and weapons training. The system also

Facing page, top: Strike students at NAS Kingsville complete their entire syllabus in the new T-45A Goshawk. The T-45 will eventually replace the older T-2C and TA-4J trainers. (U.S. Navy)

Facing page, bottom: The strike syllabus includes weapons training. This T-45A is launching 2.75-inch rockets. (U.S. Navy/Vernon Pugh)

Top: A strike student brings a Training Wing 2 T-45A to a trap on board a carrier. (U.S. Navy/PH1 Robert McRoy)

Left: The academic portion of the T-45 Training System includes the 4E10 desktop computer that has sophisticated animation to train students in such subjects as gunnery and formation flight. (McDonnell Douglas)

includes the Training and Integration System (TIS), a computer-based planning aid that schedules classrooms, simulators, and flights while tracking individual student performance and requirements.

Under the T45TS, students are exceptionally well-prepared for flight when they climb into a T-45 for their training hops. The system results in better training at lower cost.

Maritime Pipeline

Students destined for the maritime community will complete their intermediate phase at their primary training squadron. At VT primary squadrons, this phase is comprised of six weeks of training, including twenty-six hours in the T-34C, with emphasis on instrument flight and airways navigation. Intermediate students at the 35th FTS receive twenty-three hours in the T-37B, also with emphasis in instrument flying.

Maritime students proceed to VT-31 at NAS Corpus Christi, Texas, for twenty weeks of advanced multiengine propeller training, including eighty-eight flight hours in the T-44A *Pegasus*. Advanced maritime training begins with ground school, including instruction in safety, aircraft procedures, and local area familiarization. Following completion of classroom work, the student is assigned an instructor.

After the student becomes completely familiar with the peculiarities of a twin-engine airplane, including single-engine operation, the instrument phase of training begins. The student will transfer what he or she has learned here to a large, heavy, multiengined aircraft with a full crew. The novice flyer will be taught preflight planning, instrument takeoffs and departures, airway procedures, advanced patterns, partial instrument panel techniques, and approaches to a destination, as well as a variety of emergency procedures. He or she will master the use of navigation aids, the instrument landing system, and radar.

At the end of instrument training, the student will be subjected to a comprehensive instrument flight check, and, if successful, will receive an instrument rating. At this point, the student will be "turned loose" with another student of equal qualification, and the two will sharpen their skills for the operational responsibilities that will ultimately follow. Night flying is also an important part of the syllabus.

Students complete the maritime course with the confidence to carry

Wings: The Challenge 73

The T-44A is used at NAS Corpus Christi to train multiengine pilots in the maritime and E-2/C-2 pipelines. (U.S. Navy/ G. J. Spaulding)

Maritime students learn to master the complex cockpit of the T-44A. (U.S. Navy/PH2 D. MacLean)

out any assigned mission in any weather, day or night. Graduates will fill cockpits in the navy P-3 patrol plane, EP-3 electronic reconnaissance and C-130 transport communities, marine corps KC-130 refueler/transport squadrons, and coast guard HC-130 long-range search-and-rescue aircraft. VT-31 is also assuming the role of training air force student pilots destined to fly air force C-130s.

E-6 Pipeline

Navy students destined to fly the large four-engine E-6 Mercury communications aircraft will also complete their intermediate phase at their primary training squadron. At VT primary squadrons, this phase is comprised of six weeks of training, including twenty-six hours in the T-34C, with emphasis on instrument flight and airways navigation. Intermediate students at the 35th FTS receive twenty-three hours in the T-37B, with the same emphasis in instrument flying.

Once trained in the navy maritime pipeline at VT-31, prospective E-6 pilots now receive their advanced training with air force students slated to fly similar large multiengine jet aircraft. This training is conducted at the 52nd TFS at Reese AFB in Texas in the modern T-1A Jayhawk twin-turbofan jet trainer, and covers the same aspects of long-range instrument flight in any weather as are covered in the maritime pipeline. Students receive considerable instruction with classroom computer training systems and in simulators. Cockpit resource management is emphasized, as well as crew coordination.

E-2/C-2 Pipeline

E-2/C-2 students undergo their intermediate phase at NAS Corpus Christi with VT-31, flying forty-four hours in the T-44A twin-engine turboprop aircraft. The fourteen weeks of training, an abbreviated version of the maritime syllabus, includes aircraft systems lectures and simulator time.

Advanced training for prospective E-2 and C-2 pilots is conducted by VT-4 at NAS Pensacola using the T-2C. Although the T-2C is a tactical jet trainer, it is used for multiengine pilots to conduct carrier qualifications because the navy has not had any multiengine propeller-driven trainers

Advanced training for future E-6 pilots and some navigation training for naval flight officers is conducted in the air force T-1A Jayhawk. (Robert F. Dorr collection)

in inventory since the phaseout of the reciprocating engine TS-2 Tracker (see "Strike Pipeline" section for a description of carrier qualification). After completing eighty-six hours in the T-2C and twenty-three weeks with VT-4, E-2 and C-2, pilots are winged and proceed to VAW-120, the E-2/C-2 Fleet Readiness squadron at NAS Norfolk, Virginia.

Helicopter Pipeline

Students destined for the rotary-wing communities will complete their intermediate phase at their primary training squadron. At VT primary squadrons, this phase is comprised of six weeks of training, including twenty-six hours in the T-34C, with emphasis on instrument flight and airways navigation. Intermediate students at the 35th FTS receive twenty-three hours in the T-37B, with the same emphasis in instrument flying.

After mastering fixed-wing flight in basic and intermediate phases,

Student helicopter pilots practice shipboard landings in a TH-57 Sea Ranger on board the Helicopter Landing Trainer, a vessel based in Pensacola. (U.S. Navy/Art Giberson)

prospective helicopter pilots finally commence their advanced phase at NAS Whiting Field, flying 116 hours in the TH-57B/C Sea Ranger helicopter over a twenty-one-week period. Students begin by covering the aerodynamics and engineering phenomena peculiar to rotary-wing flight, moving on to commence flying, eventually soloing in the TH-57.

The helicopter student becomes proficient in basic instrument techniques, radio-navigation, cross-country flying, rough-terrain landings, night flying, rescue work, and formation flying. The student also conducts small-deck landing qualifications on board the Helicopter Landing Trainer (HLT), a vessel based at NAS Pensacola.

The naval helicopter pipeline produces the finest instrument-qualified pilots in the world. Graduates go on to fill pilot billets in navy, marine corps, and coast guard helicopter units.

Naval Flight Officer Training

An equally important member of the naval aviation team is the NFO. In the fast-moving world of aerial warfare, the need for highly skilled officers manning the aerial navigation and weapons systems has increased, and their professionalism begins in the intensive NFO training pipeline.

Like student pilot training, SNFO training is undergoing rapid computer modernization, as well as further integration with air force navigator and weapons system operator training. By 1997, all navy, marine corps, air force, and many foreign navigators will start their training with the navy at NAS Pensacola.

Primary SNFO Training

Like the student naval aviators with whom they will share cockpits in the fleet, student NFOs begin their aviation training in the six-week API at Naval Aviation Schools Command at NAS Pensacola (see section on API). Upon completion, all SNFOs report to VT-10, also at Pensacola. VT-10 is the largest squadron in the Naval Air Training Command.

At VT-10, students spend fourteen weeks learning visual flight rules and basic airmanship, racking up twenty-two hours of flight time in the T-34C TurboMentor. The SNFOs pilot the T-34Cs for eight flights, although they will not solo in the aircraft. These flights give the SNFO an enhanced awareness of the aeronautical factors affecting the pilot in flight, and better prepare the future NFO to meld with the pilot to form an integrated, effective aircrew team.

As in pilot training, computer-based training (CBT) is being introduced in VT-10, beginning with the Radio Instrument Orientation Trainer (RIOT), a personal-computer-based interactive instrument simulator, being used at individual student training stations and as a classroom lecture aid by instructors. Three T-34C courses (Emergency Procedures, Aerodynamics, and Flight Rules and Regulations) are also computer-based. CBT enhances student learning while reducing its cost.

Navigator Pipeline

Completion of the primary phase marks the first juncture of training pipeline selection. Students selected for the undergraduate navigator pipeline transfer to Randolph AFB, Texas, home of a joint training squadron, the air force's 562nd FTS. For the next twenty-two weeks, student navigators will concentrate on developing their skills in long-range, over-water navigation, using a variety of methods, including celestial, inertial, and radio navigation. Students fly eighty hours in the T-43A (a modification of the Boeing 737 airliner design). Upon graduation, students are awarded their wings and ordered to the Fleet Readiness Squadron to train for navigator slots in P-3 Orion patrol plane, EP-3 Aries electronic reconnaissance aircraft, C-130 transport, or E-6 strategic communications aircraft. While at their fleet squadrons, these navigators (P-3 and E-6) will train for and fleet up to P-3 tactical coordinator (TACCO), and E-6 airborne communications officer (ACO). The EP-3 navigators attend the electronic warfare training course at Corry Field in Pensacola, and eventually fleet up to electronic evaluator positions in their aircraft.

Tactical Navigation Intermediate Training

Students not selected for the navigator program at Randolph AFB will remain at VT-10 for fourteen weeks of training, including fifty-five hours in the T-34C and in the T-39N, a multiplace twin-jet operated by civilian contractors. In this phase, students concentrate on low-level visual navigation and airways navigation. The air force T-1A Jayhawk multiplace twin-jet is now used to augment the T-39N in this role as joint integration proceeds.

Upon completion of this intermediate phase, tactical navigation SNFOs are selected for one of three pipelines: strike; strike/fighter; and aviation tactical data system training.

Strike SNFO Pipeline

SNFOs destined to fly S-3 Vikings, ES-3 Ravens, or EA-6 Prowlers report to VT-86 at Pensacola for advanced training. They receive approxi-

Maritime navigation is taught to student naval flight officers at Randolph AFB, Texas, using the air force T-43A. (Robert F. Dorr collection)

mately eighteen weeks of intensive training, including sixty to seventy hours in the T-2C, T-39N, and T-1A. Emphasis is placed on low-level and over-water tactical jet navigation, as well as on crew coordination. Graduates destined to fly the ES-3 or EA-6 go on to the electronic warfare course at the Naval Technical Training Center at Corry Station in Pensacola before proceeding to the Fleet Readiness Squadron for their particular aircraft.

Strike/Fighter SNFO Pipeline

SNFOs leaving VT-10 for the strike/fighter pipeline at VT-86 will concentrate on many of the same areas as their counterparts in the strike pipeline, such as low-level and over-water navigation. Their training

Student naval flight officers in the Strike and Strike Fighter pipelines receive tactical navigation training in the T-2C (foreground) and T-39N (background). (U.S. Navy)

track, including about eighty hours in the T-2C, T-39N, and T-1A, is longer (about twenty-five weeks), however, in order to master the of art of airborne radar intercepts. Navy graduates go on to fly the F-14 Tomcat fighter as radar intercept officers (RIOs), while marine corps graduates will fly the two-seat F/A-18D Hornet strike fighter as weapons and sensors officers (WSOs).

Aviation Tactical Data System SNFO Pipeline

Upon completion of the intermediate phase at VT-10, students selected for the Aviation Tactical Data System pipeline leave Pensacola and report to Carrier Airborne Early Warning Squadron 120 (VAW-120), the E-2 FRS at NAS Norfolk, Virginia. This pipeline is unique in NFO flight training in that students receive their wings at the FRS rather than upon graduation from a training squadron. At VAW-120, SNFOs undergo intensive training in such subjects as radar, tactical data systems, battle force communications, and airborne intercepts. After twenty-two weeks and thirty-two flight hours in the E-2 Hawkeye, students receive their wings and continue with further FRS training before reporting to their fleet squadron.

Naval Aviation Observer Training

Earning the wings of a naval aviation observer does not involve a formal training syllabus with the Naval Air Training Command. Requirements are described in chapter 4.

Flight Surgeon and Aviation Physiologist/Psychologist Training

Flight surgeon and aviation physiologist training is described in chapter 10.

Aircrew Training

Training of enlisted aircrew is described in chapter 7.

Naval Parachutist

Naval parachutist is not an occupational specialty but is a qualification available to naval personnel. In some nonaviation forces, such as Sea-Air-Land special operations forces, parachutist qualification is necessary for performing their mission.

In years past, parachute riggers, now called aviation survival equipmentmen, were required to make at least one jump with chutes that they had packed. This is no longer a requirement.

"Jump School" for all services is located at Fort Benning, Georgia. The three-week school awards basic parachutist qualification, which is accomplished by five jumps. Five more jumps are required before the naval parachutist qualification is awarded.

Survival, Evasion, Resistance, and Escape Training

The famous SERE training is given to flyers who may find themselves in a situation with a high risk of capture or greater-than-average risk of exploitation by a captor. Navy SERE schools long established in Florida, Maine, and California will be consolidated in a joint SERE school at Fairchild Air Force Base, Washington, beginning in 1996. Personnel normally attend en route to or while in their first squadron tour.

THREE

THE SQUADRON

Revised from an original chapter written by
Capt. Richard C. Knott, USN

The squadron is the basic operational and administrative unit of naval aviation. This closely knit organization is less formal in some respects than other U.S. Navy commands. The squadron experience is characterized by a unique brand of camaraderie and a strong sense of esprit de corps, which promotes teamwork and significantly influences the quality and effectiveness of the squadron's performance, rather like that of a sports team. This environment is the one in which the first-tour aviator or naval flight officer (NFO) gets a first taste of operational flying.

Squadrons vary greatly in terms of equipment and the nature of their operations. Aircraft range from one- or two-place fighters to multiengine patrol planes with large, specialized crews. Some squadrons are carrier-based, spending approximately half of their time at sea and half ashore. Others are land-based but deploy for several months at a time to overseas areas. Some, divided into detachments, are scattered to the winds on ships or bases overseas. Still others, such as training squadrons, do not deploy at all. Whatever the case, each squadron type fulfills a necessary function, and all are essential to the successful execution of the navy's mission.

The camaraderie of squadron life enhances the discipline and teamwork required to carry out the missions of naval aviation. Here, two squadrons of F/A-18 Hornets return home in close formation from a six-month deployment. (U.S. Navy/PH1 J. F. Slaughenhaupt)

Squadron Lineage

Over 140 active navy squadrons and more than 45 naval air reserve squadrons are in existence (as of July 1995); marine corps active aircraft squadrons total 73, along with 13 reserve squadrons. Some of them have been in existence since before World War II. The number changes as new squadrons are established and old squadrons are disestablished to meet the changing needs of the navy. Squadrons are also redesignated as necessary to reflect changing missions. It should be emphasized here that the proper terminology for the origination or termination of a U.S. Navy squadron is establishment and disestablishment, respectively. The terms

The squadron is where the first-tour aviator, such as this E-2C pilot, or NFO is put in control of a multi-million dollar aircraft and the safety of his or her crew. (U.S. Navy/PH3 James E. Gallagher)

commissioned and decommissioned, used incorrectly in this regard, are properly applied to ships (including, in the past, airships).

Squadrons often carry on their heritages for decades, even after redesignation. Newly established squadrons will often adopt many traditions of previous squadrons bearing the same designation, including nicknames, call-signs, insignia, colors, and customs. Nicknames and call-signs are unofficial and can be changed at the whim of the squadron. The unit insignia, however, must be officially approved by the Office of the Chief of Naval Operations through the Special Assistant for Publications and Operational Records (N88H), who is also the Director, Naval Aviation History and Publication Division of the Naval Historical Center.

Many HC squadrons operate versions of the H-46 Sea Knight in detachments on board logistics ships, keeping the vital supplies flowing to the battle groups. (U.S. Navy/ PHAA Jeff Phillips)

Squadron Designations

Squadrons are most often identified by letter-number designations that begin with the letter *V* or *H*. The prefix *V* has been in use since the early 1920s, when it was employed to distinguish heavier-than-air aircraft from lighter-than-air aircraft, the latter type having been identified by the letter *Z*. The U.S. Navy has operated no lighter-than-air aircraft (airships, dirigibles, and blimps) since 1962, so this prefix is no longer used.

The prefix *V* is still used to identify squadrons of fixed-wing, heavier-than-air aircraft. Squadrons of rotary-wing aircraft are identified by the letter *H* for helicopters. Some squadrons include both classes of aircraft; these are normally given the prefix *V*.

The letter or letters that make up the designation suffix signify the squadron's mission. For example, the suffix *T* stands for training. When

Left: The HM squadrons that sweep for mines are the navy's first joint active/reserve squadrons. (U.S. Navy/Joe Sommers) *Right:* HS squadrons perform antisubmarine missions (this SH-60F Seahawk is dipping its sonar into the ocean), as well as plane guard, rescue, and logistics duties. (via *Naval Aviation News*)

combined, the letters *VT* identify a training squadron of fixed-wing aircraft. The letters *HT,* on the other hand, denote a training squadron of helicopters.

Two or more letter suffixes may also be used. For example, the letters *VFA* make up the letter designation of a strike fighter squadron that has both an attack and a fighter capability. Using another example, a light helicopter antisubmarine squadron is identified by the letters *HSL* (helicopter antisubmarine light). As aircraft in use and their missions change with the needs of the navy, particular squadron designations may change or fall into disuse.

To identify a specific squadron of a given type, numbers are added to the letters. Hence, VF-2 is the letter-number designation of Fighter Squadron Two. In numbering squadrons, systems are sometimes used at the outset, although often the systems lose their identities as squadrons are disestablished, redesignated, or assigned to different wings. For example, Atlantic Fleet HSL squadrons are even-numbered in the same

Top: The SH-60B Seahawk flown by HSL squadrons operates in detachments of one or two helicopters on board surface warships. (U.S. Navy/PH1 Mark Therien) *Bottom:* Squadrons vary in size. VAQ squadrons deploy on board carriers with four EA-6B electronic warfare jets. (U.S. Navy/Lt. Cdr. John Leenhouts)

VAW squadrons provide vital radar early warning and combat direction services for the carrier battle groups. (U.S. Navy/PH2 Frazier)

One fleet composite squadron, VC-6, operates no manned aircraft, but deploys detachments of unmanned reconnaissance remotely piloted vehicles (RPVs). (U.S. Navy/PHC Jeff Hilton)

series (HSL-40, -42, -44, etc.), whereas Pacific Fleet squadrons are odd-numbered (HSL-41, -43, -45, etc.). When initially established or redesignated, many current carrier-based squadrons were designated with their original carrier air wing number as the first one or two numerals in their designations (i.e., VF-21, VA-22, VA-23, VF-24, VA-25 were all originally assigned to Carrier Air Wing 2).

Squadrons also can be identified by their acronym message addresses. Within this system, for example, Patrol Squadron 30 (VP-30) becomes PATRON THREE ZERO; Fighter Squadron 14 (VF-11) becomes FITRON ELEVEN; Air Test and Evaluation Squadron 1 (VX-1) becomes AIRTEVRON ONE.

Top: The F-14 Tomcat fighters flown by VF squadrons are now capable of strike missions as well as air-to-air combat. (U.S. Navy/Lt. jg Stephen P. Davis) *Bottom:* The F/A-18 Hornet strike fighter, flown from carriers by VFA squadrons for fighter and strike missions, is the only single-seat first-line combat jet flown by the navy. (U.S. Navy/CWO2 Tony Alleyne)

Table 3-1. Squadron Designations and Missions

Designation	Name	Acronym	Mission
HC	Helicopter Combat Support Squadron	HELSUPPRON	To provide combat search and rescue, logistic and utility services, and vertical replenishment in support of fleet operations.
HCS	Helicopter Combat Support Squadron Special	HELSUPPRONSPEC	To provide combat search-and-rescue support and support of special operation forces. (Naval air reserve only.)
HM	Helicopter Mine Countermeasures Squadron	HELMINERON	To detect, sweep, and destroy mines at sea. A secondary mission is to provide logistic and utility services in support of fleet operations.
HS	Helicopter Antisubmarine Squadron	HELANTISUBRON	To conduct carrier-based all-weather antisubmarine operations, and to provide combat search and rescue and utility support to fleet operations.
HSL	Helicopter Antisubmarine Squadron Light	HELANTISUBRON LIGHT	To provide detachments of Light Airborne Multipurpose System (LAMPS) helicopters on board surface combatant ships, to conduct antisubmarine and antisurface search-and-attack operations, as well as search and rescue and utility services in support of fleet operations.

Table 3-1. *(continued)*

Designation	Name	Acronym	Mission
HT	Helicopter Training Squadron	HELTRARON	To provide rotary-wing flight training to student naval aviators.
VA	Attack Squadron	ATKRON	To conduct carrier-based all-weather offensive and defensive air-to-surface strike operations and aerial refueling support of carrier-based aircraft. (Attack squadrons are being retired with the phaseout of the A-6 aircraft.)
VAQ	Tactical Electronic Warfare Squadron	TACELRON	To conduct carrier-based tactical exploitation, suppression, degradation, and deception of enemy electromagnetic defensive and offensive systems, including communications, in support of air strikes and fleet operations.
VAW	Carrier Airborne Early Warning Squadron	CARAEWRON	To provide carrier-based early warning services to fleet forces and shore warning nets, and command and control of fleet strike and air defense operations.
VC	Fleet Composite Squadron	FLECOMPRON	To provide utility services for fleet training, including adversary services, target services, radar calibration, drone and torpedo recovery, logistics, search and rescue, and

Table 3-1. *(continued)*

Designation	Name	Acronym	Mission
			other range support services.
VF	Fighter Squadron	FITRON	To conduct carrier-based all-weather offensive and defensive air-to-air operations to establish and maintain local air superiority and to provide fleet air defense. To conduct limited carrier-based air-to-surface attack operations. (Some VF squadrons provide adversary services.)
VFA	Strike Fighter Squadron	STRIKFITRON	To conduct carrier-based offensive and defensive air-to-surface strike operations; to conduct carrier-based all-weather offensive and defensive air-to-air operations.
VFC	Fighter Composite Squadron	FITCOMPRON	To provide utility services for fleet training, including adversary services, target services, and radar calibration. To augment combat forces as directed. (Naval air reserve only.)
VP	Patrol Squadron	PATRON	To conduct land-based, all-weather maritime patrol, antisubmarine, reconnaissance, surveillance, mine warfare, and air-to-surface attack operations, and search-and-rescue operations.

Table 3-1. *(continued)*

Designation	Name	Acronym	Mission
VPU	Patrol Squadron Special Projects Unit	PATRONSPEC-PROJUNIT	To conduct land-based specialized maritime reconnaissance operations and support for special projects.
VQ	Fleet Air Reconnaissance Squadron	FAIRECONRON	To provide land-based or carrier-based electronic warfare support measures, including searching for, intercepting, locating, recording, and analyzing radiated electromagnetic signals, for the purpose of exploiting signals in support military operations.
VQ	Strategic Communications Squadron	STRATCOMMRON	To provide airborne communications relay support for land-based and sea-based strategic deterrent forces.
VR	Fleet Logistics Support Squadron	FLELOGSUPPRON	To provide land-based logistics airlift directly responsive to fleet commanders. (Currently naval air reserve only.)
VRC	Fleet Logistics Support Squadron	FLELOGSUPPRON	To provide carrier-on-board delivery logistics to aircraft carriers, and rapid-response airlift services to operating forces.
VS	Sea Control Squadron	SEACONRON	To conduct carrier-based all-weather antisubmarine and air-to-surface search-and-attack missions in support of fleet

Table 3-1. *(continued)*

Designation	Name	Acronym	Mission
			operations, and aerial refueling services to carrier-based aircraft. (Formerly designated Air Antisubmarine Squadron.)
VT	Training Squadron	TRARON	To provide basic or advanced flight training to student naval aviators or flight officers in fixed-wing aircraft.
VX	Air Test and Evaluation Squadron	AIRTEVRON	To test and evaluate operational capabilities of new aircraft and systems in an operational environment, and to develop doctrine and tactics for their most effective use.
VXE	Antarctic Development Squadron	ANTARCTIC-DEVRON	Provide logistical and utility support to the U.S. Naval Support Force and associated scientific research in Antarctica.
TACRON	Tactical Air Control Squadron	TACRON	To provide command and control of tactical aircraft in support of amphibious operations. (No aircraft are assigned.)

Note: With the disestablishment of such squadrons over the last decade, the following designations are no longer used:

HAL—Helicopter Attack Squadron Light
HMA—Marine Attack Helicopter Squadron
HML—Marine Light Helicopter Squadron
VAK—Aerial Refueler Squadron
VFP—Light Photographic Squadron
VRF—Aircraft Ferry Squadron
VXN—Oceanographic Development Squadron

Fleet Readiness Squadrons

Upon completion of flight training and before proceeding to their permanent squadron assignment, aviators, NFOs, and aircrewmen are ordered to Fleet Readiness Squadrons (FRSs) for training in the type of aircraft that they will fly in their first operational squadrons. (During the late 1950s and into the 1960s, many of these squadrons were assigned to Replacement Carrier Air Groups, hence the enduring term "RAG" as a name for an FRS.)

FRSs provide ground and flight training to new and returning aircrews, producing for most aircraft types NATOPS (naval air training and operating procedures standardization)-qualified flyers ready to deploy with their operational squadrons. FRSs, most of which report to a type wing commander, also provide tactical training and flight procedures standardization inspections for the wing's operational squadrons.

Enlisted maintenance personnel who have satisfied technical course requirements are assigned to the FRS's Fleet Replacement Aviation Maintenance Program (FRAMP) for ground maintenance training in the type of aircraft that they will maintain in their operational squadron assignment.

Fleet Readiness Squadrons are typically bigger than their operational counterparts and operate a larger number of aircraft. Their instructors are handpicked, fleet-experienced personnel; only the best can expect to be assigned to instruct the fleet's future combat flyers and ground crews. Command of an FRS is a bonus command tour for the commanding officer; in some cases, it is a major shore command.

Until 1994, in most cases, the Atlantic and Pacific fleets each had an FRS for each type of fleet aircraft. With the downsizing of the navy in the 1990s, most FRSs were consolidated, with a single FRS supporting squadrons in both fleets. In some cases, marine corps FRSs provide training to navy personnel, as does the air force in the case of the C-130 transport aircraft. Table 3-2 lists the various FRSs.

Squadron Organization

Although squadrons of different types vary in organization, they all have a common basic organization. They are organized into departments

The Squadron 97

Students at the fleet readiness squadrons receive extensive training in sophisticated simulators. This F-14D crew is practicing an approach to a dynamic image of an aircraft carrier projected on a forty-foot dome that encompasses the cockpit. (McDonnell Douglas)

Table 3-2. Fleet Readiness Squadrons

Squadron Type	Aircraft Type	FRS	Location
HC	H-3	HC-2	NAS Norfolk, Va.
	H-46	HC-3	NAS North Island, Calif.
	H-53	HMT-302*	MCAS New River, N.C.†
HM	H-53	HMT-302*	MCAS New River, N.C.†
HS	H-60	HS-1	NAS Jacksonville, Fla.
	H-60	HS-10	NAS North Island, Calif.
HSL	H-60	HSL-40	NS Mayport, Fla.
	H-60	HSL-41	NAS North Island, Calif.

Table 3-2. *(continued)*

Squadron Type	Aircraft Type	FBS	Location
VAQ	EA-6	VAQ-129	NAS Whidbey Island, Wash.
VAW	E-2	VAW-120	NAS Norfolk, Va.
VF	F-14	VF-101	NAS Oceana, Va.
VFA	F/A-18	VFA-106	NAS Cecil Field, Fla.†
		VFA-125	NAS Lemoore, Calif.
		VMFAT-101*	MCAS El Toro, Calif.†
VP	P-3	VP-30	NAS Jacksonville, Fla.
VQ	EP-3	VP-30	NAS Jacksonville, Fla.
	ES-3	VS-41	NAS North Island, Calif.
	E-6	NTSU	Tinker AFB, Okla.
VR	C-12	VRC-30	NAS North Island, Calif.
		NAS Ops	NAS Norfolk, Va.
	C-130	USAF	Little Rock AFB, Ark.
VRC	C-2	VAW-120	NAS Norfolk, Va.
VS	S-3	VS-41	NAS North Island, Calif.
NAS	H-1	HMT-303*	MCAS Camp Pendleton, Calif.

Note: The following FRSs have been disestablished since the mid-1980s:

VA-42 (A-6)	VA-122 (A-7)	VA-125 (A-7)	VA-128 (A-6)
VA-174 (A-7)	VAW-110 (E-2)	VAQ-33 (A-3)	VF-124 (F-14)
VP-31 (P-3)	VS-27 (S-3)	HM-12 (H-53)	HC-1 (H-3)
HC-16 (H-1)	HSL-30 (H-2)	HSL-31 (H-2)	

*These marine corps squadrons serve as fleet readiness squadrons for navy flyers and maintenance personnel in the respective aircraft type. Following FRS training, MH-53 crews receive mine countermeasures training at the Airborne Mine Countermeasures Weapons Systems Training School at NAS Norfolk, Va.

†These units at El Toro and Tustin, Calif., and Cecil Field, Fla., are scheduled to move to NAS Miramar, Calif., MCAS New River, N.C., and NAS Oceana, Fla., respectively.

As demonstrated by this P-3C Orion, VP squadrons now have a considerable antisurface weapons capability in addition to their traditional antisubmarine prowess. (U.S. Navy/Mark Meyer, courtesy of Naval Institute *Proceedings*)

and divisions, supervised by a commanding officer (CO) through an executive officer (XO). Both normally hold the rank of commander (or lieutenant colonel in the case of the marine corps), although some special squadrons, particularly FRSs, are commanded by captains or colonels.

The Squadron CO

The CO of a squadron may be either a pilot or an NFO. The CO is responsible for the efficient operation of the command and the successful execution of the squadron's mission. Among the CO's responsibilities outlined in U.S. Navy Regulations are morale, safety, discipline, readiness, efficiency, and operational and deployment orders. Maintaining qualifications along with the other officers, the CO flies operational and training missions with the squadron. As the most senior pilot or NFO, the CO is expected to lead the way in all major squadron events.

The Squadron XO

The executive officer is also a senior pilot or NFO who assumes the duties of CO when the CO is not present. The XO is responsible for administering the day-to-day routine of the squadron, ensuring that it functions smoothly and efficiently. The XO will normally "fleet up" to become CO when the CO's tour of duty ends.

The Squadron Departments

Regardless of mission, all navy squadrons have at least four departments: administrative, operations, maintenance, and safety. Beyond that, individual squadrons may have additional departments to suit specialized needs. Departments are divided into divisions, and divisions are divided into branches.

Administration Department

The administrative officer handles correspondence for the CO and XO. He or she also maintains officer and enlisted records; and controls classified material, educational services, legal services, and public affairs. The administrative officer also supervises the activities of the first lieutenant, who is, in turn, responsible for vehicles and the physical security, maintenance, and cleanliness of squadron spaces and equipment. In large squadrons, part of the administrative department duties are assigned to a separate department, the Command Services Department. Billets typically included in the Administration Department are:

—Assistant administrative officer
—Personnel officer
—First lieutenant
—Educational services officer
—Command security manager
—Public affairs officer
—Legal officer

Operations Department

The operations officer is charged with the proper planning and execution of squadron operations. His or her responsibilities encompass the

Top: Electronic reconnaissance performed by VQ squadrons with EP-3E Orions equipped with the Aries II system is vital to combat operations undertaken by naval forces. (Lockheed) *Bottom:* ES-3A Vikings flown by detachments from VQ squadrons give the carrier its own airborne electronic reconnaissance capability. (U.S. Navy)

areas of schedules, tactics, navigation, communications, and intelligence. The operations officer also supervises flight scheduling; training; the maintenance of logs and records; weapons employment; and defense against chemical, biological, and nuclear weapons. In some squadrons, the training functions are grouped in a separate Training Department. In a carrier squadron, the landing signal officer falls under cognizance of the "OPSO." Typical billets in the Operations Department include:

—Flight officer
—Training officer
—Communications officer
—Classified material security officer
—Intelligence officer
—Pilot training officer
—NFO training officer
—Navigation officer
—Training plans officer
—Training schedules officer
—Tactics officer
—Mine warfare officer
—Weapons training officer
—Landing signal officer

Maintenance Department

The Maintenance Department is typically the largest in the squadron. The maintenance officer is responsible for the upkeep of squadron aircraft and associated equipment at the organizational maintenance level. The technical complexity of today's weapons systems makes the maintenance officer's job especially challenging, requiring keeping a maximum number of the squadron's aircraft in an "up" status if the squadron is to perform its mission properly. Responsibilities include inspection, servicing, and maintenance of airframes, power plants, electronic equipment, instruments, electrical systems, ordnance systems, and survival equipment. The maintenance officer supervises material control (supply), and quality assurance, and ensures proper handling of a large number of aircraft records, logbooks, directives, and reports. The department's line di-

The navy operates two VQ squadrons, each using the E-6A Mercury, in the strategic communications role, supporting the strategic ballistic submarines and the air force's intercontinental ballistic missile force. (Boeing)

vision officer directs the activities of plane captains, troubleshooters, and other ground support personnel. When an aircraft is released for flight, there is the implicit assurance of the maintenance officer that it is safe to fly and ready to execute its mission. Typical junior officer billets in the Maintenance Department include:

—Assistant maintenance officer
—Maintenance administrative officer
—Maintenance/material control officer
—Maintenance control officer
—Material control officer
—Quality assurance officer
—Aircraft division officer
—Powerplants branch officer
—Airframes branch officer
—Corrosion control branch officer
—Aviator equipment branch officer

VRC squadrons deploy detachments with each carrier, using their C-2A Greyhound carrier-on-board delivery aircraft to deliver personnel, mail, and supplies to the carrier. (U.S. Navy/PHCS D. W. Holmes)

- —Avionics/armament division officer
- —Avionics branch officer
- —Armament branch officer
- —Electrical/instrument branch officer
- —Line division officer
- —Plane captain branch officer

Safety Department

Because aircraft and their associated systems are unforgiving of human carelessness, the navy assigns an officer with department head status and direct access to the CO to every squadron to deal with the aspect of safety. The safety officer's job is to prevent mishaps, mostly by promoting safety awareness. Implementing an aggressive safety program, the safety officer ensures that all personnel adhere to safety directives and

The Squadron 105

The S-3 Viking flown from carriers by VS squadrons has an impressive antisubmarine and antisurface capability. These aircraft are also used as tankers for other carrier aircraft. (U.S. Navy)

employ safe working habits. The safety officer or the safety officer's principal assistant, the aviation safety officer (ASO), is normally a graduate of the Aviation Safety Officer School at the Naval Postgraduate School in Monterey, California. The safety officer is also responsible for the squadron's NATOPS program, and has officers and enlisted personnel assigned to carry out this vital program. Typical Safety Department billets include:

—Aviation safety officer
—Ground safety officer
—Pilot NATOPS officer
—NFO NATOPS officer
—Aircrew NATOPS officer

The Command Master Chief

Each squadron has a master chief petty officer assigned as a principal advisor to the CO on matters related to the enlisted personnel in the squadron. The Command Master Chief is vital to the smooth functioning of a squadron, keeping the command attuned to the morale of the enlisted personnel and helping sailors with special problems.

Squadron Enlisted Leadership

Squadrons are no different than other navy units in relying on the experience and leadership of their chiefs and senior petty officers. The quality of leadership at this level can make or break the effectiveness of a squadron. Many a junior officer owes success to the quality of the chiefs and first-class petty officers in the officer's branch or division.

Squadron Watch Organization

Like all navy units, squadrons are manned at all times. To coordinate this, a senior watch officer is designated, normally the senior lieutenant in the squadron. A chief or senior petty officer is also assigned to coordinate the enlisted watch bill. Junior officers and enlisted personnel rotate the assignment of manning the squadron duty office or ready room at all times, ready to act in event of emergencies.

FOUR

A NAVAL AVIATION CAREER

During their first few years of service, many officers decide to make long-term commitments to naval aviation. Promotion opportunities, early responsibility, advanced education and training, and a high degree of job satisfaction are among the most frequent reasons they cite for choosing a career in naval aviation. This chapter describes naval aviation career specialties and discusses typical assignment patterns as well as professional development opportunities.

Naval Aviation Designators

All officers in the navy have four-digit designators that identify their community, specialty, and status. Every unrestricted-line officer in the naval aviation community, for example, has a designator that begins with the digits 13. The 13XX community is made up of naval aviators designated 1310, 1315, or 1317, depending on whether the pilot is a regular, reserve, or TAR (training and administration of reserves) officer, respectively. NFOs, similarly, are designated 1320, 1325, or 1327, according to duty status. All of these officers have some facet of naval aviation as a primary career pursuit. They make up approximately one-half of the

Table 4-1. Naval Aviation Designators

131X—Line officer qualified for duty piloting naval aircraft (naval aviator)
132X—Line officer qualified for duty as a weapons operator/mission specialist in naval aircraft (NFO)
137X—Line officer in training for designation as an NFO
139X—Line officer in training for designation as a naval aviator
151X—Aerospace engineering duty officer (AEDO)
152X—Aerospace maintenance duty officer (AMDO)
154X—Aviation duty officer (ADO)
161X—Cryptologic officer
163X—Intelligence officer
181X—Oceanographer
630X—Flying limited duty officer (FLDO)
631X— Aviation deck LDO
632X—Aviation operations LDO
633X—Aviation maintenance LDO
636X—Aviation ordnance LDO
638X—Aviation electronics LDO
639X—Air traffic control LDO
731X—Aviation boatswain CWO
732X—Aviation operations technician CWO
734X—Aviation maintenance technician CWO
736X—Aviation ordnance technician CWO
738X—Aviation electronics technician CWO
739X—Air traffic control technician CWO

unrestricted-line officers of the navy. Additionally, a significant number of restricted-line, limited duty (LDO), and chief warrant officers (CWO) specialize in aviation. Table 4-1 lists the various designators associated with the naval aviation community.

Naval Aviator

A naval aviator is defined in Article 1410100 of the Bureau of Personnel Manual as a "commissioned line officer in the Navy or Marine Corps

The naval aviator and the naval fight officer are a formidable war-fighting team. Their career potential includes squadron, air wing, aircraft carrier, and fleet command, as well as a variety of subspecialty opportunities. (U.S. Navy/PH3 Tom Gibbins)

who has successfully completed the course prescribed by competent authority for Naval Aviators." That course of instruction is comprised of the flight training syllabi, described in chapter 3.

In former times, the characteristic that distinguished a naval aviator from another pilot was the qualification as a carrier pilot, a "tailhooker." In this day of specialization and a high cost of training, fewer than half of naval aviators become carrier-qualified; most of the others are pilots of helicopters, patrol planes, and transports. Most naval aviators will spend their operational tours flying in the types of aircraft they were initially trained to fly; they might be able to switch communities if their aircraft type is phased from service.

Aviation Duty Officer

During the early 1980s, the navy addressed a pilot shortage by establishing a restricted line designator for naval aviators who wished to remain in flying billets and not follow a traditional line officer career pattern. The Aviation Duty Officer (ADO) program was short-lived and acquisitions were phased out by the late 1980s.

Naval Flight Officer

NFOs are unrestricted line officers qualified to operate the sophisticated navigation and weapons systems in naval aircraft. Although the need for pilots was evident as soon as the airplane was invented, the need for specialized officers to operate weapons systems in flight developed much more slowly. As far back as 1912, flying officers other than pilots were carried aloft to operate and test new equipment. The law establishing the Bureau of Aeronautics stated that the bureau's chief and 70 percent of its officers be either pilots or observers. Rear Adm. William A. Moffett, the bureau's first chief, received his naval aviation observer (NAO) wings on 17 June 1922. The need for NAOs, as they were then designated, was not great. As a result, the NAO program sustained itself strictly through volunteer efforts. The last officer so designated before World War II was "winged" about 1930.

During World War II, many aviation officer candidates were trained to be bombardiers, navigators, and meteorologists. Their outstanding performances indicated a need for qualified aircrew officers. Regulations still allowed an officer to become an NAO after completing one thousand flight hours and a course of instruction. In 1945–46, the navy divided the designation into three categories: NAO (navigation); NAO (radar); and NAO (tactical), the term for gunfire spotters.

Postwar cutbacks gradually sent the NAO program into a state of dormancy. The Korean War, which featured increasing use of search and air intercept radars as well as radar countermeasures, indicated a need for NAOs. After hostilities ceased, the program did not decline but expanded with the introduction of new, sophisticated aircraft and technology.

The rapid technological advances in naval forces during the 1950s changed the tactical employment of naval aircraft. The advances placed a heavier burden on the pilot who was expected to fly his aircraft and simultaneously operate electronic sensors. As the state-of-the-art advances progressed, it became apparent that an additional officer should operate the complex systems.

During that period, squadrons employing heavy-attack, early-warning, and antisubmarine aircraft were hard-pressed to find qualified personnel to fill positions created by avionics advancement. Personnel planners had been assigning pilots to these positions, but they soon realized this was not the answer; while temporarily solving the manpower issue, it created morale problems among the pilots that would have been difficult to rectify had the policy continued. As an interim measure, the small core of NAOs was expanded to include a mixed group of nonpilot officers, comprising an additional group of ten NAO categories. The navy supplemented these officers with highly motivated first-class and chief radiomen and radarmen, some pilots who were no longer qualified to fly because of deficient visual acuity, and many physically qualified general line officers who expressed interest in the program. The program provided little formal training; it was sustained and enlarged through need alone. The navy realized it had to establish a specific program to procure and train candidates to fill the positions. In July 1960, the Basic Naval Aviation Officer School (BNAO, or "Banana School") was established as part of NAS Pensacola. (It became a separate command and was established as Training Squadron Ten on 15 January 1968.)

Three significant milestones in the development of the NFO program occurred during the 1960s. In 1964, it was determined that an NFO, like a pilot, would remain on permanent flight pay whether on sea or shore duty. In 1965, a separate designator, 132X, was designed to distinguish the NFO from the general category of aviation officers who were not pilots. Existing NAOs were redesignated NFOs. Congressional legislation during the late 1960s removed barriers in the NFO career pattern by making NFOs eligible for command at sea, like their fellow aviators. In 1970, NFOs became eligible for command of an aviation unit. NFOs presently command approximately one-third of the aviation squadrons, as well as some aircraft carriers and other ships.

Naval Aviation Observer

Even with the establishment of the NFO program, the naval aviation observer did not disappear as a specialization. No longer a separate designator, it is a qualification available to officers who are not aviation-designated personnel but whose duties require them to fly in naval aircraft on occasion. NAOs today include patrol squadron intelligence

Keeping naval aviation as a potent force requires a high degree of professionalism and teamwork. Here, an E-2C Hawkeye radar early warning aircraft is flanked by two F/A-18C strike fighters that it would direct in a combat situation. (U.S. Navy/Cdr. John Leenhouts)

officers, fleet air reconnaissance squadron cryptologic officers, oceanographic officers, and forward air controller graduates of the Marine Corps Aviation Observer School at MCAS New River, North Carolina.

Requirements for designation as an NAO are set forth in Bureau of Personnel Manual Article 1420235: have qualified under NATOPS standards of knowledge of aircraft systems and safety procedures; successful completion of a course of instruction associated with their flying mission as prescribed by the appropriate type commander; accumulation of two hundred hours of flight time that must be directly related to the purpose of their assignment to duty; and assignment to duty involving flying for a period of not less than one year.

Aerospace Engineering Duty Officer

The advancement of aviation technology between the world wars led Congress in 1935 to authorize the assignment of line officers to aeronautical engineering duty. In 1940, the various engineering specialty groups were combined into one community. In 1948, however, Congress authorized a separate community for the aeronautical engineering duty officer (AEDO). Except for a period in the late 1950s and early 1960s when the AEDO community was combined with the ordnance engineering specialists to form the weapons engineering duty officer community, the AEDO community has remained a distinct community, which has grown to about four hundred officers. The community name was later changed to aerospace engineering duty officer.

The mission of the AEDO community is to provide professional management and technical direction in the entire air weapon system acquisition process: the design, development, procurement, production, and logistic support of naval aircraft and airborne weapons, including their related support equipment. Sponsored by the Naval Air Systems Command, the AEDO community is vital to the technological health of naval aviation.

The AEDO serves in billets that demand a combination of technical, managerial, and operational expertise. Requiring a high degree of specialization unusual for the unrestricted line community, which is devoted to warfare expertise, the AEDO relinquishes a continued operational career in order to devote full time to the technological development of naval aviation.

Because of the selection requirements for experience, education, and training, no billets below the rank of lieutenant exist for the AEDO community. Semiannual lateral transfers of naval aviators and NFOs staff the community with fleet-experienced operators possessing an acute sense of the needs of naval aviation. A master of science degree in engineering or the sciences, or a bachelor of science degree in engineering or the sciences combined with a master's degree in management or applied science is required. Aeronautical engineering is the preferred field of study. Applicants must be aviation warfare qualified; must have at least four years of sea duty in fleet units with an extensive background of operational experience; and must have attained the rank of lieutenant but must not have served more than three years as a commander. AEDOs are normally graduates of the U.S. Naval Test Pilot School or currently students at the school.

AEDOs are assigned to billets in the various research, development, test, and evaluation (RDT&E) activities in naval aviation, such as the various sites of the Naval Air Warfare Center, as well as many in Naval Air

Systems Command headquarters. They tend to specialize in the acquisition process or the fleet and product support areas. Some AEDOs are assigned to the Naval Aviation Depots (NADEPs), where their project officer duties include post-maintenance check flights for aircraft emerging from maintenance. Others are assigned to Defense Plant Representative Offices (DPROs) at the corporations that build naval aircraft and weapons, providing on-site administrative and technical representation and conducting acceptance check flights of new aircraft.

Command opportunity exists for senior AEDOs at the NADEPS, DPROs, and other field activities. At the captain level, AEDOs and aerospace maintenance duty officers are eligible to merge into a single 1500 designator as a single competitive category for flag rank.

Aerospace Maintenance Duty Officer

Studies in the late 1950s and 1960s identified a need for an officer corps dedicated to providing full-time, professional aircraft maintenance in response to the challenges presented by the sophisticated aircraft and weapons being introduced into the fleet. In March 1968, the secretary of the navy officially established the aeronautical maintenance duty officer (AMDO) designator (152X) as a restricted line officer community. A group of one hundred naval aviators, LDOs, general aviation officers, and AEDOs became the nucleus of the new community which has grown to more than six hundred officers. Entry-level accessions began in 1969. In 1990, the community expanded to the TAR program as well.

The mission of the AMDO (now named aerospace maintenance duty officer) is "to provide full-time direction in the development, establishment, and implementation of maintenance and material management policies and procedures for the support of naval aircraft, airborne weapons, attendant systems, and related support equipment." In addition to working in fleet maintenance organizations, AMDOs are heavily involved in all aspects of acquisition and support as program managers at Naval Air Systems Command, and as commanding officers at the various Naval Aviation Depots.

After commissioning, prospective AMDOs attend an eleven-week course at the Aviation Maintenance Officers School in Pensacola, Florida. Through the rank of commander, the officer rotates between sea duty and shore duty maintenance billets. The junior AMDO is normally assigned to squadron and Aircraft Intermediate Maintenance Department (AIMD) billets, serving in branch and division officer positions.

Officers from other communities can enter the AMDO community via restricted line transfer boards. Mid-grade officers attend the two-week Senior Aviation Maintenance Officers course at Pensacola. Many AMDOs earn a master's degree at the Naval Postgraduate School. The Defense Systems Management College also provides material acquisition and logistics training for many AMDOs.

Mid-grade AMDOs serve as air wing maintenance officers, assistant AIMD officers, AIMD production control officers, AIMD officers on amphibious ships, and in various staff positions. A tour of duty as an AIMD officer on an aircraft carrier or ashore at an AIMD is the equivalent of a squadron command tour for a naval aviator or an NFO. A formal selection board selects these officers for these billets.

At the captain level, AMDOs and AEDOs are eligible to merge into the 1500 designator as a single competitive category for selection to flag rank.

Aviation Supply Officer

Supply corps officers specializing in aviation logistics have been supporting naval aviation for decades. In 1984, the Chief of Naval Operations formally recognized their special brand of expertise when he approved a plan to establish a naval aviation supply officers program with their own wing insignia.

Candidates for ASO qualification must complete a comprehensive program of study of approximately 350 hours of study and experience, and pass an oral examination administered by experienced supply and maintenance officers. To be eligible, a supply officer must be serving in an aviation supply billet or have detached from one within the previous two years. OPNAV Instruction 1542.4 series contains detailed information on the ASO program.

Flight Surgeon

The Flight Surgeon program is described in chapter 10.

Naval Astronaut

Every two years a few officers from the navy, marine corps, and coast guard are selected to train in the astronaut corps of the National Aeronautics and Space Administration (NASA). Officers who complete the program will fly into space as pilots, flight engineers, and mission specialists on board the Space Shuttle.

Pilot astronaut candidates must have a minimum of five years of active commissioned service and a bachelor's degree in engineering, biological or physical science, or mathematics. They must have a minimum of one thousand hours of time as pilot-in-command in jet aircraft, with test pilot experience especially desirable. They must also pass a NASA Class I physical examination.

Mission specialists must be U.S. citizens on active duty with five years of commissioned service. A bachelor's degree is required, with three years of related experience. Advanced degrees are desired. Mission specialist candidates must pass a NASA Class II physical examination.

Candidates for the astronaut corps include naval aviators, NFOs, AEDOs, engineering duty officers (EDOs), surface warfare officers, oceanographers, and flight surgeons. After selection, the candidates undergo a year of rigorous training, including land and water survival training. Classroom instruction includes principles of space flight, astrophysics, meteorology, geology, and the specifics of the Space Shuttle systems. Flight training is conducted in NASA's fleet of T-38 aircraft.

After the first year, selection for continuation in the program is made, and training then concentrates on the Space Shuttle systems. Crews are assigned to a mission approximately one year before launch, during which time the crew trains together intensively for the specific mission. This training includes over four hundred hours in the Space Shuttle simulator.

Aviators serve as pilots and flight engineers and will wear the naval astronaut wings once they have certified for and have completed a flight in a powered vehicle designed for space flight 50 miles above the earth. NFOs serve as mission or payload specialists, and wear the naval astronaut (NFO) wings once they have completed the certification and one flight. Naval officers other than naval aviators and NFOs may be designated as naval astronaut specialists after completing one flight as a mission or payload specialist.

Once in the astronaut corps, most naval aviators and NFOs continue in the space program. Many will make more shuttle flights into space. Some will go on to assume instructor and leadership roles in the program. A few will serve in billets in the Naval Space Command at Dahlgren, Virginia, or the joint Space Command at Colorado Springs. Some continue as civilians in the space program while maintaining naval reserve affiliation.

Limited Duty Officer

Limited duty officers (LDOs) are former enlisted personnel commissioned to lead in specific technical occupational fields. They serve in billets that require authority and responsibility greater than that normally expected of a chief warrant officer (CWO), and outside a normal development pattern for unrestricted line and restricted line officers. LDOs fill the need for technical management skills, freeing line officers for broader training. They serve in a variety of assignments at sea and ashore, where their experience greatly enhances the readiness of the fleet.

LDOs are selected from the ranks of chief petty officers and first-class petty officers who have passed the chief petty officer exam, with eight to sixteen years of naval service. A small number of CWOs who have served at least two years in rank may apply for LDO selection; if selected, they are commissioned in the grade of lieutenant, junior grade.

The normal paths of advancement from enlisted specialty to LDO and CWO are shown in Table 4-2.

Flying Limited Duty Officer

The flying limited duty officer (FLDO) community (630X) was developed during the early 1980s to help offset pilot shortages and to provide instructor stability in the Naval Air Training Command. Assignments were mainly in primary flight training squadrons and in ship's company billets on board aircraft carriers, enabling them to free up naval aviators for more operational billets in the fleet. The program was terminated by the early 1990s when pilot training requirements dropped.

Chief Warrant Officer

Chief warrant officers (73XX) are former enlisted personnel who are technical specialists, performing duties limited in scope (in relation to

Table 4-2. Rating Advancement to LDO and CWO

Rating	CWO Category	LDO Category
ABE/ABF/ABH/AB	Aviation boatswain	Aviation deck
AW	Aviation operations technician	Aviation operations
AD/AME/AMH/AMS/ AM/PR/AS/AZ/AF	Aviation maintenance technician	Aviation maintenance
AE/AT/AV	Aviation electronics technician	Aviation electronics
AO	Aviation ordnance technician	Aviation ordnance
AC	Air traffic control technician	Air traffic control

other officer categories) and not significantly affected by advancement in rank. Career development is focused on increasing technical competence within the specialty of the officer.

CWOs are selected from the ranks of chief petty officers with twelve to twenty-four years of service. The technical expertise gained from years of service in their rating gives the navy many more years of valuable service. CWOs usually rotate between sea and shore duty assignments in their specialty.

Aviation Ordnance Officer Career Progression Course

In 1993 the Aviation Ordnance Officer Career Progression Course was formed at NAS Pensacola as part of Naval Aviation Schools Command. The course was designed for experienced ordnance LDOs, CWOs, and chief petty officers to enhance their professionalism. The school teaches at three levels. Level I is a six-week course aimed at senior enlisted personnel and newly commissioned LDOs and CWOs and covers administrative, technical, logistic, and safety aspects of ordnance management. Levels II and III are two-week courses for senior LDOs, CWOs, and enlisted personnel at their mid- and upper-career point, and cover such topics as air wing ordnance handling, ammunition storage activities, and aircraft intermediate maintenance departments.

Intelligence Officers

Intelligence officers (163X) comprise one community navy-wide. However, a great many junior intelligence officers begin their careers serving in squadron air intelligence officer billets. They train their aircrews in threat recognition; conduct mission briefs and debriefs; and participate in strike planning. Many will complete later tours of duty in the aviation community as air wing, aircraft carrier, and carrier group intelligence officers and assistants.

Officers bound for duty as intelligence officers in the aviation community attend the Naval Air Intelligence Officers Course conducted by Training Squadron Ten at NAS Pensacola. The course includes ground and flight instruction to familiarize the officers with aeronautical terminology and procedures. The training incorporates simulator sessions and flights in the T-34C. After the course, students proceed to intelligence training at the Navy–Marine Corps Intelligence Training Center at Dam Neck in Virginia Beach, Virginia.

Career Development

The First Sea Tour

After receiving their wings (see chapter 2) and completing type training in their fleet aircraft at the FRSs, naval aviators and NFOs begin their careers in earnest. From this point on, the responsibilities and checkpoints for pilots and NFOs are essentially the same. The Bureau of Personnel has designed a career progression pattern plan for aviators and NFOs (see page 120). It is important to stress that the career pattern is only a general progression. While it is true that most successful aviation officers will have completed most of the steps by the end of their careers, the order and timing of these steps differ from person to person. It must also be pointed out that completion of the steps outlined in no way assures success, nor does pattern alteration preclude success.

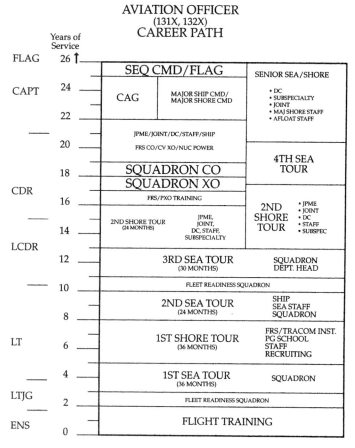

Career path for naval aviators and naval flight officers. (U.S. Navy/BUPERS)

The initial squadron tour lasts approximately three years, time enough for the aviator to learn while contributing to the attainment of the squadron's mission. Upon reporting aboard, a new officer is normally assigned as a branch or division officer. The branch officer reports to the division officer who reports to the department head, who is responsible to the executive officer and the commanding officer.

The primary duties of the junior officer are to fulfill the responsibili-

AEROSPACE ENGINEERING DUTY OFFICER
(151X)
CAREER PATH

Years of Service	Rank	Material Acquisition	Material Readiness
31 / 30 / 29	FLAG	Headquarters • RDT&E	Operational Support • Manufacturing & Production
28 / 27 / 26 / 25 / 24 / 23 / 22	CAPT	• Program Manager • CO DPRO • CO RDT&E • Division Director	• CO NADEP • CO DPRO • ACOS Material • Division Director
21 / 20 / 19 / 18 / 17 / 16	CDR	• Deputy Program Manager • Class Desk • Directorate • Department Head • Commanding Officer • PMA (F) • Branch Head	• Executive Officer • Fleet Staff • Production • Department Head • Commanding Officer • PMA (F) • Branch Head
15 / 14 / 13	LCDR	• Ass't. Class Desk • Project Officer	
12 / 11 / 10		Primary AED Accessions	• Competitive Department Head Tour • Fleet Squadron/Second Sea Tour
9 / 8 / 7 / 6 / 5 / 0	LT / LTJG / ENS	• Competitive Shore Tour/Postgraduate Education • Fleet Squadron • Aviation Training	

Career path for aerospace engineering duty officers. (U.S. Navy/BUPERS)

ties of the branch officer. The officer's performance of these responsibilities will consume the largest portion of his or her fitness report. All aviation officers must demonstrate professionalism in the air, and this is also reflected in their fitness reports.

AEROSPACE MAINTENANCE DUTY OFFICER
(152X)
CAREER PATH

EMPHASIS	YEARS TOURS	RANK	BILLETS
LOGISTICS & ACQUISITION POLICY & GUIDANCE		FLAG	AIR-00 AIR-8.0 AIR-1.0 SPAWAR-004 NAWC AD/WD PEO(CU) AIR-3.0 AIR-6.0 N-881
	5 / 2	CAPT	MPM CO FIELD ACTIVITY CO/XO NADEP SYSCOM DIV DIR TYCOM OPNAV FIELD ACTY DIV DIRECTOR ACOS MTL
EXECUTIVE LEADERSHIP OF LOGISTICS & MAINTENANCE	5 / 2	CDR	AIMD DEPT HEAD FRS MO SYSCOM BRCH HEAD APML NADEP PROJ/DEPT OPNAV TYCOM TYPE WING
MANAGEMENT OF AVIATION MAINTENANCE IN DIRECT SUPPORT OF FLEET OPERATIONS	5 / 2	LCDR	CVW MO AIMD PROD CONTROL LPH/LHA AIMD DH SQUADRON AMO SYSCOM/FIELD ACTY DPRO OPNAV TYCOM PG SCHOOL
		LT	O LEVEL - TACAIR/VP/HELO/MISC
	11 / 3-4	LTJG	I LEVEL
		ENS	STAFF - TYCOM/TYPE WING

Career path for aerospace maintenance duty officers (U.S. Navy/BUPERS)

Most junior aviation officers will have the opportunity to serve in more than one of the squadron's departments during their first tour. All squadrons have operations, administration, maintenance, and safety departments. Some have additional departments as well. Each has challenging jobs. During this tour, the junior officer will gain experience in leadership, learning to employ the squadron personnel properly. The winnowing process for advancement to squadron command also begins during the first sea tour. Few will make it, and every step counts.

The first sea tour is also the time when most aviators will attain their warfare qualifications and qualify in various positions such as mission commander; instructor pilot or NFO; maintenance check pilot; and NATOPS instructor.

Deploying overseas two or more times during a typical first sea tour, the aviator or NFO usually emerges as a mature, seasoned flyer, trusted to lead missions vital to national security and to bring his or her aircraft and crew back safely. This tour is also a time of great personal investment, and of forming friendships that will last a lifetime. The comradeship and esprit de corps enjoyed by junior officers in the wardroom of a naval aviation squadron is hard to find anywhere else and is part of the equation that makes naval aviation a potent fighting force.

The First Shore Tour

After completing the first squadron tour, an officer is available for assignment to a shore duty billet, usually for two or three years. (Though intended to be less rigorous than sea duty, many of these assignments are decidedly not so!) Many of the top-rated officers will become FRS instructors, choice billets through which they will maintain their flying skills and increase their exposure to more senior officers returning for department head and command tours. Many others will go on to become instructors in the various training squadrons and wing staffs to train their replacements in the fleet.

A wide variety of other assignments exists throughout the navy for the first shore tour. These include duty on the staffs of type wings, air stations, tactical support centers, RDT&E centers, joint commands, and flag commands, and instructor duty at the Naval Academy, Officer Candidate School, and the various ROTC units. Opportunity exists for many officers to pursue a master's degree at the Naval Postgraduate School in Monterey, California, acquiring an education, mostly in technical curricula, that will be valuable to the officer and the navy in future assignments. A small number of aviators may earn a master's degree at the Joint Military Intelligence College in Washington, D.C. Graduates of these schools receive a subspecialty code that ensures that they will be detailed to one or more tours of duty in the future that will use their subspecialty.

Many pilots will serve a rewarding tour of duty in the Naval Air Training Command as flight instructors. (via *Naval Aviation News*)

The Second Sea Tour

The second sea tour, typically two years long, comes when an officer is a senior lieutenant or a recently selected lieutenant commander. For many officers, this is the "disassociated sea tour"; they will serve in operational billets in a capacity that will broaden and deepen their warfare expertise. For example, a land-based patrol pilot or NFO may be assigned to an aircraft carrier as a catapult and arresting gear officer, carrier air traffic control officer, or assistant navigator; or to a carrier group or cruiser-destroyer group staff as an assistant air operations officer, flag secretary, flag lieutenant, or communications officer. A helicopter pilot may be assigned as the air officer or flight deck officer on an amphibious ship. A strike fighter pilot is ideal for assignment as assistant strike operations officer on a carrier or carrier group staff. An E-2 NFO may feel right at home in the combat direction center of an aircraft carrier. An S-3 or P-3 NFO or a helicopter pilot is likely to be found in a carrier's antisubmarine warfare (ASW) module, or as an ASW officer on the staff of a destroyer

Tours in the cockpit are the essence of a career in naval aviation, but many nonflying billets require the expertise of fleet-experienced, warfare-qualified aviators and NFOs. (U.S. Navy/Lt. Cdr. Dave Parsons)

squadron. An electronic warfare pilot or NFO might be assigned to the carrier's electronic warfare module, or to a battle group staff.

In some cases, if a shortage of department-head tour aviators exists in a particular community, an officer may be detailed to an operational squadron for his or her second sea tour to make up the deficit. A few other flying billets exist for some communities during this tour, especially for those in the patrol and reconnaissance communities.

The Department Head Tour

The legislation requiring officers to acquire joint service education and experience for promotion in senior grades led the navy to accelerate the department head tour and essentially eliminate the second shore tour from the career pattern. Depending upon timing, some officers may have the opportunity to attend a school such as the Armed Forces Staff College in Norfolk, Virginia, before reporting for their tour as a squadron de-

Mission commanders (whether pilots or NFOs) in large aircraft such as this P-3 patrol plane must mold their large crews into coordinated fighting teams to succeed in their assigned missions.

partment head. Before reporting to their squadrons, prospective department heads will undergo refresher training at the FRS.

The department head tour is the gateway to squadron command and thus assumes paramount importance. The Aviation Department Head Screen Board is convened in many aviation communities to consider each officer for a department head tour in an operational squadron; officers not selected on this go-round will be considered a second time for operational or special mission squadron department head billets. Those selected will normally serve two-year tours, often starting out as an assistant department head before fleeting up to department head. Some will have the opportunity to serve as head of two different departments during the tour. Those not selected will serve in other assignments.

Department heads have tremendous responsibility, leading large numbers of enlisted personnel, training and guiding junior officers, and carrying out the squadron's operations. Many will gain valuable operational experience as they serve as officers in charge of detachments away from the main squadron.

Aviation Command Screen

Near the end of the department head tour or on the follow-on shore tour, an officer comes up for selection for commander and for the aviation command screen. The majority will be promoted to commander, but only the top of that group will be selected for squadron command.

The aviation command screen board is headed by a flag officer and is comprised of a cross section of senior aviation officers who have squadron command experience. The board considers all aviation commanders for command of operational, training, and special mission squadrons. Generally, communities with larger numbers of eligible officers will offer less of a command opportunity; single-seat strike fighter squadrons, with fewer officers, generally offer greater command opportunity. If selected, an officer will then be slated for a particular squadron.

The Second Shore Tour

Department heads completing their tour normally rotate to shore duty on a wing, force, or fleet staff or one of many assignments in navy headquarters (most of which are in the Washington, D.C., area). Many officers will attend the Naval War College in Newport, Rhode Island, or the service colleges of the other departments. Many will also serve in joint commands to broaden their experience and qualify for joint-duty credit, essential for selection to flag rank. Those selected for command will begin their pipeline training for command before reporting to their squadrons.

The Squadron Command Tour

After a refresher course at the FRS, a prospective commanding officer will report to his or her squadron as XO, normally for a period of twelve to fifteen months. During this extremely challenging assignment, the XO is busily engaged in running the day-to-day affairs of the squadron to free up the CO for leadership and operational matters. All the while, the XO is an understudy preparing for the day he or she will assume command.

In squadrons with both pilots and NFOs, the navy tries to alternate them in command tours, so that a pilot CO will have an NFO for XO and vice versa.

The day finally arrives when the XO assumes command from the departing CO and welcomes his or her new XO. For an aviator in his or her late thirties or early forties, this is a crowning achievement. The responsibility that goes with it can be overwhelming: leading a squadron of hundreds of sailors and a group of multi-million dollar aircraft, molding it and maintaining it as a formidable fighting force, ready to fly into harm's way when called. It is not a job for just anyone.

Post-Command and Major Command Tours

Success as a squadron commander leads to follow-on tours for many in such duties as CO of a fleet readiness squadron; department head or executive officer on aircraft carriers or amphibious assault ships; duty as a wing, battle group, and fleet staff officer; study at a service college; embassy duty as a naval or defense attaché; and headquarters billets at the Pentagon and elsewhere. Selection for captain gives an officer an opportunity to screen for CO of a major sea or shore command, or as a major project manager. Major command opportunities include type wing, training air wing, or carrier air wing commanders; the patrol fleet readiness squadron (VP-30); and air station commanders. Major sea commands include mobile logistics force ships, amphibious force ships, carrier air wings, and patrol wings. Tour lengths vary: twenty-four months for major shore commands; and eighteen months for ships, carrier air wings, patrol wings, and subsequent commands. The exception is nuclear-powered aircraft carriers, for which the tour length is thirty months. Subsequent sea commands include amphibious assault ships and aircraft carriers. (The path to carrier command is described in chapter 6.) Selection for flag rank comes during or after a major command tour.

Shore Tour Education Opportunities

At many points during their careers, aviation warfare officers have numerous opportunities for advanced education that will broaden their background and deepen their professional knowledge. These opportunities are highly sought after and greatly benefit both the individual and the navy.

Naval Postgraduate School

The Naval Postgraduate School (NPS) in Monterey, California, is an excellent, fully accredited institution at which officers can acquire the advanced knowledge and training they need to specialize or to remain as line officers and use their education in subspecialties. Officers attending NPS normally spend eighteen to twenty-four months there while drawing full pay and allowances.

Officers from all of the uniformed services and many foreign armed services attend NPS, most earning a master's degree upon completion, and a few completing a doctorate. The NPS offers thirty programs, with most degrees awarded in technical fields. All students must complete a thesis. A tour at NPS also counts toward the Joint Professional Military Education promotion requirement.

The navy also offers other opportunities for postgraduate study in a number of different fields at several civilian universities.

Service Colleges

All naval officers (O-4 and O-5) within an annual eligibility zone are considered for selection to attend an intermediate or senior (as appropriate) service college. (O-6 and O-6 selectee officers are automatically eligible to attend.) The Naval War College in Newport, Rhode Island, is the navy's primary service college, but programs at the other service colleges are available as well, including those of foreign nations. Service colleges in the United States are listed below.

Intermediate (Phase I Joint Professional Military Education):
—Naval Command and Staff College, Naval War College*
—Air Command and Staff College, Maxwell AFB, Alabama
—Army Command and General Staff College, Ft. Leavenworth, Kansas
—USMC Command and Staff College, Quantico, Virginia
Senior (Phase II Joint Professional Military Education):
—College of Naval Warfare, Naval War College*
—Air War College, Maxwell AFB, Alabama*

—Army War College, Carlisle Barracks, Pennsylvania
—National War College, Ft. McNair, Washington, D.C.
—Industrial College of the Armed Forces, Ft. McNair, Washington, D.C.*
—USMC Top Level School, Quantico, Virginia

Other service colleges:
—Armed Forces Staff College, Norfolk, Virginia (Phase II JPME)
—Joint Military Intelligence College, Washington, D.C.*
—Defense Language Institute, Monterey, California.

Note: Asterisks indicate that a master's program is available on site or with an affiliated civilian college or university.

Test Pilot Schools

One of the outstanding opportunities available to naval aviators and NFOs is the chance to attend one of three test pilot schools available: the U.S. Naval Test Pilot School, the U.S. Air Force Aerospace Research Pilot School, and the British Empire Test Pilot School. A board convened by the Bureau of Personnel selects the candidates for these schools.

U.S. Naval Test Pilot School

Located at the Naval Air Warfare Center, Patuxent River, Maryland, the U.S. Naval Test Pilot School (USNTPS) has the mission of training highly motivated fleet pilots and NFOs to become fully qualified naval test pilots and naval test flight officers. Young naval aviation officers highly prize assignment to this school. Upon graduation, officers normally complete a shore tour at one of the Naval Air Warfare Center sites or with a VX squadron as a project officer to test and evaluate new aircraft, components, and weapons. Graduation from USNTPS is especially desirable for applicants for the astronaut program or for designation as an AEDO.

USNTPS has a tough, eleven-month curriculum in fixed-wing, rotary-wing, or airborne systems. The school is the only military test pilot school that offers academic courses on rotary-wing aircraft. USNTPS trains all army and marine corps test pilots, some civilian engineers and foreign students, and runs an exchange program with the air force.

A Naval Aviation Career   131

The U.S. Naval Test Pilot School is one of many educational opportunities that await the fleet-experienced aviator or NFO. (U.S. Navy/Robert L. Lawson)

Acceptance into USNTPS requires college-level algebra, calculus, and physics; engineering is also helpful. Normally, USNTPS requires fifteen hundred hours of flight time, although exceptions have been made. Applicants should achieve as many flight qualifications as possible during their first tour. The academic course of instruction includes aerodynamics, aircraft and engine performance, and related aeronautical engineering subjects. Students learn to write reports detailing the flight characteristics of the aircraft they fly at the school, which include strike fighters, helicopters, gliders, and even old radial-engine "tail draggers."

USNTPS also has a cooperative program with the Naval Postgraduate School; a student can study for a year at NPS, earning a master's degree in aeronautical engineering, and then go straight to USNTPS.

USAF Aerospace Research Pilot School

The navy has a small number of quotas for students at the USAF Aerospace Research Pilot School at Edwards Air Force Base in California. The mission of this school is to train pilots in the latest methods of testing and evaluating aircraft, manned space vehicles, and related aerospace equipment. Selection criteria include a bachelor's degree in engineering, mathematics, or physical science, and a minimum of one thousand hours of pilot time, including five hundred hours of jet time.

British Empire Test Pilot School

The British Empire Test Pilot School at Boscombe Down in Salisbury, England, trains British Commonwealth pilots to test-fly experimental aircraft. Two U.S. naval aviators are selected each year for the school's test pilot course. Candidates must have completed college-level algebra and physics, and have recent operational flight experience.

Aviation Pay

Aviation Career Incentive Pay

Originating in the early days of aviation as an incentive to volunteer for the dangers inherent in flying, "flight pay" remains an attractive benefit of a career in naval aviation. Today it is called Aviation Career Incentive Pay (ACIP). ACIP increases with promotion over time to a maximum after six years of aviation service, and begins to decline after eighteen years of commissioned service in accordance with the reduced flying by senior officers. The law governing ACIP is complicated, however, and its details require the attention of every naval flyer in order to avoid disqualification for it.

At certain checkpoints ("gates") an aviation officer must have achieved a prescribed ratio of operational flying time to total aviation service. The following applies to officers who had less than six years of aviation service as of 1 October 1991. To meet the first gate, a flyer must have served as an officer in an operational flying billet for nine of the first twelve years of aviation service (including flight training); this entitles the officer to receive ACIP through the eighteenth year of aviation service, whether or not the officer is actually assigned to a flying billet. (A proposal under consideration in 1995 would, if approved, reduce the requirement to eight years in a flying billet.) If an officer fails to meet this gate, ACIP will thereafter be paid only when the officer is actually assigned to a flying billet.

The second gate is measured at the completion of eighteen years of aviation service. If, at this gate, the officer has accumulated ten years in flying assignments, entitlement continues through the twenty-second year of commissioned service. If the officer has accumulated twelve years in flying assignments, entitlement continues through the twenty-fifth year of commissioned service. Completion of less than nine years in flying assignments in the first eighteen years of aviation service authorizes ACIP to be paid only when the flyer is actually filling an operational flying billet.

ACIP is based on completion of months in flying billets, and pilots and NFOs have specified annual flight time requirements to qualify for ACIP. Simulator time can make up a certain portion of flight time. All squadron billets for pilots and NFOs count as flying assignments, including training and fleet readiness squadron billets. Many disassociated sea-tour billets on aviation ships and staffs also count as flying billets; officers assigned to these units must arrange for flight time with aircraft assigned to associated squadrons. Because of the difficulty in arranging flight time due to operational commitments, the officer can request a waiver. Other flying billets are found at the Naval Air Warfare Center and at naval air stations.

Aviation Continuation Pay

Starting in the late 1970s, the navy attacked a pilot retention problem by offering Aviation Officer Continuation Pay (AOCP) for aviators and NFOs to continue in service. These considerable sums of money, called "bonuses," incurred a service requirement well beyond initial service obligation. The program succeeded and was replaced in 1988 by the Aviation Continuation Pay (ACP) program, now targeted to officers below the rank of O-5 in specific pilot and NFO communities. It varies from year to year according to the needs of the navy and marine corps.

Though the specifics vary, an officer generally must meet the following criteria to be eligible for ACP:

—Be in a paygrade below O-5
—Serving with a regular commission or selected to augment the regular navy
—Already be receiving ACIP
—Have not previously participated in ACP
—Be qualified for operational flying
—Completed at least six years but less than thirteen years of commissioned service
—Completed active-duty service obligation
—Agree to serve through fourteen years of commissioned service

Fitness Reports

In periods specified by the Bureau of Personnel, each officer is evaluated in writing by his or her CO or reporting senior. The officer is evaluated on performance in primary assignments, such as that of division officer, and in collateral duties. Flight performance is also evaluated in the same fitness report.

Fitness reports form the most important part of an officer's record. They receive careful consideration by promotion boards, selection boards (for special programs such as augmentation and postgraduate education), and by officer detailers when considering an officer for a new assignment. Fitness reports evaluate performance and personal character traits in specific areas. Skills and qualifications are carefully evaluated so that the most skilled aviation officers will be chosen for the most demanding flying assignments.

Selection Boards

Selection boards are a mystery to most naval officers. However, their importance to an officer's career is paramount: They will determine the future of each officer.

Composition of selection boards is regulated by law; members are carefully selected to give a wide range of experience and diversity of background. The secretary of the navy approves the composition of each board. The board members' names are kept confidential until the board convenes in order to avoid undue influence in advance.

When each board meets, officials in the Bureau of Personnel give a presentation on the needs of the navy as a whole for officers in the grade under consideration, the distribution requirements, and the laws and regulations governing selection. Career patterns are discussed in light of the navy's present and future requirements, and board members are reminded that there are no fixed career patterns, and that there are many avenues to success. No attempt is made to establish finite guidelines or to dictate who or what type of person is to be selected; that responsibility is left to the board, which is free to act within the scope of the precept (a letter from the secretary of the navy to the board president).

Upon convening, the board members and recorders are sworn in and the precept is read. The precept informs the board which officers are in the promotion zone, above the zone, and the number who can be selected for early promotion. Board members are charged with the solemn responsibility of selecting, to the best of their collective ability, those officers who have the greatest potential for service in the next grade.

Each officer's record is briefed before the board, then each member assigns a score to the record. The scores are tabulated and averaged, and each record assumes a place on a continuum ranked by their score. At the end of the scoring, the records within a certain range of the "crunch-zone" (cutoff score), above and below, are reconsidered to establish the final cut.

Officers are considered for promotion at certain points in their career, usually based on their year of commissioning. An officer is normally considered for promotion twice before being considered for separation. In reality, the first "look" is crucial; chances of selection during the second "look" are very small. Each promotion board is allowed to select a few outstanding officers for early promotion ("deep selects"). Since the navy is awash in talented officers, selection is a very difficult, hair-splitting process. There simply are not enough promotion slots for every qualified officer. The competition for promotion is very keen, and small distinctions make the difference.

Once selected, the selectee list must be approved by the secretary of the navy and ratified by the Senate. Usually within a year, the selectees are promoted in order of seniority as senior officers in their grade leave the service or are promoted. The number of officers allowed on active duty in each grade is strictly governed by law.

FIVE

NAVAL AVIATION ORGANIZATION

Although U.S. naval aviation has long maintained a strong identity, it is not a separate corps within the navy. Its identity is strong at lower levels of administrative organization, such as squadrons and wings. In most cases of operational organization, however, naval aviation forces are integrated with other operating forces across the spectrum of naval warfare or joint warfare.

The operating forces of the navy are responsible for conducting naval operations in support of U.S. national policy and interests. They are supported by a large shore establishment of bases, stations, depots, test centers, laboratories, hospitals, and other support and training organizations.

Chain of Command

Command of the navy's operating forces is exercised through two chains of command. The administrative chain is responsible for manning, equipping, training, supplying, and maintaining the operating forces. The operational chain, which is the war-fighting organization, assumes command of the forces provided by the administrative chain and directs them in the execution of national policy objectives. In many cases, the administrative and operational commanders may be the same individual, wearing "two hats" as commander of both. The administrative chain is largely permanent, while the operational chain, except at the higher levels, is task oriented and is restructured to meet changing operational requirements.

Almost all administrative commanders of naval operating forces are naval officers. Operational commanders above the unit level of naval aviation are likely to be naval officers but may be army, air force, marine corps, or coast guard officers. In fact, all naval operations are conducted under a joint chain of command, even when other services are not part of the operational forces.

For naval aviation personnel, the administrative chain of command is the one that most affects their day-to-day activities. At the squadron level, the operational chain of command is largely indistinguishable from the administrative chain of command.

For the operating forces, the administrative chain runs from the President of the United States (as Commander in Chief) through the secretary of defense, the secretary of the navy, the chief of naval operations (CNO), and the fleet commanders (Commander in Chief, U.S. Atlantic Fleet [CINCLANTFLT], or Commander in Chief, U.S. Pacific Fleet [CINCPACFLT]). Fleet type commanders, such as Commander, Naval Air Force, U.S. Atlantic Fleet (COMNAVAIRLANT) and Commander, Naval Air Force, U.S. Pacific Fleet (COMNAVAIRPAC), or numbered fleet commanders, such as commanders of the Second (COMSECONDFLT), Third (COMTHIRDFLT), Fifth (COMFIFTHFLT), Sixth (COMSIXTHFLT), and Seventh (COMSEVENTHFLT) fleets, exercise administrative command of battle groups, ships, wings, and squadrons assigned.

The Chief of Naval Operations

The CNO (N00), an admiral who may or may not be an aviator or NFO, administrates the navy from a headquarters in the Pentagon in Arlington, Virginia, the Office of the Chief of Naval Operations (OPNAV). The CNO's title is technically a misnomer, since the CNO is not in charge of any operations but oversees the manning, training, supply, and administration of naval forces, making them available to the joint unified and specified commands for war-fighting. The CNO is assisted by a principal and senior deputy, the vice chief of naval operations (VCNO [N09]).

OPNAV is a vast, complex, often changing organization, responsible for handling a multitude of details concerning the world's largest navy and, at the same time, keeping abreast of rapid changes in ship, weapons, aircraft, and space technology. The OPNAV staff makes or resolves all policy matters affecting the navy; although far from the flight-line, it is a fascinating place to work and gives one an opportunity to put fleet experience to work, carrying ideas forward to the highest decision-making echelons. Listed below are the principal deputy chiefs of naval operations (DCNOs) and OPNAV directorates and assistants:

N1—DCNO (Manpower and personnel)
N2—Director of naval intelligence
N3/N5—DCNO (Plans, policy, and operations)
N4—DCNO (Logistics)
N6—Director, space and electronic warfare
N7—Director of naval training
N8—DCNO (Resources, warfare requirements, and assessments)
N00N—Director of naval nuclear propulsion
N09B—Assistant VCNO
N091—Director of test and evaluation and technology requirements
N093—Director of navy medicine/surgeon general of the navy
N095—Director of naval reserve
N096—Oceanographer of the navy
N097—Chief of chaplains/director of religious ministries
N09C—Special assistant for public affairs
N09F—Special assistant for safety matters
N09G—Special assistant for inspection support
N09J—Special assistant for legal services
N09L—Special assistant for legislative support
N09N—Special assistant for naval investigative matters & security
N09P—Special assistant for material inspection and surveys

Director, Air Warfare (N88)

In the decades following World War II, the CNO had a principal naval aviation advisor, a vice admiral aviator or NFO serving as deputy chief of naval operations for air, or later as assistant chief of naval operations (air warfare), more familiar by its OPNAV office code, OP-05. In 1992, however, the OPNAV staff was extensively reorganized in line with its counterparts on the Joint Staff. In part a reduction of flag billets, the reorganization recognized naval warfare as a spectrum, diminishing the distinctions between the three traditional "platform" sponsors (air, surface, and submarine).

Under the reorganization, the three former "platform" sponsors report to the deputy chief of naval operations for resources, warfare requirements, and assessment (N8), a vice admiral billet. N8 reviews mission areas, force levels, types of weapons platforms, and future weapons systems, improving decision-making and coordinating in the context of joint mission areas.

The assistant chief of naval operations (air warfare) was reduced to a two-star billet, becoming director, air warfare (N88). N88 is the principal naval aviation advisor to N8 and is his representative in all naval aviation matters, including those involving other government and civil agencies. N88 is responsible for overall planning, budgeting, and managing of naval aviation programs, including aircraft, weapons, manpower, training, facilities, and aircraft carriers. N88 is also the principal advisor in strike warfare.

The director, air warfare has a staff of approximately two hundred military and civilian personnel organized in functional and support branches and sections. The marine corps deputy chief of staff for aviation serves on additional duty with the N88 staff as a principal advisor in marine corps aviation matters (N882). The principal offices within N88 are:

N88A—Executive assistant
N88C—Assistant for aviation budget requirements
N88H—Special assistant for publications and operational records
N88I—Intelligence officer
N88M/N882—Program advisor, marine corps aviation
N88R—Coordinator, naval air reserve
N88W—Advanced systems development/plans/analysis
N880—Aviation plans and requirements
N881—Aviation logistics
N885—Carrier and air station programs
N889—Aviation manpower and training

Type Commanders

Most navy aviation commands such as aircraft carriers, carrier air wings, type wings, and certain squadrons come under the direct or concurrent administrative command of aviation type commanders. The main two are Commander, Naval Air Force, U.S. Atlantic Fleet (COMNAVAIRLANT), headquartered at NAS Norfolk, Virginia, and Commander, Naval Air Force, U.S. Pacific Fleet (COMNAVAIRPAC), based at NAS North Island, San Diego, California. Each commander, a vice admiral, reports to the respective fleet commander. Training wings report administratively and operationally to the Chief of Naval Air Training at NAS Corpus Christi, Texas. A few test-and-evaluation squadrons (VX) report administratively to the type commanders but operationally to the Commander, Operational Test and Evaluation Force. Amphibious assault ships, while primarily involved in helicopter operations, are under administrative control of the fleet surface type commanders, COMSURFLANT and COMSURFPAC.

COMNAVAIRLANT and COMNAVAIRPAC exercise administrative control over such forces as aircraft carriers, wings, and squadrons. (Until 1993, naval air stations and other aviation shore activities in the Atlantic came under COMNAVAIRLANT command; Commander Naval Shore Activities, U.S. Atlantic Fleet became the type commander for air stations as well as other bases.) The type commanders standardize aviation operational, training, maintenance, supply, and administrative procedures, and recommend aviation policy to fleet commanders on matters concerning the organization, maintenance, distribution, and employment of fleet aviation. They are responsible for the flight training of air wings, squadrons, and aircraft carriers undergoing shakedown and refresher training and have access to the substantial budget required to fund such a large-scale force. Their staffs contain the wealth of technical expertise necessary to support the operation and training of their ships and aircraft.

Fleet Air Commanders

Fleet air commanders, subordinate to numbered fleet commanders, coordinate the administration of aviation units assigned to areas outside

The navy's striking power is concentrated in its carrier battle groups. Seen here are three of the six battle groups that struck Iraq during the Persian Gulf War. (U.S. Navy)

the United States. While they report only for additional duty to their type commanders, their tasks and responsibilities closely parallel those of functional wing commanders. In addition, they act as agents for the type commanders in supporting wings and squadrons assigned or deployed within a particular geographic area. They coordinate aviation matters and logistic support to fleet aviation units in the area and advise the fleet commander and type commander on such matters.

Fleet air commanders include Commander Fleet Air Mediterranean (COMFAIRMED, headquartered at NSA Naples, Italy), Commander Fleet Air Keflavik (COMFAIRKEF, at Keflavik, Iceland), Commander Fleet Air Caribbean (COMFAIRCARIB, at NS Roosevelt Roads, Puerto Rico), and Commander Fleet Air Western Pacific (COMFAIRWESTPAC, at NAF Atsugi, Japan). Many of these commanders are "dual-hatted" with operational roles as task force commanders or antisubmarine sector commanders.

Wings

Below the type commander level are the navy's various wings. Wings are groups of squadrons and other units conveniently organized with common missions, similar aircraft, or based on the same aircraft carrier. Wings are administrative organizations designed to provide administrative, training, maintenance, supply, and standardization to subordinate squadrons. In some cases, wings also have operational command responsibilities. There are four types of wings: functional wings, type wings, training air wings, and carrier air wings.

Functional Wings

Until recently, much of naval aviation was organized in functional wings, flag-level commands that spanned two or more type wings. They descended from the old Fleet Air organizations and retained many of their geographical administrative responsibilities, similar in function to the Fleet Air Commanders overseas.

During a large-scale reorganization of U.S. naval aviation in 1992 and 1993, most functional wings were disestablished, with the type commanders assuming direct echelon over the type wings. The one exception was Commander Patrol Wings Pacific (COMPATWINGSPAC), now based at NAS Barbers Point, Hawaii. With the realignment of patrol bases in the Pacific, COMPATWINGSPAC replaced a subordinate type wing, Patrol Wing Two in Hawaii, and assumed geographical area responsibilities as a de facto Fleet Air Commander. It also retained its position as administrative commander over Patrol Wing Ten at NAS Whidbey Island, Washington, and Strategic Communications Wing One at Tinker AFB, Oklahoma, as well as rotating patrol squadrons to Patrol Wing One (under COMFAIRWESTPAC) in the western Pacific.

In October 1994, Commander Patrol Wings Atlantic (COMPATWINGSLANT) was established at Norfolk, Virginia, resurrecting a functional wing for Atlantic Fleet patrol squadrons that had been dises-

Table 5-1. Type Wings—Atlantic Fleet

Commander Airborne Early Warning Wing Atlantic	
COMAEWWINGLANT	NAS Norfolk, Va.
Commander Attack Wing Atlantic*	
COMATKWINGLANT	NAS Oceana, Va.
Commander Fighter Wing Atlantic	
COMFITWINGLANT	NAS Oceana, Va.
Commander Helicopter Antisubmarine Wing Atlantic	
COMHSWINGLANT	NAS Jacksonville, Fla.
Commander Helicopter Antisubmarine Light Wing Atlantic	
COMHSLWINGLANT	NS Mayport, Fla.
Commander Helicopter Tactical Wing Atlantic	
COMHELTACWINGLANT	NAS Norfolk, Va.
Commander Patrol Wing Five	
COMPATWING FIVE	NAS Brunswick, Me.
Commander Patrol Wing Eleven	
COMPATWING ELEVEN	NAS Jacksonville, Fla.
Commander Sea Control Wing Atlantic†	
COMSEACONWINGLANT	NAS Cecil Field, Fla.
Commander Strike Fighter Wing Atlantic‡	
COMSTRIKFIGHTWINGLANT	NAS Cecil Field, Fla.

* Slated for disestablishment upon retirement of the A-6 attack squadrons.

† Slated to move to NAS Jacksonville, Fla., upon closure of NAS Cecil Field.

‡ Slated to move to NAS Oceana, Va., upon closure of NAS Cecil Field.

tablished only two years earlier at Brunswick, Maine. The new wing not only exercises administrative command over Commander Patrol Wing Five, Commander Patrol Wing Eleven, and the P-3 fleet readiness squadron, VP-30, but it also absorbed the operational antisubmarine responsibilities for the Atlantic area formerly exercised by a part of the staff of CINCLANTFLT, Commander Task Force 84.

Type Wings

Type wings, as the name implies, are organizations of squadrons with identical roles that generally operate the same type aircraft, usually based

Table 5-2. Type Wings—Pacific Fleet

Commander Carrier Airborne Early Warning Wing Pacific*	
COMCAEWWINGPAC	NAS Miramar, Calif.
Commander Attack Wing Pacific†	
COMATKWINGPAC	NAS Whidbey Island, Wash.
Commander Electronic Combat Wing Pacific	
COMVAQWINGPAC	NAS Whidbey Island, Wash.
Commander Fighter Wing Pacific‡	
COMFITWINGPAC	NAS Miramar, Calif.
Commander Helicopter Antisubmarine Wing Pacific	
COMHSWINGPAC	NAS North Island, Calif.
Commander Helicopter Antisubmarine Light Wing Pacific	
COMHSLWINGPAC	NAS North Island, Calif.
Commander Helicopter Tactical Wing Pacific	
COMHELTACWINGPAC	NAS North Island, Calif.
Commander Patrol Wing One	
COMPATWING ONE	Kamiseya, Japan
Commander Patrol Wing Ten	
COMPATWING TEN	NAS Whidbey Island, Wash.
Commander Strategic Communications Wing One	
COMSTRATCOMWING ONE	Tinker AFB, Okla.
Commander Strike Fighter Wing Pacific	
COMSTRIKFIGHTWINGPAC	NAS Lemoore, Calif.

* Slated to move to NAS North Island, Calif.

† Slated for disestablishment upon retirement of the A-6 attack squadrons.

‡ Slated for disestablishment upon wing consolidation with Fighter Wing Atlantic.

together at the same air station. The type wings provide administrative, training, maintenance, and supply support to their squadrons. The type wings in the Atlantic and Pacific fleets generally mirror each other. With the exception of patrol wings, of which there are two in each fleet, and the Pacific Fleet's electronic combat wing and strategic communications wing, each fleet has one of each type wing. (See Tables 5-1 and 5-2.)

The type wing commander is a captain who has a large staff to support the myriad of functions involved in supporting the combat readiness of the dozens of planes and hundreds of personnel assigned to the wing's squadrons. In most cases, type wings also include the Fleet Readiness Squadrons for each type of aircraft. Type wings work closely with the FRSs to develop standardized training, procedures, and tactics. Type wings also maintain and operate flight simulators, weapons system trainers, and crew positional trainers.

In addition to type wing responsibilities, patrol wings also have operational responsibilities, particularly as antisubmarine sector commanders. In this role, they report operationally to their respective fleet commanders and maintain Tactical Support Centers at their bases to support their operations as well as to train their squadrons.

In the case of carrier-based squadrons, type wings provide a community of training and administrative support, but the carrier squadrons report directly to the carrier wing commander.

Training Air Wings

The navy has five training air wings (CTWs) organized under the chief of naval air training (CNATRA). (See Table 5-3.) Each wing, commanded by a captain with prior squadron command experience, has two or three squadrons assigned at a given base. With the exception of the two wings devoted to strike training, each wing provides a different training pipeline in different classes of aircraft. Each wing gives the instructors, support personnel, and students assigned to each training squadron administrative and logistical support.

Carrier Air Wings

The navy's carrier air wings (CVWs) contain much of the nation's power projection capability. There are ten active carrier air wings and one reserve carrier air wing. Each operational aircraft carrier has one wing assigned. Every wing has about eight squadrons and one or more detachments of various types of aircraft. (See Table 5-4.)

The carrier air wing commander (or "CAG," an acronym hangover from the years before the early 1960s when the wings were designated carrier air groups) was upgraded in echelon during the mid-1980s from a senior commander-level command to a captain-level major command.

Table 5-3. Training Air Wings

Training Air Wing One	Tail Code: A
TRAWING ONE	NAS Meridian, Miss.
Training Air Wing Two	Tail Code: B
TRAWING TWO	NAS Kingsville, Tex.
Training Air Wing Four	Tail Code: G
TRAWING FOUR	NAS Corpus Christi, Tex.
Training Wing Five	Tail Code: E
TRAWING FIVE	NAS Whiting Field, Fla.
Training Air Wing Six	Tail Code: F
TRAWING SIX	NAS Pensacola, Fla.

Note: TRAWING THREE (C) and NAS Chase Field, Tex., were disestablished in 1992 and 1993, respectively.

Unlike before, when the wing was a department of the aircraft carrier, the CVW is a tenant on board the carrier. The CAG is an operational commander who reports directly to the battle group commander and serves as his primary advisor in strike warfare matters. The CAG, an aviator or NFO with previous carrier squadron command experience, is normally qualified to fly two or more types of aircraft assigned to the wing.

The CAG has a small staff of approximately thirty to thirty-five experienced officers and enlisted personnel to assist in coordinating the operations and training of the air wing. Directed by the Deputy Air Wing Commander, or "Deputy CAG," a senior commander or junior captain who will fleet up to become CAG after eighteen months, the staff includes six department heads (operations, administration, intelligence, weapons, maintenance, and safety) as well as their officer and enlisted assistants. The CAG staff also includes special assistants, including a command master chief, two flight surgeons, and several landing signal officers.

Operational Chain of Command

The operational chain of command runs from the president of the United States (as commander in chief) through the secretary of defense directly to the various unified and specified commanders. Most naval avi-

Table 5-4. Active Carrier Air Wings

Atlantic Fleet Carrier Air Wings

Commander Carrier Air Wing One	Tail Code: AB
COMCARAIRWING ONE	NAS Oceana, Va.
Commander Carrier Air Wing Three	Tail Code: AC
COMCARAIRWING THREE	NAS Oceana, Va.
Commander Carrier Air Wing Seven	Tail Code: AG
COMCARAIRWING SEVEN	NAS Oceana, Va.
Commander Carrier Air Wing Eight	Tail Code: AJ
COMCARAIRWING EIGHT	NAS Oceana, Va.
Commander Carrier Air Wing Seventeen	Tail Code: AA
COMCARAIRWING SEVENTEEN	NAS Oceana, Va.

Note: CVW-6 (AE) and CVW-13 (AK) have been disestablished since 1992.

Pacific Fleet Carrier Air Wings

Commander Carrier Air Wing Two*	Tail Code: NE
COMCARAIRWING TWO	NAS Miramar, Calif.
Commander Carrier Air Wing Five	Tail Code: NF
COMCARAIRWING FIVE	NAF Atsugi, Japan
Commander Carrier Air Wing Nine	Tail Code: NG
COMCARAIRWING NINE	NAS Lemoore, Calif.
Commander Carrier Air Wing Eleven*	Tail Code: NH
COMCARAIRWING ELEVEN	NAS Miramar, Calif.
Commander Carrier Air Wing Fourteen*	Tail Code: NK
COMCARAIRWING FOURTEEN	NAS Miramar, Calif.

Note: CVW-10(NM) and CVW-15(NL) have been disestablished since 1988.

*Slated to move to another base upon transfer of NAS Miramar to the marine corps.

ation units would fall under the operational command of Commander in Chief, U.S. Pacific Command (USCINCPAC) or Commander in Chief, U.S. Atlantic Command (CINCUSACOM). Units assigned to the Sixth Fleet fall under Commander in Chief, U.S. Forces, Europe (CINCEUR), through Commander in Chief, U.S. Naval Forces, Europe (CINCUSNAVEUR). Units deployed to the Middle East fall under Commander in

Naval Aviation Organization 149

Naval aviation's striking power is concentrated in the eleven carrier air wings. (U.S. Navy/PH2 Mark Kettenhoffen)

The carrier air wing carries a blend of about seventy-five aircraft, organized into squadrons with operational, administrative, training, and maintenance responsibilities. (U.S. Navy/PH2 Dennis D. Taylor)

Chief, U.S. Central Command (CINCUSCENTCOM). A few units might find themselves under the control of U.S. Transportation Command (US-TRANSCOM), U.S. Special Operations Command (SOCOM), or U.S. Strategic Command (STRATCOM).

Many commands assigned to the Atlantic and European areas are also part of the North Atlantic Treaty Organization (NATO) command structure, adding a "third hat" for some individuals. For example, Commander Carrier Group Four serves as commander of Second Fleet's Carrier Striking Force, and also as NATO's Commander Carrier Striking Force Atlantic.

Numbered Fleets

The Atlantic and Pacific fleets together have five numbered fleets assigned under administrative command. Each numbered fleet is also "dual-hatted" as an operational commander in its geographical area under command of a joint unified commander.

The U.S. Second Fleet

The U.S. Second Fleet, headquartered on board a flagship based at Norfolk, Virginia, controls all operational naval units in the Atlantic Ocean area and trains units for rotation to the Mediterranean Sea under Sixth Fleet control, and to the Indian Ocean under Seventh Fleet control. Second Fleet also has an important operational role with NATO as Striking Fleet Atlantic.

The U.S. Third Fleet

The U.S. Third Fleet, headquartered on board a flagship based at San Diego, California, has a similar role in the Pacific. The Third Fleet exercises operational control over all naval units in the eastern Pacific area. It also trains units for rotation to the western Pacific and Indian Ocean under Fifth Fleet or Seventh Fleet control.

The U.S. Fifth Fleet

Formed in 1995, the U.S. Fifth Fleet replaced Commander Middle East Force in the Persian Gulf as the commander of ships deployed to the Per-

Naval aircraft, such as this SH-60B Seahawk taking off from a frigate, often deploy in detachments of one or two aircraft. The detachment officer in charge shoulders tremendous responsibility for the success of the deployment. (U.S. Navy/PH2 Joseph Horner)

sian Gulf, Arabian Sea, the western Indian Ocean, and the Red Sea. This fleet was formed in recognition of the strategic importance of the region and the permanence of a sizeable U.S. naval force there, often including carrier battle groups. COMFIFTHFLT also doubles as Commander Naval Forces, U.S. Central Command. Most of the Fifth Fleet's ships and aircraft are on rotation from the Second, Third, and Seventh fleets.

The U.S. Sixth Fleet

Permanently deployed to the Mediterranean Sea, the U.S. Sixth Fleet, headquartered at Gaeta, Italy, controls units deployed to the area from the Second Fleet, as well as a flagship and two squadrons permanently assigned there. The Sixth Fleet also has a NATO operational role as Naval Striking and Support Forces South.

The U.S. Seventh Fleet

In the western Pacific, the U.S. Seventh Fleet is permanently headquartered on board a flagship based at Yokosuka, Japan, and controls units deployed from the Third Fleet to the western Pacific and Indian Ocean. Because it is so far from the United States, many squadrons and ships, including one aircraft carrier and one amphibious assault ship, are permanently deployed to the Seventh Fleet. During Operation Desert Storm, COMSEVENTHFLT served as naval forces component commander under Commander in Chief, U.S. Central Command.

Task Forces

Every numbered fleet has several operational task forces, each composed of assigned units and usually commanded by a senior group or wing commander. The Sixth Fleet, for example, has nine task forces. Commander Task Force 60 (CTF-60) is the senior battle group commander deployed to the Mediterranean and can be either a carrier group commander or a cruiser-destroyer group commander. This admiral is the operational commander of the fleet's battle force, normally a carrier battle group.

The fleet also has an amphibious force (CTF-61), a landing force (CTF-62), a service force (CTF-63), a ballistic missile submarine force (CTF-64), an area antisubmarine force (CTF-66), a maritime surveillance and reconnaissance force (CTF-67), a special operations force (CTF-68), and an attack submarine force (CTF-69). In this fleet, the submarine squadron commander serves as both CTF-64 and CTF-69. Commander, Fleet Air Mediterranean serves as CTF-67, and if senior to the submarine squadron commander, as CTF-66.

Battle Force Organization

The navy's major offensive element is the battle force. Naval aviation units comprise a major portion of the concentrated striking power of the

The air wing commander will frequently fly with his wing, both to train the wing and to provide inspirational leadership. (U.S. Navy/Lt. Gerald B. Parsons)

battle force. As with the other task forces, it is a fluid, semipermanent organization composed of various types of ships, submarines, and aircraft. The battle force fluctuates in size as ships and squadrons join the command, detach for other operations, or return to bases for training and upkeep. It may be reconstituted from within or subdivided to meet various operational requirements. The battle force commander is normally the numbered fleet commander or the senior battle group commander.

The basic tactical unit of the battle force is the carrier battle group. In 1992, the navy organized its ships into permanent battle groups, each centered around an aircraft carrier and composed of several cruisers, destroyers, frigates, and submarines. The battle group works together in its training cycle, and most of it deploys together to the Mediterranean Sea, western Pacific, or Indian Ocean. The battle group's flexible organization allows it to be tailored for action against any set of targets, including enemy surface ships, submarines, aircraft, coastal defenses, or targets well inland.

The battle group commander is a carrier group commander (an aviator or NFO), with a surface warrior as chief of staff. It can also be a cruiser-destroyer group commander (a surface warrior), with an aviator or NFO as chief of staff. The group staffs are similar. They function in both an administrative and an operational capacity as part of a fleet and task force. They are responsible for the operational planning and coordination of the air, surface, and subsurface operations of their assigned units. Under the fleet type commanders, they are responsible for the readiness, training, administration, and supply of assigned units.

The aircraft carrier falls under the administrative and operational control of the battle group commander, whether that individual is a carrier group commander or a cruiser-destroyer group commander. The carrier commanding officer is responsible for training, readiness, operations, and maintenance of the carrier, and for supporting the embarked carrier air wing and its squadrons.

Under the Composite Warfare Commander doctrine, the staffs and ships of the battle group are assigned day-to-day execution or coordination of certain warfare responsibilities. The battle group commander serves as the composite warfare commander. The commanding officers of various ships or destroyer squadron staffs serve as antiair, antisubmarine, or antisurface warfare commanders. Some serve as electronic warfare coordinators, helicopter element coordinators, screen coordinators, and submarine element coordinators. The carrier air wing commander normally serves as strike warfare commander and air resources coordinator.

The Naval Doctrine Command

A vigorous discussion within the navy on maritime strategy during the 1980s and into the post–Cold War 1990s caused the navy to establish the Naval Doctrine Command, headquartered at Norfolk, Virginia. This flag-level command develops naval war-fighting doctrine across the spectrum of naval warfare, promoting operational integration of the aviation, surface, subsurface, and special warfare communities within the navy and within joint operations.

The Center for Naval Tactical Warfare

In response to the increased integration of naval warfare communities at the doctrinal level the navy established the Center for Naval Tactical

More and more, navy units are operating jointly with those of other services. Here, a navy F-14A Tomcat fighter takes on fuel from an air force KC-135 tanker. (U.S. Navy/PH3 Chester D. Falkenhainer)

Warfare at NAS Fallon, Nevada, in 1995, thus consolidating tactical development under one flag-level command. The center is the navy's first foray into extending tactical development across the spectrum of naval warfare, including aviation, surface, subsurface, and special warfare.

The Center for Naval Tactical Warfare represents an evolution of the success of the Naval Strike Warfare Center (NSWC, or "Strike University"), established during the mid-1980s to improve the tactical integration of naval power projection, of which naval aviation is a key component. The navy incorporated NSWC into the center, along with several other existing tactical schools, including the famous Naval Fighter Weapons School ("Topgun") and the Carrier Airborne Early Warning Weapons School (both relocating to Fallon), the Sea-based Weapons and Advanced Tactics School at NAS North Island, California, and the Electronic Combat Weapons School at NAS Whidbey Island, Washington.

SIX

THE AIRCRAFT CARRIER

Revised from an original chapter written by
Rear Adm. Jeremy D. Taylor, USN

> An aircraft carrier is a noble thing. It lacks almost everything that seems to denote nobility, yet deep nobility is there.
>
> A carrier has no poise. It has no grace. It is top-heavy and lop-sided. It has the lines of a well-fed cow.
>
> It doesn't cut through the water like a cruiser, knifing romantically along. It doesn't dance and cavort like a destroyer. It just plows. You feel it should be carrying a hod, rather than wearing a red sash.
>
> Yet a carrier is a ferocious thing, and out of its heritage of action has grown nobility. I believe that today every navy in the world has as its No. 1 priority the destruction of enemy carriers. That's a precarious honor, but it's a proud one.
>
> —Ernie Pyle

An aircraft carrier is an impressive sight by anyone's standards. A ship of gigantic proportions, it is a carefully engineered and highly mobile strike platform, an armored shell containing an extraordinary complex of powerful machinery and electronic sophistication. But a carrier is much more than a technical marvel; it is a floating city of some five to six thousand teammates who are trained to work and fight with split-second timing.

With its embarked air wing of some seventy-five tactical aircraft, the big-deck carrier is a weapons system of such awesome power that its very location or direction of movement on the world's oceans can have a significant effect on the course of international events. Mobile and flexible, it permits the United States to project its presence and power virtually anywhere in the world. With its tremendous war-fighting capabilities, the carrier is intended to deter aggression, and failing this, to prevail over the most powerful and determined adversary.

The aircraft carrier, which first saw combat with the Royal Navy in World War I, came into its own during World War II, and by the end of 1946, the United States had more than one hundred carriers of all types in service, epitomized by the *Essex*-class fleet carriers that led the carrier offensives against Japan during the last half of the war. By that time, the concept of war had changed dramatically. It was clear that, for the foreseeable future, the aircraft carrier would be the focal point of naval warfare.

An important product of the war was the development of the three large carriers of the *Midway* class (commissioned after the war), two of which were in service until the early 1990s. Larger and heavier than their predecessors, with armored flight decks and better compartmentalization for damage control, the *Midway* class was the transitional step between the *Essex* class and the supercarriers of today.

After World War II, the advent of jet aircraft, heavier and faster than piston-engine aircraft, gave rise to the idea that the days of the aircraft carrier were numbered. This was not to be the case, however; the navy adapted existing carriers to deal with the new requirements. At the navy's behest shipbuilders strenghthened flight decks, installed catapults, and built in jet-blast deflectors, which muted some of the new flight deck hazards. Eventually, the angled deck came into being, which permitted the carrier to launch and land high-performance aircraft simultaneously, and mirror and lens visual landing systems replaced the landing signal officer's "paddles."

The era of the supercarrier began with the USS *Forrestal* (CVA 59), commissioned in 1955. Larger than the *Midway* class, this carrier had four catapults instead of two, and four elevators instead of three. The *Forrestal* was followed by three sister ships, the USS *Saratoga*, *Ranger*, and *Independence*, of which only the last remains in service today. A variation of the *Forrestal* class, the *Kitty Hawk* class, included the sister ships *Constellation* and *America*, followed by the similar *John F. Kennedy*, the last con-

The USS *George Washington* (CVN 73), one of the navy's most modern aircraft carriers, represents, with her embarked air wing, the "tip of the spear" of naval power projection. (U.S. Navy)

ventionally powered carrier built. Through the 1960s and into the 1970s, these ships were backed up by about ten *Essex*-class ships, many of which became antisubmarine carriers (CVSs) and the three *Midway*-class carriers.

The world's first nuclear-powered carrier, the USS *Enterprise* (CVAN 65), was commissioned in 1961. She was unique until the commissioning of the USS *Nimitz* (CVN 68) in 1975, the first of nine nuclear-powered carriers (CVNs) of that class built or planned into the next century. Her sister ships, the USS *Dwight D. Eisenhower* (CVN 69), *Carl Vinson* (CVN 70), *Theodore Roosevelt* (CVN 71), *Abraham Lincoln* (CVN 72), *George Washington* (CVN 73), and *John C. Stennis* (CVN 74), each an improvement over its predecessor, were in service by the end of 1995; construction or funding had begun on the *Harry S Truman* (CVN 76) and *Ronald Reagan* (CVN 77).

The Aircraft Carrier   161

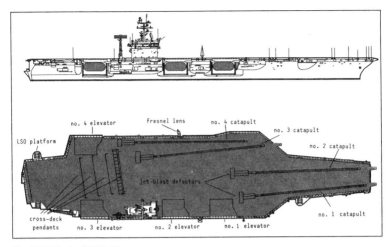

The USS *Nimitz* (CVN 68)

The Modern Aircraft Carrier

As of the end of 1995, the United States had thirteen aircraft carriers (seven of which are nuclear-powered). One carrier, the *John F. Kennedy,* is part of the Naval Reserve Force and serves as a training carrier, but she is available for deployment. The USS *America* (CV 66) and *Independence* (CV 62) are slated for decommissioning during the late 1990s, with current plans calling for a force of eleven front-line carriers and one reserve/training carrier.

The nuclear-powered carriers have the important advantage of being able to steam greater distances at higher speeds without having to refuel. The nuclear-powered carrier is supplied with enough nuclear fuel to operate for more than twelve years without refueling. It is limited in its operations only by crew fatigue and the need to replenish supplies, jet fuel, and ordnance. Conventional carriers must have more than ten million gallons of fossil fuel; the fuel on a nuclear carrier is contained within the reactors, allowing more room for the crew, and for jet fuel, ammunition, and other consumables. (See Table 6-1.)

Table 6-1. Characteristics of a *Nimitz*-Class CVN

Propulsion: Two nuclear reactors, which permit the ship to steam more than 1,000,000 miles before refueling.
Length of flight deck: 1,094 feet
Width of flight deck: 257 feet
Height (keel to mast): 244 feet (equal to a 24-story building)
Flight deck area: 4.5 acres
Combat load displacement: 97,000 tons
Number of aircraft: About 80
Aircraft elevators: Four, each 3,880 square feet
Number of catapults: Four
Ship speed: Over 30 knots
Number of propellers: Four, each weighing 66,200 pounds
Number of anchors: Four, each weighing 30 tons
Accommodations: 6,250 personnel
Meals served daily: 18,150
Number of compartments and spaces: 3,360
Number of telephones: 2,000
Capacity of air conditioning: 2,250 tons (enough to serve more than 2,000 homes)
Daily capacity of distilling plants: 400,000 gallons (enough to supply the daily needs of 2,000 homes)
Lighting fixtures: Nearly 30,000
Length of wiring and cable: More than 900 miles
Amount of structural steel: More than 60,000 tons
Required technical manuals: A stack as high as the Washington Monument (555 feet)
Bed mattresses: If lined up end to end, they would stretch more than 9 miles.
Sheets: 28,000
Pillow cases: 14,000

Note: All data applies to the USS *George Washington* (CVN 73) as built.

The Aircraft Carrier 163

Carriers (the USS *Abraham Lincoln* [CVN 72] shown here) operate as the centerpiece of battle groups, accompanied by escorting cruisers, destroyers, frigates, and logistics ships. (U.S. Navy/PH2 Tracy Lee Didas)

The modern, multipurpose, big-deck aircraft carrier embarks about seventy-eight aircraft of differing types. These are the carrier's striking arm, and they have a long reach. Air-to-air refueling enables carrier aircraft to fly over 85 percent of the earth's surface. They can detect and locate hostile forces; attack and destroy surface, subsurface, and air targets at sea; support ground forces; and interdict enemy forces ashore when land-based airpower is not available. In addition, they can provide protective cover for land-based maritime patrol aircraft and other operations at sea.

The twelve carriers afford flexibility in a variety of peacetime operations or limited-war situations as well as in the event of a major conventional or nuclear war. They have a formidable nuclear strike capability that an enemy must reckon with should the circumstances arise. Whatever the circumstances, these ships are an essential element in the sea-power equation.

In an all-out conflict, the aircraft carrier would be the unit around which we would array much of our naval might. Its purpose would be to ensure unimpeded use of the world's life sustaining maritime arteries and to attack enemy targets best reached from the sea. The modern aircraft carrier is equipped to deal effectively with the air, surface, and subsurface forces of any conceivable enemy. Further, because of its size, structural strength, extensive compartmentalization, massive protective armor, and sophisticated damage control systems, it is the least vulnerable of all surface ships to sinking and destruction. It is also most likely to weather all but a direct hit or very near miss.

"Where Are the Carriers?"

Experience over the past forty-five years suggests that limited war is the type of conflict in which the United States is most likely to become involved. In 1950, the communist forces of North Korea struck South Korea with lightning speed and captured most of the airfields capable of launching air strikes and supporting United Nations troops on the ground. Carrier aircraft conducted all tactical air operations during the first stages of that conflict and remained a critical part of the U.N. effort until the end of the war. The importance of attack carriers during this period was evidenced by an increase in their numbers from seven to nineteen. Carriers were also used to thwart communist China's designs on Formosa in the latter half of the 1950s.

Carriers operating in the Tonkin Gulf were indispensable to the conduct of the war in Vietnam, especially when the war was carried to North Vietnam during Operations Rolling Thunder and Linebacker. During the 1980s, carriers were called into action against hostile forces in Libya, Grenada, Lebanon, and in the Persian Gulf. In Operation Desert Storm in 1991 the navy brought six carriers to bear against Iraqi forces, launching their aircraft in the successful action to expel Iraq from Kuwait.

Since World War II, even excluding the Korean War, the Vietnam War, and the Persian Gulf War, American forces have been called into crisis areas around the globe over 250 times; aircraft carriers were part of half of those responses.

The Aircraft Carrier 165

In an international crisis, the President of the United States is likely to ask, "Where are the carriers?" Shown here is the USS *Constellation* (CV 64). (U.S. Navy/PH2 Heuser)

It is predicted that wars in the next few decades are likely to occur between smaller countries; in such conflicts the mobile, flexible, self-sufficient aircraft carrier reigns supreme in the projection of U.S. power. It has no peer. As in the past when presented with crises, present and future U.S. presidents are likely to ask first, "Where are the carriers?"

A carrier need not actually engage in hostilities to produce the desired result. Aggressors who look upon neighboring countries as easy marks for a quick military takeover are likely to have second thoughts when they see a carrier battle group appear on the horizon. In this role, the job of a carrier is to prevent war. Steaming through narrow straits, cruising offshore, or lying at anchor in a foreign port, the aircraft carrier is a highly visible and impressive symbol of U.S. power—on call and ready on arrival anywhere, anytime. It is a comforting symbol to friends and a warning to potential adversaries; it says in no uncertain terms that the price of aggression may be unacceptably high.

Carrier Organization

An aircraft carrier is organized much like other U.S. Navy combatant ships. The commanding officer has absolute responsibility for the safety, well-being, and efficiency of the ship. He is also provided with the authority to deal with his awesome responsibility. The carrier CO is always a captain and is normally addressed as "The Captain" on a ship that may have as many as ten people with the rank of captain on board.

Carriers are all commanded by naval aviators or naval flight officers in compliance with the act of Congress that followed recommendations made by the president's aircraft board in November 1925. Chaired by Dwight Morrow, the board considered a wide number of aviation issues arising from the early military application of aircraft. The issue of carrier command was one of the most difficult issues considered by the board.

On the basis of testimony from military and civilian aviation leaders, the Morrow board recommended that selections for command or general line duty on aircraft carriers or tenders, for command of flying schools, or for other important duties requiring immediate command of flying activities be confined to navy pilots. Congress enacted a law in 1926 (Public Law, Title 10, U.S. Code, Section 5942) that stated that the CO of an aircraft carrier or tender must be a line officer who is designated a naval aviator or naval aviation observer. A February 1970 amendment substituted the phrase naval flight officer for naval aviation observer.

The executive officer of an aircraft carrier acts as the CO's direct representative. The XO is primarily responsible for the organization, performance, good order, and discipline of the command and is prepared to assume command of the ship should the need arise. For this reason, the XO normally would be stationed, during hostile action, in some position where he would not be subject to any casualty that might disable the CO.

Few navy billets are as demanding as that of XO of a carrier, or as effective in preparing a successful aviation squadron CO for ship or carrier command. A relentless schedule of operational and administrative activity must be carefully executed so that operational readiness, safety, and welfare of the crew and material condition of the ship reach and remain at high levels. The XO is an experienced carrier airman who can effectively manage extensive human and material resources, and is also an expert in solving problems and getting things done.

The aircraft carrier is organized into departments and divisions for maximum efficiency. The typical nuclear-powered carrier has the following departments:

—Air
—Operations
—Engineering
—Reactor
—Weapons
—Supply
—Deck (First Lieutenant)
—Navigation
—Administration
—Aircraft Intermediate Maintenance
—Legal
—Medical
—Dental
—Training
—Safety
—Religious Ministries

Unlike most other navy ships, the carrier has an air department and an aircraft intermediate maintenance department.

Air Department

The air department is headed by the air officer, who is known in carrier parlance as the air boss. The air boss is responsible under the CO for all local air operations, including launching and recovery, and for the handling and servicing of aircraft on board the ship. The air boss's principal assistants are the assistant air officer ("mini boss"), flight-deck officer, catapult officer, arresting-gear officer, hangar-deck officer, aviation-fuels officer, aircraft handling officer ("handler"), and administrative and training assistants. The air department itself has five divisions, totaling over six hundred personnel.

Aircraft Intermediate Maintenance Department

The aircraft intermediate maintenance department (AIMD) officer is responsible for the supervision and direction of the ship's maintenance effort in direct support of the embarked air wing aircraft readiness. The AIMD is divided into divisions manned by skilled technicians whose primary function is to troubleshoot and repair avionics, airframes, and jet engines used by squadron aircraft. Additionally, the AIMD maintains and repairs ground-support equipment (GSE) used to maintain, start, and move embarked aircraft.

The Carrier Air Wing

Each carrier air wing (CVW) is typically composed of eight squadrons and two detachments of different types of aircraft. This mix of aircraft provides the carrier's search, surveillance, and strike capability, as well as fighter protection for the strike aircraft and battle group itself. Included in the capabilities of the modern air wing are strike, airborne early warning, electronic jamming and reconnaissance, in-flight refueling, photo-reconnaissance, antisubmarine warfare, search and rescue, and logistics. There are ten active carrier air wings in the fleet and one reserve carrier air wing. (See chapter 5.)

The Aircraft Carrier   169

The carrier air wing gives the aircraft its offensive striking punch and much of its defensive capability. (U.S. Navy)

Table 6-2. Typical Carrier Air Wing

Squadron	Function	Aircraft Type	Aircraft Number
VF	Interceptor; strike; photo-reconnaissance	F-14	14
VFA	Strike fighter	F/A-18	12
VFA	Strike fighter	F/A-18	12
VFA	Strike fighter	F/A-18	12
VAW	Early warning	E-2	4
VAQ	Electronic warfare	EA-6	4
VS	ASW; strike; refueling	S-3	8
HS	ASW; strike rescue	SH-60/HH-60	6/2
VQ*	Electronic reconnaissance; refueling	ES-3	2
VRC*	Carrier on-board delivery logistics	C-2	2

* Detachments.

The CVW is headed by an air-wing commander, who is called the "CAG," an acronym carryover from the early 1960s, when wings were called groups, and the air-wing commander was known as the air group commander.

A department of the carrier until the mid-1980s, the carrier air wing is now a separate entity under the battle group commander, with the carrier acting as host to the wing. Once a commander, the CAG (once called the Super CAG to reflect the increased responsibility) is a full captain, with a deputy who is a captain or senior commander. (See chapter 5 for a discussion of the CAG command relationships.) Although the CAG now reports directly to the battle group commander and has battle group operational planning responsibilities, the CAG must still maintain an extremely close working relationship with the carrier CO in order to keep the ship/air wing team functioning smoothly.

The CAG is responsible for the leadership and management of the squadrons under his command. The CAG supervises training and indoctrination; coordinates the activities of the squadrons and detachments; ensures material readiness; and oversees communications, intelligence, and other wing functions.

The CAG is a unique warrior. As the oldest and most senior combat leader in the wing, the CAG is the first to meet the enemy. He thrives on tough missions, including night and all-weather flying. He leads. He is a tactician and operator, with a bold and aggressive fighting spirit tempered by judgment. He is savvy in naval warfare, including antiair warfare, antisubmarine warfare, and strike warfare. He is a weapons expert who knows how to fight and win. He is an experienced survivor in a profession unforgiving of human error. The CAG billet is the ultimate flying billet in the navy and is one of the prime tracks to flag rank.

Flight Operations

Preparations for flight operations usually begin the night before with the distribution of the air plan. An outline of the coming day's events, it includes launch and recovery times and information about the mission, number of sorties, fuel and ordnance loads, and tactical frequencies.

Flight quarters are announced over the ship's 1MC announcing circuit and manned as prescribed by the ship's watch, quarter, and station bill. Crew members not directly involved in flight operations are not permitted on the flight deck or in the deck-edge catwalks. Those who are have specific, clearly defined functions. They are recognizable at a glance by their colored jerseys that denote their roles. (See Table 6-3.)

Pilots and aircrews, meanwhile, have received comprehensive briefings and understand clearly the sequence of events that will take place. They usually man their aircraft forty-five minutes prior to launching. Before they receive word to start engines, they conduct preflight inspections of their aircraft to ensure that all is in order.

Flight-deck and squadron maintenance personnel also have been busy readying their equipment and conducting a FOD (foreign object damage) walk-down, in which they systematically comb every inch of the deck for loose material that could be blown about by jet engines or prop wash and cause injury to personnel or aircraft engines. Only after the FOD walk-down is complete the order is given to start engines. Plane guard helicopters are launched and orbit in a "Starboard Delta"—a

Table 6-3. Flight Deck Jersey Colors

Blue	Plane handlers
	Aircraft elevator operators
	Tractor drivers
	Messengers/Phone talkers
Brown	Air wing plane captains
	Air wing line leading petty officers
Green	Catapult and arresting gear crews
	Air wing maintenance personnel
	Air wing quality assurance (QA) personnel
	Cargo-handling personnel
	Ground support equipment (GSE) troubleshooters
	Hook runners
	Photographers
	Helicopter landing signal enlisted personnel (LSE)
Purple	Aviation fuel personnel ("Grapes")
Red	Ordnancemen
	Crash and salvage crews
	Explosive ordnance disposal (EOD) personnel
White	Squadron plane inspectors
	Landing signal officers (LSO)
	Air transfer officer (ATO)
	Liquid oxygen (LOX) crews
	Safety observers
	Medical personnel
Yellow	Aircraft handling officers
	Catapult and arresting gear officers
	Plane directors

"D"-shaped flight path making them available to rescue a crewman in event of a mishap.

By this time the carrier has been turned to a course that will provide approximately 30 knots of wind over the flight deck for launch. Aircraft are directed forward by yellow-shirted plane directors and precisely positioned on the steam catapults. As an aircraft is "spotted" on the "cat," a

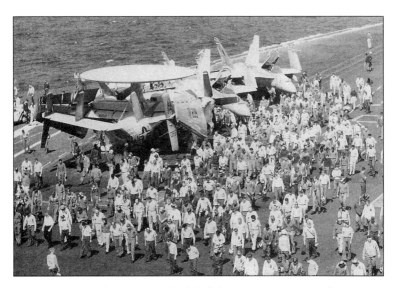

An FOD walk-down always precedes the day's flight operations on an aircraft carrier. It is an all-hands evolution for the flight deck personnel and air wing. (U.S. Navy/PH2(AW) Tim W. Tow)

A flight deck officer surveys a spotting board in a carrier's Flight Deck Control space. Parking and moving aircraft on a crowded deck require precision planning and execution. (U.S. Navy/PH2 John Rivera)

Carrier flight operations always begin with the launch of the plane guard helicopter, ready to rescue a crew in distress. (U.S. Navy/PHAN James E. Gallagher)

blast deflector rises from the deck behind it to protect personnel and aircraft aft of the catapult.

A green-shirted aviation boatswain's mate (AB) hookup man attaches the nose gear of the aircraft to the catapult shuttle by means of nose-tow and hold-back bars. When all is ready, the pilot, on signal from the yellow shirt, releases the brakes and applies full power. At this time the catapult officer signals with a rotating hand motion, two fingers extended. After a final check to see if the aircraft is functioning correctly, the pilot salutes to indicate that all is ready, and braces for the launch. The catapult officer makes final checks on the cat's readiness and confirms from other deck personnel that the aircraft is ready for flight. He then touches the deck, signaling to an AB in the catwalk (or "bubble," an enclosed launch station on *Nimitz*-class carriers) to press the steam catapult firing button. The

The Aircraft Carrier 175

The starboard deck-edge catapult operator gives the first ready signal to the catapult officer during the launch sequence for an F/A-18C Hornet on board the USS *Kitty Hawk* (CV 63). (U.S. Navy/PHAN James E. Gallagher)

aircraft is shot into the air ahead of the ship, accelerating from zero to a normal "end speed" of 150 knots. The acceleration from zero to safe flying speed puts tremendous pressure on the aircraft and crew. This spectacular achievement, which is usually duplicated more than one hundred times per day during peacetime carrier operations, is the product of brilliant engineering, careful and skilled maintenance of equipment, effective training of intelligent and motivated personnel, and relentless attention to detail and safety.

As the aircraft becomes airborne, the catapult crews are already scrambling into position to hook up the next plane. A proficient team of four catapult crews can launch an aircraft every twenty to thirty seconds. In a matter of five minutes, the ship can launch twenty aircraft and commence recovery of aircraft launched earlier in the day.

A catapult officer signals to pilot preparing for launch. (U.S. Navy/JO1(SW) Eric S. Sesit)

The airborne aircraft, meanwhile, are under the control of the carrier air traffic control center (CATCC), which guides them in the carrier control area around the ship. As planes are launched, they join up at a designated rendezvous area and proceed to carry out various missions as directed by the air plan.

When the aircraft return to the ship and weather precludes a safe visual approach, CATCC controls their arrival and clears each aircraft for approach at one minute intervals. It is the landing signal officer (LSO) who becomes the key player in assisting the pilot in his or her final approach to landing. The LSO is a carefully selected, seasoned carrier pilot—a "tailhooker"—who has had extensive training at LSO school and on board ship. The LSO operates from a well-equipped platform abeam the landing area on the aft port side of the ship. The LSO and assistants, as well as LSOs under training, correlate factors such as wind, weather,

The catapult officer gives the signal to launch an EA-6B Prowler. (U.S. Navy/PH2 Coss)

aircraft characteristics, deck motion, and individual pilot experience to guide the pilot on final approach. The LSO is an expert whose judgment is fine-tuned and rarely questioned.

For recovery in visual conditions, the aircraft return to an overhead "stack" at altitudes prescribed by air-wing doctrine. Individual flight leaders "take interval" on the flights at lower altitudes in the stack. Aircraft in formations of two or four normally enter the break for landing astern of the ship, on the same heading and slightly to the starboard side, at an altitude of 800 feet. The flight leader will break left upon reaching a position projected ahead of the ship, establish the aircraft in the downwind leg, descend to 600 feet, and complete the landing checklist. For final approach, the pilot will normally use the Fresnel lens optical landing system, a combination of lenses and lights located on the port edge of the angled deck. This is an automatic, gyrostabilized system; should it fail, or if the ship is rolling and pitching beyond the limits of gyrostabilization, a manual optical visual landing aid system (MOVLAS) will be

An F-14 Tomcat leaps into the sky after a catapult shot from the USS *Theodore Roosevelt* (CVN 71). (U.S. Navy)

quickly installed and used instead. In good weather conditions, this entire operation—the recovery of approximately twenty aircraft—is conducted "zip-lip," with no radio communication.

As the aircraft lines up for its final approach at somewhere between 120 and 150 knots (depending on aircraft type), the pilot will observe and fly the "meatball." The "meatball" is an amber light that appears at the center of a "mirror," which in reality is a stack of five lenses. If the aircraft is properly positioned on the glide path, the "meatball" will be aligned with a horizontal line of green reference lights on either side of the center lens. If the aircraft is above the glide path, the "ball" will appear on one of the upper lenses; if below, on one of the lower lenses. The pilot's objective is to keep the ball centered all the way to touchdown and to engage the "three-wire"—the third of four cross-deck pendants (wires) extending across the aft end of the flight deck—ahead of the "ramp," as "tailhookers" refer to the rounded aft end of the flight deck.

While it is the pilot's responsibility to fly the "ball," the LSO may also give light signals or voice instructions until touchdown. If the approach

An F-14 fighter, its hook lowered for landing, heads for the break to enter the carrier's visual landing pattern. (U.S. Navy/Lt. Cdr. Dave Parsons)

is unsafe, the LSO will press the "pickle" switch, which activates flashing red lights and orders a wave-off. The pilot has no option in this situation; he or she must comply with the order to take the aircraft around the landing pattern for another approach. If low on fuel and with no options to refuel in flight, the aircraft must head for the nearest "bingo" airfield and return to the ship at some future time.

The aircraft normally will land on the angled deck, hook a wire, and be brought to a halt within a few hundred feet. The cross-deck wires are attached to cables that are rigged through pulleys and around the drums of the ship's four arresting-gear engines. Hydraulic dampeners are adjusted for each aircraft according to its weight, so that the arrestment does not exceed the aircraft's structural limits but does stop the aircraft within the landing area.

As the landing aircraft makes contact with the deck, the pilot moves the throttle to the full-power position. If the aircraft's tailhook engages one of the cross-deck wires, the pilot immediately retards the power so the engines idle as the aircraft is brought to an abrupt stop. This is an ar-

With hook down, an S-3B heads for an arrested landing on board the USS *Theodore Roosevelt* (CVN 71). (U.S. Navy/PHC Denis Keske)

rested landing—a "trap." If the landing aircraft does not engage one of the four cables, the throttle remains in the full-power position, the engine accelerates, and the aircraft becomes airborne again for another try. This event, called a "bolter," is the principal reason for designing the carrier with an angled deck. If the aircraft has been successfully trapped, the plane is permitted to roll back a few feet so that the wire can be disengaged from the hook. The hook is raised and the aircraft is then taxied forward and parked. The arresting gear is quickly reset for the next aircraft. During recovery operations, a proficient crew will complete the recovery of twenty aircraft in fifteen to eighteen minutes.

A pilot making a good approach snags either the number two or number three wire. Catching the number four wire is the result of an approach that was probably too high or too fast on the glideslope; a trap on the number one wire indicates an approach that was too low or too slow. The LSO grades every approach on a carrier trend analysis form so that there is a continuing record of each pilot's performance. Competition among pilots is keen.

A landing signal officer and his backup each hold a pickle switch, ready to signal a wave-off to the pilot of an approaching aircraft. (U.S. Navy/PH2 Tracy Lee Didas)

Last resort. The carrier's barricade can be rigged in less than two minutes to receive an aircraft with an in-flight emergency. (U.S. Navy/PH3 Leonard J. Filion)

When recovering aircraft in foul weather, a variety of systems are available to aid landings, including the instrument landing system (ILS), tactical air navigation system (TACAN), carrier-controlled approach (CCA), and the automatic carrier landing system (ACLS).

The ACLS is capable of bringing an aircraft to touchdown when a pilot has no visual contact with the landing area. A computer takes information from the ship's precision radar and sends signals to the aircraft's automatic pilot, which in turn flies the aircraft and executes the approach. In ACLS landings, the pilot does not have to touch the controls.

The Path to Carrier Command

The path to carrier command, rather broad at junior levels, narrows considerably with seniority. Repeated superior performance in assignments as a carrier aviator or NFO and as CO of at least one aviation unit, normally a carrier-based squadron, invariably precedes selection for major command of an amphibious or support force "deep draft" ship. Selection for carrier command is made from the survivors of this winnowing process, and each year only five to ten contenders are screened for such assignments. There is no more prestigious, responsible, or challenging captain's assignment in naval aviation. It is a goal that the most ambitious seek but only a few attain.

Contenders for carrier command will typically have on their record between eight hundred and twelve hundred carrier landings (except helicopter pilots), between four thousand and six thousand flight hours, and six to eight extended deployments during three or four squadron and afloat staff tours. Most will qualify as underway officer of the deck and command duty officer before completing a tour as a department head on board a carrier. Some will also have served on a major afloat staff. Many will have ascended to that highly sought position via selection and assignment as carrier executive officers.

From these billets, prospective carrier skippers enter training pipelines that will prepare them for ship command. Before they take over a deep-draft major command, they will complete additional courses in shipboard engineering, ship handling, tactics, and leadership.

Some will assume command of amphibious ships, while others will command support ships such as oilers and replenishment ships. Operat-

The Aircraft Carrier   183

An aviation boatswain's mate waits to chain down an aircraft being parked on a carrier deck. (U.S. Navy/PHCS D. W. Holmes II)

ing with battle groups and amphibious ready groups, they will make more than fifty port entries in these large ships, and operate them in heavily trafficked waters, steaming both independently and in formation. All this will be done in numerous exercises that show the flag in several countries. In short, contenders for carrier command must master the heavy responsibility of a captain.

For those selected for nuclear-power training following a squadron command tour, the route to carrier command is especially arduous. They

Lulls in flight activity are rarely a let-up for the Air Department on a carrier. The ABE is tightening a cross-deck pendant (arresting wire). (U.S. Navy/PH3 Borbely)

complete sixteen months of intensive nuclear-engineering training. They then serve two to three years as operations and executive officers on nuclear-powered carriers. Carrier command ensures these extraordinary performers two or three more years of sea duty.

Carrier command is likely to come to only those aviators and NFOs who set their sights early and who pursue, with unswerving perseverance and skill, the proven paths established by Congress in 1926.

Flagship

As the centerpiece of a battle group, every carrier is equipped to accommodate a battle-group commander and the staff. The battle-group commander is normally a rear admiral who commands a carrier group (as an aviator or NFO) or a cruiser-destroyer group (as a surface warrior). In virtually every case, a carrier group commander is a former carrier skipper. It is highly unusual for a carrier to be deployed away from home waters without a battle-group commander and his staff embarked. The carrier thus becomes the host for officers who plan, coordinate, and direct the operations of the entire battle group. These operations include strike, antiair, antisubmarine, and electronic warfare, as well as reconnaissance and logistics.

The embarked admiral and the staff, along with the carrier's crew and the air wing, constitute a team that must work in close harmony if the capability of the carrier is to be realized. This harmony is quickly developed during predeployment training—the six-month period of underway and in-port training that precedes a carrier's deployment to either the Fifth, Sixth, or Seventh Fleet.

Carrier Rotation

After returning from a forward deployment, a carrier enters a period of restricted availability largely determined by its material condition. While this is normally a short period of two to four months, a carrier that has been repeatedly deployed for extended periods with minimum voyage repairs can require several additional months of shipyard repairs before commencing pre-deployment training.

New personnel and new equipment are integrated into the carrier during the first months after a deployment. This is the period of refresher training during which the crew drills for all contingencies and the air wing returns to the ship to regain carrier landing and operations proficiency. For the next three or four months, the tempo and complexity of training is intensified in preparation for the battle-group commander's final test of the ship and air wing readiness.

The battle-group commander and staff put the ship and air wing through a complex simulated battle scenario. Around-the-clock operations are sustained for several days. When the exercise is completed, the carrier is certified as ready for deployment.

An additional predeployment period of about one month is normally scheduled to enable the ship and air-wing personnel to top off provisions, to wrap up personal and family affairs, to peak out material readiness, and to solve other last-minute problems.

Carriers normally deploy for six-month periods, although world crises often demand that they remain on station for longer periods. The turnaround predeployment period normally lasts about a year but can last longer if extensive shipyard periods are involved. Periodically, carriers spend much longer durations in shipyards, such as for comprehensive overhauls. Nuclear-powered carriers require refueling about every twelve years, a process that can take well over a year as the reactors are replaced.

First In, Last Out

Carrier battle groups are the favorite instrument of U.S. presidents when they want a show of military presence and power to some area of the globe. Carriers are usually the first ships in and the last out in situations in which U.S. national interests are threatened. Carriers, which, unlike overseas bases, do not require host nation approval, can be ready on arrival to perform a variety of missions—presence, reconnaissance, show of force, or power projection. Because they can be easily resupplied, carriers are able to remain on station indefinitely.

The mighty aircraft carrier is the weapon of choice, lending support to diplomatic efforts to achieve peaceful solutions or favorable outcomes to problems involving U.S. national interests.

SEVEN

AVIATION ENLISTED RATINGS

Revised from an original chapter written by
Journalist Senior Chief Kirby Harrison, USN

While the tip of the naval aviation spear is composed mostly of the naval aviators and naval flight officers who fly aircraft into harm's way, the enlisted men and women who launch, fuel, fix, track, and fly in naval aircraft are an indispensable part of naval aviation. The plane captain of an F/A-18 Hornet strike fighter, responsible for ensuring that his or her aircraft is properly serviced and ready for flight, or the flight engineer who shares the cockpit with the pilots of a P-3 Orion are two obvious examples of such personnel. In addition to the plane captain and flight engineer, ordnancemen, avionics technicians, structural mechanics, air-traffic controllers, aerographers, and many other ratings make up this large, highly skilled support force. Still other enlisted men and women who are not technically part of the naval aviation rating structure are nonetheless involved in essential support activities in naval aviation units.

Enlisted personnel make important contributions to the daily routine of flight operations. A minimum of eleven enlisted personnel, each with different skills, are required to get each aircraft off the ground; with some aircraft, the number is much larger. A squadron of ten tactical jet aircraft

188   The Naval Aviation Guide

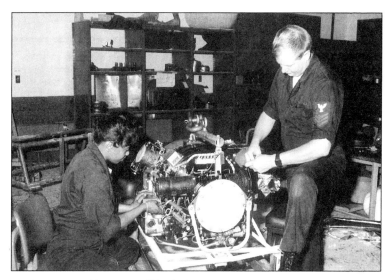

Naval aviation would never get off the deck without its highly skilled, hard-working maintenance and support enlisted men and women. These aviation machinist's mates are servicing an auxiliary power unit for a P-3 patrol plane at NAS Brunswick, Maine. (U.S. Navy/PH2 Scruggs)

typically may have some 250 enlisted personnel. Overall, there are more than one hundred thousand enlisted men and women in aviation-specific ratings, ranging from the nonrated airman apprentice right out of basic training to the master chief petty officers.

From 1916 until the late 1940s, the navy trained more than five thousand navy, marine corps, and coast guard enlisted men as pilots, designating them as naval aviation pilots, who served alongside their officer counterparts. Since that time, only officers (and a limited number of midshipmen) have been trained as pilots. The number of aircraft types that are crewed by enlisted personnel has declined over the years with the increasing performance of aircraft and sophistication of electronics. Today, most enlisted flyers serve in helicopters and in patrol, reconnaissance, antisubmarine, and transport aircraft.

Responsibility comes early to enlisted personnel in naval aviation. This airman, a plane captain for a fighter squadron, signals an F-14 pilot for engine start. (U.S. Navy/Lt. Joseph E. Higgins)

Training for Aviation Ratings

Enlisted aviation personnel normally complete basic training as airmen recruits (AR, pay grade E-1), and progress through airman apprentice (AA, E-2) and airman (AN, E-3). After completion of basic training, they attend a four-week course on basic theory in aviation fundamental skills. Airman apprentices are usually assigned to aviation squadrons, ships, or stations based on the needs of the navy. They will work with qualified personnel to gain job experience and perform such duties as repairing, maintaining, and stowing aircraft and support equipment; loading ordnance and preparing aircraft for flight; standing security watch on flight lines; and serving on crash rescue crews.

While assigned to their first commands, these personnel may obtain authorization to "strike" in specific ratings based on formal study and/or

An aviation machinist's mate refuels a UC-12B transport aircraft. (U.S. Navy/PH2 Robert Joyal)

on-the-job training. (Personnel in the seaman or fireman tracks may, in some cases, "cross-rate" and strike for aviation ratings as well.) There are eighteen aviation-specific ratings at the third-class petty officer (E-4) level for which an airman can "strike." Most of these strikers will receive training in their rates at Class A technical schools, most of which are located at NAS Memphis at Millington, Tennessee, or NAS Meridian, Mississippi. (See individual ratings later in this chapter for locations of specific schools. The schools at NAS Memphis and NAS Meridian are slated for relocation to NAS Pensacola, Florida, in 1997.)

A-school graduates slated for assignment to an operational squadron may be ordered to an FRS (or its Fleet Replacement Aviation Maintenance Program) for training specific to a certain fleet aircraft before reporting to their operational squadrons. Others will be assigned directly to aviation ships or air stations.

As with officers, training is a constant companion for enlisted ratings. In addition to on-the-job training, advanced and specialized training is available at many Class C technical schools, and at short functional Class F schools. The many Naval Air Maintenance Training Group detachments located at air stations fleet-wide offer on-site training on specific aircraft and their support systems.

As an individual is promoted to the level of senior or master chief petty officer, some ratings merge. For example, aviation boatswain's mates will specialize at the third-class petty officer level in launching and recovery equipment (ABE), fuels (ABF), or aircraft handling (ABH). Upon promotion to master chief petty officer (E-9), these individuals are considered to have sufficient experience to take on a supervisory role in any or all of these areas, and assume the rating of aviation boatswain's mate master chief (ABCM).

All aviation units have nonaviation ratings assigned, generally to perform administrative support functions. Squadrons typically have yeomen, personnelmen, disbursing clerks, intelligence specialists, and hospital corpsmen. Aircraft carriers and air stations incorporate virtually the entire range of enlisted ratings.

Upon assignment to an aviation unit, a pilot, NFO, or intelligence, maintenance, or supply officer will invariably have the job of supervising enlisted personnel. Because officers in a flying status spend so much time flying and studying, they rely heavily on senior enlisted personnel to see that the squadron's day-to-day business is conducted efficiently and effectively.

An officer's interest in and attitude toward enlisted personnel can have a positive effect, resulting in enthusiasm that is contagious. A genuine respect for subordinates and the importance of their contributions to the team effort is an essential element of effective leadership in naval aviation.

Naval Enlisted Classification Codes

As with other ratings, aviation ratings include numerous specialties, organized in a system of over nine hundred navy enlisted classification (NEC) codes. These codes identify individuals with specialized expertise

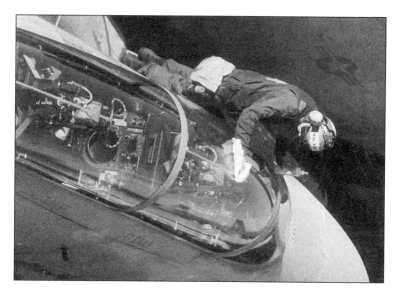

A plane captain polishes the canopy of an F-14 fighter. Attention to detail in this task can mean life or death for a fighter crew in combat. (U.S. Navy/CWO2 Ed Bailey)

within individual ratings, even down to specific aircraft, engines, systems, and components. The aviation electronics technician rating, for example, includes more than seventy separate NECs. NECs are added and dropped as technology changes in naval aviation. Primary and secondary NECs and their job descriptions can be found in the Manual of Enlisted and Personnel Classification and Occupational Standards (NAVPERS 18068D).

Naval Aircrewmen

Since the early years of naval aviation, enlisted personnel have served with distinction as crewmen in naval aircraft. For many years, the naval aviation pilot (NAP) program allowed a limited number of enlisted personnel to pilot naval aircraft. Enlisted aircrewmen have long served on board airplanes and helicopters in such roles as gunners, radiomen, ob-

Daily inspections of aircraft are required to ensure that they are safe and ready for flight. (U.S. Navy/JO3 Cyndi Reilly)

servers, flight engineers, radar and sonar operators, ordnancemen, loadmasters, in-flight technicians, and rescue swimmers.

Personnel volunteering for duty as naval aircrewmen are assigned under permanent flight orders, must be physically fit for flight duty as set forth in the Manual of the Medical Department (NAVMED P117), and must meet minimum qualifications for second-class swimmer. (The specific requirements are detailed in Article 9.12 of the Enlisted Transfer Manual.) Those who are accepted attend the six-week Naval Aircrewman Candidate School at NAS Pensacola, Florida, where they undergo training in physical fitness, land and sea survival, first aid, and aircraft familiarization.

Upon graduation, most personnel receive training in their specific type aircraft at the appropriate FRS, followed by assignment to an operational squadron or other flying unit. The individual then has eighteen

Enlisted personnel in some ratings have the opportunity to qualify as naval aircrewmen. This flight engineer, who is preparing his P-3 patrol plane for engine start, also serves as plane captain and is a vital part of the P-3's crew. (U.S. Navy/PHCS Ron Bayles)

months to qualify in aircraft type. Upon completion of all requirements, the individual is granted the appropriate NEC and is entitled to wear the naval aircrewman wings. Personnel designated as naval aircrewmen hold NECs in the 78XX or 82XX series.

Aircrewmen represent a cross section of many of the aviation ratings. The aircrew NEC is mandatory for the aviation warfare systems operator (AW) rating. Also, several nonaviation ratings serve as crew members in certain naval aircraft. These include the hospital corpsman (HM), who often flies on rescue helicopters; radioman (RM), who serves on strategic communications aircraft; and ratings in the cryptologic technician series (Communications [CTO]; Collection [CTR]; Interpretive [CTI]; and Technical [CTT]), who fly in fleet air reconnaissance aircraft). A few mess specialists (MSs) also serve as aircrewmen on executive transport aircraft.

Naval aircrewman earn hazardous duty pay while in a flying status.

Enlisted Aviation Warfare Specialist

In 1980, the navy established a program with an appropriate wing emblem for those enlisted personnel qualifying as enlisted aviation warfare specialists (EAWS). Those desiring to win their wings in this program normally come from the aviation ratings, but the program is open to other ratings in billets that provide exposure to naval aviation. Designation as an EAWS signifies that an individual has attained significant professional skills, knowledge, and experience in direct support of the naval air warfare mission.

Candidates for EAWS must be permanently assigned to a naval aviation command and serving in a billet that directly, routinely, and actively supports aviation activities. Candidates must be E-4 or above; be recommended by the chain of command; successfully complete EAWS Personnel Qualification Standard (NAVEDTRA 43423C) within twenty-four months of entry into the program (forty-eight months for Selected Reserve personnel), and be qualified in the Maintenance Training Improvement Program. Most of the candidates must complete a major deployment before becoming qualified. Final qualification comes when the candidate passes an oral examination given by a command review board and is designated by the commanding officer.

Personnel who qualify are authorized to wear the EAWS wings, and the letters AW are added to their rating designation. The EAWS program is not open to officers; however, officers who qualified prior to commissioning retain the privilege of wearing the EAWS wings.

Rescue Swimmer

The navy maintains a rescue swimmer program designed to maintain a capability to rescue aircrew and other personnel from the ocean. Aircrewmen from all ratings within the helicopter communities and, as of 1994, all aviation warfare systems operator (AW) personnel, complete this four-week school. The students attend either the East Coast school at HS-1, based at NAS Jacksonville, Florida, or HC-3 at NAS North Island, San Diego, California.

Rescue swimmer training is rigorous, and students must be in top physical condition. Prospective students must have a good disciplinary

All aviation warfare systems operators and many helicopter crewmen become qualified as rescue swimmers. (via *Naval Aviation News*)

record and be able to complete a rigorous physical fitness test (including sit-ups, a run, and a swim). Rescue swimmers who have been away from rescue swimmer duty for a year or more must complete a two-week refresher course before returning to swimmer duty.

Aviation Boatswain's Mate

Aviation boatswain's mates (AB-ABE, ABF, ABH) are responsible for launching and recovering naval aircraft quickly and safely, afloat and ashore. By its very nature, the daily routine of the AB is physically demanding and involves hazardous duty on the flight deck of the aircraft carrier. The day-to-day safety and successful operation of naval aviation depends largely on the professionalism of the ABs in the aircraft carrier's air department; they routinely put in eighteen-hour workdays during sustained flight operations.

The AB rating is divided into three specialties. The ABE (launching

Above: An ABH (aviation boatswain's mate-handler) (background) directs an aircraft to a catapult while an ABE (aviation boatswain's mate-launching and recovery equipment) (foreground) monitors the readiness of the catapult. (U.S. Navy/PHAN James E. Gallagher

Left: Aviation boatswain's mates (ABF) fuel aircraft and operate the aircraft carrier's aviation fuel system. (U.S. Navy/PH3 Paul Hawthorne)

and recovery equipment) rating is responsible for operating and maintaining the aircraft carrier's catapults and arresting gear. The ABF (fuels) rating has the tasks of fueling and defueling aircraft, and maintaining a ship's aviation fueling and lubrication transfer systems and spaces. The ABH (aircraft handling) rating involves directing and handling aircraft on a flight deck or airfield, and operating crash and fire rescue vehicles and equipment. At the E-9 level, the three rating specialties combine as ABs, capable of supervising in any or all of these specialties.

The AB Class A and C technical schools are located at NAS Memphis, Tennessee (scheduled to move to Pensacola, Florida, in 1997), with some Class C schools located at Naval Air Warfare Center Aircraft Division Lakehurst, New Jersey. Class A school, varying in length from four to eight weeks, is followed by intensive on-the-job training on board ships or shore stations. ABs may attend Class C school after reenlistment for further training. ABs can expect to spend 50 percent or more of a twenty-year career on arduous sea duty.

Air Traffic Controller

Like their civilian counterparts, navy air traffic controllers (AC) are responsible for the safe, orderly, and speedy movement of aircraft into and out of landing areas. Unlike civilian controllers, they also control aircraft movement around ships at sea.

ACs direct air traffic in and out of airfields and aircraft carriers by means of radio, radar, and light signals, and they plot aircraft positions on radar screens. They provide aircrews with information regarding air traffic, navigation and weather conditions, and airfield status. They also operate carrier-controlled and ground controlled approach systems, and field lighting systems, and maintain aeronautical charts and flight information publications for use by flight crews.

AC candidates must be at least eighteen years old upon entering school, and they must pass a flight physical, even though their duties do not involve flying in aircraft. They must be U.S. citizens eligible for a security clearance and have no history of drug abuse. The ability to speak clearly is essential in this rating.

The AC Class A Technical School involves approximately sixteen weeks of training at NAS Memphis, Tennessee (scheduled to move to

Aviation machinist's mates (AD) repair the engine of an A-6 attack aircraft. (U.S. Navy/PH2 Willie V. Davis)

Pensacola, Florida, in 1997). New ACs undergo one to two years of on-the-job training at their first duty station before achieving qualification. ACs can expect to serve 30 percent of a twenty-year career on sea duty.

Aviation Machinist's Mate

Aviation machinist's mates (AD) serve as aircraft engine mechanics. They inspect, adjust, repair, and overhaul aircraft engines, propellers, drive-shafts, gear-boxes, rotors, and fuel systems. They perform spectrometric oil analysis and evaluate engine performance. They also carry out routine maintenance, prepare aircraft for flight, and assist in aircraft ground handling.

AD Class A Technical School at NAS Memphis, Tennessee (scheduled to move to Pensacola, Florida, in 1997) lasts eight to ten weeks, followed by training at Naval Air Maintenance Training Groups and Fleet Replacement Air Maintenance Programs. An AD can expect to spend 50 percent of a twenty-year career assigned to deploying fleet squadrons and ships. At the E-9 level, the AD rating merges with the aviation structural mechanic (AM) ratings to form the aircraft maintenanceman (AF) rating.

Many ADs also serve as plane captains and loadmasters on board transports and helicopters, as well as flight engineers on board patrol, reconnaissance, and transport aircraft. They must pass a flight physical and eventually qualify as naval aircrewmen with aircraft-specific NECs after training with an FRS and on-the-job training.

Aviation Electrician's Mate

Aviation electrician's mates (AE) maintain and repair a wide range of aircraft electrical and navigational systems. These include power generation and distribution systems; lighting systems; flight instruments; automatic flight control systems; fuel, temperature, and pressure indicating systems; compasses; motors; and inertial navigation systems.

Candidates for the AE rating must be U.S. citizens eligible for a security clearance. AE Class A Technical School at NAS Memphis, Tennessee (scheduled to move to Pensacola, Florida, in 1997), lasts twenty-seven weeks, followed by training at Naval Air Maintenance Training Groups and Fleet Replacement Air Maintenance Programs. An AE can expect to spend 60 percent of a twenty-year career assigned to deploying fleet squadrons and ships. At the E-9 level, the AE rating merges with the avionics electronics technician (AT) rating to form the avionics technician (AV) rating.

Many AEs also serve as plane captains and loadmasters on board transports and helicopters, as well as flight engineers on board patrol, reconnaissance, and transport aircraft. They must pass a flight physical and eventually qualify as naval aircrewmen with aircraft-specific NECs after training with a Fleet Readiness Squadron and on-the-job training.

Aircraft Maintenanceman

The aircraft maintenanceman (AF) rating is a "compressed" rating, formed by a merger of the aviation machinist's mate (AD) and aviation structural mechanic (AM) ratings at the E-9 level only. At this level, ADs

An aviation electrician's mate (AE) repairs electrical equipment in a carrier's Aircraft Intermediate Maintenance Department. (U.S. Navy/PHAN A. D. Smith)

and AMs are considered qualified to supervise maintenance in both fields of expertise.

Aerographer's Mate

Aerographer's mates (AG) are the navy's meteorologists and oceanographers. Trained in aviation meteorology and physical oceanography, AGs collect, record, analyze, and disseminate data on historical and current weather conditions and forecasts to aircrews, ships, staffs, and shore installations.

AGs use and maintain instruments to measure air temperature, pressure, humidity, and wind speed and direction, as well as ocean temperature profiles, sound velocity profiles, currents, and ice formations. They

An aerographer's mate (AG) monitors radar for approaching rain and snow. (U.S. Navy/JO1(SW) Eric Sesit)

prepare weather maps and information and conduct briefings for fleet users. Their products are used for planning fleet movements, aircraft and ship navigation, and antiaircraft and antisubmarine search tactics.

AG candidates must be U.S. citizens eligible for a security clearance and have normal color perception. The AG Class A and C Technical Schools are located at Keesler Air Force Base in Biloxi, Mississippi. Class A school lasts thirteen weeks, after which AGs are assigned to ships, air stations, or other shore facilities. A few proceed directly to Class C school, which lasts eight and a half months. During a twenty-year career, AGs can expect to spend 60 percent of their time assigned to deploying fleet units.

Aviation Storekeeper

Aviation storekeepers (AK) are the aviation community's supply clerks, with duties similar to their surface and submarine counterparts, storekeepers (SK). They are responsible for ordering, tracking, storing, and issuing the hundreds of thousands of parts and supplies needed to keep naval aviation flying and fighting.

AKs prepare and maintain procurement records; order, store, and issue parts, supplies, and flight clothing; maintain stock control records and inventories; and maintain fiscal records of unit expenditures. AKs use sophisticated computer technology to track the large volume of data inherent in their specialty.

The AK Class A technical school is located at NAS Meridian, Mississippi (scheduled to move to Pensacola, Florida) and is eight weeks in duration. Upon completion, AKs can expect to be assigned to squadrons, aviation and supply ships, naval air stations, and supply depots. An AK will spend 45 percent of a twenty-year career assigned to deploying fleet units.

Aviation Structural Mechanic

The aviation structural mechanic (AM-AME, AMH, AMS) rating is responsible for the maintenance and repair of aircraft structures, including airframes, hydraulic systems, and safety equipment. Personnel in this field are crucial to the structural soundness and flight capabilities of naval aircraft, as well as the safety of the crews that fly in them.

The AM rating is divided into three specialties. The aviation structural mechanic-safety equipment (AME) maintains and repairs aircraft systems necessary to the safety of flight of the aircrew. These systems include canopy and seat ejection systems; oxygen systems; life raft kits; air conditioning and heating systems; and pressurization and ventilation systems.

The aviation structural mechanic-hydraulics (AMH) maintains and repairs the complex hydraulic systems in naval aircraft. The AMH is responsible for such systems as landing gear, brakes, flight controls, weapons bay doors, and their pumps, actuating systems, accumulators, valves, regulators, lines, and fittings.

The aviation structural mechanic-structures (AMS) is responsible for maintaining and repairing airframes and associated aircraft structures. The AMS is responsible for such components as wings, fuselages, control surfaces, wheels, tires, and airfoils, including fabricating metal parts and

AMEs (aviation structural mechanic-safety equipment) perform corrosion control maintenance on the ejection seat of an F/A-18C Hornet strike fighter. (U.S. Navy/PH3 Harold J. Walsh)

making repairs to the aircraft skin if necessary. AMHs also oversee the painting and corrosion control of naval aircraft.

At the E-8 level, the AME, AMH, and AMS ratings combine to form the aviation structural mechanic rating (AMCS), which at the E-9 level combines with the aviation machinist's mate (AD) rating to form the aircraft maintenanceman (AFCM) rating.

Class A technical schools for all three AM specialties last eight to ten weeks at NAS Memphis, Tennessee (scheduled to move to NAS Pensacola, Florida, in 1997). Upon completion, students will be assigned to squadrons, aviation ships, or air stations and can expect to spend about 50 percent of a twenty-year career with deploying fleet units.

Many AMEs, AMHs, and AMSs also serve as plane captains and load-

Left: An AMH (aviation structural mechanic-hydraulics) removes a panel to service an aircraft's flap system. (U.S. Navy/JO3 Cyndi Reilly)

Below: A maintenance chief petty officer monitors the work of AMSs (aviation structural mechanic-structures) as they repair the wing of an F-14 fighter. (U.S. Navy/PH1 Michael D. P. Flynn)

masters on board transports and helicopters, as well as flight engineers on board patrol, reconnaissance, and transport aircraft. They must pass a flight physical and eventually qualify as naval aircrewmen with aircraft-specific NECs after training with a Fleet Readiness Squadron and performing on-the-job training.

Aviation Ordnanceman

Aviation ordnancemen (AO) are naval aviation's armament specialists. Their professionalism is crucial to the combat effectiveness of naval aircraft. Ordnancemen are in charge of storing, servicing, inspecting, preparing, and handling all types of weapons, ammunition, search stores, flares, and smoke markers carried on board naval aircraft.

AOs inspect, maintain, and repair the mechanical and electrical systems armament systems, such as bomb racks, weapons pylons, and guns. They also assemble and fuse weapons, such as bombs, missiles, mines, and torpedoes. AOs supervise the operation of armories, magazines, and weapons elevators on aviation ships. AOs work on the flight and hangar decks of aircraft carriers.

The AO Class A technical school is located at NAS Memphis, Tennessee (scheduled to move to NAS Pensacola, Florida, in 1997). The A school lasts nine to eleven weeks; upon completion, the graduates are assigned to aviation squadrons, ships, air stations, or weapons stations. During a twenty-year career, an AO can expect to spend about 60 percent of his or her career assigned to deploying fleet units.

Aviation ordnancemen must be U.S. citizens and eligible for a security clearance. (Until 1995, many AOs also served as patrol plane in-flight ordnancemen, earning designation as naval aircrewmen with aircraft-specific NECs.)

Aviation Support Equipment Technician

Aviation support equipment technicians (AS) are naval aviation's automotive mechanics who operate, maintain, test, and repair the ground support equipment that service the navy's aircraft.

ASs maintain the electrical, engine, hydraulic, and pneumatic systems

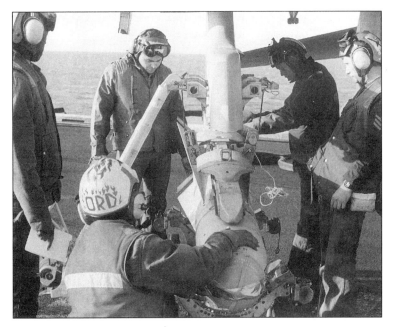

Aviation Ordancemen (AO) load a Maverick missile on an aircraft pylon. (U.S. Navy/PH2 Charles Stover)

in the support equipment, which includes tow tractors, aircraft starting carts, ground air conditioning carts, flight deck fire-fighting vehicles, flight deck cranes, bomb hoists, weapons loader trucks, and a variety of other equipment. They work on systems such as air conditioning, gas turbine compressors, generators, transmissions, brakes, and hydraulic lifts. The AS rating also includes metal fabrication and body work. On aircraft carriers and other aviation ships, many AS ratings work on the flight deck, as well as the hangar deck.

The AS Class A technical school is sixteen weeks in duration at NAS Memphis, Tennessee (scheduled to move to NAS Pensacola, Florida, in 1997). After completion, ASs can expect assignments to aviation ships or air stations, in particular at Aircraft Intermediate Maintenance Depots.

During a twenty-year career, ASs can expect to spend about 50 percent of their time with deploying fleet units.

Aviation Electronics Technician

The navy's aviation electronics technician (AT) rating is responsible for repairing and maintaining some of the most sophisticated electronic systems in the world. The ever-increasing complexity of aircraft avionics makes it a constant challenge to maintain competence in this rating.

ATs troubleshoot and repair the computers, consoles, displays, circuitry, antennas, and associated components on board naval aircraft. The systems that ATs maintain include communication, navigation, infrared detection, radar, acoustic sensing, laser, and fiber-optic systems.

In recent years the AT rating absorbed the more-specialized aviation fire control technician (AQ) and aviation antisubmarine warfare technician (AX) ratings. At the E-9 level, the rating is merged with the aviation electrician's mate rating to form the avionics technician (AV) rating.

Following a five- to six-week course in basic electricity and electronics, the prospective AT undergoes a tough twenty-seven-week curriculum at the AT Class A technical school at NAS Memphis, Tennessee (scheduled to move to NAS Pensacola, Florida, in 1997). For some, this is followed by an eleven-week Advanced Class A technical school. Upon completion, the AT can expect to be assigned to an aviation ship, squadron, or naval air station. In the course of a twenty-year career, an AT can expect to spend about 60 percent of his or her career with deploying fleet units.

Many ATs also serve as radiomen, sensor operators, and in-flight technicians on board patrol, reconnaissance, communications, and transport aircraft. They must pass a flight physical and eventually qualify as naval aircrewmen with aircraft-specific NECs after training with a Fleet Readiness Squadron and performing on-the-job training.

Avionics Technician

The avionics technician (AV) rating is a "compressed" rating, formed by a merger of the aviation electrician's mate and aviation electronics technician (AT) ratings at the E-9 level only. At this level, AEs and ATs are considered qualified to supervise maintenance in both fields of expertise.

Many aviation warfare systems operators (AW) serve as sonar operators, door gunners, and rescue swimmers on board helicopters. (U.S. Navy/Lt. Gerald B. Parsons)

Aviation Warfare Systems Operator

Known until November 1993 as the aviation antisubmarine warfare operator (AW) rating, the aviation warfare systems operator (AW) rating was renamed because of its broadened scope in naval warfare, particularly in recent years. Unlike other enlisted aviation ratings, AWs are primarily equipment operators rather than maintainers.

AWs operate aircraft sensor systems in antisubmarine, antisurface, electronic, and mine warfare. They are also employed in drug interdiction missions and serve as helicopter door gunners and rescue swimmers. They operate radar, infrared, acoustic, and electronic surveillance systems

These AZs (aviation administrationmen) are using the Naval Aviation Logistics Command Management Information System (NALCOMIS) computer to keep track of aircraft maintenance records. (U.S. Navy/JO1(SW) Eric Sesit)

on board patrol and carrier-based antisubmarine aircraft, as well as antisubmarine helicopters. Much of their time is spent studying equipment operating procedures and the threat parameters of potentially hostile ships, submarines, aircraft, and their equipment.

AWs attend Class A technical school at NAS Memphis, Tennessee (scheduled to move to NAS Pensacola, Florida, in 1997). All AWs must pass a flight physical exam, complete Aircrew Candidate School, and eventually qualify as naval aircrewmen. Current policy also requires that all AWs complete Rescue Swimmer School. Aircraft-specific NECs are assigned after training with a Fleet Readiness Squadron and on-the-job training. AWs can expect assignment to patrol, sea control, helicopter antisubmarine, and helicopter antisubmarine light squadrons, as well as aircraft carrier ASW modules and shore-based Tactical Support Centers. In a twenty-year career, an AW can expect to spend 60 percent of his or her career with deploying fleet units.

Aviation Maintenance Administrationman

Aviation maintenance administrationmen (AZ) perform a variety of clerical and managerial duties necessary for the maintenance of naval aircraft and associated weapons systems. The records that they maintain are essential to the practice of efficient maintenance and help to ensure that aircraft are safe for flight.

AZs organize and operate libraries of technical publications and reports. They collect data and maintain charts that show trends in aircraft reliability and maintainability. AZs issue work orders and schedule aircraft inspections, and maintain aircraft and engine logbooks.

The AZ Class A technical school at NAS Meridian, Mississippi (scheduled to move to Pensacola, Florida) lasts five-and-one-half weeks, following which AZs are assigned to squadrons, aviation ships, air stations, or repair activities ashore. During a twenty-year career, AZs will typically spend 55 percent of their time assigned to deploying fleet units. AZs must pass a typing test during training and must be U.S. citizens eligible for security clearances.

Photographer's Mate

Photographer's mates (PH) serve in a wide variety of naval assignments, but the PH is considered an aviation rating because of a long association with aerial reconnaissance, both as camera operator and maintainer. Until the rate was merged with the general PH rating in 1952, the aviation photographer's mate was a separate rating, with a winged rating badge. Wings were added to the PH insignia in 1993 to reflect its status as an aviation rating.

PHs are the navy's professional photographers, operating and maintaining still, motion, and video cameras. Their work includes news photography, portraits, copying, aerial and underwater photography, training films, news films, and other audiovisual presentations. They also operate darkrooms and photo-processing equipment.

A photographer's mate (PH) on board a P-3 patrol plane photographs a surface contact during a surveillance flight. (U.S. Navy)

After completing a ten-week Class A technical school at NAS Pensacola, Florida, PHs are normally assigned to ships or shore stations, though some serve with aviation squadrons with a photo-reconnaissance role, such as the F-14 fighter squadrons equipped with the Tactical Air Reconnaissance Pod System. PHs must be U.S. citizens eligible for security clearances and can expect to serve 50 percent of their career assigned to deploying fleet units.

Aircrew Survival Equipmentman

Aircrew survival equipmentmen (PR) were originally designated parachute riggers, hence the PR rating designation. As naval aircraft became more sophisticated, their duties expanded to include maintaining all types of aviation clothing and personal flight and survival equipment.

PRs are responsible for outfitting naval flyers with properly fitting and operating parachutes, survival vests, helmets, life rafts, flight suits, boots, gloves, oxygen masks, and other survival equipment. They inspect, maintain, and repack parachutes and life rafts. PRs also maintain the sewing

Aviation Enlisted Ratings 213

machines used in their work. They become quite skilled in sewing and manufacturing various types of fabric work and webbing assemblies.

PRs attend eleven weeks of Class A technical school at NAS Memphis, Tennessee (scheduled to move to NAS Pensacola, Florida, in 1997). Afterward, they are assigned to squadrons, aviation ships, and air stations, spending about 40 percent of a twenty-year career assigned to deploying fleet units. Unlike in the past, PRs are no longer required to become qualified parachute jumpers.

Editor's note: Much of the material in this chapter is derived from the Navy Retention Team Manual.

Naval Aircrewman

Enlisted Aviation Warfare Specialist

Rescue Swimmer

Aviation Boatswain's Mate

Air Traffic Controller

Aviation Machinist's Mate

Aviation Electrician's Mate

Aerographer's Mate

Aviation Storekeeper

Aviation Structural Mechanic

Aviation Ordnanceman

Aviation Support Equipment Technician

Aviation Electronics Technician

Aviation Warfare Systems Operator

Aviation Maintenance Administrationman

Photographer's Mate

Aircrew Survival Equipmentman

EIGHT

ACQUISITION AND SUPPORT: THE NAVAL AVIATION SYSTEMS TEAM

By William J. Armstrong

The Naval Aviation Systems Team is the element of the Navy Department responsible for the development, acquisition, supply, and support of all aviation systems, related equipment, and services required by the navy and marine corps. Included are aircraft engines, electronics, air-launched weapons, ship and shore equipment, and all spares. The work of the Naval Aviation Systems Team begins with naval aviation's technology base and covers the full spectrum, from research and development through engineering, test and evaluation, procurement, supply, maintenance, upgrade and modification, and, ultimately, disposal.

Like all elements of the navy's materiel community, the team produces in-house only a small portion of what it provides; most is procured from private industry. In addition, while the team is made up of many systems operators with extensive experience, it actually operates none of the systems that it furnishes. Its primary concern is fulfilling the fleet's aviation requirements. The team does not establish these requirements; they are established by the chief of naval operations (CNO) and the commandant of the marine corps and are based on the existing and projected needs of the fleet. Once a requirement for aviation materiel is established, the team is responsibile for meeting it.

The Naval Aviation Systems Team is a new concept developed in the early 1990s in response to a changing geopolitical structure and declining financial resources. (See Figure 1.) To perform its vast job, the team is composed of the following organizations:

— The Naval Air Systems Command
— Four Program Executive Officers (PEO)
    (1) Air ASW, Assault & Special Mission Programs (PEO[A])
    (2) Tactical Aircraft Programs (PEO[T])
    (3) Cruise Missiles Project and Unmanned Aerial Vehicle (UAV) Joint Project (PEO[CU])
    (4) Joint Advanced Strike Technology Program (PEO[JAST])
— The Naval Aviation Supply Office

The Naval Air Systems Command

From the time that the navy first procured airplanes, some organization in the Navy Department has been charged with developing the best technology and hardware for integrating aeronautics and the fleet. From 1911 to 1921, the navy administered aircraft responsibilities as though aircraft were small ships; authority for them was divided among various bureaus. The Bureau of Construction and Repair was responsible for airframes; the Bureau of Steam Engineering for aircraft engines; and the Bureau of Ordnance for aircraft weaponry.

In 1921, when the navy acknowledged that this system was unsatisfactory, it created the Bureau of Aeronautics (BUAER). Virtually all elements of naval aviation were drawn into this bureau, and the organization had a direct voice in operations. The bureau's plans division established naval aviation's requirements; the materiel division was charged with meeting them. The only exception was ordnance: BUAER established aviation's requirements for weapons, but the Bureau of Ordnance continued to develop ordnance. This arrangement prevailed until 1943, when the navy transferred four BUAER divisions—plans, flight, training, and personnel—to the Office of the Chief of Naval Operations (OPNAV). These divisions form what is today the office of Director, Air Warfare (N88). This transfer of functions left BUAER with its materiel division; all responsibility for operations was vested in OPNAV.

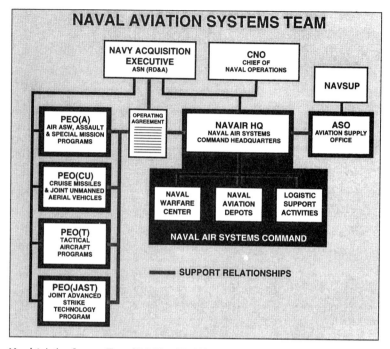

Naval Aviation Systems Team (U.S. Navy/NASC)

The Bureau of Aeronautics's responsibility for aviation materiel remained basically unchanged until 1959. In the meantime, however, a question arose between the Bureaus of Aeronautics and Ordnance over guided missiles. Because early guided missiles were primarily aircraft loaded with explosives, BUAER developed them and referred to them as pilotless aircraft. Nonetheless, the Bureau of Ordnance was responsible for developing and furnishing naval weapons. In 1959, in an effort to resolve the difficulties posed by divided cognizance over a system of growing importance, the two bureaus merged to form the Bureau of Naval Weapons. This bureau was disestablished in 1966, and in its place the navy created three systems commands: air, ordnance, and electronics.

NAVAIRSYSCOM is organized as a three-star headquarters in the Washington, D.C., area. The commander reports directly to the assistant

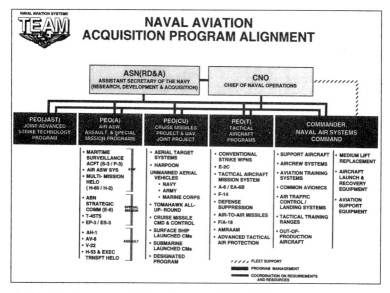

Naval Aviation Program Acquisition Alignment (U.S. Navy/NASC)

secretary of the navy (research & development) (ASN[RD&A]) for procurement issues and to the CNO for military affairs.

When established in 1966, NAVAIRSYSCOM was a program-functional matrix organization; all aviation programs (PMAs) reported at that time to the Commander, NAVAIRSYSCOM and received support from the command's functional groups. This structure changed in 1990 with the creation of the Program Executive Officers (PEOs). Ordered by the Defense Management Review (DMR), the PEOs took over the management and fiduciary responsibility of major and related non-major acquisition category programs. Some PMAs, those managing commodities and out-of-production aircraft, remained within NAVAIRSYSCOM reporting to the Deputy Commander for Acquisition and Operations, who performs in a manner analogous to a PEO under COMNAVAIRSYSCOM. All PMAs continued to receive their functional support as always from NAVAIRSYSCOM by way of a formal operating agreement. (See the figure above.)

Another major development started in 1994, with a target completion date of 1997: NAVAIRSYSCOM is being engineered into a new operating concept. This new concept centers on two key elements: (1) Integrated Program Teams as the primary avenue for developing, acquiring, and supporting products for naval aviation, and (2) the realignment from a program functional matrix organization to a competency-based organization.

This reengineering was undertaken in response to the decisions of the Base Closure and Realignment Commission (BRAC) and the outlook for the national defense budget. The command had to concentrate its dwindling resources more effectively on the present needs of its customers and organize itself to preserve and regenerate resources to meet the future needs of naval aviation. The restructured NAVAIRSYSCOM will focus on Integrated Program Teams (IPTs) that are fully empowered under PMA leadership to manage their assigned programs from initiation to disposal. Many of these IPT leaders will reside in the PEOs as a component of the Naval Air Systems Team. The reengineered team will be a Competency-Aligned Organization (CAO) developing and sustaining the team's resources in support of IPTs and other needs.

At the heart of this new concept of operations are the IPTs whose responsibilities span the complete program life cycle. The CAO will link people with like capabilities across all NAVAIRSYSCOM sites and competencies. The Naval Aviation Systems Team will move from an organization based on a program-functional matrix that is site-oriented to one based on pools of organization-wide talent and the leadership opportunity to unite people doing similar work by common processes. Instead of thinking of a specific site's personnel and capital resources to solve a problem, the new approach will use the strength of the Naval Aviation Systems Team to determine each solution.

NAVAIRSYSCOM includes its Headquarters element, the Naval Aviation Depots, the Logistics Support Activities, and the Naval Air Warfare Center.

Naval Air Systems Command Headquarters

NAVAIRSYSCOM's Headquarters is the team's focus for functional support and acquisition policy. Although many functions that were formerly part of Headquarters have now moved to the Naval Aviation Depots (NADEPs), to the operating sites of the Naval Air Warfare Center (NAWC), or to the Aviation Supply Office (ASO), sufficient expertise remains at Headquarters to provide leadership for all technical, logistic, and other service areas that are provided by the team to the fleet and to the more than two hundred acquisition programs that the team manages.

Headquarters contains NAVAIRSYSCOM's commander, vice commander, and the deputy commander (the team's senior civilian). Also located in Headquarters are the following organizations currently providing leadership in their key areas:

— Deputy Commander for Acquisition and Operations (AIR-1.0)
— Assistant Commander for Contracts (AIR-2.0)
— Assistant Commander for Logistics (AIR-3.0)
— Assistant Commander for Engineering (AIR-4.0)
— Assistant Commander for Test and Evaluation (AIR-5.0)
— Deputy Assistant Commander for Industrial Capabilities (AIR-6.0)
— Assistant Commander for Corporate Operations (AIR-7.0)
— Shore Station Management (AIR-8.0).

Deputy Commander for Acquisition and Operations

The Deputy Commander for Acquisition and Operations (AIR-1.0) serves on behalf of NAVAIRSYSCOM as the acquisition executive for programs assigned to the command. AIR-1.0 provides leadership for team acquisition operations and provides program support for all naval aviation programs. As acquisition executive, AIR-1.0 performs acquisition functions analogous to the naval aviation PEOs overseeing cost, schedule, and performance of the programs under his or her control. AIR-1.0 also chairs the Naval Aviation Acquisition Operation Council as the team's forum to review and improve processes used to acquire and support aviation systems. This deputy commander also provides program support for the entire team in the key areas of acquisition policy and operations, defense security assistance programs, production management, configuration management, and test-and-evaluation policy and planning. In addition, AIR-1.0 has a major role in writing the Test and Evaluation Master Plan (TEMP), a document under the program manager's responsibility.

Assistant Commander for Corporate Operations

The Assistant Commander for Corporate Operations (AIR-7.0) is the team's primary resource integrator, facilitating the planning, allocation, and execution of manpower, information, and fiscal resources for the team. In this organization are strategic management, congressional liaison, comptroller and financial management, the office of council, human resources, military manpower and personnel, security, public affairs, and information resources management. Each of these elements is aligned to support corporate operations throughout the team.

Assistant Commander for Engineering

The team exists to provide for the aeronautical needs of the fleet. It must consider various approaches to satisfying an operational requirement, and it must test and refine the emerging designs to ensure the correct choice of a weapon system. The research, development, and engineering of these systems and their related equipment is the responsibility of the Assistant Commander for Engineering (AIR-4.0). The AIR-4.0 group develops and publishes the specifications for the procurement and production of aircraft and airborne weapon systems and evaluates systems proposals from the industrial sector to determine to what extent they meet systems and engineering requirements. It also analyzes and evaluates design, cost, and mission effectiveness of each component of an aviation system, which it then studies, engineers, and integrates into a system. The group also develops and conducts planning for the engineering, development, technical evaluation, and production management of all systems and equipment being acquired. Once a system is acquired and furnished to the fleet, AIR-4.0 provides the necessary engineering support throughout the system's life-cycle.

Within AIR-4.0, Assistant Program Managers for Systems Engineering (APMSE) act as focal points for the program managers to provide technical support for the programs. Known specifically as "Class Desk" Officers, APMSEs are assigned to each aircraft and guided weapon for which the team has a designated program manager. Other APMSEs are assigned throughout the various divisions of AIR-4.0 and may be responsible for commodities rather than for major platform or weapons programs.

Another of the team's responsibilities is managing the technology base of naval aviation. AIR-4.0's Naval Aviation Science and Technology Office manages the general areas of naval aviation's research and technology. The specialists in this function do not develop systems because their work is mainly with research and exploratory and advanced development of the concepts used by the team in the actual development of systems. However, they are dispersed and colocated among the engineering functions to ensure that this work is done with a continuing knowledge of aviation systems needs, and to provide insight into the availability of emerging technology for aircraft or weapons application.

Assistant Commander for Logistics

As an integral part of the acquisition process, logistics support is designed into systems from the start. The Assistant Commander for Logistics (AIR-3.0) is responsible for preparing an integrated logistics support plan for each aviation and weapon system. AIR-3.0 prepares these plans in coordination with practically all elements of the team. Each integrated logistics support plan developed by AIR-3.0 addresses the maintenance, facilities, support equipment, parts, manpower, technical publications, and training needed by a system or commodity.

Within AIR-3.0, assistant program managers for logistics (APML) are assigned to a program as core members of a PMA's team and are leaders of the integrated logistics support management team for their programs. They are responsible for defining the in-service maintenance plan, coordinating its implementation, and ensuring its currency. There are APMLs for aircraft, weapons, and several commodities for which the team has a designated program manager. All logistic support for the fleet's aviation needs is developed and provided throughout each system's life cycle by AIR-3.0 and the Aviation Supply Office.

Assistant Commander for Test and Evaluation

In NAVAIRSYSCOM, the competency leader for test and evaluation is the Assistant Commander for Test and Evaluation (AIR-5.0). This competency has the technical knowledge, processes, and facilities that are required to support the planning, conduct, monitoring, and reporting of tests that are necessary for the development, production, evaluation, and fielding of air warfare systems, subsystems, and support systems.

Naval Aviation Depots overhaul aircraft (such as the P-3 Orions shown here) and fit them with the latest modifications. (Merco Corporation)

Assistant Commander for Industrial Capabilities

Within NAVAIRSYSCOM, the competency leader for maintenance is the Assistant Commander for Industrial Capabilities (AIR-6.0). This assistant commander controls a major aviation maintenance, logistics, and engineering services organization. (See Figure 3.) For over half a century, these industrial facilities have specialized in maintaining, repairing, and modifying military aircraft, engines, components, ordnance, and support equipment, and in providing associated engineering, logistics, and training support. There are six Naval Aviation Depots (NADEPs) within the United States, fleet repair sites in Italy and Japan, and the NADEP Operations Center at NAS Patuxent River, Maryland. These facilities provide the full range of aviation maintenance services to the team and its customers.

Acquisition and Support 223

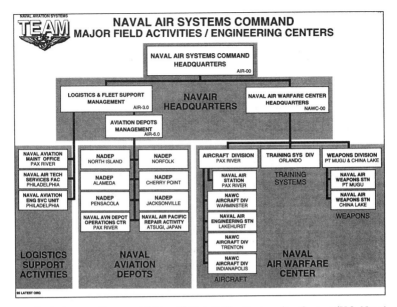

Naval Air Systems Command Major Field Activities/Engineering Centers (U.S. Navy/NASC)

The six NADEPS are best known for their depot-level overhauls of naval aircraft. Fleet squadrons and other units send aircraft to the depots to be overhauled, refurbished, repainted, and modified if necessary. Aircraft are normally stripped to have their components refurbished and/or replaced, a process that normally takes several months. The aircraft are repainted and test-flown before returning to fleet service. Some of this work, especially for minor aircraft types, is contracted out to private companies. Indeed, the NADEPS themselves have for some years competed with private companies for contracts to complete major depot-level maintenance work on naval aircraft. Some NADEPS also overhaul some army and air force aircraft types.

The NAVAIRSYSCOM industrial strategy, developed to optimize the balance between public and private facilities, will result in the closure of the NADEPs at Alameda, California; Norfolk, Virginia; and Pensacola, Florida. The closure of these depots is being accomplished through the

The skilled industrial workforce at the Naval Aviation Depots provides the fleet's aircraft with support that extends their useful life and saves the taxpayers many dollars. (U.S. Navy)

Base Realignment and Closure Commission. A restructuring of the three remaining depots within a CAO will provide depot capability in support of IPTs.

Assistant Commander for Contracts

As mentioned earlier, only a very small portion of the hardware that the team develops and furnishes is built in-house. With only a few exceptions, the navy has always procured its aviation material from private industry. Consequently, one of the team's major functions involves developing contractual agreements between the government and the private sector. The team has such a large number of contracts in force—or pending award—at any given time that a functional group in Headquarters is devoted entirely to contracts. The Assistant Commander for Contracts (AIR-2.0) coordinates contractual matters between private industry and public activities, the PEOs, and NAVAIRSYSCOM offices. AIR-2.0 negotiates contracts, awards the Command's and PEO's contracts, and represents the Command and the PEOs in the development of procurement policy at the highest levels of government. Procuring contracting officers (PCOs) focus the expertise of the group. Each PCO is designated to support a program. For example, there is a PCO for the F/A-18 Hornet strike fighter, another for the AIM-9 Sidewinder missile, and another for antisubmarine warfare.

The Comptroller

AIR-2.0 commits the government to financial obligations, but it is the NAVAIRSYSCOM Comptroller (AIR-7.6) who acts as senior financial adviser to the team. The comptroller develops and implements policies and procedures for financial and resource management, and sees that financial management supports the team's mission and conforms to laws and regulations. The comptroller's duties include budget formulation, financial execution, and reporting.

The Naval Air Warfare Center

The Naval Air Warfare Center (NAWC) was created in January 1992 as an initiative of the Defense Management Review; the purpose was to consolidate and streamline research, development, test, and evaluation (RDT&E), and engineering facilities. (See Figure 3.) The NAWC is the navy's center for aeronautical RDT&E and engineering facilities. It provides a central focus for all naval aeronautical weapon systems technical activities.

The NAWC has three divisions: the Aircraft Division (NAWC AD), headquartered at NAS Patuxent River, Maryland; the Weapons Division (NAWC WD) at NAWS Point Mugu and NAWS China Lake in California; and the Naval Training Systems Division at Orlando, Florida. The commanders of each division report directly to a small NAWC headquarters commanded by a rear admiral located in the Washington, D.C., area who reports directly to Commander, NAVAIRSYSCOM.

The Naval Air Warfare Center's fleet of aircraft are used to test and develop new weapons and systems. This F-14, based at Patuxent River, Maryland, drops laser-guided bombs in a test to clear the weapons for fleet use. (U.S. Navy/Vernon Pugh)

Once all of naval aviation's RDT&E and engineering facilities were consolidated under a single organization, the foundation was laid for establishing the NAWC as a fully integrated command. The NAWC is responsible for full life-cycle technical development, testing, and support of air platforms, unmanned aerial vehicles, missiles, missile subsystems, air warfare weapon systems, and airborne antisubmarine warfare sensor systems. Specific mission leadership areas across the navy under NAWC cognizance include air warfare analysis and modeling; airborne electronic warfare, and aircraft and missile survivability and vulnerability.

The Aircraft Division (NAWC AD) is responsible for all aspects of RDT&E and engineering for aircraft, aircraft engines, avionics, and aircraft support equipment. In addition to its headquarters at NAS Patuxent

Test pilot duty with one of the Naval Air Warfare Center's operating sites gives an officer unique opportunities to influence the development of naval aircraft and weapons. (U.S. Navy/Vernon Pugh)

River, NAWC AD has operating sites at Trenton, New Jersey; Lakehurst, New Jersey; Warminster, Pennsylvania; and Indianapolis, Indiana. (The Warminster and Indianapolis sites are scheduled for closure and consolidation at other sites.)

The Weapons Division (NAWC WD) is responsible for the RDT&E and engineering for air-launched weapons and targets. Besides its major sites at Point Mugu and China Lake, California, NAWC AD maintains a detachment at the Naval Ordnance Missile Test Station at White Sands, New Mexico.

Both the NAWC AD and NAWC WD maintain a fleet of aircraft for test-and-evaluation purposes. Fleet-experienced aviators, NFOs, and AEDOs fly these aircraft. Assignment to one of these divisions gives an aviation officer unique opportunities to influence the development of naval aircraft and weapons.

The third NAWC division, the Training Systems Division at Orlando, Florida, fulfills the team's responsibility to provide for the training systems used by navy and marine corps military and civilian personnel. It was set up to be the principal navy center for RDT&E, acquisition, and product support for all navy training systems. The Training Systems Division also provides interservice coordination and training systems support to the army and air force, both of which have major systems in the Orlando area.

Logistics Support Activities

The Logistics Support Activities include the:

Naval Aviation Maintenance Office (NAMO)—Patuxent River, Md.
Naval Air Technical Services Facility (NATSF)—Philadelphia, Pa.
Naval Aviation Engineering Service Unit (NAESU)—Philadelphia, Pa.
Naval European Rework and Repair Activity (NERRA)—Naples, Italy
Naval Air Pacific Repair Activity (NAPRA)—Atsugi, Japan

The Program Executive Officers

The navy established three aviation Program Executive Officers (PEOs) in April 1991 in response to an initiative of the Defense Management Review: Tactical Aircraft Programs (PEO T); Air ASW, Assault, & Special Mission Programs (PEO A); and Cruise Missiles Project and Unmanned Air Vehicle Joint Project (PEO CU). A fourth, PEO(JAST), was established in 1994. (See page 217.) Operating with relatively small staffs, the PEOs oversee acquisition management of all aspects of cost, schedule, and performance of the PMAs assigned to them. The PEOs have fiduciary responsibility for their programs, but their functional support comes from NAVAIRSYSCOM. The program managers within a PEO report directly to their PEO who in turn reports to the assistant secretary of the navy (research, development, and acquisition). To achieve a pure alignment, all programs have been grouped in PEOs according to their warfare areas.

Naval Aviation Supply Office

The Naval Aviation Supply Office (ASO) in Philadelphia, Pennsylvania, is an element of the Naval Supply Systems Command (NAVSUP). Created during World War II as a joint office for the Bureau of Supplies and Accounts and the Bureau of Aeronautics, ASO is dedicated to meeting naval aviation's supply requirements. An integral member of the Naval Aviation Systems Team, it provides the vital element of supply that the fleet needs to assure maintenance of a high level of readiness. ASO plans, develops, employs, and controls supply systems worldwide, and in support of the team carries out procurement and supply actions for navy and marine corps aircraft and support equipment. ASO receives command authority and functional direction from NAVSUP and technical direction from NAVAIRSYSCOM on logistical and supply issues. Logistics and maintenance planning are done with NAVAIRSYSCOM, but systems planning and supply policy are carried out with NAVSUP.

NINE

SAFETY AND NATOPS

By Capt. Rosario Rausa, USNR (Ret.)

> *"Every man and woman in the navy is a safety manager!"*
> *"Know your emergency procedures!"*
> *"Safety saves!"*

These slogans would become platitudes in the world of naval aviation if the message they conveyed were not so important. From the outset in the flight training program, safety is emphasized; eventually it becomes a daily ruling principle of every navy, marine corps, and coast guard flyer.

Mishaps Are Costly

As of this writing, the navy's aviation mishap rate is the lowest it ever has been. Compared with activities during World War II, today's flight activities are, indeed, safe. Nevertheless, too many pilots and aircrewmen, men and women, are lost each year. Even though the declining rate of mishaps is a welcome reflection of the continuing attention placed on safety, there can be no slackening of precaution. The cost of mishaps in lives and funds spent for aircraft, training, and maintenance is simply too

Safety and NATOPS (Artist: Robert Osborn)

high. A single F/A-18D Hornet, for example, costs approximately $35 million. It takes $800,000 to train an F/A-18 pilot through the Fleet Readiness Squadron stage, a price tag that rises with each passing year. The cost of human life is, of course, incalculable.

So, for fledglings and veterans alike, including flag officers at the upper echelons of command, safety considerations are critical and second in importance only to mission accomplishment in "real-world" combat operations.

The Naval Aviation Safety Program

The Naval Aviation Safety Program is described in the OPNAVINST 3750.6 series, 3750.6Q as of this writing. Its chief purpose is to preserve human life and material resources by eliminating hazards. All aviation personnel should be familiar with its directives. Normally, when an officer checks into a squadron, the indoctrination briefings include reviews of pertinent safety instructions and safety "rules of the road" for operations in the air and on the ground. A successful safety program has three main functions:

— Hazard detection
— Hazard elimination
— Safety information management

A naval aircraft mishap is defined as an unplanned event or series of events, directly involving naval aircraft, which results in injury or property damage exceeding $10,000. A Class A mishap is one in which the total cost of property damage or injury is greater than $1 million and/or in which a person receives a fatal or permanently disabling injury. The mishap classes are listed as follows:

Class A: >$1,000,000
Class B: $200,000–$1,000,000
Class C: >$10,000–<$200,000

The main injury classifications are:

Good safety practices are vital to the readiness of naval aviation, conserving expensively trained, highly skilled personnel, aircraft, and ships for combat operations. (U.S. Navy/CWO2 Tony Alleyne)

— Alfa: fatal injury
— Bravo: permanent total disability
— Charlie: permanent partial disability
— Delta: lost workday injury

A common acronym in safety parlance is AMB—Aircraft Mishap Board. An AMB consists of several officers, including a flight surgeon, and is convened to examine a mishap thoroughly and to record its findings in a mishap investigation report to be submitted to higher authority.

If disciplinary measures were taken against those who provide information to an AMB, it would impede the flow of critical facts and observations from witnesses or those involved in mishaps, thus reducing the value of the investigation. The primary purpose of the investigation is to prevent or reduce the likelihood of future mishaps. The information supplied by witnesses and participants, therefore, is privileged and cannot be revealed to the public or to sources other than designated officials.

The Aviation Safety Officer

Each aviation squadron has an aviation safety officer (ASO). The ASO is the CO's principal advisor on all aviation safety matters. The ASO is usually a lieutenant or lieutenant commander on a second tour of flying duty who has graduated from the five-week ASO course at the Naval Postgraduate School in Monterey, California.

The ASO is usually the squadron Safety Department head and thus has direct access to the CO. This reflects the importance that both the navy and individual units place on safety. Detachments or units smaller than squadrons may not have a full-time ASO; however, at least one officer will have ASO responsibilities on a collateral-duty basis. Aircraft carriers and air stations have full-time safety officers with department-head status.

The Naval Postgraduate School also offers a five-day Aviation Safety Command Course designed for prospective squadron executive officers and commanding officers, as well as staff safety officers.

The Naval Safety Center

The U.S. Naval Safety Center, located at NAS Norfolk, Virginia, is a flag-level command with the mission of collecting, evaluating, and disseminating safety information. It also develops aviation, submarine, surface ship, and shore establishment safety programs. The aviation division is further divided into aircraft and facilities operations, maintenance and material activities, mishap investigations, and aerospace medical matters.

The Naval Safety Center produces several publications, one of which is a familiar item in virtually every ready room and maintenance shop throughout the naval aviation community: *Approach/Mech* magazine, a bimonthly combination of the former *Approach* and *Mech* magazines, which features first-person accounts of mishaps and near-mishaps and articles on safety, hazards, policies, and equipment pertinent to readiness and safety in naval aviation at all levels.

Anymouse

For navy and marine corps flyers and their support crews, the term Anymouse has nothing to do with rodents; it is a comic substitute for the word anonymous. Anyone who wants to say something about aviation safety without revealing his or her identity can submit an Anymouse report. Anonymity is important; without it, the perpetrator of a near-mishap might keep silent. First-person-singular "confessions" tend to be candid descriptions of human error which, when passed on to others, are extremely valuable training tools. Learning from the mistakes of others is beneficial. Anymouse reports can be submitted to *Approach/Mech* magazine (which features a section on them in each issue); to squadron/unit safety officers; or to the CO directly.

Grampaw Pettibone

Published for Director, Air Warfare by the Naval Historical Center, *Naval Aviation News* is the oldest U.S. Navy publication (first appearing in 1917). Although not a safety publication per se, it does feature the most widely recognized character in naval aviation safety: Grampaw Pettibone.

In each issue, several mishaps are described in narrative form (followed by caustic commentary from "Gramps") in the magazine's popular Grampaw Pettibone section. The accounts are accompanied by illustrations from the talented hand of Ted Wilbur, who in 1994 succeeded Robert Osborn. (Osborn, who helped create "Gramps" during World War II, drew the character for over fifty years, long after he left active duty to become a prominent artist in his own right.)

A naval flyer is bombarded by many safety axioms throughout his or her career. Regardless of the programs of a particular command, one axiom, sooner or later, becomes imbedded in the aviator's mind: "Flying in itself is not dangerous, but it is mercilessly unforgiving of human error." Good words to remember.

NATOPS and Safety

Naval Air Training and Operating Procedures Standardization Program is an unwieldy title, easier to manage as an acronym: NATOPS. This staple of U.S. naval aviation has far-reaching, long-lasting connotations for each and every naval flyer. NATOPS sets down, lucidly and intelligently, step-by-step procedures for operating aircraft and accomplishing other aeronautical functions.

236   The Naval Aviation Guide

Flying is not inherently dangerous, but it is mercilessly unforgiving of human error. (U.S. Navy)

The importance of NATOPS may not reach biblical dimensions, but a thorough, if not commanding, knowledge of NATOPS procedures is essential for the flyer who wants to become a genuine professional. Two facts demonstrate the value of NATOPS:

— Before the navy established the NATOPS program in 1961, the aviation mishap rate was nearly twenty mishap rates per one hundred thousand flight hours.
— In 1994, that rate had dipped to below two mishaps per one hundred thousand flight hours.

In large part, NATOPS is credited for this substantial reduction in loss of aircraft, not to mention the savings in terms of lives.

NATOPS Manuals

Instrumental to NATOPS is the NATOPS flight manual. One flight manual is published for each model of aircraft, and for aircraft with several crew positions, a manual is published for each position. Every flight manual contains standardized ground and flight operating procedures, training requirements, safety and emergency procedures, and technical data necessary for the safe and effective operation of the aircraft. Flight manuals also have indispensable pocket checklists for use during flight, and for ground operations, such as fueling and arming.

A NATOPS manual, as differentiated from a NATOPS flight manual, is issued for particular operations that lend themselves to standardization, such as aircraft carrier flight operations, aerial refueling, instrument flight, and landing signal officer activities.

Key NATOPS Groups and Individuals

NATOPS Advisory Group

The NATOPS Advisory Group is comprised of representatives from the staffs of the chief of naval operations, the commandant of the marine corps, and other commands subordinate to these two. It monitors NATOPS to ensure that it functions properly. The Naval Safety Center, as an advisory group member, is responsible for apprising other members of the effectiveness of the program. A cognizant command is an advisory group member designated by the CNO and responsible for specific portions of the program.

CNO NATOPS Coordinator

The CNO NATOPS coordinator is an experienced aviator tasked with overall NATOPS duties. While this aviator monitors virtually all phases of the NATOPS program for the CNO, he or she also works in conjunction with the navy Tactical Support Activity (NAVTACSUPPACT). Selected NAVTACSUPPACT officers act as CNO NATOPS coordinators and actively participate in NATOPS review conferences. NAVTACSUPPACT produces NATOPS manuals, coordinates the production of NATOPS flight manuals with various commands and contractors, and monitors the production, printing, and distribution of all NATOPS publications. It also promulgates a report of cognizant-command and model-manager assignments.

NATOPS Coordinator

Like his CNO-level counterpart, a NATOPS coordinator is a veteran flyer. Assigned to advisory-group member staffs, this officer coordinates the command's NATOPS program and maintains liaison with other coordinators as well as with NAVTACSUPPACT. The coordinator sees to it that an annual review is made of each NATOPS evaluator's activities.

Model Manager

A model manager is a unit designated by a cognizant command to administer the NATOPS program for a specific aircraft model. The model manager compiles proposed NATOPS changes and recommends the convening of review conferences when appropriate. Model managers review publications for accuracy and to ensure that they are in accordance with the latest approved operating procedures. Model managers coordinate the efforts of other NATOPS evaluators working on the same aircraft model to achieve standardization. The NATOPS evaluator for an aircraft model within the cognizant command is attached to the model-manager unit of that model.

Evaluator Unit

An evaluator unit is a squadron, unit, or air station that has been assigned responsibilities for NATOPS matters by the advisory group member. The Fleet Readiness Squadrons are normally the evaluator units.

NATOPS Evaluator

A NATOPS evaluator is a pilot or crew member, highly qualified in a specific model of aircraft, who occupies a primary billet in an evaluator unit. Every year he or she evaluates NATOPS instructors in squadrons or units of the same model within the same major command. The evaluator conducts written examinations of the squadron personnel and check flights of crews selected at random to measure overall adherence to NATOPS procedures. The evaluator is also responsible for continuously reviewing manuals and certain maintenance and warfare publications to achieve standardization.

NATOPS Instructors

A NATOPS instructor evaluates all flight crew members within the instructor's squadron or unit and keeps the CO informed of all NATOPS matters.

NATOPS—Everyone's Business

All members of the naval aviation community are encouraged to help update the NATOPS program. Procedural flaws or conflicts can be reported anonymously if an individual desires. OPNAV Instruction 3710.7 series is the guiding directive for the program. It states, "NATOPS publications must have inputs from many sources in order to maintain the effectiveness of the program. To accomplish this, anyone in the naval establishment who notes a deficiency or error is obliged to submit a change recommendation. The participation of the individual in this program of continual manual improvement is imperative."

The instruction outlines steps for initiating changes. There are two ways to initiate a change to a specific NATOPS manual or flight manual. Routine changes are submitted to the model manager for consideration at a NATOPS review conference. Urgent changes are submitted through the cognizant command and approved by the CNO NATOPS coordinator for quick distribution to the fleet.

The essential purpose of the NATOPS program has not changed since its inception. It was created to provide the safest and best aircraft training and operating procedures. It has proven to be an all-encompassing management tool that continues to enhance the operational readiness of naval aviation.

TEN

AEROSPACE MEDICINE

Revised by Cdr. John W. Mills, MC, USN

Aerospace medicine is a specialized field dedicated to the safe adaptation of men and women to flight, be they aviators or astronauts. Once airborne, an individual is subjected to the stresses of acceleration, deceleration, thermal extremes, radiation, vibration, weightlessness, and confinement. The ultimate goal of the flight surgeon is to maintain the health, safety, and well-being of the flight crew, thus maximizing and preserving the operational readiness of the command.

Flight Surgeons

The question is often asked, "Who do flight surgeons operate on?" The answer is, "Usually no one." The use of the term *surgeon*, especially in a military context, goes back well over one hundred years, when all military doctors were called surgeons. The word *surgeon* was also used as part of a rank. Considering that a surgeon's main task was amputations, the term was appropriate. Until World War II, all naval physicians were commissioned as surgeons, assistant surgeons, or acting assistant surgeons.

The navy's interest in aviation medicine dates back to 29 April 1922, when five navy medical officers graduated from the U.S. Army School of Aviation Medicine at Mitchell Field, Long Island, New York. The navy trained its own flight surgeons at the Naval Medical School at Bethesda, Maryland, from 1927 until 1935, when the army resumed training navy flight surgeons. In November 1939, the navy opened the School of Aviation Medicine at NAS Pensacola, Florida.

Becoming a Flight Surgeon

Today, the young medical officer who wants to become a flight surgeon must first volunteer for such duty and then complete an internship. The candidate, like his or her line-officer counterpart, must then be found aeronautically adaptable and physically qualified to fly. The prospective flight surgeon must pass the same flight physical standards that are applied to all aviators, except for modified requirements for visual acuity. Failure to meet the visual acuity standards does not disqualify the candidate for flight training but may preclude solo flights.

Once chosen, the student is ordered to the Naval Aerospace and Operational Medicine Institute (NAOMI) in Pensacola and receives six months of training in the U.S. Navy Flight Surgeon program. The emphasis is on safety and the occupational and preventative medicine aspects of the military aviation environment, as well as the aeromedical disposition of medical cases. The first five weeks of the course are devoted to officer indoctrination, and completion of the swimming and water survival prerequisites for flying. The following twelve weeks are spent in classroom instruction and clinical practice at NAOMI, covering many topics in operational medicine, environmental physiology, and aeromedical disposition of cases.

Environmental physiology gives the student a firm understanding of the hazards inherent in aviation—including hypoxia, decompression, and other dangers—and how to minimize them. In operational medicine, the student encounters a wide range of potential medical considerations that may affect the aviation operational forces, such as flight physical standards, night vision, mass casualties, chemical weapons, and nuclear weapons. The clinical segment offers both lectures and clinical exposure to give the student practical experience in the aeromedical disposition of cases and an understanding of the impact of medical conditions and their treatment on flight qualifications. Areas of exposure include internal medicine; ophthamology; neurology; ear, nose, and throat; and psychiatry.

The final phase of training consists of seven weeks of flight training at NAS Whiting Field at Milton, Florida, including about a dozen flights in fixed- and rotary-wing training aircraft. The navy is the only service that provides flight familiarization to prospective flight surgeons. Aeromedical students receive training right alongside student naval aviators and are treated identically. They experience the same intensity and stresses in order to give them a realistic perspective of military aviation; by doing so, they can better relate to the stresses and dangers that the flight environment holds for all aviators.

All flight surgeons must successfully complete all phases of training. Designated flight surgeons are then assigned to a variety of navy and marine corps activities. These include air stations, major air command staffs, aircraft carriers, air wings, large squadrons, and some specialized units such as the Blue Angels.

The physician attracted to aviation medicine is commonly not one who seeks a career in that specialty. More often than not, one chooses a flight surgeon tour when sifting options or eager for adventure, travel, or interaction with exciting people in an exciting business. At the end of the first tour, the flight surgeon may apply for residence training in aerospace medicine or almost any other medical specialty, an option most flight surgeons exercise. A small percentage continue in aviation medicine. Following three years as a resident in aerospace medicine (RAM), including earning a master's degree in Public Health and successfully completing an exam, one is certified as an Aerospace Medicine Specialist by the American Board of Preventative Medicine. The total number of flight surgeons will vary with the needs of the service, but there are normally about three hundred.

Aviation Physiologists, Experimental Psychologists, and Optometrists

The navy's flight surgeons are augmented by a small group of Medical Service Corps officers who have also completed the syllabus at NAOMI.

Prospective aviation physiologists, aviation experimental psychologists, and aviation optometrists participate only in those phases of classroom instruction and clinical practice pertinent to their respective specialty, but otherwise complete all of the program.

Aviation Medical Safety Officer

Aviation Medical Safety Officer (AMSO) billets are filled by either experienced flight surgeons or aviation physiologists, who have also attended the Aviation Safety School in Monterey, California. These officers are very active in safety programs, accident investigations, physiology training and equipment programs, survival training, anthropometry fit checks, and design and testing of egress systems and aviation life support systems. AMSOs are valuable members of the naval aviation safety team and a ready resource in any of those programs.

The Flight Surgeon's Role

The flight surgeon's job is multidimensional. His or her primary role is to be totally involved with the primary goal of the aviation community—takeoff, completion of an assigned task, and safe return to ship or base. This requires more than just healthy, qualified aviators. Aircrews and ground personnel must be just as qualified, motivated, and healthy as pilots. To accomplish the primary goal, all aviation personnel should be knowledgeable in those areas where psychological, medical, and/or physiological phenomena affect flight performance and mission accomplishment. The flight surgeon is the natural interface between the practice of medicine, the science of safety, and the business of naval aviation.

The flight surgeon is responsible for all aspects of the practice of aerospace medicine, including outpatient and inpatient care; preventative medicine programs; required physical examinations; sanitation and habitability inspections; industrial hygiene; mass casualty readiness; continuing training of hospital corpsmen; medical supply and repair; and record keeping and reporting. Accident prevention and membership in aviation mishap boards (AMBs), field flight evaluation boards (FFEBs), and field naval aviator evaluation boards (FNAEBs) are collateral tasks.

As one who is qualified to analyze the human body, the flight surgeon is a very important link in the navy's aviation safety program.

To accomplish these tasks and to be effective, the flight surgeon must work, play, and fly with the unit's personnel, knowing their problems and being able to detect departures from normal patterns.

Relations with the Flight Surgeon

One of the special associations navy and marine corps flyers have is their close association with their flight surgeon. Unfortunately, many young aviators—and a few old ones—mistakenly see the flight surgeon as a police officer, the "company doc." No doubt this erroneous impression is in part fostered by the fact that the flight surgeons have to decide who is physically qualified to enter into or stay in aviation. Once in naval aviation, the flight surgeon's job is to keep flight personnel alive, safe, and flying. He or she is their personal consultant on all medical and aeromedical problems.

The flight surgeon is also available to discuss a variety of topics, whether it is a child's immunization schedule or how to combat fatigue on long-range flights. Aviation personnel should take advantage of their flight surgeon's presence.

Annual Physical Examination

One of the certainties of life for naval flyers is the annual flight examination. Whether a person is a candidate for flight training or an old hand with four thousand hours in the logbook, the examinee should look upon a flight physical not with apprehension but with confidence.

If a candidate is not able to meet the physical requirements, it is better to know it and not add unnecessary risk to the risky business of flying. The seasoned flyer should keep in mind that a flight surgeon is committed to keeping as many aviators healthy and flying as possible. Experience has shown that most problems detected in a physical exam can be corrected or waived. It is better to spend some time resolving a minor health problem than to ignore it until it becomes major.

The aviation physical is a thorough general examination during which particular attention is given to the eyes, ears, and circulatory system. Blood is drawn and urine is checked for signs of conditions that affect the whole body, such as diabetes, which frequently show up first in the urine. A chest X-ray is taken every three years until age forty-five, and yearly thereafter. Weight is checked and must conform to Bureau of Medicine guidelines.

The hearing test is important because flyers are subject to a great deal of high-frequency and high-intensity noise, often causing early loss of hearing in higher ranges. Using extra hearing protection can halt the damage to a person experiencing hearing loss in the high frequencies.

Visual acuity, obviously necessary to safe flight, is also measured. For entry into the flight training program, 20/30 vision corrected to 20/20 is required. However, service group 1 aviators whose vision has changed with age are usually allowed waivers that require them to wear glasses while flying. Tests are designed to detect eyes that may not, under all circumstances, be able to maintain a single image. No aviator, for obvious reasons, can have double vision. The standards for flying personnel will vary with their specific jobs. Perfect color and depth perception are also required. Also measured is accommodation, the ability of the eyes to adjust from scanning the horizon to scanning the cockpit instruments, and to comfortably maintain that scan. Peripheral fields of vision, so necessary to the fighter pilot, are outlined; then the size and shape of the peripheral field for each eye is examined and interpreted. A glaucoma test is performed for persons thirty-five and older.

The remainder of the exam is a simple complete physical from head to foot. It is an opportunity to discuss with the flight surgeon medical problems revealed in the physical's questionnaire and to determine corrective courses of action.

It is the responsibility of the individual flyer to arrange an appointment with the flight surgeon for an annual physical exam during the month before or of the flyer's birthday. Should an officer fail to receive an exam within ninety days after his or her birthday, he or she must write a letter to the Bureau of Personnel explaining the delay. Moreover, aviation personnel need to be aware that auditors periodically document the status of flight physicals. Those unfortunates who received flight pay for periods during which they were not administratively qualified (i.e., their physicals were sixty days overdue) are forced to repay the money.

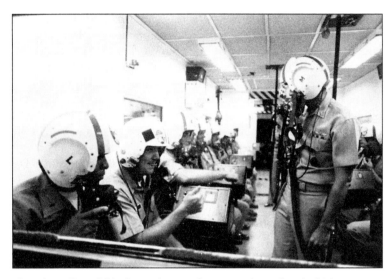

The various effects of altitude on aviators, as demonstrated to students in this low-pressure chamber, are of primary concern to flight surgeons and aviation physiologists. (U.S. Navy/JO1 Jim Bryant)

Flight Physical Standards

The Bureau of Medicine prescribes the flight physical standards for each of three service groups of pilots. When a pilot fails to meet the standards of a group, the flight surgeon prepares a report of medical examination (Standard Form 88) and submits it to the command with his or her recommendation. The command reviews the case and makes a recommendation to the Bureau of Personnel (BUPERS). The recommendation may:

— Permit the pilot to continue in an unrestricted flight status if BUPERS waives the standards
— Restrict the pilot to flight duty in the next service group
— Restrict the pilot to a light tempo of flight activity (when a pilot is recuperating from illness or injury)

— Restrict the pilot to service group 3, requiring the presence of a service group 1 or 2 pilot when flying (See BUPERS Manual 1410100)

Revoking Flight Status for Medical Reasons

When a physical or mental condition may be cause to revoke the flying authority and change the designator of an aviator, the Bureau of Personnel will usually request the nearest air command to appoint a board consisting of three flight surgeons to review the facts, examine the individual, and make a recommendation from a medical standpoint. If three flight surgeons are not available, the board may consist of other medical officers as long as at least one is a flight surgeon.

The board then submits its report to the Bureau of Personnel via the Bureau of Medicine and the NAOMI for disposition. When it appears that special studies or a more in-depth look is required, the NAOMI will recommend that the aviator in question be ordered to appear before the Special Board of Flight Surgeons at the NAOMI.

When the aviator requests appeal of a recommendation or decision of the board, the Bureau of Personnel may convene a formal board of senior flight surgeons at BuMed. The decision of this board is final. In cases where recommendations are made to terminate flight status, the chief of naval personnel determines if the individual should be retained in the aeronautical organization or assigned outside the aeronautical organization.

Attitudes Toward Hazardous Duty

Flying may appear glamorous, but it is often hazardous. Landing an aircraft on a rolling, pitching deck on a moonless night calls for the highest order of airmanship, alertness, and courage.

The pilot must perform his or her duties with a healthy respect for their inherent hazards, yet if hazards dominate one's thoughts, faith in oneself and in one's aircraft will suffer, adversely affecting airmanship. A proper perspective is beneficial; it discourages dangerous maneuvers and flight operations that demand too much of the pilot or the aircraft.

One keeps hazards at a minimum by continually adhering to safe rules of flight, by demanding sound maintenance procedures, and by respecting aircraft and individual limitations. Statistics have proven that all but a small percentage of naval aircraft mishaps can be prevented.

Fear

Fear is an emotion that all men and women experience, and aviators are no exception. In fact, the "fearless" aviator is a potentially dangerous pilot, tempted to exceed the limits of aircraft limits or personal abilities. There are two kinds of fear—the immediate fear that comes when an emergency arises, or the subconscious fear, whose effects on a person are more subtle and long-term.

The first kind of fear may be beneficial. It is the body's way of summoning together all of its resources to meet an emergency. It can make an individual sharp and enhance alertness at the controls. It can make one work harder and longer. On the other hand, this kind of fear may cause vertigo, nausea, or blurred vision. It may seize the mind and cut the individual off from one's environment, possibly causing incapacitation. The aviator must recognize these symptoms and take control, making fear work in favor of the situation. Once the emergency has passed, he or she must recognize what has occurred and learn from it. Denial of fear is a liability that one cannot afford in naval aviation.

The second type of fear may become chronic, expressing itself indirectly in various neurotic symptoms and attitudes. Unlike the cause of immediate fear, the cause of subconscious fear is usually not apparent. Its symptoms are more prolonged; they follow a person around, making life miserable. Sometimes they drive one to have the very mishap one fears. Some of the more common symptoms of subconscious fear are loss of appetite, bad dreams, and depression. A flight surgeon can help the individual deal with such problems by talking with that person. With improved insight, the individual's fears may cease to exist. But if the individual ignores these types of problems, he or she may endanger themselves, family members, and squadron mates.

Flying Fitness—Personal Choices

To fly today's high-performance aircraft and stay alive, flight crews must be as fit as their aircraft. The common cold, indigestion, and other minor illnesses that do not seriously impair individuals in other pursuits may be incapacitating in flight. Inadequate nourishment, lack of sleep, excesses that lower efficiency, and preoccupation with extraneous matters are incompatible with flight safety and mission accomplishment.

Fatigue, Rest, and Sleep

Fatigue is a significant problem in naval aviation and all too frequently a contributing factor in mishaps. Three main causes of fatigue are generally recognized: stress, anxiety, and fear. There are three types of stress:

— Physical stress, caused by heat, noise, vibration, and poor lighting
— Physiological stress, caused by hypoxia, lack of sleep, and strenuous work
— Emotional stress

Certain types of particularly stressful flying result in fatigue, even though they require little physical activity; formation flying, night flying, and flying in bad weather are a few examples.

Some of the more significant effects of fatigue are lowered physical efficiency, reduced night vision, decreased "G" tolerance, increased susceptibility to vertigo, and an unconscious decrease in performance standards. Many of these effects feed upon themselves. Fortunately, evidence shows that a fatigued but sufficiently motivated individual has the ability to mobilize the necessary skills for brief critical periods, such as during landing.

Fatigue can be either temporary or chronic. Unlike temporary fatigue, the chronic type is not relieved by a good night's sleep. Chronic fatigue may induce any or all of the following symptoms: increased tension, irritability, reduced aggressiveness, loss of appetite, lowered morale, and insomnia.

To increase resistance to fatigue, a flyer must recognize its existence and its ramifications. Maintaining good physical fitness through proper sleep, diet, exercise, and recreation, and the use of proper flight equipment and strict adherence to NATOPS procedures are a must. If tactical jet crews wear properly fitted G-suits and strictly adhere to the rules of oxygen mask, these measures should also reduce fatigue. On long flights, when it is not possible to move about frequently, stretching the neck, back, and leg muscles can fight fatigue.

Adequate sleep and rest restore the body's mental and physical energy. While "combat naps" can help eliminate temporary fatigue, approximately six to eight hours of uninterrupted sleep a night are usually needed to prevent the onset of chronic fatigue. Flight schedules should accommodate this need. No flight personnel should be scheduled for continuous alert and/or flight duty for more than eighteen hours. A crew rest of fifteen hours minimum should be provided following such duties.

Exercise

There is no question that a planned exercise program contributes to one's physical well-being by relieving nervous tension and mental fatigue and improving morale. The flight surgeon can give advice on exercise programs geared to a person's needs and age. Experience shows that spurts of exercise may be harmful and are less effective than a planned, regularly scheduled program. For those engaged in highly competitive and tiring sports, adequate rest (at least twelve hours) is essential before flying.

Physical Fitness Requirements

Flight crewmen should be aware that all naval personnel must maintain certain physical standards, as delineated in the SECNAV Instruction 6100.1 and BUPERS 6100.2 series.

Diet

A flyer should eat a balanced diet that fulfills his or her daily caloric and nutritional needs. Two or three meals per day should be eaten in relaxed and pleasant surroundings. Flyers should not attempt to lose weight by skipping meals but rather by reducing their caloric intake at every meal. Skipping meals merely reduces alertness and therefore increases the hazards of flying. Time and money should not be wasted on diet pills, sweat belts, and vitamins. Fads do not work, and many have adverse physiological effects. Over the years, a significant number of mishaps occurred partly because of missed meals or unwise diet practices.

Flight Lunches and Food Poisoning

The flight or box lunches used for in-flight meals are a potential source of food poisoning, which causes nausea, diarrhea, and vomiting. Food poisoning can readily disable an aircrew and result in mission abort or worse. The most common form of food poisoning, that caused by toxins produced in food contaminated with the staphyloccus bacteria, commences about two to four hours after the food is eaten. However, symptoms may appear as early as one hour after eating. Food is usually contaminated during its handling or preparation; the contaminating organisms continue to grow, particularly when the food is not refrigerated. Food kept at a temperature above 40 degrees Fahrenheit should be eaten within three to four hours. To avoid food poisoning, flyers should follow these simple rules:

— Do not consume food after the expiration date stamped on the box
— Store box lunches in a cool place, not near hot electronic equipment
— Order two kinds of lunches so the pilot can eat one and the copilot the other, thus lessening the possibility that both will eat contaminated food
— Separate eating times of the pilot and copilot by at least one hour

Medication

Taking medication without a prescription is foolhardy for anyone; for flyers it can be extremely hazardous. Flyers should even avoid taking over-the-counter drugs. After one mishap, a pilot's personal effects were found to include muscle relaxant pills of a type known to reduce "G" tolerance significantly. After another fatal mishap, the deceased pilot was found to have taken a common over-the-counter cold remedy. Although the Aviation Mishap Board could not state that these mishaps were actually caused by the medications, they were considered to be contributory factors. Even such simple remedies as aspirin or cold tablets can impair the fine coordination and concentration required in flight. It is foolish to fly with a cold or a case of "GIs" (gastrointestinal disorder); it is irresponsible to fly with a minor illness under the influence of medication.

A flyer who has seen a physician not trained in aviation medicine should report back to a flight surgeon prior to resuming flight. While most physicians are well trained and competent, few are aware of all the medical problems peculiar to the aviation environment.

In general, a flyer should not fly for twenty-four hours after taking any medication unless the flight surgeon prescribing it has indicated otherwise. When one is sick, one should not fly; if one flies, one should not take medications without consulting a flight surgeon.

Alcohol

Alcohol is a potentially addictive drug that affects memory, muscular skill, sensory acuity, and judgment. In addition, it can dehydrate the body. Alcohol therefore has no part in aviation, which requires the highest alertness, muscular coordination, and judgment. Even being hungover can degrade these skills. Personnel in a flying status whose faculties are impaired even to the slightest degree by alcohol or its aftereffects should be grounded until fully recovered. At least twelve hours should elapse between the consumption of alcohol and the assumption of aircraft control.

Tobacco

Tobacco smoke contains a number of irritating substances, such as aldehydes, ammonia, and tobacco tars, which account for the burning effect it has upon the eyes. Smoke also irritates the membranes lining the mouth, upper air passages, and lungs. This may cause inflammatory reactions, which include the simple "smoker's hack," bronchitis, chronic thickening of the lining of the bronchial tubes, and, most serious of all, emphysema. However, just the simple cough can prove to be a real problem for an aviator on 100 percent oxygen.

There is no question that cigarette smoking helps cause lung cancer as well as cancers of the lip, mouth, and larynx. Children of smoking parents are more prone to respiratory disease than those of parents who do not smoke. Personnel working in cold environments are more susceptible to hypothermia and frostbite if they smoke. Chewing tobacco clearly causes lip and mouth cancer.

Coffee/Caffeine

Coffee contains caffeine, a substance that affects the muscles, nervous system, kidneys, and heart. An excess of caffeine can reduce muscle coordination and cause tremors, heart irregularities, irritability, and, in some people, depression. Ten cups per day is considered the maximum that most people can tolerate without adverse effects. Caffeine is also present in tea, chocolate, and some cola drinks.

Eye Care

Good eyes and excellent vision are prerequisites for aviation. Tips for eye protection include:

— Using adequate lighting for reading
— Using protective gear when operating power tools and participating in certain sports
— Avoiding exposure to direct sunlight or overexposure on the beaches, ski slopes, etc.
— Using oxygen over ten thousand feet
— Eliminating extraneous light from the cockpit
— Avoiding rapid change and marked contrast in radar scope intensity gain
— Avoiding cheap sunglasses

One of the most useful items an aviator has in the air and on the ground is a pair of sunglasses. Even though sunglasses could possibly reduce the distance at which the pilot can detect other aircraft, the reduction of glare, lessened eye strain, and generally increased comfort compensate for this. Thus, sunglasses may give an aviator an even greater detection distance during extended periods of flight. The following points apply to sunglasses and tinted helmet visors:

— Sunglasses should be worn when flying in the glare at high altitudes, above cloud cover, or on clear, sunny days. They should be removed when moving from bright illumination to dim light.

— Studies have shown that night vision decreases with age, especially after age forty, and that night vision can be impaired by as much as 30 to 50 percent if the eyes are exposed to high-level illumination during the day. Hence, personnel who will be flying at night should wear sunglasses during the day if they are on beaches, ski slopes, etc.
— Polaroid sunglasses should not be used when flying; they only reduce glare when the head is in certain positions, and they leave blind spots.
— Official flight sunglasses of the highest optical quality are available through the supply system. The flight surgeon can order prescription sunglasses if necessary.

Hypoxia and Hyperventilation

Hypoxia is defined as the lack of oxygen in the bloodstream which if uncorrected leads to severe bodily disturbances. Hyperventilation—excessive respiration that leads to abnormal loss of carbon dioxide from the blood—may cause dizziness, "air hunger," and unconsciousness. Flyers should have an understanding of both conditions.

During normal ground-level activities, the rate and depth of breathing are controlled by changes in the acidity of the blood. Physical activity causes both carbon dioxide and lactic acid to be produced in large quantities, slightly increasing blood acidity. The blood passes through the brain and stimulates the "breathing center," which increases the respiratory rate. This increase in breathing in response to muscular work is known as physiological hyperventilation and will not, under normal circumstances, produce any unpleasant or abnormal sensations.

The body's regulation of breathing under conditions of rest and physical activity operates effectively until the plane reaches an altitude of approximately ten thousand feet. Above this altitude, if the person is relatively inactive, breathing automatically increases in response to a significant drop in the oxygen content of the blood. This less efficient mechanism of breathing control operates through reflex centers in the blood vessels of the neck and results also in physiological hyperventilation, but at a time when the person is not producing excessive carbon dioxide.

During normal flight conditions, the body tends to limit the breathing rate to avoid excessive loss of carbon dioxide. If a person does not consciously or unconsciously interfere with breathing, the adverse symptoms of hyperventilation should not occur. However, if a flyer suffers from anxiety, fear, extreme stress, or unusual resistance to oxygen flow, the excessive loss of carbon dioxide may cause the blood to become slightly alkaline and the blood vessels in the brain to constrict, reducing the amount of available oxygen. He or she may experience, singly or in combination, dizziness, tingling in the hands and feet, visual distortion, and the inability to think clearly—the most common symptoms of hyperventilation. These symptoms are commonly noted during hypoxia, also, and to a certain degree are produced by the same phenomenon—a reduction in the oxygen supply to the brain. Consequently, a flyer may think he or she is suffering from hypoxia. Numerous studies and experiences have shown that the most common symptoms of hypoxia are visual distortion, dizziness, lack of muscular coordination, inability to think clearly, tingling in the arms and legs, apprehension, and, in moderately advanced cases, characteristic bluish discoloration of the lips and fingernails.

Every pilot is aware of the insidious and potentially serious effects hypoxia has on alertness. Much of the physiological training the pilot receives acquaints him or her with the symptoms of hypoxia and the measures to counteract it. But pilots do not receive as much training on the effects of hyperventilation. Consequently, they are not always aware that this condition, while closely resembling hypoxia, is not as critical and may be fairly easily corrected. Inexperienced or inadequately trained airmen experience hyperventilation most often. It also frequently occurs in students using oxygen systems for the first time, either in the air or in a low-pressure chamber during physiological training. In addition, it can happen when a flyer is pressure-breathing and any time the body resists the movement of oxygen through the system. Regulated breathing is the remedy for hyperventilation.

Since hyperventilation is frequently precipitated by anxiety, it occurs frequently in pilots under extreme emotional stress who are very tense and worried. To prevent or alleviate the symptoms of hyperventilation, a flyer must be able to recognize them or at least suspect their presence, and must be well-trained in breathing control. The pilot can easily reproduce the symptoms of hyperventilation on the ground or in a low-pressure chamber by simply taking four or five very deep breaths and noting the rapid onset of such effects as the tingling in arms and legs. These symptoms should be contrasted to the symptoms of hypoxia experienced by all flyers in low-pressure chamber indoctrination.

Altitude hypoxia rarely occurs below ten thousand feet and seldom results during exposure times of less than thirty minutes between ten thousand and fifteen thousand feet. At higher altitudes, symptoms of hypoxia may occur very rapidly; above forty thousand feet, they may show up within twelve to fifteen seconds. Since altitude hypoxia is critical, the pilot should immediately switch the oxygen regulator to 100 percent and emergency settings and take a single deep breath and hold it for about ten seconds. At the same time, he or she should bring the aircraft to a lower and safer altitude. As soon thereafter as possible, the pilot should make a rapid but thorough oxygen-equipment check. The pilot should reduce the breathing rate to six or eight breaths per minute. If hypoxia or hyperventilation is the problem, the flyer will note improvement within fifteen or twenty seconds.

By this time, the flyer should be closer to knowing whether the difficulty is hypoxia, hyperventilation, or contamination of the oxygen system. If the pilot suspects hypoxia, he or she should use 100 percent oxygen with or without the emergency setting, depending on the cause. If hyperventilation is the problem, breathing control alone will suffice. If it is contamination, the pilot should use the emergency oxygen system for the duration of the flight, which should be terminated as soon as possible.

Blood Donations

Because the flyer's physical fitness is directly dependent upon the oxygen-carrying capacity of the blood, naval aviation personnel are grounded for four days after donating one unit of blood. Carrier aviators are prohibited from donating blood less than four weeks before they begin carrier operations.

Vertigo

Vertigo involves dizziness, spatial disorientation, or a "feeling" that an aircraft is flying in one attitude when it is actually flying in another. Vertigo has been a flight hazard since the first days of aviation and can occur under the following conditions:

— Flying in instrument flight rules (IFR) conditions.
— Rotating the head when pulling Gs or during a turn, causing a tumbling, or coriolis, effect.

- Flying in marginal visual flight rules (VFR) conditions where the horizon is indistinct or absent. In this case, confusion results from conflicting cues and information transmitted through sight, inner ear, balance, and receptors in the muscles and skin—what flight surgeons call the proprioceptive sense.
- Flying by IFR and VFR at the same time. (This should never be attempted.)
- Flying out of a set of flares into darkness after a night dive-bombing mission.
- Target fixation, overeagerness, and overconcentration on low bombing runs, causing late pull-outs.
- Night aerial refueling.
- Moonless-night carrier landings.
- Wearing gas-mask goggles, which distort depth perception.

Regardless of skill or experience, every pilot has vertigo from time to time. Good physical health and plenty of rest will go far to combat it. The pilot should avoid rapid head movement when maneuvering and should not turn his or her head while pulling Gs. At the onset of vertigo, a pilot must not panic but should go to the instruments and believe what they indicate. Attention to scan is important, as is straight and level flight. The flyer should minimize head movements until things quiet down. The movement of fluid in the semicircular canals of the ears can give false signals, and it takes time to return to equilibrium. If the pilot is flying in formation, the wingman should be made aware of the problem. Later, the pilot can discuss the incident with a flight surgeon and squadron safety officer. Education about and recognition of vertigo offers the best insurance against mishaps caused by vertigo.

Heat Injury

During the summer months or in tropical areas, aviation personnel run the risk of heat injury. The primary injuries of concern are: heat cramps, which can be incapacitating; heat exhaustion, which can be incapacitating and may lead to heatstroke; and heatstroke, which can be fatal. Since 15 percent of heatstroke victims die, and since naval aviators who survive a heatstroke are permanently grounded, it is worth taking the time to understand heat injury.

The body defends against a rise in core temperature by increasing the blood flow to the skin and by sweating. Environmental temperature, relative humidity, irradiation from the sun, and air movement determine the degree of heat to which a person is exposed. In an area of 100 percent humidity, where the temperature is higher than that of the body and there are no air currents, the body cannot lose heat.

Any conditions that reduce the body's salt and water content make a person more susceptible to heat injury. Some common conditions are diarrhea, fever, recent immunizations, some medications, excessive alcohol consumption, and sunburn. Poor physical conditioning and lack of acclimatization also contribute to heat injury. Studies done during July in Pensacola have shown that pilots in full gear have lost up to 1.5 percent of body weight during a routine sortie. If an aviator loses 3 percent of body weight, heatstroke is a danger.

Symptoms of heat injury include cramps, lack of coordination, muscular weakness, poor judgment, mental dullness, irrational behavior, dizziness, throbbing headaches, and chilling sensations. These symptoms may be present singly or in any combination. If sweating stops, heatstroke has begun.

Scuba Policy

Scuba diving increases the amount of nitrogen dissolved in the tissues of the body. For aviators in flight, exposed to decreased barometric pressure, or in low-pressure chamber runs, there is an increased tendency for symptoms of "bends" (decompression sickness) to occur following diving. Therefore, naval aviation personnel should not fly within twenty-four hours of scuba diving or other compressed-air dives. Although a twenty-four hour period may appear ultraconservative, it takes under consideration the general fatigue that normally accompanies such activities. On one occasion, serious decompression sickness afflicted several divers when they flew home at twelve thousand feet, forty-eight hours after scuba diving. If circumstances dictate, an aviator may fly within twelve hours of scuba diving if examined and cleared for flight by a flight surgeon. (See OPNAVINST 3710.7 series.)

ELEVEN

THE NAVAL AIR RESERVE

Revised from an original chapter written by
Cdr. Peter B. Mersky, USNR

Readiness is the hallmark of any good military organization, and readiness is what the naval air reserve is all about. The purpose of the naval air reserve is to maintain a civilian force of qualified aviation officers and enlisted personnel who are trained and prepared for mobilization and immediate action. The reserve is expected to keep abreast of changing technology and to maintain its proficiency so that in times of national emergency it can respond to any contingency. In a large-scale conflict, it must be able to augment the existing active-duty force to meet the expanding needs of naval aviation while new personnel are being trained.

Aviators, NFOs, aircrewmen, and maintenance technicians are expensive commodities. The investment in both time and money for training aviation personnel and maintaining their operational skills is considerable, and it is lost when personnel are released from active duty. The cost, however, of maintaining a large active-duty force in time of peace is prohibitive. The solution to the problem, and one that has proven itself on numerous occasions, is the maintenance of a naval air reserve force.

The naval air reserve maintains a civilian force of qualified personnel, such as this F-14 crew, who can be called upon at a moment's notice in wartime or national emergency. (U.S. Navy/JOC Rich Beth)

A Distinguished History

Until World War I, the only naval reserve forces in the United States were the naval militia of various states. Naval militia were originally sponsored by civilian amateur sailors and naval enthusiasts rather than by federal or state governments. As naval militia proved effective, some states began to purchase clothing and equipment to help defray the expense to the members of the militia organizations.

In 1891, as part of a naval appropriations act, Congress allocated twenty-five thousand dollars for arming and equipping naval militia. Ships were loaned to these organizations, and training assistance was given by the bureaus of the Navy Department. The program was administered by the Office of the Naval Militia. With annual practice cruises, training gradually progressed.

During the Spanish-American War of 1898, the naval militia proved its value and efficiency in time of national emergency. Because of this, the Navy Department recommended the organization of a national naval reserve. In February 1914, the Naval Militia Act became law, with states being required to organize their naval militia in consonance with the Navy Department's prescribed plans.

In April 1914, plans were initiated for the establishment of an aeronautical force in the naval militia. During the following year, the navy's General Order 153 established the practice of lending aircraft to the states that had an aeronautical corps in their naval militia.

Earlier, in May 1911, the state of New York had established an aviation militia at Bay Shore, Long Island. In July 1911, the Massachusetts militia, including an aeronautical branch at Squantum, was mustered into federal service. Local authorities supplied the field and facilities. The Aero Club of America assisted in the administration of the program; this group offered the services of its members to the militia and sought ways to contribute to the meager funds from the navy for the purchase of aircraft.

The naval appropriations act for fiscal year 1917 provided funds for the establishment of a naval reserve flying corps and the purchase of twelve airplanes for the naval militia. The naval reserve flying corps was designed to attract civilian aviators, designers, and aircraft workers. It also attracted many college student groups. The first of these was the "Yale unit," organized in 1916 by F. Trubee Davison, who later became assistant secretary of war. (An annual trophy given to the best naval air reserve squadrons in various categories is named in his honor.) The organization of the First Yale Unit is considered the official beginning of the naval air reserve.

After U.S. entry into World War I in 1917, as one of several actions taken immediately after the declaration of war to expand the air training program while more permanent bases were built, the First Naval District assumed control of the naval militia station at Squantum for use as an air training station. Other college flying units were brought under control of the navy, and these units formed the basis for an aviation training program that trained more than two thousand aviators and four thousand other aviation specialists, with the naval reserve flying corps comprising over 75 percent of naval aviation strength during World War I. These aviators made impressive contributions to the war; their members included the first naval aviator to destroy an enemy submarine; the first to shoot down an enemy seaplane; the first to become an ace; and the only naval aviator to be awarded the Medal of Honor for action during the war.

By mid-1922, the naval reserve flying corps had been reduced to practically nothing in the postwar demobilization. Early in 1923, Rear Adm. William A. Moffett, chief of the Bureau of Aeronautics, submitted to the CNO a plan to correct the deficiencies in the naval air reserve, recommending that at least one naval air reserve unit be located in each naval district. On 13 August 1923, Squantum became the first organized naval air reserve establishment. In 1926, Admiral Moffett instigated a plan to raise the number of naval reserve aviation units to seven. In July 1927, the first group of fifty newly commissioned ensigns in the naval air reserve was ordered to one year of training duty with the fleet. The naval air reserve continued to expand and, immediately prior to World War II, consisted of sixteen activities spread throughout the United States.

In October 1940, the secretary of the navy placed all organized reserve aviation squadrons on short notice for recall. By January 1941, all units had been ordered to active duty. During World War II, members of the naval air reserve took their place beside their regular navy counterparts and made significant contributions to the final victory.

After World War II, a substantial portion of naval aviation was relegated to the reserve. The Naval Air Reserve Training Command, with twenty-one activities, was formally activated as a component of the Naval Air Training Command.

After the Korean conflict broke out in June 1950, fourteen naval air reserve squadrons were activated in July for duty. Reserve patrol squadrons deployed to the war zone, and one carrier air group, made up entirely of recalled reservists, established an impressive combat record. By the end of the conflict, over forty reserve squadrons had been activated. Many of them were absorbed into the regular navy force structure.

As the naval air reserve grew and entered the jet age, up-to-date fleet training and equipment was clearly needed to maintain the reserve in a high state of readiness. In November 1957, reserve squadrons first began firing guided missiles as part of their regular training. In 1959, naval air reserve units participated for the first time in a full-scale exercise. Also that year, the navy announced that the reserve would receive Sidewinder air-to-air missiles. Training benefited by the establishment of the Training and Administration of Reserves (TAR) program, which set aside a cadre of reservists on continual active duty to provide training continuity in reserve units.

The Berlin Crisis in 1961 saw the mobilization of eighteen selected air reserve squadrons (thirteen antisubmarine and five patrol squadrons) involving 4,000 reservists and 190 aircraft; this was the first partial mobilization of selected reservists.

In early 1965, Commander in Chief, U.S. Pacific Fleet, asked for the support of the naval air reserve in logistics operations to Southeast Asia. The voluntary response of the selected air reservists, who delivered vital cargo to Saigon and Da Nang in Vietnam, was overwhelming.

The war effort in Southeast Asia demanded so much of the navy's resources that modernization and training of the naval air reserve suffered considerable neglect. In January 1968, in response to the Pueblo Crisis, six attack and fighter squadrons were recalled to active duty; however, their equipment and training deficiencies were so marked that they were demobilized without augmenting the fleet. This embarrassment, however, was the impetus to modernize the naval air reserve into the effective force that it remains today.

During 1970, the naval air reserve was reorganized into a mirror image of the fleet aviation forces. Two attack-carrier air wings, two antisubmarine-carrier air groups, and two patrol wings were created, one each earmarked to augment the Atlantic and Pacific fleets. In addition, transport squadrons were reorganized and located across the United States. In February 1973, the Naval Air Reserve Command at NAS Glenview, Illinois, consolidated with the Naval Surface Reserve Force Command, then located in Omaha, Nebraska, to form the Chief of Naval Reserve, headquartered in New Orleans, Louisiana. The Chief, Naval Air Reserve, became a subordinate command.

Though never mobilized during the 1970s and 1980s, the naval air reserve underwent tremendous growth in capability, especially in terms of aircraft modernization and training. In November 1976, a reserve carrier wing completed two weeks of flight operations on board the USS *Ranger* (CV 61), a dramatic demonstration of readiness.

The structure of the naval air reserve kept pace with fleet developments. The two carrier antisubmarine air groups were disestablished as the navy phased out its antisubmarine carriers. Patrol squadrons led the

The naval air reserve provides 100 percent of the navy's organic airlift support, with transport aircraft such as this C-9B, and the C-130T. (U.S. Navy/McDonnell Douglas)

way in fleet integration, operating detachments in direct support of fleet patrol aviation operations. By the late 1970s, they were assuming complete responsibility of some forward operating sites for months at a time. Patrol and airborne early warning aircraft also became heavily involved in the drug interdiction effort in the Caribbean. Reserve fleet logistics squadrons gradually assumed 100 percent of the navy's organic airlift responsibilities, performing with dependable distinction on overseas rotating detachments. By the beginning of the 1990s, the naval air reserve's carrier air wings finally achieved an inventory of aircraft on par with the fleet standard.

The naval air reserve was ready when called to action in 1990 for Operation Desert Shield and combat operations against Iraqi forces in Operation Desert Storm in January 1991. Over two thousand naval air reservists were called to active duty. Four fleet logistics squadrons deployed to bases in Europe to support the war effort. A detachment from one patrol squadron operated in the Persian Gulf; one from a helicopter squadron rescued the crew of an air force bomber returning to Diego Garcia; and two special operations helicopter detachments conducted operations behind enemy lines. The nation's investment in the naval air reserve was vindicated manyfold.

With the end of the Cold War, the naval air reserve underwent significant force-level reductions in concert with reductions in the active forces. One of the two carrier air wings was disestablished during 1994–95, as were four of thirteen patrol squadrons, three of nine helicopter squadrons, and two of fourteen fleet logistics squadrons. Helicopter minesweeping squadrons were merged with active-duty squadrons. At the same time, however, the naval air reserve completely assumed airborne adversary fleet electronic warfare training responsibilities from the active fleet, and, as of this writing, was well on its way to assuming the air combat adversary role from active squadrons. The carrier *John F. Kennedy* assumed her new duties in 1995 as a deck dedicated to training with a reserve combat role. Also in 1995, a reserve tactical electronic warfare squadron, VAQ-209, deployed two EA-6B aircraft to a carrier enforcing U.N. sanctions in Bosnia-Herzegovina; the detachment integrated with the regular VAQ squadron on board the carrier and carried out its combat mission in the true "one-navy" tradition.

Organization

The naval air reserve and its programs are directed by the Chief of Naval Reserve, with the Commander Naval Air Reserve (COMNAVAIRES) as one of his principal deputies. Reporting to COMNAVAIRES are the five reserve wings, five air stations, and several naval air reserve units, training sites, and centers.

The five naval air reserve wings are:

Commander Reserve Carrier Air Wing 20 (NAS Cecil Field, Fla.)
Commander Reserve Patrol Wing Atlantic (NAS Norfolk, Va.)
Commander Reserve Patrol Wing Pacific (also named Commander Patrol Wing Four) (Moffett Federal Airfield, Calif.)

A helicopter pilot preflights his HH-60H special warfare helicopter at Point Mugu, California. Reserve crews maintain skills during monthly drills and annual periods of active duty for training. (U.S. Navy/Robert L. Lawson)

Commander Helicopter Wing Reserve (NAS North Island, Calif.)
Commander Fleet Logistic Support Wing (NAS Fort Worth, Tex.)

The reserve's single carrier air wing, CVWR-20 (slated to move from its home at Cecil Field), includes the following types of squadrons: one VF, two VFA, one VAW, one VAQ, and two VFC adversary squadrons, with one marine corps reserve VMFA squadron attached. The wing lacks a VS squadron. The Helicopter Wing Reserve provides the HS squadron for CVWR-20, and also includes two HSL, two HCS, and one HC squadron. The two reserve patrol wings command nine VP squadrons between them. Fleet Logistics Support Wing commands twelve VR squadrons.

Though many reserve force squadrons and training units are usually tenant commands located at regular naval air stations and facilities, five air stations are dedicated to naval air reserve activities:

— NAS Atlanta, Georgia
— NAS Fort Worth, Texas
— NAS New Orleans, Louisiana
— NAS South Weymouth, Massachusetts (slated for closure)
— NAS Willow Grove, Pennsylvania

The major naval air reserve activities are located within major population centers of the United States to eliminate many problems associated with extensive travel to weekend drill sites.

The naval air reserve has some thirty-four squadrons (see Appendix D for a list of squadrons), providing the following percentages of naval aviation's overall force:

— 9 percent of carrier air wings
— 40 percent of patrol squadrons
— 100 percent of fleet logistic support squadrons
— 100 percent of special combat support helicopter squadrons
— 100 percent of adversary squadrons (by 1997)

Augment Activities

Although the squadron augmentation units and master augmentation units were mostly disestablished early in the 1990s for budget reasons, many naval air reserve personnel are assigned to various reinforcing and sustaining units, which will augment existing regular commands and activities during a mobilization. These units include:

— Aircraft carrier units
— Air station units
— Air staff units
— Tactical air control squadrons
— Maritime tactical support centers
— Oceanographic units
— Aviation supply units

Some naval air reserve squadrons mobilized for the Persian Gulf War. Helicopter squadrons flying the HH-60H deployed detachments to the war zone to support special operations forces. (U.S. Navy)

— Audiovisual units
— Naval Air Systems Command units

Some reserve aviators serve as flight instructors with the Naval Air Training Command during their active-duty training periods.

Affiliation

Individuals who wish to affiliate with the naval air reserve can do so through the reserve activity nearest their active-duty station, residence, or intended residence. Active-duty personnel can apply ahead of time for immediate assignment to a naval air reserve unit upon release from active duty; this eliminates administrative delays in training and pay.

P-3 Orions flown by reserve squadrons (VP-68 shown here) regularly augment active-duty patrol squadrons at deployment sites around the world. (U.S. Navy)

The youngest, best-qualified personnel have priority for assignment to pay billets in the naval air reserve. These pay billets are limited in number by regulation.

Most officers who affiliate with the naval air reserve are reserve or former regular officers who join after completing a tour of active duty. Hence, most are lieutenants with extensive fleet experience. A small number of junior officers are acquired each year who complete flight training and affiliate immediately with a reserve unit.

Terminology

Like any other organization, the naval air reserve has its own distinctive jargon. Some of the more common terms are discussed below.

Active duty for training (ACDUTRA)—Full-time training duty with a regular component of the navy, usually for a period of twelve to fourteen days.

Ready Reserve—A category comprising all reservists liable for active duty in time of war or national emergency. Reservists in this category are in an active status; only ready reservists may receive pay for taking part in training.

A reserve Aviation Warfare Systems Operator monitors sensor systems on board his SH-2 helicopter during drug interdiction operations. Naval air reserve crews are regular participants in the drug interdiction effort. (U.S. Navy/JOC Rich Beth)

Retired Reserve—Reservists on the retired list who can be ordered to active duty only in time of war or national emergency. Retired reservists include members retired with or without pay.

Selected Reserve—Ready reservists in a drill-pay status. Selected reservists are issued mobilization orders in time of peace and are to report to specified activities in time of war or national emergency.

Selected Air Reservist—A member, officer or enlisted, of a naval air reserve force squadron. The term specifically applies to reservists in a drill-pay status.

Training and Administration of Reserves (TAR)—TARs are personnel on active duty with special designators involved with the reserve training program.

The TAR Program

Operating and maintaining a naval air reserve base, squadron or training activity is a full-time affair, and one that does not begin and end with weekend drills and two-week active training periods. The drilling reservist cannot be with the unit throughout the week, so a special kind of reservist called a TAR deals with the day-to-day operations and provides vital continuity.

TARs are the nucleus of a reserve unit. TAR duties typically include training, organizing, recruiting, instructing, and administering the reserve unit. A typical reserve force squadron may have a drilling reservist as a commanding officer but will have a TAR lieutenant commander as the officer-in-charge running the squadron in the CO's absence.

Regular or reserve officers in the unrestricted line, restricted line (intelligence), aviation maintenance, or in the supply corps in the grades from lieutenant (jg) to lieutenant commander are eligible for conversion to the TAR program. Officers must have completed their initial active-duty obligation to be eligible. Applications are considered by a TAR selection board, which evaluates the applicant's previous experience, performance, and qualifications, in accordance with the needs of the navy.

TAR officers compete only among themselves for promotion. They are eligible for selection for command of reserve force squadrons and other commands. Some serve tours of duty within regular navy commands.

Training and Pay

Normally, all naval reservists attached to drilling units are expected to attend a minimum specified number of drills per year—usually forty-eight—and one twelve- to fourteen-day period of annual active duty for training. A drill weekend usually consists of four four-hour drills. There are two categories of drills, pay and nonpay. Naturally, the pay billets are the most sought after; a lieutenant or lieutenant commander can earn several thousand dollars per year in a pay billet.

Like their active-duty counterparts, Naval Air Reserve LAMPS helicopters deploy on board surface warships. Two reserve helicopter squadrons fly the SH-2G Seasprite. (U.S. Navy)

Reservists in a drill-pay status receive one day's base pay (plus flight pay, if eligible) for each drill performed. Normally, two drills are held on Saturday and two on Sunday, one weekend per month. Thus, the naval air reservist is paid four days' pay for each weekend of drills, plus pay for any additional drills. Only basic pay and flight pay are earned during regular weekend drills. Full pay and allowances are earned during the annual two-week active-duty training periods and any other periods of temporary active duty.

Most reserve squadrons have additional active-duty training periods when time and resources allow. For tactical air units, these extra stints often involve short detachments to ranges or competitions to further hone war-fighting skills. Patrol squadrons often send detachments to operational deployment sites.

Reservists are eligible to use most of the exchange and recreational facilities on military bases. While on active duty for training, the full range of military benefits are available to them.

Many reservists are willing and able to devote more than the required amount of time to their reserve responsibilities. Additional drill and active-duty opportunities are frequently offered to keep skills honed.

Promotion

Naval reserve officers are eligible for promotion all the way up to rear admiral. Selection procedures are similar to those used for regular personnel. Reserve selection boards are composed of active-duty and inactive-duty officers. As with active-duty personnel, reserve officers are selected primarily on the basis of fitness reports.

Retirement

Reservists become eligible for retirement pay after completing twenty years of "qualifying service." In order to be credited with a year of qualifying service, the reservist must accumulate a minimum of fifty retirement points in a year.

Retirement points are earned as follows:

— One point for each day of active duty or active-duty training, including travel time
— One point for each authorized drill attended in a pay or non-pay status
— Points for completion of approved correspondence courses
— Fifteen points credited for each year on active status in a naval reserve component

Retirement pay starts at age sixty, provided the retiree, during the last eight years of qualifying service, served as a member of a reserve component. These eight years need not be continuous, nor is it necessary that participation for the last years be with a drilling unit. A reservist is not eligible for retired pay if eligible for or receiving any other retired pay for military service.

After retirement with pay, a reservist is eligible to use the full range of military retiree benefits, subject to availability of space. Retired reserve officers are not subject to many of the employment restrictions imposed by law on retired regular officers.

A Total Force

In some respects, the responsibilities of a naval reservist are greater than those of his or her active-duty counterpart. A reservist holds two or more jobs, and, to keep them, must satisfy civilian and military bosses. The naval air reserve flier must keep current in a particular aircraft and its assigned missions. It is a demanding regimen that an active reservist sets for oneself.

Naval air reservists are highly motivated. Whatever a reservist's civilian occupation, when on duty he or she is a dedicated navy professional. Reservists enjoy the pursuit of a civilian career while maintaining the rewards of service in naval aviation. Many reserve aviators are civilian pilots whose skills in each job are enhanced by the other.

In recent years, with decreasing defense resources, the navy has greatly increased its reliance on the naval air reserve to meet the demands of national requirements. More and more, the naval air reservist augments and serves alongside active-duty counterparts, strengthening the total force concept that the nation relies on for an effective national defense.

TWELVE

Marine Corps Aviation

Revised from an original chapter written by
Maj. John M. Elliott, USMC (Ret.)

A Proud Tradition

Since the establishment of marine corps aviation, all marine corps aviators have been designated naval aviators. The first marine corps aviator was 1st Lt. Alfred A. Cunningham, who entered the Corps in 1909 after serving in the U.S. Army during the Spanish-American War. The date upon which he reported to the aviation camp at the Naval Academy, 22 May 1912, came to be recognized as the birthday of marine corps aviation. Upon soloing, Cunningham became naval aviator number 5 and marine corps aviator number 1.

Progress was slow in marine corps aviation, primarily because of a limited amount of equipment and personnel. During the early years, however, several operations were carried out with the fleet, including reconnaissance patrols and early shipboard catapult testing. Marine aviators saw their first combat in support of landing parties during operations at Tampico and Veracruz, Mexico.

With U.S. entry into World War I, a rapid buildup in marine corps aviation occurred. The Marine Aeronautic Company was activated at Philadelphia, Pennsylvania, and within six months was divided into the

First Aviation Squadron, which flew land planes, and the First Marine Aeronautic Company, which flew seaplanes. The latter group shipped overseas on 9 January 1918, the first fully equipped and trained American aviation unit to go overseas. Equipped with N-9, R-6, and HS-2L seaplanes, the company conducted antisubmarine patrols from Ponta Delgada in the Azores for the duration of the war.

The First Aviation Squadron, which eventually moved to Miami, Florida, evolved during the buildup to become the First Aviation Force with four squadrons. The force arrived in France in August 1918 with three of its squadrons to become the day wing of the Northern Bombing Group. While awaiting aircraft, many marines flew with British squadrons. With enough aircraft on hand by mid-October 1918, the marines were flying missions on their own.

While the First Marine Aviation Force was small, its members compiled an enviable record in a three-month period; flying in forty-three missions with the British and in fourteen of their own, they dropped almost thirty-four thousand pounds of bombs on the enemy and shot down four enemy aircraft (and claimed eight others). The force lost four pilots killed in action.

With the rapid demobilization following the war, marine corps aviation was reorganized. New squadrons were formed and deployed to Haiti and the Dominican Republic to support marines employed in establishing order in those countries. A flight was stationed at Sumay, Guam, as the first marine corps aviation unit in the Pacific.

Cunningham, as director of marine corps aviation, led the way as he continued to develop his concept of the airplane in the marine corps mission. Support of ground troops is still the primary purpose of marine corps aviation and the basis of the tried and proven air-ground team.

Even in those early days, Cunningham visualized the value of radio communication between the aircraft and ground units. He understood the concept of isolating a beachhead by bombing roads, railroads, and reinforcements, and of suppressing beach defenses by bombs and machine-gun fire. All of these ideas were soon to be tried in actual combat operations.

The outbreak of civil war in Nicaragua in 1927 led to the introduction of marines in an attempt to stabilize the government. This small-scale, drawn-out guerrilla war provided the opportunity to practice some of the theories of close-air support. Dive-bombing, air-ground communi-

U.S. Marine Corps DH-4 aircraft at Yorktown, Virginia, in 1921. (U.S. Navy)

cations, and aerial delivery of troops and supplies were all utilized in support of marine patrols on the ground. The lessons learned in Nicaragua led to doctrines used in the Pacific during World War II and also produced some of the most successful leaders both in the air and on the ground.

Although the Great Depression caused considerable reduction in strength and consolidation in marine corps aviation during the 1930s, two squadrons were formed as part of the new navy aircraft carrier force. Marines were rotated through these squadrons so that by the time they were deactivated three years later, two-thirds of the marine aviators had served on board aircraft carriers. (Marines were not to have regular carrier-based squadrons again until 1945.) Marine corps aviation was strengthened during the 1930s by a reserve force that eventually mobilized into thirteen squadrons at the beginning of World War II.

The Japanese sweep of the Pacific in December 1941 virtually wiped out marine corps aircraft there. A marine fighter squadron put up a valiant defense of Wake Island with five surviving aircraft, managing to destroy eight Japanese aircraft and one destroyer before the unit was put out of action. Marine squadrons on the East Coast were rapidly transferred to the Pacific, and marine fighters and dive-bombers participated

Marines, flying aircraft such as this F4F Wildcat fighter from Henderson Field at Guadalcanal, held the line against great odds and provided a foothold from which to launch an offensive and push the enemy up the Solomon Islands. (U.S. Navy)

in the defense of Midway Island in June 1942 that turned the tide against the Japanese advance.

Marine corps aviation came into its own during the Guadalcanal campaign that began in August 1942. Marine fighters, dive-bombers, and torpedo bombers formed the core of the joint "Cactus Air Force" that operated on a shoestring while beating back repeated Japanese attacks. With Guadalcanal finally secured in February 1943, marine squadrons spearheaded the two-year march up the Solomon island chain and isolation of the Japanese stronghold at Rabaul in New Britain. As the fighting progressed, more effort was devoted to the development of air-ground tactics, though not necessarily in support of ground marines. Marine SBD dive-bombers gave sterling close-air support to army troops during the liberation of the Philippines during 1944–45.

In late 1944, a program was initiated to put marine squadrons on escort carriers (CVEs). The desperate need for more fighter aircraft on board carriers to combat the Japanese kamikaze threat resulted in ten marine F4U fighter squadrons serving on board five fleet aircraft carriers. These units flew missions against Japanese targets in French Indochina, the Philippines, Formosa, China, and Japan itself. Other marine squadrons provided close-air support during the battle for Okinawa, and kept Japanese forces isolated in bypassed Pacific islands.

By the end of World War II, marine corps aviation had grown to 5 air wings, 29 air groups, 132 tactical squadrons, and 116,628 personnel. Some squadrons participated in the occupation of Japan and in the attempt to prevent a communist takeover in China. But with the end of the war and the subsequent de-mobilization, the marine corps phased out its dive-bomber, torpedo bomber, medium bomber, and observation squadrons, retaining only fighter and transport capabilities. A few fighter squadrons continued to serve as the air complements on board escort carriers. Despite the austere force levels, the seeds of future progress were being sown as helicopters entered marine corps service in 1947, followed by jet fighters in 1948, and specialized attack aircraft in 1950. A strong marine air reserve program reinstated at twenty-one naval air stations in 1946 grew steadily, enabling the marine corps to mobilize twenty squadrons after the North Korean army invaded South Korea in June 1950.

After a feverish period of activating reserve units and bringing regular units up to full strength, marine squadrons were in action against North Korean forces on 6 August 1950. For the duration of the conflict, marine aircraft flew close-air support, night attack, and night interception missions. Marine night fighters escorted air force B-29 bombers on strikes against North Korea. Some marine pilots flew missions on exchange duty with air force jet fighter squadrons. Marine corps aviation has remained on station in the Far East—long after the end of the Korean War.

The concept of vertical envelopment using helicopters was tried and proven in Korea. Casualty rates were reduced rapidly by evacuating the wounded to rear medical facilities; combat units were lifted into place; and downed aircrews were rescued. Despite the success of helicopters in Korea, it was not possible to integrate these aircraft fully into amphibious operations because of a lack of vessels to support them. As an interim measure, carriers being phased out of fixed-wing service were pressed into service as helicopter carriers (designated landing platform helicopters, or LPHs). The first ship designed and built specifically for this task was the USS *Iwo Jima* (LPH 2), which entered service in August 1961.

The need for marine corps aviation to operate in forward areas where few or no facilities existed had been recognized early in World War II. It

Marine corps F4U-4 Corsair fighters prepare to launch on a strike from a carrier off the coast of Korea. (U.S. Marine Corps)

was not until 1958 that a short airfield for tactical support (SATS) was constructed. This installation consisted of an aluminum plank mat and catapult and arresting equipment that could be transported easily and constructed in a minimum amount of time. Three experimental sites were built, and tests continued for five years. In March 1965, the concept was put into combat use with the installation of a SATS at Chu Lai, Vietnam. Eventually, a permanent concrete airfield was constructed farther inland.

By 1959, marine fighter and attack squadrons completed transition to an all-jet force. Improved turbine-powered helicopters entered service in the early 1960s, greatly improving lift capability. Marine corps aviation entered the space age in 1962 when Lt. John H. Glenn orbited the earth three times in the first American manned orbital space flight. Later that year, marine corps reconnaissance pilots flew dangerous missions in their

Marine Corps Aviation 281

A bomb-laden marine corps A-6A Intruder prepares for launch on a strike in Vietnam. Marine squadrons have often deployed on navy carriers. (U.S. Navy)

RF-8 Crusaders over Cuba to monitor the buildup of Soviet nuclear missiles during the Cuban Missile Crisis.

In April 1962, marine corps aviation began its thirteen-year participation in the Vietnam War with the introduction of a transport helicopter squadron as a component of an advisory program. In April 1965, elements of the First Marine Air Wing began arriving in Vietnam to provide tactical air support for ground troops.

Every type of aircraft in the marine corps's operational inventory was utilized in Vietnam. Tactical squadrons supported troops on the ground in South Vietnam, struck enemy targets in North Vietnam and Laos, and engaged in air-to-air combat. Some marine tactical jet squadrons operated from navy aircraft carriers offshore. Transport units kept busy ferrying troops and supplies to and from Japan, providing in-flight refueling for tactical aircraft, and supplying bases such as the besieged Khe Sanh. Marine helicopters operating from bases in Vietnam and LPHs offshore were essential to the war effort; it was in Vietnam that the armed helicopter came into its own. Marine helicopters were also instrumental in evacuating the last Americans from Vietnam and Cambodia in 1975.

In the ensuing years, marine aviation often has been called into action to defend Americans and their interests abroad, during hostilities and humanitarian efforts. Marine helicopter crews participated in the aborted attempt to rescue American hostages in Tehran, Iran. Marine helicopters saw combat against Cuban forces during the 1983 invasion of Grenada which freed a large number of American hostages and prevented a communist takeover of the island. During 1987–88, helicopter gunships countered Iranian threats to shipping in the Persian Gulf during Operation Earnest Will. In 1990, when Liberia was racked with civil war, marine helicopters evacuated Americans and other foreigners.

The Iraqi invasion of Kuwait in 1990 precipitated the largest deployment of marine corps aviation forces since World War II. Some 70 percent of marine corps aviation squadrons were positioned in the Arabian peninsula and in amphibious ships offshore during Operation Desert Shield. In January and February 1991, these well-trained forces, including some reserve units called to active duty, played a major role during Operation Desert Storm, striking Iraqi forces in Kuwait and supporting coalition troops as they liberated Kuwait from enemy control. (Also, just days prior to the war, marine helicopters supported by aerial refueling tankers carried out the daring evacuation of Americans and other foreigners from strife-torn Somalia.)

The end of the lightning war in Kuwait did not bring any rest for marine aviation during 1991. Marine helicopters were immediately called into Operation Provide Comfort, the effort to relieve suffering among the Kurdish minority in northern Iraq. Other helicopter units returning from the Persian Gulf War executed Operation Sea Angel to assist storm-ravaged Bangladesh. Operation Fiery Vigil involved marine helicopters assisting relief efforts in the Philippines after the eruption of Mount Pinatubo.

Marine helicopters again saw action during 1992 as they participated in a search-and-rescue effort for an Italian aircrew downed during the civil war in Bosnia-Herzegovina. Later that year and into 1993, marine helicopters and transports were back in Somalia, this time to protect

Much of marine corps aviation has the mission of amphibious assault; helicopters such as these CH-46E Sea Knights are used to transport troops to the battle area. (U.S. Navy/PH3 Jerry M. Ireland)

U.N.-sponsored relief efforts. Helicopter gunships were called into action several times to counter hostile forces. (Marine transport helicopters supporting U.N. peacekeeping forces in Cambodia also came under hostile fire during early 1993.) In 1994, marine helicopters supported the movement of U.S. troops into Haiti in support of the U.S. effort to restore the elected Haitian president to power. In 1995, marine corps F/A-18 strike fighters under NATO command flew strikes in support of U.N. peacekeeping forces in Bosnia-Herzegovina, where marine CH-53 helicopters also rescued a downed air force pilot.

Marine Corps Aviation Today

Today's marine corps is still very much an air-ground team. The noteworthy characteristic of marine corps aviation is that it is an inseparable part of marine corps infantry. Its basic purpose since its inception is clear—to support marines on the ground.

The role of marine corps aviation is to provide close-air support, bat-

UH-1N helicopters are used for observation and forward air control. (U.S. Navy/PH1 D. Brockschmidt)

tlefield airlift, and air defense of marine corps ground forces ashore and during amphibious operations. A secondary role, and one that became increasingly important during the force restructuring of the 1990s, is to augment navy carrier air wings, as marines have been called upon to do from time to time since the latter half of World War II.

Organization

At Headquarters Marine Corps in Arlington, Virginia, the deputy chief of staff (DC/S) for aviation plans and supervises all matters relating to the organization, personnel, operational readiness, and logistical requirements of marine corps aviation. He also serves as an advisor for marine corps aviation requirements to the CNO through the CNO's Director, Air Warfare.

Marine corps aviation is organized administratively into three active Marine Aircraft Wings (MAW) and one reserve MAW. The 2nd MAW,

Marine corps helicopters and AV-8B VTOL attack aircraft deploy on board amphibious ships such as the USS *Saipan* (LHA 2). (U.S. Navy/PH1(AW) Raymond H. Turner II)

headquartered at MCAS Cherry Point, North Carolina, is based on the East Coast and supports the Atlantic Fleet's Fleet Marine Force. The 3rd MAW, headquartered at MCAS El Toro, California (moving to Miramar, California) is based on the West Coast and supports the Pacific Fleet's Fleet Marine Force. The 1st MAW, headquartered at MCAS Futemna, Okinawa, is based in Japan, also in support of the Pacific Fleet Marine Force; most of its assigned squadrons are on six-month rotation from the 2nd and 3rd MAWs, as well as from the 1st Marine Air Wing Aviation Support Element at Marine Corps Base Hawaii.

The 4th Marine Aircraft Wing, headquartered at New Orleans, Louisiana, reports to the Marine Corps Reserve Forces. Its aircraft and personnel are located mostly at navy and marine corps air stations throughout the United States.

AV-8B Harrier II VTOL attack jets position for launch from an amphibious ship during Operation Desert Shield. (U.S. Navy/PH2 Charles Stover)

Although no two wings are identical in structure, a typical wing would consist of a Marine Air Control Group (MACG); a Marine Wing Support Group (MWSG); one or two fixed-wing Marine Aircraft Groups (MAG); and one or two rotary-wing MAGs.

> MACG—Assigned Marine Air Control Squadrons (MACS) provide air surveillance and control of aircraft and surface-to-air missiles for antiair support of marine forces. Assigned Marine Air Support Squadrons (MASSs) provide facilities for control of aircraft in close or direct support of ground forces. Assigned Marine Tactical Air Command Squadrons (MTACS) have the mission of planning for and coordinating the Tactical Air Command Center (TACC) for the Aviation Combat Element (ACE), and providing personnel and

facilities as components for a Marine Expeditionary Force or Marine Expeditionary Force (Forward) TACC. (The TACC is the operational command post of the ACE Commander and is the facility from which command and control of all marine air operations in support of the Marine Air-Ground Task Force are conducted.) Assigned Marine Wing Communications Squadrons (MWCS) provide communications for wing headquarters and the wing's air command-and-control system. Also assigned for air base defense are a Light Anti-Aircraft Missile Battalion (LAAM) or a Low-Altitude Air Defense Battalion (LAAD).

MWSG—Its assigned Ground Support Elements or Marine Wing Support Squadrons (MWSSs) provide supply, logistic, medical, and meteorological support for the wing's groups and squadrons, including such support as motor transport and refueling for ground support equipment and aircraft.

MAG—Active MAGs are generally organized with three or more squadrons with similar type aircraft and located at a single base. (For administrative geographic convenience, many reserve MAGs and their permanent detachments are assigned both fixed-wing and rotary-wing squadrons.) Each MAG has a Marine Air Logistics Squadron (MALS) which provides repair of avionics, airframes, and engines for the group's aircraft squadrons. Some MAGs also host replacement training squadrons.

During the 1980s, Marine Air Weapons and Tactics Squadron (MWTS) 1 was formed at MCAS Yuma, Arizona, to develop and refine tactical doctrine and weapons employment, and train selected aircrews from all three Marine Aircraft Wings.

Aircraft Squadrons

The types of squadrons listed below are basic tactical and administrative units that operate aircraft to accomplish their assigned missions and are subordinate to the MAGs or, in a few cases, to the air stations to which they are assigned.

HMLA (Marine Helicopter Light Attack Squadron)—Provides close-in fire support of ground forces; attacks and destroys surface tar-

Refueling CH-53E Super Stallion helicopters from KC-130 Hercules transports gives the marine corps the ability to fly long-range troop insertion missions. (via *Naval Aviation News*)

gets; escorts other helicopters; provides utility combat support to ground forces, including light transport and battle command and control.

HMH (Marine Heavy Helicopter Squadron)—Provides assault helicopter transport of combat troops, heavy weapons, equipment, and supplies during amphibious operations and operations ashore.

HMM (Marine Medium Helicopter Squadron)—Provides assault transport of combat troops during amphibious operations and operations ashore.

HMT (Marine Helicopter Training Squadron)—Provides flight training in aircraft type to helicopter pilots and crewmen; provides technical training in aircraft type to maintenance personnel.

HMX (Marine Helicopter Squadron)—Provides helicopter transportation for the president and vice-president of the United States, members of the president's cabinet, and foreign dignitaries; pro-

The marine corps operates four squadrons of EA-6B Prowler electronic warfare aircraft. (U.S. Marine Corps)

vides helicopter support to Headquarters Marine Corps; provides helicopter support for the development of helicopter tactics, techniques, and landing force equipment, and for student indoctrination and demonstration.

SOES (Station Operations and Engineering Squadron)—Provides rapid-response airlift of personnel and cargo and local search and rescue from selected marine corps air stations, as well as airfield services.

SOMS (Station Operations and Maintenance Squadron)—Provides limited airlift and local search and rescue from selected marine corps air stations, as well as airfield services.

The F/A-18 Hornet strike fighter gives the marine air wing the capability of hitting targets in the air or on the ground with equal agility. (McDonnell Douglas)

VMA (Marine Attack Squadron)—Attacks and destroys surface targets; escorts helicopters.

VMAQ (Marine Tactical Electronic Warfare Squadron)—Neutralizes enemy defenses and control systems with electronic jamming and antiradiation missiles.

VMAT (Marine Attack Training Squadron)—Conducts attack training in aircraft type for pilots, with emphasis upon weapons delivery; conducts technical training for attack aircraft maintenance personnel.

VMFA (Marine Fighter Attack Squadron)—Attacks and destroys surface targets; intercepts and destroys enemy aircraft under all-weather conditions.

VMFA(AW) (Marine All-Weather Fighter Attack Squadron)—Attacks and destroys surface targets under all-weather conditions; inter-

cepts and destroys enemy aircraft under all-weather conditions; conducts reconnaissance, observation, and forward air control operations in support of ground forces.
VMFAT (Marine Fighter Attack Training Squadron)—Conducts attack and intercept training for VMFA pilots and VMFA(AW) pilots and weapons systems operators in aircraft type, with emphasis on all-weather operations; conducts technical training for fighter attack maintenance personnel.
VMFT (Marine Fighter Training Squadron)—Provides adversary aircraft services to train squadrons in air combat maneuvering and tactics.
VMGR (Marine Aerial Refueler Transport Squadron)—Provides aerial refueling to tactical jets and helicopters; provides air assault transport for personnel, equipment and supplies.
VMGRT (Marine Aerial Refueler Transport Training Squadron)—Provides flight training in aircraft type to pilots, navigators, and loadmasters; provides technical training to VMGR maintenance personnel.

Marine Corps Air Stations

The marine corps maintains its own air stations and air facilities in the continental United States, in Hawaii, and in Japan to support active aviation units (see Appendix G for a list of air stations, facilities, and outlying fields). Most reserve groups and squadrons are stationed at naval air stations and facilities and at Air National Guard bases. Most marine corps air stations have a Headquarters and Headquarters Squadron (H&HS) assigned, as well as an SOES or SOMS.

Marine Corps Aircraft

The marine corps operates approximately one thousand aircraft, mostly tactical jets and helicopters. The marine corps has steadily modernized its aircraft force and is gradually "necking down" the number of different type/model/series in order to maintain a lean, economical, hard-hitting air arm. (For example, such long-serving types as the A-6 Intruder, F-4 and RF-4 Phantom II, and OV-10 Bronco were completely

The two-seat F/A-18D Hornet performs strike, reconnaissance, and forward air control missions. (Robert L. Lawson)

phased out of service in the early 1990s, all replaced by versions of the F/A-18 Hornet.) Some types are also operated by the navy, while some are flown only by the corps. Whatever their function, marine corps aircraft have as their ultimate purpose the support of marine ground forces.

Aircraft types in marine corps service include:

— Strike Fighter: F/A-18 Hornet (F/A-18A/B/C/D)
— Attack: AV-8 Harrier (AV-8B; TAV-8B)
— Electronic Warfare: EA-6B Prowler
— Adversary Fighter: F-5 Tiger II (F-5E/F)

The marine corps reserve's 4th Marine Air Wing is available for call-up in a national emergency. The F/A-18A Hornet of reserve squadron VMFA-321 climbs out for a close-air support mission loaded with four napalm fire bombs. (U.S. Navy/PH2 Bruce Trombecky)

— Assault Helicopters: CH-46E Sea Knight
　　　　　　　　　　　H-53D Sea Stallion (CH-53D; RH-53D)
　　　　　　　　　　　CH-53E Super Stallion
— Attack Helicopter: AH-1W Super Cobra
— Utility Helicopter: UH-1N Iroquois ("Huey")
— Rescue Helicopter: HH-1N Iroquois ("Huey")
　　　　　　　　　　HH-46D Sea Knight
— Executive Helicopter: VH-3D Sea King
　　　　　　　　　　　　VH-60N Seahawk
— Refueler/Transport: KC-130 Hercules (KC-130F/R/T)
— Transport: C-9B Skytrain II
　　　　　　　C-20G Gulfstream IV
　　　　　　　CT-39G Sabreliner
　　　　　　　UC-12B Huron

Marine corps aviation is dependent on its skilled mechanics to keep aircraft operating in the forward battle areas. Here, two mechanics perform maintenance on an AH-1 gunship helicopter. (U.S. Navy/PHC Ken A. George)

Table 12-1. Replacement Training Squadrons

Squadron	Location	Aircraft
VMFAT-101	MCAS El Toro, Calif.	F/A-18
VFA-106*	NAS Cecil Field, Fla.	F/A-18
VFA-125*	NAS Lemoore, Calif.	F/A-18
VMAT-203	MCAS Cherry Point, N.C.	AV-8B; TAV-8B
VAQ-129*	NAS Whidbey Is., Wash.	EA-6B
VMGRT-253†	MCAS Cherry Point, N.C.	KC-130
HMT-204	MCAS New River, N.C.	CH-46
HMT-301	MCAF Kaneohe Bay, Hawaii	CH-53D
HMT-302‡	MCAS New River, N.C.	CH-53E; MH-53E
HMT-303‡	MCAS Camp Pendleton, Calif.	AH-1; UH-1; HH-1

*Navy fleet readiness squadrons which also train marines. (VFA-106 is slated to move to NAS Oceana, Virginia.)

†VMGRT-253 also trains enlisted marine aerial navigators, flight engineers, radio operators, and loadmasters in the KC-130.

‡HMT-302 (relocating from MCAS Tustin, Calif.) also trains navy crews to fly the CH-53E and MH-53E. HMT-303 also trains navy crews to fly the UH-1N and HH-1N.

Replacement and Type Training

Upon completion of training in the Naval Air Training Command and winning their wings (see chapter 2), marine corps naval aviators and naval flight officers report to replacement training squadrons, in the same manner as their navy counterparts, to learn to fly the tactical aircraft that they will operate in the Fleet Marine Force. In some cases, the training for marines is conducted by navy fleet readiness squadrons, and vice versa. These training squadrons also train mechanics and avionics technicians on the type of aircraft that they will maintain during their squadron assignment. The replacement training squadrons are listed in Table 12-1.

THIRTEEN

Coast Guard Aviation

Revised from an original chapter written by
Cdr. Jess C. Barrow, USCGR (Ret.)

The U.S. Coast Guard adopted the airplane soon after the navy did, and coast guard aviation grew alongside naval aviation as the importance of maritime aviation expanded during this century. Coast guard pilots have been trained by the navy since the beginning and are designated naval aviators. The smallest of the nation's military air arms, coast guard aviation has performed splendidly in proportion far greater than its size would suggest, both in times of peace and augmenting the navy in times of war.

The Beginning

Coast guard aviation officially began on 30 March 1916, when 2d Lt. Charles E. Sugden and 3d Lt. Elmer F. Stone were selected by the Treasury Department to report to the naval air station at Pensacola, Florida, for flight training. On 29 August of that year, Congress passed the Naval Deficiency Act, which authorized the Treasury Department to establish ten coast guard air stations along the Atlantic and Pacific coasts, the Great Lakes, and the Gulf of Mexico. The legislation also authorized a coast guard aviation school, and an aviation corps of ten flight officers, five engineering officers, and forty mechanics. Congress, however, failed to appropriate funds to carry out the legislation, and the program was shelved until the termination of World War I.

In the meantime, the coast guard sent four additional officers and twelve enlisted men to Pensacola, all receiving their wings in 1917. During World War I, coast guard pilots were attached to navy units, serving in aviation billets. One coast guard officer served as commanding officer of the naval air station at Ille Tudy, France, during the war.

After the war, coast guard aviators continued to fly with the navy. One of the pilots of the NC-4 flying boat that made the first crossing of the Atlantic Ocean by air was Lt. Elmer F. Stone.

In March 1920 the first coast guard air station was established at Morehead City, North Carolina, with six airplanes borrowed from the navy. Although it was closed after fifteen months of operations because of a lack of funds, the Morehead City experiment convinced the Treasury Department that the coast guard air arm was a vital necessity.

In 1925 a new air station was established at Gloucester, Massachusetts, from which Lt. Cdr. Carl C. von Paulson and Aviation Pilot Leonard M. Melca flew many thousands of miles on patrol, locating rum-running boats, directing patrol boats in distress, carrying out experiments in two-way radio communications, and performing many other duties. These results convinced Congress to give the coast guard $152,000 to purchase five airplanes of its own. Within a short time, the coast guard placed contracts for three Loening OL-5 amphibians and two Chance Vought UO-4 floatplanes.

During the 1930s, coast guard aviation grew rapidly and steadily, becoming an integral part of the coast guard in carrying out its traditional and time-honored rescue and law enforcement duties. Air stations, their number increased to nine, were strategically located to enable the greatest service to the public and the military. By 1939, the number of cases of coast guard assistance and of hours flown by coast guard pilots had increased tenfold, amassed with only 63 pilots, 180 enlisted men, and 50 airplanes on strength.

Coast Guard Aviation in World War II

Several months prior to the attack on Pearl Harbor in December 1941, coast guard cutter-based planes began operating in the Greenland area,

The first aircraft built for the coast guard was the Loening OL-5 amphibian, delivered in October 1926. (U.S. Coast Guard)

carrying out antisubmarine and coastal patrols and making heroic rescues. In October 1941, the Greenland Patrol was inaugurated by Capt. Edward H. Smith, USCG, to operate as part of Task Force 24 of the U.S. Atlantic Fleet.

On 1 November 1941, with war imminent, President Franklin Roosevelt put the coast guard under the operational control of the navy. Rapidly expanded in both planes and personnel, the efforts of coast guard air stations through early 1944 were primarily directed at antisubmarine patrols, particularly against the German submarine threat. Daily inshore patrols protected the important harbors and approaches to the sea, while offshore patrols covered other sections of the nation's coast. By June 1943, coast guard aircraft had made sixty-one attacks against enemy submarines; on 1 August 1942, while flying a Grumman J4F amphibian, Chief Aviation Pilot Henry C. White attacked and sank German submarine U-166 in the Gulf of Mexico, about one hundred miles south of Houma, Louisiana.

In the summer of 1943, the coast guard was directed to establish a special patrol squadron to augment the Greenland Patrol. Flying the PBY-5A

Catalina, Patrol Bombing Squadron Six became the most colorful of all World War II coast guard squadrons. Based in Greenland, it provided air cover for ship convoys plying the North Atlantic between the United States and Great Britain; carried out antisubmarine patrols; surveyed ice conditions for shipping; made hundreds of dramatic rescues; and carried mail and supplies to remote regions. In addition to covering the vast Greenland area, the squadron's operations ranged south to Newfoundland, west to the Hudson and Baffin bay regions, and east to Iceland. In 1943, the squadron assisted coast guard cutters in destroying a German weather station in northeast Greenland.

During World War II, the coast guard was a leader in the development of a technology that would prove a boon to both military and civilian aviation: the helicopter. In November 1943, Coast Guard Air Station Brooklyn, New York, was designated a helicopter training base. By February 1945 the school had trained 102 helicopter pilots (72 coast guard, 6 navy, 5 army, 12 British, 4 Canadian, and 3 civilian). A deck landing platform was installed at the base to simulate a rolling ship deck, and a cutter was assigned to provide actual landings at sea under varying weather conditions.

The coast guard undertook other important training assignments. A preflight training school was established at Elizabeth City, North Carolina, as was a school for pilots and mechanics bound for Greenland duty with Patrol Bombing Squadron Six. At the air station at St. Petersburg, Florida, the coast guard trained Mexican pilots in antisubmarine warfare.

The coast guard also led the way in institutionalizing the coordination of air-sea rescue efforts among the various armed forces. In December 1943, in response to the increasing number of air mishaps in the southern California region, a new rescue organization formed at CGAS San Diego. This unit, the first of its kind in the United States, incorporated surface craft, airplanes, blimps, and other rescue equipment used by the army, navy, marine corps, and other maritime agencies. The Air-Sea Rescue Agency was established in February 1944, and the coast guard, which had been organizing toward this end for a long time, was the logical administrator for this new agency.

Coordination of rescue activities was conducted by joint operation centers, while actual rescues were the responsibility of each regional air-sea task unit, headed by the commanding officer of the coast guard air station within that region. The national organization was headed by the commandant of the coast guard, advised by representatives from the other services.

Besides rescue operations, air-sea rescue services trained personnel engaged in search-and-rescue duties, and the coast guard carried on experimental work in using blimps in rescue work. Actual rescues were made from raft to blimp, and a small number of officers and enlisted personnel were trained in blimp operations.

The rescue service also included a special parachute unit, trained at the Forest Service smoke jumper school in Montana. Another unique rescue training program was conducted at CGAS Port Angeles, Washington, where special air-land rescue ski squads were trained to render service in snow-covered mountain areas.

The outstanding work of coast guard aviation during World War II remained little known to the general public. Its activities went far beyond the capabilities envisioned for it during peacetime. In performance of its missions, the coast guard exceeded even its own high standard of excellence and devotion to duty.

The Post–World War II Years

In January 1946, control of coast guard operations again returned to the Treasury Department. Congress, recognizing the need for an expanding coast guard aviation role, asked the Treasury Department to determine its future aviation needs. The task was somewhat difficult, as many of the coast guard's missions were under review or yet undefined. Issues included the future extent of the nation's territorial waters, and, given the rapid expansion of transoceanic air travel, how far out search-and rescue attempts would be undertaken. To accomplish its missions, the coast guard would require long-, medium-, and short-range aircraft.

During the 1950s, the coast guard relied mostly on a fleet of flying boats and amphibians but increased the integration of the helicopter as a rescue platform. Coast guard aircraft still operated in the western Pacific, including rescue operations under combat conditions in the Formosa Strait. By the 1960s, the coast guard cutter/helicopter team emerged as a highly effective part of the service's search-and-rescue, law enforcement, and military missions. Many new cutters, in the medium- and high-endurance class, all with new landing pads in their design, were commissioned. These new teams developed advanced techniques for the use of helicopters, and the helicopter gradually replaced the flying boat as the coast guard's primary rescue aircraft. The helicopter demonstrated its value during the 1950s when helicopters were used to perform many spectacular rescues of civilians from floods.

Coast guard aircraft did not participate in the air war over Vietnam during the 1960s, but some coast guard aviators did. Serving on exchange duty with the air force's rescue service, coast guard aviators flew combat rescue missions in air force HH-3 and HC-130 aircraft similar to their own aircraft.

The 1970s marked an ongoing era of vastly expanded mission requirements for the coast guard. In 1976, the implementation of the 200-mile fishery conservation zone off U.S. shores exponentially increased the demand upon the coast guard's long-range HC-130 and medium-range HU-16 aircraft. The tremendous distances involved in the enforcement of the 200-mile zone created the need for a high-speed aircraft capable of covering hundreds of square miles in a relatively short period of time. The HU-25 Guardian, an adaptation of an executive transport jet, eventually replaced the coast guard's last amphibian, the HU-16E Albatross.

In addition to increased fisheries patrol requirements, the 1970s brought new responsibilities in environmental protection. An aerial oil-pollution surveillance system was installed on some aircraft; this sophisticated electronic system can detect the presence of oil on the ocean's surface under all weather conditions, day or night.

The 1980s and 1990s provided no letup in tempo for coast guard aviation. Waves of migrants sailing by boat and raft from Cuba and Haiti demanded increased rescue and surveillance efforts. The major increase in operations came, however, from a massive national effort to interdict drugs being smuggled by boat and aircraft into the United States, mostly in the Caribbean and Gulf of Mexico. This effort led to the acquisition of several navy E-2C radar early-warning aircraft and RG-8 powered gliders; the modification of an HC-130 into a radar early-warning EC-130V version; and the development of a version of the HU-25 (the HU-25C) with an airborne interceptor radar. In 1987, coast guard aircraft became an integral part of OPBAT (Operations in the Bahamas, Turks, and Caicos Islands), a multi-agency effort to interdict drug smuggling operating through those islands into the United States.

Environmental missions came into spectacular view in 1989 with the massive oil spill in Alaska's Prince William Sound from the tanker *Exxon Valdez*; ten coast guard aircraft were involved in the clean-up operations. In 1990, Congress passed the Oil Pollution Act, which gave the coast guard increased environmental mission responsibility and additional funds to carry it out.

The coast guard was ready to go when called to a war zone in 1991. Three HU-25Bs, equipped with an oil-pollution surveillance radar, and supported by an HC-130, deployed to the Persian Gulf to map the extent of the damage to the gulf after Iraqi forces blew up Kuwaiti oil wells.

Like the other U.S. services in the mid-1990s, the coast guard faced severe budgetary pressures, with no letup in mission requirements. This caused the coast guard to retire some aircraft, realign the assignment of others among its air stations, close an air station and an air facility, reduce the number of aviation personnel, acquire fewer pilots (temporarily closing its Direct Commission Aviator program), and increasing the length of time helicopter detachments are deployed on board ships.

Coast Guard Aviation Today

The coast guard today, perhaps more than ever, operates in support of a myriad of national missions, and its aviation component continues to perform a vital part of those missions.

Maritime Safety

Search and rescue is the mission for which coast guard aviation is the most famous and which endears it most to the public. The scope of this mission increased as recreational boating expanded dramatically after World War II. The advent of the helicopter gave the coast guard the ideal aircraft with which to assist and rescue boaters along the nation's coasts. Although the coast guard no longer operates flying boats and amphibians, its fixed-wing aircraft carry inflatable life rafts and other survival equipment to drop to persons in distress until they can be rescued by other means. Each year thousands of Americans are assisted by coast guard aircraft in many thousands of rescue responses.

Since 1946, coast guard aircraft have supported the International Ice Patrol, established as a result of the *Titanic* disaster. The Ice Patrol observes icebergs drifting into the Grand Banks area of the North Atlantic and plots their positions in order to warn maritime shipping of their location.

Maritime Law Enforcement

The coast guard enforces U.S. laws and treaties in coastal waters and in international waters. Coast guard aviation has long been instrumental in the drug interdiction campaign of recent years, and it has also participated in operations against other types of smuggling, as well as against illegal immigration and piracy.

Maritime Environmental Protection

The coast guard has been given primary responsibility for maritime environmental protection, and its aircraft play a large part in this program. They conduct offshore and port patrols to see that laws are obeyed and to monitor environmental disasters. Coast guard cutters with helicopters conduct polar and domestic ice-breaking operations and support marine science operations.

Maritime Defense

Coast guard aviation assists in patrolling the Maritime Defense Zones, which extend 200 miles from the coast. This mission would become more visible in event of war, during which the coast guard would come under operational control of the navy. During the early 1990s, the coast guard gave up antisubmarine warfare entirely to the navy as a mission because of the increasing cost of technology and training required to maintain an edge in this area of naval warfare.

Organization

Coast guard aviation is not a separate corps within the coast guard. Its operations at every level are integrated with the other coast guard forces. Chief, Coast Guard Aviation, is a senior captain who advises the commandant in aviation matters. The Atlantic and Pacific area commanders

The HC-130H Hercules serves as the coast guard's long-range surveillance aircraft. (Robert F. Dorr collection)

are under the commandant. Under the commanders are the ten numbered districts. The air stations in each district normally conduct air missions as assigned by their district.

Aviation personnel comprise approximately 13 percent of all coast guard men and women, and will total approximately twenty-eight hundred personnel by the late 1990s.

Coast Guard Air Stations

Coast guard aviation has no squadrons; all aircraft are assigned directly to the twenty-six coast guard air stations and the Aviation Training Center (at Mobile, Alabama). (See Appendix H for a list of coast guard air stations and assigned aircraft types). Some air stations have only helicopters assigned; others only fixed-wing aircraft assigned. The air stations are located along the coasts of the United States in areas of heavy maritime activity. Even so, the small number of aircraft available stretches the coast guard very thin as it performs all of its responsibilities.

The pilots and crewmen assigned to each air station perform administrative duties and stand alert for quick reaction missions when they are not flying scheduled missions. Coast guard air station commanding officers have both administrative and operational responsibility over the aircraft assigned to their station, as well as all of the myriad maintenance, supply, and personnel support functions of a base. Some air station COs also have responsibility over all boats and small cutters assigned within their geographic area.

Aviation Training Center

Although the Coast Guard Aviation Training Center (ATC) at Mobile, Alabama, carries out the functions of a normal air station, its primary mission is training coast guard aviators and aircrewmen to operate the aircraft in the coast guard inventory and to become familiar with coast guard standard operational procedures.

The ATC also provides qualification courses for fixed-wing pilots making the transition to instrument-qualified rotary-wing aircraft, and provides comprehensive refresher training. Pilots return to the ATC frequently to review and update their knowledge of air traffic control procedures, air operations, in-flight emergency procedures, and other aviation matters. ATC also provides an aviation orientation program for Coast Guard Academy cadets to acquaint them with the capabilities of coast guard aviation and to stimulate interest in aviation careers.

One of the unique functions of the ATC is to train coast guard helicopter pilots for shipboard operations. A division of the ATC trains the pilots and crews to be deployed on board coast guard cutters and icebreakers for polar missions, including scientific research, supply of remote stations, logistic support, ice observations, search and rescue, and law enforcement.

Aviation Technical Training Center

The coast guard operates the Aviation Technical Training Center at CGAS Elizabeth City, North Carolina. The mechanics and techni-

The HU-25 Guardian is a high-speed, medium-range surveillance jet. This HU-25B version is equipped with side-looking aircraft radar (SLAR) to track oil slicks. (U.S. Coast Guard)

cians that maintain coast guard aircraft are trained there in a variety of courses.

Aviation Repair & Supply Center

Also located at Elizabeth City is the coast guard's Aviation Repair & Supply Center. This facility overhauls the service's aircraft and serves as a centralized supply depot.

Coast Guard Aircraft

The coast guard operates a relatively modern fleet of high-performance, turbine-powered, multimission aircraft. A focused procurement program has achieved great economies by "necking down" the number of different types in operation and ensuring that each type in service is capable of a wide variety of missions. The coast guard operates four main types:

The HH-60J Jayhawk is used for medium-range search-and-rescue missions. (U.S. Coast Guard)

Helicopters:
HH-60J Jayhawk—medium-range rescue
HH-65A Dolphin—short-range rescue; shipboard operations

Fixed-wing aircraft:
HC-130H Hercules—Long-range surveillance. The HC-130H fleet was modified with APS-137 inverse synthetic aperture radar (ISAR), greatly increasing the aircraft's surface ship detection capability.
HU-25 Guardian—Medium-range surveillance. The HU-25 is operated in three versions. The HU-25A is the standard surveillance aircraft. The HU-25B can carry a pod-mounted APS-131 SLAR which can be used to map oil spills. The HU-25C is equipped with an APG-66 air intercept radar and a WF-360 infrared sensor to enable the aircraft to intercept smuggler aircraft.

The coast guard also operates a handful of specialized aircraft. These include:

RG-8A Condor—Two powered gliders able to soar quietly over smuggler watercraft. These are being replaced by RU-38A twin-boom monoplanes.

RU-38A—A follow-on to the RG-8A Condor powered glider which is able to soar quietly over smuggler watercraft. These are tandem-engine, twin-boom monoplanes with increased capability.

C-20B Gulfstream III—A single long-range command-and-control and executive transport aircraft for the commandant that replaced a VC-11A in 1995.

VC-4A Gulfstream—A single logistics transport.

Coast Guard Aviators

Coast guard pilots are designated naval aviators. Most are designated as they complete the navy helicopter or maritime syllabi but some are commissioned directly from other services. The coast guard acquires approximately fifty aviators each year.

Approximately two-thirds of potential coast guard pilots are graduates of the Coast Guard Academy. Others come from the Officer Candidate School. They must pass an academic qualification test, flight aptitude rating, and a flight physical examination in order to be selected for flight training.

A third source of pilots is the Direct Commission Aviator Program. A board selects prior military pilots who have a college degree and are graduates of a U.S. military pilot training program. Age and flight time requirements also govern the selection, and selectees are commissioned as active-duty reservists, many of whom eventually become regular coast guard officers. The direct commission program is used to augment the regular path through naval aviator training; therefore, the number of individuals selected every year varies, and the program was temporarily suspended in 1994 because of an excess of pilots. Direct commission aviators are designated naval aviators and wear wings of gold.

The coast guard does not use specialized navigators, so all of its long-range fixed-wing pilots receive maritime navigation training alongside air force navigators and naval flight officers at Randolph Air Force Base in Texas. (The coast guard designated a few naval flight officers to operate

The HH-65A Dolphin is used for short-range search-and-rescue missions, shipboard operations, and polar ice operations. (U.S. Coast Guard)

the radars on board the E-2C and EC-130V aircraft, but these programs were terminated during the early 1990s.)

Coast Guard Aviation Enlisted Ratings

Unlike the navy, which has twenty-one aviation ratings (see chapter 7), the coast guard has only five aviation ratings:

— Aviation Machinist's Mate (AD)
— Aviation Electrician's Mate (AE)
— Aviation Structural Mechanic (AM)
— Aviation Electronics Technician (AT)
— Aviation Survivalman (ASM)

Of these ratings, three (AD, AE, and AT) are equivalent to their navy counterparts. The AM rating combines the duties of the navy AMH,

What it's all about—an HH-60J comes to the rescue of persons in distress. (U.S. Coast Guard)

AMS, and AME ratings. The aviation survivalman rating is unique to the coast guard, and combines many of the duties of the navy's PR and AW ratings, including the rescue swimmer role. Rescue swimmers are graduates of the navy rescue swimmer school and are also trained as emergency medical technicians.

The Class A schools for all of the coast guard aviation ratings are located at the Aviation Technical Training Center at Elizabeth City, North Carolina.

A

NAVY WINGS

The origin of distinctive insignia for naval aviators and other aviation personnel is somewhat obscure, but the idea was undoubtedly influenced by the fact that U.S. Army aviators had been wearing badges since 1913. The first correspondence on the subject appears to have been a letter from the CNO to the Bureau of Navigation, dated 19 July 1917, which forwarded a suggestion from the G. F. Hemsley Company for aviators' caps and collar ornaments, with the comment that the navy did not especially want them, but since foreign countries and the U.S. Army had adopted aviation insignia, naval aviators should also be given "some form of mark or badge to indicate their qualifications, in order that they have standing with other aviation services." The letter enclosed a sample design.

The aviator wing insignia was officially adopted on 7 September 1917, when the secretary of the navy approved Change 12 to the uniform regulations. The pertinent portion read: "A Naval Aviator's device, a winged fouled anchor with the letters *U.S.*, is hereby adopted to be worn by qualified Naval Aviators. This device will be issued by the Bureau of Navigation to Officers and Men of the Navy and Marine Corps who qualify as Naval Aviators, and will be worn on the left breast." Before any such wings were issued, the design was modified by another change dated 12 October 1917, which deleted the letters *U.S.*

One early design for naval aviator's wings may have looked like this.

Correspondence continued with a number of firms concerning the design and production of the insignia. The first wings, made by Bailey, Banks & Biddle of Philadelphia, were received by the navy in December 1917 and issued early the following year. The design was described in more detail in uniform regulations approved on 20 December 1922. Since then, the original design has undergone only a few minor changes.

NFOs can trace the origin of their wings to Rear Adm. William A.

Naval Aviator

Moffett, the first chief of the Bureau of Aeronautics and the first naval aviation observer. NAO wings consisted of a single anchor encompassed by a circle to which wings were affixed. During World War II, specialized NAO wings were used for various NAO specialities (such as radar and navigation). In 1968, most NAOs were redesignated NFOs and the new community adopted a new wing design, featuring a shield with two crossed fouled anchors. NAO wings continued to be worn by certain navy intelligence officers and meteorologists who qualified as aerial observers, as well as marine corps officers who graduated from the Marine Corps Naval Aviation Observer School at New River, North Carolina, and served as aerial spotters.

Marine corps enlisted men and warrant officers serving as navigators wear Marine Aerial Navigator wings, consisting of wings attached to a compass rose on a circular plate with crossed fouled anchors.

Aircrew wings first came into use during World War II. These wings were designated combat aircrew insignia in 1958 and are still worn by marine corps enlisted men and women who qualify by virtue of service as aircrewmen in combat situations. (In 1995, eligibility to wear these wings was expanded to include

Naval Flight Officer

Naval Aviation Observer

Marine Aerial Navigator

Combat Aircrew

sailors who served as aircrewmen in marine corps aircraft in combat situations.) Combat aircrew wings consist of wings attached to a circle encompassing a fouled anchor, with a banner above with three stars, and a banner below with the inscription *AIRCREW*.

Navy personnel who are designated naval aircrewmen wear wings that resemble NAO wings but have the letters *AC* straddling the anchor.

Aircrewman

Navy enlisted personnel, including naval aircrewmen, who have met the requirements (see chapter 7), may wear the wings of the aviation warfare specialist. This insignia consists of wings attached to a shield bearing a fouled anchor, with a banner below inscribed *AIR WARFARE*.

Aviation Warfare Specialist

Flight surgeons' wings have changed several times over the years. The present design features wings attached to an oval bearing the oak leaf with acorn insignia of a physician.

Flight Surgeon

Wings are also worn by a small group of medical service corps personnel designated naval aviation physiologists and naval aviation experimental psychologists. Their wings are similar to those of the flight surgeon, minus the acorn attached to the oak leaf.

Naval Aviation Experimental Psychologist/Physiologist

Special wings are worn by individuals who have qualified as naval parachutists. Their insignia features gold wings attached to an open parachute.

Special variations of the naval aviator and naval flight officer wings are worn by naval astronauts. A shooting star is superimposed on the respective traditional wing designs to symbolize their special qualifications. The naval astronaut (pilot) wings were first pinned on then-commander Alan B. Shepard, the nation's first astronaut, in 1961. Naval astronaut (NFO) wings came into use in 1980.

In 1984, a wing design was created for supply corps officers who qualified as naval aviation supply officers. The design consists of wings attached to the traditional supply corps "pork-chop" oak leaves insignia.

Naval Astronaut

Naval Aviation Supply Officer

B

Naval Aircraft

Prior to 1962, the individual services devised their own alphanumeric systems to identify aircraft and their functions. Since October 1962, all U.S. military aircraft have been designated under a relatively simple common system, albeit with some inconsistencies. The military has adopted a few commercial designs, and these aircraft retain their company designations in military use. Designations are assigned by the Department of Defense in DOD Directive 4120.15 series, published by the air force in cooperation with the other services.

Each aircraft type is assigned a basic mission designator letter and, except in the case of conventional airplanes, a vehicle-type letter symbol, followed by a dash and a numeral indicating the design model. If the aircraft's mission is modified, a mission modification letter will precede the basic mission designator. If the aircraft is modified to or assigned a special status, a status prefix precedes all symbols. A design modification letter will follow the design model number. For example, an F-14D is the fourth modification of the original F-14 fighter. An NTA-4J is the tenth (J) modification of the A-4 attack aircraft, modified to a trainer (T), and modified for permanent special test (N).

Model Designation Series

Status Prefixes

G — Permanently grounded (normally an instructional airframe)
J — Special test (temporary)
N — Special test (permanent)
X — Experimental
Y — Prototype
Z — Planning

Modified Mission Prefixes

A — Attack
C — Transport
D — Drone director
E — Special electronic installation
F — Fighter
H — Search and rescue
K — Tanker
L — Cold weather
M — Multimission
O — Observation
P — Patrol
Q — Drone
R — Reconnaissance
S — Antisubmarine
T — Trainer
U — Utility
V — Staff transport
W — Weather reconnaissance

Basic Mission Designators

A — Attack
B — Bomber
C — Transport
E — Special electronic installation
F — Fighter
O — Observation
P — Patrol
R — Reconnaissance
S — Antisubmarine
T — Trainer
U — Utility
X — Research

Vehicle type

Note: The Vehicle Type symbol is not used for fixed-wing conventional airplanes.

G — Glider
H — Helicopter
S — Spaceplane
V — VSTOL/STOL (vertical short takeoff and landing/ short takeoff and landing)
Z — Lighter-than-air vehicle

In recent years, the trend has been to avoid new series designations of improved designs, instead adding unofficial designation modifiers to denote upgrades (for example, P-3C Update III, EA-6B ICAP II, A-6E SWIP, etc.). This reluctance is in part due to the vast amount of support and paperwork involved in publishing technical manuals for new models. (The trend now is a far cry from the World War II era, when, for example, the sole difference between the SBD-3 and SBD-4 versions of the "Dauntless" dive-bomber was the voltage of the aircraft's electrical system.)

Most military aircraft have popular names, usually created by the manufacturer and approved by the service. In some cases aircraft designs used by more than one service will have a different popular name for each service (the H-3 is a "Sea King" in the navy and was a "Pelican" in coast guard service); in other cases, a formal name used by one service is rarely or never used by another. (In the army, the C-12 is a "Huron," a name rarely used in the navy, whose crews call it by its civilian name, "Super King Air.") Some basic models that undergo radical modification are given new popular names. (For example, the EA-6B "Prowler" vice A-6A "Intruder" and the AH-1 "Sea Cobra" vice UH-1 "Iroquois.") Some designs come to be better known by their nickname than by their assigned popular name. (The use of "Huey" instead of the name "Iroquois" for the H-1 is a famous example.)

Current Inventory of Navy, Marine Corps, and Coast Guard Aircraft

Attack

A-4 Skyhawk

TA-4J—Two-place advanced strike trainer

TA-4J Skyhawk (McDonnell Douglas/ Harry Gann)

Naval Aircraft

A-6 Intruder/Prowler

EA-6B—Carrier-based electronic countermeasures
NEA-6B—EA-6B permanently modified for test roles
A-6E—Long-range medium attack
NA-6E—A-6E modified for permanent test roles

Cargo Transport

C-2 Greyhound

C-2A—Carrier logistics

C-9 Skytrain II

C-9B—Cargo/personnel transport
DC-9—Converted airliner similiar to C-9B

C-12 Huron

UC-12B—Utility transport
RC-12F—Range control aircraft
UC-12F—Utility transport
RC-12M—Range control aircraft
UC-12M—Utility transport

EA-6B Prowler (U.S. Navy/Lt. Cdr. John R. Leenhouts)

A-6E Intruder (U.S. Navy)

C-2A Greyhound (U.S. Navy/Lt. Cdr. John R. Leenhouts)

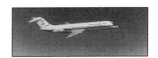

C-9B Skytrain II (McDonnell Douglas/Harry Gann)

UC-12B Huron (Beech Aircraft Corp.)

C-20 Gulfstream III/IV

C-20B—USCG executive transport Gulfstream III
C-20D—Executive transport Gulfstream III
C-20G—Executive transport Gulfstream IV

C-20D Gulfstream III

C-130 Hercules

DC-130A—Drone launch and control (contract)
KC-130F—Tanker/transport
LC-130F—Ski-equipped transport
TC-130G—Logistics for Blue Angels
HC-130H—USCG long-range rescue
KC-130R—Improved tanker/transport
LC-130R—Improved ski-equipped transport
KC-130T—Improved tanker/transport
C-130T—Improved logistics transport

KC-130T Hercules (Lockheed Aeronautical Systems)

Early Warning/Communications

E-2 Hawkeye

E-2C—Carrier-based early warning
TE-2C—Pilot trainer for E-2C

E-6 Mercury

E-6A—Strategic communications relay
E-6B—E-6A with expanded mission avionics

E-2C Hawkeye (U.S. Navy/CWO2 Tony Alleyne)

E-6A Mercury (Boeing)

Fighter

F-5 Tiger II

F-5E—Adversary aircraft
F-5F—Two-place adversary

F-5E Tiger II (Northrop)

F-14 Tomcat/Super Tomcat

F-14A—Carrier-based interceptor
NF-14A—F-14A modified for permanent test roles
F-14B—Interceptor with improved engines
NF-14B—F-14B modified for permanent test roles
F-14D—Interceptor with improved engines and avionics
NF-14D—F-14D modified for permanent test roles

F-14A Tomcat (U.S. Navy/Lt. Cdr. Dave Parsons)

Strike Fighter

F/A-18 Hornet/Super Hornet

F/A-18A—Carrier-based strike fighter
NF/A-18A—F/A-18A modified for permanent test roles
F/A-18B—Two-place version of F/A-18A
F/A-18C—Improved version of F/A-18A
NF/A-18C—F/A-18C modified for permanent test roles
F/A-18D—Two-place version of F/A-18C
NF/A-18D—F/A-18D modified for permanent test roles
F/A-18E—Improved, enlarged strike fighter
F/A-18F—Two-place version of F/A-18E

F/A-18C Hornet (U.S. Navy/CWO2 Tony Alleyne)

Patrol

P-3 Orion

TP-3A—Pilot trainer for P-3
UP-3A—Utility transport
VP-3A—Executive transport
P-3B—P-3A with improved engines
NP-3B—P-3B modified for permanent test roles

P-3C Orion

UP-3B—Utility transport
P-3C—ASW patrol with integrated avionics
NP-3C—P-3C modified for permanent test roles
NP-3D—EP-3A, RP-3A, EP-3B, RP-3D modified for research
EP-3E—Aries I/II electronic reconnaissance
EP-3J—Electronic aggressor

EP-3E Orion

Antisubmarine Warfare

S-3 Viking

S-3A—Carrier-based ASW aircraft
ES-3A—Carrier-based electronic reconnaissance
US-3A—Carrier logistics
S-3B—Improved S-3A

ES-3A Viking (Lockheed)

S-3B Viking (U.S. Navy/CWO2 Tony Alleyne)

Trainer

T-2 Buckeye

T-2C—Basic jet trainer

T-34 Turbo-Mentor

T-34C—Primary trainer
NT-34C—T-34C modified for avionics test

T-39 Sabreliner

T-39D—Utility transport or research
CT-39E—Rapid-response airlift
CT-39G—Stretched CT-39E
T-39N—Contract trainer for flight officers

T-2C Buckeye

T-34C Turbo-Mentor

CT-39G Sabreliner (Harry Gann)

Naval Aircraft

T-44 Pegasus

T-44A—Advanced multiengine trainer

T-45—Goshawk

T-45A—Advanced strike trainer

T-44A Pegasus (Beech Aircraft)

Utility

U-25 Guardian

HU-25A—Medium-range search and rescue
HU-25B—HU-25A equipped with side-looking airborne radar (SLAR)
HU-25C—HU-25A with airborne intercept radar

T-45A Goshawk (McDonnell Douglas)

V/STOL

AV-8 Harrier II

AV-8B—V/STOL attack aircraft
TAV-8B—Two-place trainer for AV-8B

V-22 Osprey

MV-22A—Tilt-rotor assault transport

HU-25A Guardian (U.S. Coast Guard)

Helicopter

H-1 Iroquois

HH-1N—Search and rescue
UH-1N—Utility transport/observation

AV-8B Harrier II+ (McDonnell Douglas)

MV-22A Osprey

UH-1N Iroquois (U.S. Navy/PH3 Henry Cleveland)

AH-1 Super Cobra

AH-1W—Improved gunship with TOW/Hellfire missiles

AH-1W Super Cobra (Bell Textron)

H-2 Seasprite

SH-2G—SH-2F LAMPS with improved engines and avionics

SH-2G Seasprite (Kaman Corp.)

H-3 Sea King

VH-3A—Executive transport
NVH-3A—Test platform for VH-3A/D
VH-3D—Executive transport
SH-3H—Carrier-based ASW/rescue
UH-3H—Utility/rescue/range support

SH-3H Sea King (U.S. Navy)

H-46 Sea Knight

CH-46D—Vertical replenishment
HH-46D—Utility/rescue
UH-46D—Vertical replenishment
CH-46E—Assault transport

CH-46E Sea Knight (U.S. Navy/OS2 John Bouvia)

H-53 Sea Stallion/Super Stallion/Sea Dragon

CH-53D—Heavy assault transport
RH-53D—Mine countermeasures/transport
CH-53E—Three-engine assault transport
MH-53E—Mine countermeasures version of CH-53E

CH-53E Super Stallion (U.S. Navy/CWO Ed Bailey)

MH-53E Sea Dragon

H-57 Sea Ranger
TH-57B—Basic helicopter trainer
TH-57C—Advanced instrument trainer

H-60 Seahawk/Jayhawk/Blackhawk
UH-60A—Trainer for Test Pilot School
SH-60B—Sea-based LAMPS ASW helicopter
NSH-60B—SH-60B modified for permanent test roles
SH-60F—Carrier-based ASW helicopter
YSH-60F—Prototype for SH-60F
HH-60H—Strike rescue version
HH-60J—USCG rescue version
VH-60N—Executive transport
SH-60R—Proposed remanufactured SH-60B/F

H-65 Dolphin
HH-65A—USCG short-range rescue

TH-57 Sea Ranger (Bell Textron)

SH-60B Seahawk (U.S. Navy/PH2 Dave Loveall)

HH-60H Seahawk (U.S. Navy/PH1 David Miller)

HH-65A Dolphin (U.S. Coast Guard)

Miscellaneous Aircraft

The types listed below are mostly non-naval designs used in limited numbers mainly by test establishments. Some are on loan to the navy from other services, and some are operated for the navy by contractors:

VC-4A Gulfstream—USCG Logistics Support
TC-18F (Boeing 707)—Crew trainer for E-6
EC-24A (DC-8)—Electronic aggressor
NKC-135A Stratotanker—Electronic aggressor
YF-4J Phantom II—Ejection-seat test

QF-4N Phantom II—Target drone
QF-86F Sabre—Target drone
RG-8A Condor—USCG surveillance
T-38A Talon—Test Pilot School trainer
T-38B Talon—Test Pilot School trainer
U-6A Beaver—Test Pilot School trainer
NU-1B Otter—Test Pilot School trainer
U-21A Ute—Test Pilot School trainer
RU-38A Twin Condor—USCG surveillance
X-26A—Test Pilot School powered glider
X-31A—Research aircraft
OH-6B Cayuse—Test Pilot School trainer
OH-58A Kiowa—Test Pilot School trainer

C

Naval Aviation Ships

Active Aircraft Carriers

| Hull | Ship Name | Commissioned | Home Port |

Forrestal Class
CV 62 *Independence* 10 Jan. 1959 Yokosuka, Japan

Note: The *Independence* is slated for decommissioning in fiscal year 1998.

***Enterprise* Class**
CVN 65 *Enterprise* 25 Nov. 1961 Norfolk, Va.

***Kitty Hawk* Class**
CV 63 *Kitty Hawk* 29 Apr. 1961 North Island, Calif.
CV 64 *Constellation* 27 Oct. 1961 North Island, Calif.
CV 66 *America* 23 Jan. 1965 Norfolk, Va.

Note: The *Constellation* is slated to replace the *Independence* in Japan when the *Independence* is decommissioned. The *America* is slated to be decommissioned in 1996. The *Kitty Hawk* is scheduled for decommissioning in fiscal year 2002.

| Hull | Ship Name | Commissioned | Home Port |

John F. Kennedy Class

| CV 67 | John F. Kennedy | 7 Sep. 1968 | Mayport, Fla. |

Note: The *John F. Kennedy* is a Naval Reserve Force ship whose primary mission is training. It remains a deployable combatant.

Nimitz Class

CVN 68	*Nimitz*	3 May 1975	North Island, Calif.
CVN 69	*Dwight D. Eisenhower*	18 Oct. 1977	Norfolk, Va.
CVN 70	*Carl Vinson*	13 Mar. 1982	Alameda, Calif.
CVN 71	*Theodore Roosevelt*	25 Oct. 1986	Norfolk, Va.
CVN 72	*Abraham Lincoln*	11 Nov. 1989	Alameda, Calif.
CVN 73	*George Washington*	4 July 1992	Norfolk, Va.
CVN 74	*John C. Stennis*	9 Dec. 1995	Norfolk, Va.
CVN 75	*Harry S. Truman*	(under construction)	
CVN 76	*Ronald Reagan*	(under construction)	

Note: The *Nimitz* will change home port to North Island in fiscal year 2001 after a refueling overhaul in Newport News, Va. The *Carl Vinson* is scheduled to change home port to Bremerton, Wash., in late 1996. The *Abraham Lincoln* will change home port to Everett, Wash., in late 1996. The *John C. Stennis* will work up at Norfolk, Va., before moving to North Island during fiscal year 1998. The *Harry S. Truman* and *Ronald Reagan* are slated to be based at Norfolk and North Island, respectively.

Amphibious Assault Ships

Iwo Jima Class

| LPH 9 | *Guam* | 16 Jan. 1965 | Norfolk, Va. |
| LPH 11 | *New Orleans* | 16 Nov. 1968 | San Diego, Calif. |

Note: These LPHs are scheduled for decommissioning as LHDs join the fleet. The *Inchon* (LPH 12) was redesignated a mine countermeasures support ship (MCS) in March 1995.

Tarawa Class

LHA 1	*Tarawa*	29 May 1976	Long Beach, Calif.
LHA 2	*Saipan*	15 Oct. 1977	Norfolk, Va.
LHA 3	*Belleau Wood*	23 Sep. 1978	Sasebo, Japan

Hull	Ship Name	Commissioned	Home Port
LHA 4	*Nassau*	28 July 1979	Norfolk, Va.
LHA 5	*Peleliu*	3 May 1980	San Diego, Calif.

Wasp Class
LHD 1	*Wasp*	29 July 1988	Norfolk, Va.
LHD 2	*Essex*	19 Oct. 1992	San Diego, Calif.
LHD 3	*Kearsarge*	25 Sep. 1993	Norfolk, Va.
LHD 4	*Boxer*	11 Feb. 1995	San Diego, Calif.
LHD 5	*Bataan*	(under construction)	
LHD 6	*Bon Homme Richard*	(under construction)	
LHD 7	(unnamed)	(construction authorized)	

Mine Countermeasures Support Ships

***Inchon* Class** (Modified *Iwo Jima* Class LPH)
MCS 12	*Inchon*	20 June 1970	Ingleside, Tex.

Surface Warships

The following classes of surface warfare ships routinely operate with detachments of SH-60 or reserve SH-2 LAMPS helicopters on board:

Ticonderoga-class guided-missile cruisers (CG)
Arleigh Burke-class guided-missile destroyers (DDG) (Flight IIA)
Kidd-class guided-missile destroyers (DDG)
Spruance-class destroyers (DD)
Oliver Hazard Perry-class guided-missile frigates (FFG)

Replenishment Ships

The following classes of replenishment ships routinely operate with H-46 vertical replenishment helicopters on board:

Kilauea-class ammunition ships (AE)
Ex-British combat stores ships (T-AFS)
Mars-class combat stores ships (AFS)

Supply-class fast combat support ships (AOE)
Sacramento-class fast combat support ships (AOE)
Wichita-class replenishment oilers (AOR)

Aviation Logistic Ships (AVB)

The following ships provide maintenance and logistic support for forward-deployed marine corps aircraft units. They have helicopter pads but do not regularly embark helicopters.

Converted *Seabridge*-class ships (AVB)

D

Naval Aircraft Squadrons

Designation	Nickname	Homeport	Code	Aircraft
Helicopter Combat Support Squadrons (HC)				
HC-2	Circuit Riders	NAS Norfolk	HU	VH-3A, UH-3H
HC-3†	Pack Rats	NAS North Island	SA	CH/HH/UH-46D
HC-4	Black Stallions	NAS Sigonella	HC	MH-53E
HC-5	Providers	NAS Agana, Guam	RB	HH-46D
HC-6	Chargers	NAS Norfolk	HW	CH/HH/UH-46D
HC-8	Dragon Whales	NAS Norfolk	BR	CH/HH/UH-46D
HC-11	Gunbearers	NAS North Island	VR	CH/HH/UH-46D, UH-3H
HC-85*	Golden Gaters	NAS North Island	NW	UH-3H, SH-3H

Note: HC-2 also serves as an FRS for the H-3 helicopter. HC-5 is slated to move from NAS Agana when the base is closed.

Helicopter Combat Support Special Squadrons (HCS)

Designation	Nickname	Homeport	Code	Aircraft
HCS-4*	Red Wolves	NAS Norfolk	NW	HH-60H
HCS-5*	Firehawks	NAWS Point Mugu	NW	HH-60H

* = Reserve squadron
† = Fleet Readiness Squadron
‡ = Uses code of wing to which assigned

Designation   Nickname   Homeport   Code Aircraft

Helicopter Mine Countermeasures Squadrons (HM)

Designation	Nickname	Homeport	Code	Aircraft
HM-14	Vanguard	NAS Norfolk	BJ	MH-53E
HM-15	Blackhawks	Moffett Field	TB	MH-53E

Note: Both HM squadrons are joint active/reserve squadrons.

Helicopter Antisubmarine Squadrons (HS)

Designation	Nickname	Homeport	Code	Aircraft
HS-1†	Sea Horses	NAS Jacksonville	AR	SH-60F
HS-2	Golden Falcons	NAS North Island	‡	SH-60F, HH-60H
HS-3	Tridents	NAS Jacksonville	‡	SH-60F, HH-60H
HS-4	Black Knights	NAS North Island	‡	SH-60F, HH-60H
HS-5	Night Dippers	NAS Jacksonville	‡	SH-60F, HH-60H
HS-6	Indians	NAS North Island	‡	SH-60F, HH-60H
HS-7	Dusty Dogs	NAS Jacksonville	‡	SH-60F, HH-60H
HS-8	Eightballers	NAS North Island	‡	SH-60F, HH-60H
HS-10†	Warhawks	NAS North Island	‡	SH-60F
HS-11	Dragonslayers	NAS Jacksonville	‡	SH-60F, HH-60H
HS-14	Chargers	NAF Atsugi	‡	SH-60F, HH-60H
HS-15	Red Lions	NAS Jacksonville	‡	SH-60F, HH-60H
HS-75*	Emerald Knights	NAS Jacksonville	NW	SH-3H

Helicopter Antisubmarine Squadrons Light (HSL)

Designation	Nickname	Homeport	Code	Aircraft
HSL-37	Easy Riders	NAS Barbers Point	TH	SH-60B
HSL-40†	Air Wolves	NS Mayport	HK	SH-60B
HSL-41†	Seahawks	NAS North Island	TS	SH-60B
HSL-42	Proud Warriors	NS Mayport	HN	SH-60B
HSL-43	Battlecats	NAS North Island	TT	SH-60B
HSL-44	Swamp Foxes	NS Mayport	HP	SH-60B
HSL-45	Wolfpack	NAS North Island	TZ	SH-60B
HSL-46	Grandmasters	NS Mayport	HQ	SH-60B
HSL-47	Saberhawks	NAS North Island	TY	SH-60B
HSL-48	Vipers	NS Mayport	HR	SH-60B
HSL-49	Scorpions	NAS North Island	TX	SH-60B
HSL-51	Warlords	NAF Atsugi	TA	SH-60B
HSL-84*	Thunderbolts	NAS North Island	NW	SH-2G
HSL-94*	Titans	NAS Willow Grove	NW	SH-2G

Designation   Nickname   Homeport   Code   Aircraft

Helicopter Training Squadrons (HT)

HT-8	Eightballers	NAS Whiting Field	E	TH-57B/C
HT-18	Vigilant Eagles	NAS Whiting Field	E	TH-57B/C

Attack Squadrons (VA)

VA-34	Blue Blasters	NAS Oceana	‡	A-6E
VA-75	Sunday Punchers	NAS Oceana	‡	A-6E
VA-115	Eagles	NAF Atsugi	‡	A-6E
VA-165	Boomers	NAS Whidbey Is.	‡	A-6E
VA-196	Main Battery	NAS Whidbey Is.	‡	A-6E

Note: With the planned phaseout of the A-6 aircraft from carrier air wings by 1997, all attack squadrons will be disestablished, or redesignated as they re-equip with F/A-18 aircraft (as VA-34, VA-75, and VA-115 are slated).

Tactical Electronic Warfare Squadrons (VAQ)

VAQ-129†	Vikings	NAS Whidbey Is.	‡	EA-6B
VAQ-130	Zappers	NAS Whidbey Is.	‡	EA-6B
VAQ-131	Lancers	NAS Whidbey Is.	‡	EA-6B
VAQ-132	Scorpions	NAS Whidbey Is.	‡	EA-6B
VAQ-133	Wizards	NAS Whidbey Is.	‡	EA-6B
VAQ-134	Garudas	NAS Whidbey Is.	‡	EA-6B
VAQ-135	Black Ravens	NAS Whidbey Is.	‡	EA-6B
VAQ-136	Gauntlets	NAF Atsugi	‡	EA-6B
VAQ-138	Yellowjackets	NAS Whidbey Is.	‡	EA-6B
VAQ-139	Cougars	NAS Whidbey Is.	‡	EA-6B
VAQ-140	Patriots	NAS Whidbey Is.	‡	EA-6B
VAQ-141	Shadowhawks	NAS Whidbey Is.	‡	EA-6B
VAQ-209*	Star Warriors	NAF Washington	‡	EA-6B

Note: VAQ-137, VAQ-142, and one additional squadron are slated to be established to provide electronic support to air force wings along with VAQ-134.

Airborne Early Warning Squadrons (VAW)

VAW-77*	Night Wolf	NAS Atlanta	AF	E-2C

Note: Although it bears the VAW designation, VAW-77 is not a carrier-capable squadron, hence its Airborne Early Warning Squadron designation. VAW-77 has replaced VAW-122 in drug interdiction and fleet support roles.

Designation	Nickname	Homeport	Code	Aircraft

Carrier Airborne Early Warning Squadrons (VAW)

Designation	Nickname	Homeport	Code	Aircraft
VAW-78*	Fighting Escargots	NAS Norfolk	‡	E-2C
VAW-112	Golden Hawks	NAS Miramar	‡	E-2C
VAW-113	Black Hawks	NAS Miramar	‡	E-2C
VAW-115	Sentinels	NAF Atsugi	‡	E-2C
VAW-116	Sun Kings	NAS Miramar	‡	E-2C
VAW-117	Wallbangers	NAS Miramar	‡	E-2C
VAW-120†	Cyclones	NAS Norfolk	‡	E-2C, C-2A
VAW-121	Bluetails	NAS Norfolk	‡	E-2C
VAW-123	Screwtops	NAS Norfolk	‡	E-2C
VAW-124	Bear Aces	NAS Norfolk	‡	E-2C
VAW-125	Tigertails	NAS Norfolk	‡	E-2C
VAW-126	Seahawks	NAS Norfolk	‡	E-2C

Note: The Miramar-based squadrons will move to NAS North Island with the change of Miramar from a naval air station to a marine corps air station.

Composite Squadrons (VC)

Designation	Nickname	Homeport	Code	Aircraft
VC-6	Skeet for the Fleet	NAS Norfolk	JG	Drones
VC-8	Redtails	NS Roosevelt Rds.	GF	TA-4J, UH-3H

Fighter Squadrons (VF)

Designation	Nickname	Homeport	Code	Aircraft
VF-2	Bounty Hunters	NAS Oceana	‡	F-14D
VF-11	Red Rippers	NAS Miramar	‡	F-14D
VF-14	Tophatters	NAS Oceana	‡	F-14A
VF-24	Fighting Renegades	NAS Miramar	‡	F-14A
VF-31	Tomcatters	NAS Miramar	‡	F-14D
VF-32	Swordsmen	NAS Oceana	‡	F-14A
VF-41	Black Aces	NAS Oceana	‡	F-14A
VF-101†	Grim Reapers	NAS Oceana	‡	F-14A/B/D, T-34C
VF-102	Diamondbacks	NAS Oceana	‡	F-14B
VF-103	Jolly Rogers	NAS Oceana	‡	F-14B
VF-143	Dogs	NAS Oceana	‡	F-14B
VF-154	Black Knights	NAF Atsugi	‡	F-14A
VF-201*	Hunters	NAS Ft. Worth	‡	F-14A
VF-211	Fighting Checkmates	NAS Miramar	‡	F-14A

Designation	Nickname	Homeport	Code	Aircraft
VF-213	Black Lions	NAS Miramar	‡	F-14A

Note: VF squadrons assigned to NAS Miramar are slated to move to NAS Oceana by 1997. VF-24 is slated for disestablishment by 1997.

Strike Fighter Squadrons (VFA)

Designation	Nickname	Homeport	Code	Aircraft
VFA-15	Valions	NAS Cecil Field	‡	F/A-18C
VFA-22	Fighting Redcocks	NAS Lemoore	‡	F/A-18C
VFA-25	Fist of the Fleet	NAS Lemoore	‡	F/A-18C
VFA-27	Chargers	NAS Lemoore	‡	F/A-18C
VFA-37	Bulls	NAS Cecil Field	‡	F/A-18C
VFA-81	Sunliners	NAS Cecil Field	‡	F/A-18C
VFA-82	Marauders	NAS Cecil Field	‡	F/A-18C
VFA-83	Rampagers	NAS Cecil Field	‡	F/A-18C
VFA-86	Sidewinders	NAS Cecil Field	‡	F/A-18C
VFA-87	Golden Warriors	NAS Cecil Field	‡	F/A-18C
VFA-94	Mighty Shrikes	NAS Lemoore	‡	F/A-18C
VFA-97	Warhawks	NAS Lemoore	‡	F/A-18C
VFA-105	Gunslingers	NAS Cecil Field	‡	F/A-18C
VFA-106†	Gladiators	NAS Cecil Field	‡	F/A-18A/B/C/D, T-34C
VFA-113	Stingers	NAS Lemoore	‡	F/A-18C
VFA-125†	Rough Riders	NAS Lemoore	‡	F/A-18A/B/C/D, T-34C
VFA-131	Wildcats	NAS Cecil Field	‡	F/A-18C
VFA-136	Knighthawks	NAS Cecil Field	‡	F/A-18C
VFA-137	Kestrels	NAS Lemoore	‡	F/A-18C
VFA-146	Blue Diamonds	NAS Lemoore	‡	F/A-18C
VFA-147	Argonauts	NAS Lemoore	‡	F/A-18C
VFA-151	Vigilantes	NAS Lemoore	‡	F/A-18C
VFA-192	World Famous Golden Dragons	NAF Atsugi	‡	F/A-18C
VFA-195	Dambusters	NAF Atsugi	‡	F/A-18C
VFA-203*	Blue Dolphins	NAS Cecil Field	‡	F/A-18A
VFA-204*	River Rattlers	NAS New Orleans	‡	F/A-18A

Note: All active squadrons based at Cecil Field are slated to move to NAS Oceana by the end of the 1990s.

Designation Nickname   Homeport   Code Aircraft

Fighter Composite Squadrons (VFC)
Designation	Nickname	Homeport	Code	Aircraft
VFC-12*	Fighting Omars	NAS Oceana	‡	F/A-18A/B
VFC-13*	Saints	NAS Fallon	‡	F-5E/F

Patrol Squadrons (VP)
Designation	Nickname	Homeport	Code	Aircraft
VP-1	Screaming Eagles	NAS Whidbey Is.	YB	P-3C
VP-4	Skinny Dragons	NAS Barbers Pt.	YD	P-3C
VP-5	Mad Foxes	NAS Jacksonville	LA	P-3C
VP-8	Tigers	NAS Brunswick	LC	P-3C
VP-9	Golden Eagles	NAS Barbers Pt.	PD	P-3C
VP-10	Lancers	NAS Brunswick	LD	P-3C
VP-11	Proud Pegasus	NAS Brunswick	LE	P-3C
VP-16	Eagles	NAS Jacksonville	LF	P-3C
VP-26	Tridents	NAS Brunswick	LK	P-3C
VP-30†	Pro's Nest	NAS Jacksonville	LL	P-3C, TP-3A, UP-3A, VP-3A
VP-40	Fighting Marlins	NAS Whidbey Is.	QE	P-3C
VP-45	Pelicans	NAS Jacksonville	LN	P-3C
VP-46	Grey Knights	NAS Whidbey Is.	RC	P-3C
VP-47	Golden Swordsmen	NAS Barbers Pt.	RD	P-3C
VP-62*	Broadarrows	NAS Jacksonville	LT	P-3C
VP-64*	Condors	NAS Willow Grove	LU	P-3C
VP-65*	Tridents	NAWS Point Mugu	PG	P-3C
VP-66*	Liberty Bells	NAS Willow Grove	LV	P-3C, EP-3J
VP-68*	Blackhawks	NAF Washington	LW	P-3C
VP-69*	Totems	NAS Whidbey Is.	PJ	P-3C
VP-91*	Stingers	Moffett Fld.	PM	P-3C
VP-92*	Minutemen	NAS Brunswick	LY	P-3C
VP-94*	Crawfishers	NAS New Orleans	PZ	P-3C

Note: Squadrons based at NAS Barbers Pt. are slated to move to MCAF Kaneohe Bay when Barbers Pt. closes. VP-11 and VP-68 are slated for disestablishment.

Patrol Squadron Special Projects Units (VPU)
Designation	Nickname	Homeport	Code	Aircraft
VPU-1	Old Buzzards	NAS Brunswick	–	P-3B/C
VPU-2	Wizards	NAS Barbers Pt.	SP	P-3C, UP-3A

Fleet Air Reconnaissance Squadrons (VQ)
Designation	Nickname	Homeport	Code	Aircraft
VQ-1	World Watchers	NAS Whidbey Is.	PR	EP-3E, UP-3A/B

Designation	Nickname	Homeport	Code	Aircraft
VQ-2	Batmen	NS Rota	JQ	EP-3E, P-3C
VQ-5	Black Ravens	NAS North Island	SS	ES-3A, S-3A
VQ-6	Sea Shadows	NAS Cecil Field	‡	ES-3A

Strategic Communications Squadrons (VQ)

VQ-3	Ironmen	Tinker AFB	TC	E-6A
VQ-4	Shadows	Tinker AFB	HL	E-6A

Note: Strategic Communications Squadrons retain the VQ designation associated with their former designations as Fleet Air Reconnaissance Squadrons.

Fleet Logistic Support Squadrons (VR, VRC)

VR-46*	Peach Airlines	NAS Atlanta	JS	DC-9
VR-48*		NAF Washington	JR	C-20G
VR-52*	Taskmasters	NAS Willow Grove	JT	DC-9
VR-53	Capital Express	NAF Washington	WV	C-130T
VR-54*	Revelers	NAS New Orleans	CW	C-130T
VR-55*	Bicentennial Minutemen	Moffett Field	RU	C-130T
VR-56*	Globemasters	NAS Norfolk	JU	C-9B
VR-57*	Conquistadors	NAS North Island	RX	C-9B
VR-58*	Sun Seekers	NAS Jacksonville	JV	C-9B
VR-59*	Lone Star Express	NAS Ft. Worth	RY	C-9B
VR-61*	Islanders	NAS Whidbey Is.	RS	DC-9
VR-62*	Mass Transit	NAS Brunswick	JW	C-130T
VRC-30	Fighting Providers	NAS North Island	RW	C-2A, UC-12B, CT-39E
VRC-40	Rawhides	NAS Norfolk	JK	C-2A

Sea Control Squadrons (VS)

VS-21	Fighting Redtails	NAF Atsugi	‡	S-3B
VS-22	Vidars	NAS Cecil Field	‡	S-3B
VS-24	Scouts	NAS Cecil Field	‡	S-3B
VS-29	Screaming Dragonfires	NAS North Island	‡	S-3B
VS-30	Diamondcutters	NAS Cecil Field	‡	S-3B
VS-31	Topcats	NAS Cecil Field	‡	S-3B
VS-32	Maulers	NAS Cecil Field	‡	S-3B
VS-33	Screwbirds	NAS North Island	‡	S-3B
VS-35	Blue Wolves	NAS North Island	‡	S-3B

Designation	Nickname	Homeport	Code	Aircraft
VS-38	Red Griffins	NAS North Island	‡	S-3B
VS-41†	Shamrocks	NAS North Island	‡	S-3B, S-3A

Note: VS squadrons based at NAS Cecil Field are slated to move to NAS Jacksonville when Cecil Field closes.

Training Squadrons (VT)

Designation	Nickname	Homeport	Code	Aircraft
VT-2	Doer Birds	NAS Whiting Field	E	T-34C
VT-3	Red Knights	NAS Whiting Field	E	T-34C
VT-4	Warbucks	NAS Pensacola	F	T-2C
VT-6	Shooters	NAS Whiting Field	E	T-34C
VT-7	Eagles	NAS Meridian	A	TA-4J
VT-10	Wildcats	NAS Pensacola	F	T-34C, T-39N
VT-19	Attack Frogs	NAS Meridian	A	T-2C
VT-21	Red Hawks	NAS Kingsville	B	T-45A
VT-22	King Eagles	NAS Kingsville	B	T-45A
VT-23	Professionals	NAS Meridian	A	T-2C
VT-27	Boomers	NAS Corpus Christi	G	T-34C
VT-28	Rangers	NAS Corpus Christi	G	T-34C
VT-31	Wise Owls	NAS Corpus Christi	G	T-44A
VT-86	Sabre Hawks	NAS Pensacola	F	T-2C, T-39N

Air Test and Evaluation Squadrons (VX)

Designation	Nickname	Homeport	Code	Aircraft
VX-1	Pioneers	NAS Patuxent River	JA	P-3C, SH-3H, SH-60B/F, HH-60H
VX-9	Evaluators	NAWS China Lake NAWS Point Mugu (detachment)	XE	F-14A/B/D, F/A-18A/B/C/D, A-6E, AV-8B, AH-1W, TA-4J, EA-6B

Antarctic Development Squadrons (VXE)

Designation	Nickname	Homeport	Code	Aircraft
VXE-6	Puckered Penguins	NAWS Point Mugu	XD	LC-130F/R

E

MARINE CORPS AIRCRAFT SQUADRONS

Squadron   Nickname   Home Base   Code   Aircraft

Marine Heavy Helicopter Squadrons (HMH)

Squadron	Nickname	Home Base	Code	Aircraft
HMH-361	Flying Tigers	MCAS Tustin	YN	CH-53E
HMH-362	Ugly Angels	MCAF Kaneohe Bay	YL	CH-53D
HMH-363	Red Lions	MCAS Tustin	YZ	CH-53D
HMH-366		MCAF Kaneohe Bay	HH	CH-53D
HMH-461	Sea Stallions	MCAS New River	CJ	CH-53E
HMH-462	Heavy Haulers	MCAS Tustin	YF	CH-53E
HMH-463	Heavy Haulers	MCAF Kaneohe Bay	YH	CH-53D
HMH-464	Condors	MCAS New River	EN	CH-53E
HMH-465	Warhorses	MCAS Tustin	YJ	CH-53E
HMH-466		MCAS Tustin	YK	CH-53E
HMH-769*	Roadhogs	NAS Alameda	MS	RH-53D
HMH-772*		NAS Willow Grove	MT	RH-53D

Note: HMH-363 is slated to move to MCAF Kaneohe Bay during 1996. All other Tustin-based units will move to other bases in southern California. HMH-769 is slated to move from NAS Alameda when that base closes.

* = Reserve squadron
† = Fleet Readiness Squadron
‡ = Detachment at NAS New Orleans

Squadron   Nickname   Home Base   Code   Aircraft

Marine Helicopter Squadron (HMX)

HMX-1		MCAF Quantico	MX	VH-3D, VH-60N, CH-46E, CH-53D/E

Marine Helicopter Light Attack Squadrons (HMLA)

Squadron	Nickname	Home Base	Code	Aircraft
HMLA-167		MCAS New River	TV	UH-1N, AH-1W
HMLA-169	Vipers	MCAS Camp Pendleton	SN	UH-1N, AH-1W
HMLA-267	Black Aces	MCAS Camp Pendleton	UV	UH-1N, AH-1W
HMLA-269	Sea Cobras	MCAS New River	HF	UH-1N, AH-1W
HMLA-367	Scarface	MCAS Camp Pendleton	VT	UH-1N, AH-1W
HMLA-369	Gunfighters	MCAS Camp Pendleton	SM	UH-1N, AH-1W
HMLA-773*	Cobras	NAS Atlanta	MP	UH-1N, AH-1W
HMLA-775*‡	Coyotes	MCAS Camp Pendleton	WR	UH-1N, AH-1W

Marine Medium Helicopter Squadrons (HMM)

Squadron	Nickname	Home Base	Code	Aircraft
HMM-161		MCAS Tustin	YR	CH-46E
HMM-162		MCAS New River	YS	CH-46E
HMM-163	Ridgerunners	MCAS Tustin	YP	CH-46E
HMM-164		MCAS Tustin	YT	CH-46E
HMM-165		MCAF Kaneohe Bay	YW	CH-46E
HMM-166	Sea Elk	MCAS Tustin	YX	CH-46E
HMM-261		MCAS New River	EM	CH-46E
HMM-262	Flying Tigers	MCAS Futenma	ET	CH-46E
HMM-263		MCAS New River	EG	CH-46E
HMM-264		MCAS New River	EH	CH-46E
HMM-265		MCAF Futenma	EP	CH-46E
HMM-266	Griffins	MCAS New River	ES	CH-46E
HMM-268		MCAS Tustin	YQ	CH-46E
HMM-364		MCAF Kaneohe Bay	PF	CH-46E
HMM-365		MCAS New River	YM	CH-46E
HMM-764*		MCAS El Toro	ML	CH-46E
HMM-774*		NAS Norfolk	MQ	CH-46E

Note: All Tustin- and El Toro-based HMM squadrons are slated to move to other bases in southern California. The two Kaneohe Bay-based HMM squadrons are slated to move to bases in the CONUS.

Squadron   Nickname   Home Base   Code   Aircraft

Marine Helicopter Training Squadrons (HMT)
Squadron	Nickname	Home Base	Code	Aircraft
HMT-204		MCAS New River	GX	CH-46E
HMT-301		MCAF Kaneohe Bay	SU	CH-53D
HMT-302		MCAS New River	UT	CH-53E, MH-53E
HMT-303		MCAS Camp Pendleton	QT	UH-1N, AH-1W

Note: HMT-302 is slated to move to MCAS New River from MCAS Tustin in 1996.

Marine Attack Squadrons (VMA)
Squadron	Nickname	Home Base	Code	Aircraft
VMA-211	Wake Island Avengers	MCAS Yuma	CF	AV-8B
VMA-214	Black Sheep	MCAS Yuma	WE	AV-8B
VMA-223	Bulldogs	MCAS Cherry Point	WP	AV-8B
VMA-231	Ace of Spades	MCAS Cherry Point	CG	AV-8B
VMA-311	Tomcats	MCAS Yuma	WL	AV-8B
VMA-513	Flying Nightmares	MCAS Yuma	WF	AV-8B
VMA-542	Flying Tigers	MCAS Cherry Point	WH	AV-8B

Marine Attack Training Squadrons (VMAT)
Squadron	Nickname	Home Base	Code	Aircraft
VMAT-203	Hawks	MCAS Cherry Point	KD	AV-8B, TAV-8B

Marine Tactical Electronic Warfare Squadrons (VMAQ)
Squadron	Nickname	Home Base	Code	Aircraft
VMAQ-1	Banshees	MCAS Cherry Point	CB	EA-6B
VMAQ-2	Panthers	MCAS Cherry Point	CY	EA-6B
VMAQ-3	Moon Dogs	MCAS Cherry Point	MD	EA-6B
VMAQ-4	Seahawks	MCAS Cherry Point	RM	EA-6B

Marine Fighter Attack Squadrons (VMFA)
Squadron	Nickname	Home Base	Code	Aircraft
VMFA-112*	Cowboys	NAS Dallas	MA	F/A-18A
VMFA-115	Silver Eagles	MCAS Beaufort	VE	F/A-18A
VMFA-122	Crusaders	MCAS Beaufort	DC	F/A-18A
VMFA-134	Smokes	NAS Miramar	MF	F/A-18A
VMFA-142*	Flying Gators	NAS Cecil Field	MB	F/A-18A
VMFA-212	Lancers	NAS Miramar	WD	F/A-18C

Squadron	Nickname	Home Base	Code	Aircraft
VMFA-232	Red Devils	NAS Miramar	WT	F/A-18C
VMFA-235	Death Angels	NAS Miramar	DB	F/A-18C
VMFA-251	Thunderbolts	MCAS Beaufort	DW	F/A-18C
VMFA-312	Checkerboards	MCAS Beaufort	DR	F/A-18C
VMFA-314	Black Knights	NAS Miramar	VW	F/A-18C
VMFA-321*	Hell's Angels	NAF Washington	MG	F/A-18A/B
VMFA-323	Death Rattlers	NAS Miramar	WS	F/A-18C
VMFA-451	Warlords	MCAS Beaufort	VM	F/A-18A

Note: VMFA-235 and VMFA-451 are slated for deactivation during fiscal year 1998.

Marine All-Weather Fighter Attack Squadrons (VMFA(AW))

Squadron	Nickname	Home Base	Code	Aircraft
VMFA(AW)-121	Green Knights	NAS Miramar	VK	F/A-18D
VMFA(AW)-224	Bengals	MCAS Beaufort	WK	F/A-18D
VMFA(AW)-225	Vikings	NAS Miramar	CE	F/A-18D
VMFA(AW)-242	Batmen	NAS Miramar	DT	F/A-18D
VMFA(AW)-332	Polka Dots	MCAS Beaufort	EA	F/A-18D
VMFA(AW)-533	Hawks	MCAS Beaufort	ED	F/A-18D

Marine Fighter Attack Training Squadrons (VMFAT)

Squadron	Nickname	Home Base	Code	Aircraft
VMAT-101†	Sharpshooters	MCAS El Toro (moving to NAS Miramar)	SH	F/A-18A/B/C/D, T-34C

Marine Fighter Training Squadron (VMFT)

Squadron	Nickname	Home Base	Code	Aircraft
VMFT-401*	Snipers	MCAS Yuma	WB	F-5E/F

Marine Aerial Refueler Transport Squadrons (VMGR)

Squadron	Nickname	Home Base	Code	Aircraft
VMGR-152		MCAS Futenma	QD	KC-130F
VMGR-234*	Thundering Herd	NAS Ft. Worth	QH	KC-130T
VMGR-252	Heavy Haulers	MCAS Cherry Point	BH	KC-130F/R
WMGR-352		MCAS El Toro	QB	KC-130F/R
VMGR-452*	Yankees	Stewart Field	NY	KC-130F/T

Marine Aerial Refueler Transport Training Squadrons (VMGRT)

Squadron	Nickname	Home Base	Code	Aircraft
VMGRT-253†	Titans	MCAS Cherry Point	GR	KC-130F

F

SQUADRON AIRCRAFT MARKINGS

Tail Codes

Navy and marine corps aircraft assigned to squadrons or units are usually marked with one-letter, two-letter, or number-letter combination codes displayed on vertical tail surfaces and upper starboard wing surfaces. The Office of the Chief of Naval Operations (OPNAV code N880G) assigns these codes in accordance with the visual identification system, and they are promulgated annually in the Naval Aeronautical Organization publication (OPNAV Notice 5400). Once assigned to a wing or squadron, codes are rarely changed, even if the unit is transferred from one fleet to the other. (This is most noticeable among marine corps squadrons.) When a unit is disestablished, its tail code can be reassigned.

Navy and marine corps units assigned to the Atlantic Fleet have two-letter codes with the first letter taken from the first half of the alphabet (A through M). Units assigned to the Pacific Fleet use codes with the first letter taken from the second half of the alphabet (N through Z). In both fleets, the second letter may be any letter of the alphabet. The letters I and O are not used in either first or second position because they can be mistaken for the numerals 1 and 0.

Units assigned to the Naval Air Training Command, including air stations, use single letter codes taken from letters A though G. Other air stations and naval air reserve units use number-letter combinations (i.e., 5F, 8G, etc.).

Most navy carrier squadrons do not have individual tail codes assigned; they wear the code of the carrier air wing to which they are assigned. Carrier squadrons that deploy in detachments either wear their unit-assigned tail code, or wear the code of the carrier air wing to which they are assigned. Marine Corps squadrons assigned to carrier air wings will usually temporarily adopt the code of that wing.

Aircraft assigned to carrier air wings and air stations will usually display the name of the ship or station to which they are assigned (i.e., USS *George Washington,* or NAS Jacksonville).

Side Numbers

Required by a navy instruction (OPNAVINST 3710.7 series), most navy aircraft have a one-, two-, or three-digit number painted on the side of the fuselage, usually on the nose of the aircraft, and often repeated in total or in part on the flaps, vertical stabilizer, or nose landing gear doors. These numbers are used extensively as call-sign suffixes, for easy identification within the squadron for ground and deck handling, and for air traffic control. Many squadrons, such as patrol and transport squadrons, use the last three digits of the aircraft's Bureau Number as the side number.

Carrier squadrons, which share the same tail code, are required to bear side numbers according to a standard system as laid forth in the 3710.7 instruction. The system, detailed below, is occasionally changed or temporarily modified to adjust for changes in air wing structure. (The numerals 8 and 9 are not supposed to be used on operational carrier air wing aircraft and other combat aircraft because the side numbers are used in air traffic control Identification Friend-or-Foe (IFF) systems, which are binary-octal coded and do not recognize those numerals.) The system also specifies an assigned color, often applied to aircraft fin caps and other markings.

Carrier Air Wing Side Number and Color Assignments

Squadron	Side Number Series	Color
VF	100-117	Insignia Red
First VFA	200-217	Orange-Yellow
Second VFA	300-317	Light Blue
Third VFA	400-417	International Orange
VA	500-524	Light Green
VAW	600-603	Insignia Blue
HS	610-617	Magenta
VAQ	620-624	Maroon
VS	700-713	Dark Green
VQ detachment	720-727 or 760-767	
VRC detachment	various	

Although largely symbolic, the squadron aircraft bearing the side numbers ending in 00 are assigned for use by the carrier air wing commander. Those with numbers ending in 01 are assigned to the squadron commanding officers, and those ending in 02 are assigned to squadron executive officers.

Individual Unit Markings

Naval aircraft have a long tradition of wearing the insignia, logo, or some other stylized markings identifying them with the squadron nickname or other tradition. These markings are unofficial, and their splendor is determined and often limited by the squadron, wing, or fleet commander. The advent of the low-visibility Tactical Paint Scheme on combat aircraft in the 1980s severely limited the colorful markings for operational reasons. Many wings will allow one aircraft to bear full-color markings, with the rest of the squadron aircraft bearing much more subdued equivalents.

Many squadrons allow crew members and plane captains to paint their names along canopy rails, on the fuselage underneath cockpits, on nose landing gear doors, and in other locations. Assignment of aircraft to pilots and NFOs is strictly nominal; the crewmen will usually fly whatever aircraft is available at the time of the mission.

G

NAVY AND MARINE CORPS AIR STATIONS AND FACILITIES

Revised from an original chapter written by
Capt. Paolo E. Coletta, USNR (Ret.)

Evolution of the Naval Air Station

The first naval aviation "station" was in fact no more than an experimental camp established in August 1911 at Greenbury Point, Maryland, across the Severn River from the U.S. Naval Academy. Aircraft were housed in ten hangars, and the navy's first aviators were assigned there under Capt. Washington Irving Chambers, who was then in charge of naval aviation. Operations had barely gotten under way when the camp was packed up in January 1912 and moved to North Island, San Diego, California, where the weather was more hospitable and where Glenn H. Curtiss, who had built the navy's first aeroplanes, had established his winter camp.

In May of that year, the aviators and their equipment returned to Greenbury Point, where experiments in both day and night operations continued. There were a number of accomplishments at the camp, including notable altitude, distance, and endurance flights. Here, too, the first fatal mishap involving a naval aviator occurred when Ens. W. D. Billingsly, the navy's ninth aviator, was thrown from his aircraft by a sudden downdraft. To prevent a recurrence of this unfortunate event, Glenn Curtiss designed a safety belt.

The first permanent facility was the naval aeronautic station established at Pensacola, Florida, in January 1914 for the purpose of conducting ground and flight training. While the marine corps aviators at Greenbury Point went to exercise with the advance base unit off Culebra, the aviation camp moved to Pensacola to open a flight school.

When the United States entered World War I, naval air stations were established along the Atlantic Coast from Key West, Florida, to Halifax, Nova Scotia. In between, "rest stations" were created which were, for the most part, merely beaches where seaplanes could come ashore to refuel. Some thirty stations were established on foreign soil in the Azores, Britain, and France, as well as one in Central America to guard the Panama Canal.

With victory, the naval air stations abroad were returned to their host countries. The station at Pensacola and another at San Diego became permanent training bases. Other stations continued in operation as the requirements of naval aviation grew.

Several naval reserve air stations were built during the 1930s, and in 1938 some $68 million were appropriated for a building program. Funds were also made available through the Works Progress Administration, other depression-era agencies, and the Civil Aeronautics Administration.

In September 1940, an agreement with Britain granted many overseas base sites to the United States. Others were obtained from Pan American Airlines.

World War II brought an urgent need for more and better basing facilities for training, antisubmarine warfare operations, and support of carrier-based aircraft. Existing air stations were expanded and a score of new ones built throughout the country. Facilities for blimp operations also were increased. Overseas stations were built in Greenland, Iceland, Britain, and the Azores; their emphasis was on convoy protection and antisubmarine warfare. Stations in North Africa supported the assault on Axis forces there and in Sicily and Italy. Aircraft from bases in the Caribbean and in Central and South America flew endless hours of antisubmarine patrol against the German submarine menace to shipping. Other stations sprang up on islands across the Pacific as the Allies drove toward Japan.

When the war ended, many air stations were quickly disestablished. However, by 1947, a naval air reserve program saved many of them from extinction and even called for some new construction. Meanwhile, jet aircraft demanded longer runways as well as improved fuel storage and maintenance facilities, which provided a new impetus for upgrading and growth. The Korean and Vietnam wars made it necessary to maintain and improve a respectable array of naval air stations and facilities at home and abroad, many of which remain in service today. The military drawdown of the 1990s, however, brought the consolidation, closure, or planned closure of many air stations and facilities.

Modern Naval Air Stations and Facilities

Navy and marine corps airfields support fleet users, aviation training activities, research-and-development centers, test centers, and the naval air reserve. Most coast guard air stations are separate facilities, but a few are hosted on military airfields of other services.

Naval air stations and facilities differ in size and capability as well as in the activities they support. Air stations offer the most extensive facilities and complete support, while naval air facilities are generally smaller in size, have less support capability, and are often tenants of airfields operated by other U.S. services or the military services of other countries. Some air stations are operated by and are primarily used for the naval air reserve. Other air stations support naval air weapons development and are designated naval air weapons stations. Some naval stations, primarily used for ship support, also have airfields that function as operational air stations. Stations are constantly changing to adapt to technological and organizational changes within naval aviation.

Not listed in this book are many outlying landing fields (OLFs) and auxiliary landing fields (ALFs) generally associated with specific naval air stations and primarily used for training, particularly "bouncing," or touch-and-go landings, including practice carrier landings.

Naval Air Stations

NAS Alameda, California*
NAS Atlanta, Marietta, Georgia

---

* Slated for closure.
† Slated to be downgraded to an NAF.
‡ Scheduled to become an MCAS.

NAS Barbers Point, Hawaii*
NAS Brunswick, Maine
NAS Cecil Field, Jacksonville, Florida*
NAS Corpus Christi, Texas
NAS Fallon, Nevada
NAS Fort Worth-Joint Reserve Base, Texas
NAS Jacksonville, Florida
NAS Keflavik, Iceland
NAS Key West, Florida†
NAS Lemoore, California
NAS Meridian, Mississippi
NAS Miramar, San Diego, California‡
NAS New Orleans, Louisiana
NAS Norfolk, Virginia
NAS North Island, San Diego, California
NAS Patuxent River, Maryland
NAS Pensacola, Florida
NAS Oceana, Virginia Beach, Virginia
NAS Sigonella, Sicily, Italy
NAS South Weymouth, Massachusetts*
NAS Whidbey Island, Washington
NAS Whiting Field, Milton, Florida
NAS Willow Grove, Pennsylvania

Naval Air Facilities

NAF Atsugi, Japan
NAF Diego Garcia, B.I.O.T.
NAF El Centro, California
NAF Kadena, Okinawa, Japan (Kadena AB)
NAF Mildenhall, England
NAF Misawa, Japan (Misawa AB)
NAF Washington, D.C.(at Andrews AFB, Maryland)

Other Airfields Hosting Naval Aviation

Moffett Federal Airfield, Mountain View, California (former NAS)
NAWC AD Lakehurst, New Jersey (former NAEC)
NAWS China Lake, California (former NWC)
NAWS Point Mugu, California (former NMC, PMTC)

NS Guantanamo Bay, Cuba (former NAS)
NS Mayport, Jacksonville, Florida (former NAF)
NS Roosevelt Roads, Puerto Rico
NS Rota, Spain
NSA Naples, Italy
PMRF Barking Sands, Kuaui, Hawaii

Marine Corps Air Stations and Facilities

MCAS Beaufort, South Carolina
MCALF Bogue Field, North Carolina
MCAS Camp Pendleton, California
MCAS Cherry Point, North Carolina
MCAS El Toro, California*
MCAS Futemna, Okinawa, Japan*
MCAS Iwakuni, Japan
MCAF Kaneohe Bay, Hawaii (at MCB Hawaii)
MCAS New River, North Carolina
MCAF Quantico, Virginia
MCAS Tustin, California*
MCAS Yuma, Arizona

H

Coast Guard Air Stations and Facilities

Base	Assigned Aircraft
CGAS Astoria, Oregon	HH-60J
CGAS Barbers Point, Hawaii * (NAS Barbers Point)	HC-130H, HH-65A
CGAS Biloxi, Mississippi (Keesler AFB)	HC-130H
CGAS Borinquen, Puerto Rico	HC-130H, HH-65A
CGAS Brooklyn, New York † (Floyd Bennett Field)	HH-65A
CGAS Cape Cod, Massachusetts (Otis ANGB)	HH-60J, HU-25B
CGAS Cape May, New Jersey†	HH-65A
CGAS Clearwater, Florida (St. Petersburg International Airport)	HC-130H, HH-60J
CGAS Corpus Christi, Texas (NAS Corpus Christi)	HU-25B, HH-65A
CGAS Detroit, Michigan (Selfridge ANGB)	HH-65A

* Slated to move, possibly to Marine Corps Base Hawaii.
† CGAS Cape May and CGAS Brooklyn are slated to close and combine aircraft at a new facility in Atlantic City, New Jersey.

Base	Assigned Aircraft
CGAS Elizabeth City, North Carolina	HC-130H, HH-60J
CGAF Glenview, Chicago, Illinois (ex-NAS Glenview)	HH-65A (seasonal)
CGAS Houston, Texas (Ellington ANGB)	HH-65A
CGAS Humbolt Bay, California	HH-65A
CGAS Kodiak, Alaska	HC-130H, HH-60J, HH-65A
CGAS Los Angeles, California (Los Angeles International Airport)	HH-65A
CGAS Miami, Florida (Opa Locka Airport)	HH-65A, RU-38A, HU-25C, VC-4A
CGATC Mobile, Alabama (Aviation Training Center)	HH-60J, HH-65A, HU-25B/C
CGAS New Orleans, Louisiana (NAS New Orleans)	HH-65A
CGAF Newport, Oregon (supported by North Bend)	HH-65A
CGAS North Bend, Oregon	HH-65A
CGAS Sacramento, California (McClellan AFB)	HC-130H
CGAS San Diego, California (Lindbergh Field)	HH-65A, HH-60J
CGAS San Francisco, California (San Francisco International Airport)	HH-65A
CGAS Savannah, Georgia (Hunter AAF)	HH-65A
CGAS Sitka, Alaska	HH-60J
CGAS Traverse City, Michigan (Cherry Capitol Airport)	HH-65A
CGAS Washington, D.C. (Washington National Airport)	C-20B

I

THE BLUE ANGELS

One unusual navy squadron familiar to many Americans and others is the Navy Flight Demonstration Squadron, known universally as the Blue Angels. The Blue Angels trace their lineage back to 1946, when the team, made up of World War II veterans, began performing in F6F Hellcat fighters, and shortly thereafter in F8F Bearcat fighters. The team made the transition to the jet age in 1949, flying the F9F Panther. In 1950, the team was organized into Fighter Squadron 191 and served in combat over Korea. The team was reformed in 1951, eventually flying F9F Cougars, followed by F11F Tigers, F-4J Phantom IIs, A-4F Skyhawks, and presently F/A-18A Hornets.

The Blue Angels are based at NAS Pensacola, Florida, but spend little time at home. Training during winter is conducted at NAF El Centro, California, followed by a long airshow performance season that runs through October. Aircraft complement includes six F/A-18A Hornets, one F/A-18B two-seat Hornet, and one marine corps TC-130G Hercules transport for the support crew.

To be selected for assignment to the Blue Angels is a signal honor. There are only a few openings available each year, and competition is keen.

Demonstration pilot applicants must be navy or marine corps tactical

The Blue Angels Flight Demonstration Team puts naval aviation in the spotlight before millions of spectators each year. (U.S. Navy/Bruce Trombecky)

jet pilots with fifteen hundred hours of flight time. Navy applicants must also be carrier qualified. Preferably, the applicant is rotating from sea duty or has done so within twelve months. Marine corps applicants must have completed at least one extended overseas deployment.

Marine corps C-130 pilot applicants must be C-130 plane commanders and have fifteen hundred hours of flight time.

Events coordinator applicants must be designated naval flight officers.

Flight surgeon applicants must be qualified navy flight surgeons and must have completed or be in the midst of an operational fleet tour.

Maintenance officer applicants must be qualified AMDOs and be on or have completed one operational tour.

The Blue Angels also employ first-rate enlisted personnel in the squadron's departments.

While the Blue Angels are clearly an elite group, the basic flying techniques they employ are taught to every naval aviator. They have simply expanded their skills and honed them to a peak of perfection during one or more operational tours and a grueling team training schedule. Their performances at airshows across the United States introduce the American taxpayer to naval aviation at its finest and serve as an indispensable tool for recruiting the finest possible applicants for flight training.

J

NAVAL AVIATION IN SPACE

Although space operations are not the exclusive purview of naval aviation in an organizational, administrative, or operational sense, naval aviation personnel and organizations have made sterling contributions to the U.S. space program. A naval aviator was the first American in space; another was the first to walk on Earth's moon; others were the first to fly the space shuttle.

Naval aviators were in the forefront of the Mercury, Gemini, and Apollo programs. With the advent of the Space Shuttle, opportunities for other naval personnel, including naval flight officers, flight surgeons, and engineering duty officers, opened up to become Mission Specialists. Today, present and former naval aviators and naval flight officers of the navy, marine corps, and coast guard are heavily represented in the National Aeronautics and Space Administration's astronaut corps. They wear the gold wings of the naval astronaut (see Appendix A).

Naval Aviation Milestones in Space

1. Alan B. Shepard, Jr., navy pilot, was the first American in space (suborbital flight); Mercury capsule Freedom 7, 5 May 1961.

Naval aviation has provided many of the astronauts and mission specialists that take the space shuttles into orbit.

2. John H. Glenn, Jr., marine corps pilot, was the first American to orbit the earth; Mercury capsule Friendship 7, 20 February 1962.

3. John W. Young, navy pilot, was one of two crewmen on the first multi-person space flight; Gemini 3, 23 March 1965.

4. James A. Lovell, Jr., navy pilot, was one of three crewmen on the first flight to orbit the moon; Apollo 8, 21 December 1968.

5. Neil A. Armstrong, former naval aviator, was the first man to walk on the moon; Apollo 11, 20 July 1969.

6. The first U.S.-manned orbiting space station had an all-navy crew: Charles Conrad, Jr., and Paul J. Weitz, both navy pilots, and Joseph P. Kerwin, navy flight surgeon; Skylab, 22 June 1973.

7. Vance D. Brand, navy pilot, participated in the first joint manned mission involving rendezvous, docking, crew transfer, and undocking of U.S. and Soviet spacecraft; Apollo-Soyuz Test Project, 15–24 July 1975.

8. The Space Shuttle's first flight into space was made by an all-naval aviator crew consisting of John W. Young and Robert L. Crippen; Space Shuttle Columbia, 12–14 April 1981.

9. Bruce McCandless, navy pilot, made the first untethered space walk using a nitrogen-propelled manned maneuvering suit from Space Shuttle Challenger, February 1984.

10. Captain Robert "Hoot" Gibson made the first docking of the Space Shuttle with the Russian *Mir* Space Station, July 1995.

(See chapter 4 for a description of the navy's astronaut program, and Appendix L for a list of winners of the Congressional Space Medal of Honor.)

K

NAVAL AVIATION HALL OF HONOR

On 10 July 1980, the CNO approved the names of the first twelve distinguished persons to be enshrined in the Naval Aviation Hall of Honor. Most were early naval aviators, but the list also included the first naval aviation observer and two civilians. All were enshrined at a ceremony opening the hall at the Naval Aviation Museum (now the National Museum of Naval Aviation) in Pensacola, Florida, on 6 November 1981.

Since that time others have been added to the list. All are carefully chosen by a special selection committee appointed by the CNO. The committee makes its selections, normally every two years, based on the following criteria:

— Sustained superior performance in or for naval aviation
— Superior contributions in the technical or tactical development of naval aviation
— Unique and superior flight achievement in combat or noncombat flight operations

A bronze plaque commemorating the achievements and/or special contributions of each honoree is placed on display in the Hall of Honor following the ceremonies, held in recent years in conjunction with the

The Naval Aviation Hall of Honor is part of the National Museum of Naval Aviation in Pensacola, Florida.

Naval Aviation Symposium sponsored by the Naval Aviation Museum Foundation and the U.S. Naval Institute.

Members of the Naval Aviation Hall of Honor

Enshrined 1981

Admiral John H. Towers, USN—Naval aviator no. 3; pioneer of naval aviation; officer in charge of the navy's first formal flying school at Pensacola; headed the navy Curtiss NC flying boat project; first commander, Seaplane Division 1; commanded NC-3 in a transatlantic attempt; chief of the Bureau of Aeronautics during World War II buildup.

Eugene Burton Ely—Civilian pioneer of naval aviation; first to take off in an aircraft from a ship (USS *Birmingham*); made the first landing-takeoff cycle to and from a ship (USS *Pennsylvania*).

Lieutenant Colonel Alfred A. Cunningham, USMC—Naval aviator no. 5; marine corps aviator no. 1; commanded the first marine corps aviation squadron; commanding officer of the First Marine Aviation Force, in Europe during World War I.

Rear Admiral Richard E. Byrd, USN—Naval aviator no. 608; devoted more than thirty years to polar exploration.

Commander Theodore G. Ellyson, USN—Naval aviator no.1; pioneer of naval aviation; involved in the earliest efforts to win acceptance of aviation in the navy.

Glenn Hammond Curtiss—Civilian pioneer of naval aviation; built the navy's first aircraft (A-1 Triad); trained the navy's first pilot; leading designer and manufacturer of early naval aircraft; codesigner of the NC flying boats.

Vice Admiral Patrick N.L. Bellinger, USN—Naval aviator no. 8; pioneer of naval aviation; first naval aviator to come under hostile fire (Vera Cruz, Mexico); commander of NC-1 in a transatlantic attempt; flag rank leader during World War II.

Rear Admiral William A. Moffett, USN—Naval aviation observer no. 1; first chief of the Bureau of Aeronautics; strong advocate of naval aviation between the two world wars.

Rear Admiral Albert C. Read, USN—Naval aviator no. 24; pilot in command of NC-4 during the world's first flight across the Atlantic; flag rank leader during World War II.

Lieutenant Commander Godfrey de C. Chevalier, USN—Naval aviator no. 7; commanded the Northern Bombing Group in France during World War I; first U.S. naval aviator to land on board an aircraft carrier (USS *Langley*).

Captain Holden C. Richardson, USN—Naval aviator no. 13; early aircraft designer; supervised construction of the NC flying boats; served as pilot of NC-3 in a transatlantic attempt.

Warrant Officer Floyd Bennett, USN—Early naval aviation pilot; served as pilot for Lt. Cdr. Richard E. Byrd during the first flight over the North Pole.

Enshrined 1983

General Roy M. Geiger, USMC—Naval aviator no. 49; marine corps aviator no. 5; pioneer of marine corps aviation; commanded the First Marine Air Wing at Guadalcanal and held the line against the Japanese onslaught there during World War II.

Glenn L. Martin—Civilian aviation pioneer and founder of the Glenn L. Martin Company; produced many successful naval aircraft designs; especially known for his giant flying boats.

Admiral Marc A. Mitscher, USN—Naval aviator no. 33; pioneer of naval aviation; pilot of NC-1 during a transatlantic attempt; commanding officer of the aircraft carrier *Hornet* that launched the Halsey-Doolittle raid on Japan; outstanding commander fast carrier task forces in the Pacific during World War II.

Admiral Arthur W. Radford, USN—Director of naval air training at the outset of World War II; carrier division commander in the Pacific; first naval officer to serve as Chairman of the Joint Chiefs of Staff; outspoken defender of naval aviation.

Vice Admiral Charles E. Rosendahl, USN—Pioneer of the navy's great rigid airships of the 1920s; survivor of the crash of the airship *Shenandoah* and commander of the airships *Akron* and *Macon*; outspoken navy advocate of lighter-than-air operations.

Commander Elmer F. Stone, USCG—Naval aviator no. 38; coast guard aviator no. 1; one of the pilots of NC-4 during the world's first flight across the Atlantic; strong proponent of coast guard aviation.

Enshrined 1984

Captain Kenneth Whiting, USN—Naval aviator no. 16; commanded the First Aeronautical Detachment in Europe and developed U.S. base structure overseas during World War I; influential in the development of carrier operations on board the USS *Langley*.

Leroy R. Grumman—Naval aviator no. 1216, cofounder of Grumman Aircraft Engineering Corporation; manufacturer of many successful naval aircraft designs, including the F4F Wildcat, F6F Hellcat, and TBF Avenger.

Vice Admiral James H. Flatley, Jr., USN—Fighter ace, air group commander, and aggressive combat leader during World War II; involved in the development of the "Thach Weave" fighter tactic.

Admiral John S. Thach, USN—Fighter ace; renowned air combat tactician; originator of the "Thach Weave" tactic for engaging the maneuverable Japanese Zero fighter.

Enshrined 1986

Major General Marion E. Carl, USMC—Fighter ace; led valiant aerial defenses of Midway Island and Guadalcanal; made the navy's first carrier landings and takeoffs in a pure-jet aircraft; the first marine corps helicopter pilot; set a world speed record in 1947 in the Douglas Skystreak; commanded the marine corps' first jet fighter squadron.

Fleet Admiral William F. "Bull" Halsey, USN—Carrier task force commander and fleet commander during World War II; conducted the first U.S. offensive against the Japanese after Pearl Harbor and launched the Halsey-Doolittle Raid against Japan; defeated the Japanese fleet at the battles of Santa Cruz and Guadalcanal; led the Third Fleet in the destruction of Japanese forces in the Palaus, the Philippines, Formosa, Okinawa, and the South China Sea; launched the final carrier raids against Japan.

Edward H. Heinemann—Outstanding aircraft designer, most famous for his successful naval aircraft designs produced by Douglas Aircraft Company, including the SBD Dauntless, AD Skyraider, F3D Skyknight, A3D Skywarrior, F4D Skyray, and A4D Skyhawk.

Rear Admiral David S. Ingalls, USNR—The navy's only ace in World War I; served as assistant secretary of the navy for aeronautics; returned to active duty during World War II and was instrumental in the extension of air transportation throughout the Pacific and the development of the Naval Air Transport Service.

Captain Donald B. MacDiarmid, USCG—Coast guard aviator who developed open-ocean seaplane landing techniques; pioneered development of a rational doctrine for seaplane offshore landing and takeoff adopted by the coast guard and navy.

Vice Admiral Robert B. Pirie, USN—Executive officer of an escort carrier in Atlantic hunter-killer operations during World War II; as carrier division chief of staff participated in the capture of the Marianas and Palau, and in the raids on the Philippines, Formosa, and Okinawa, and in the Battle of Leyte Gulf; first head of the Department of Aviation at the Naval Academy; Deputy Chief of Naval Operations (Air).

First Lieutenant Robert G. Robinson, USMCR—Air observer with the First Marine Aviation Force in France during World War I; awarded the Medal of Honor for helping his pilot bring their aircraft to safety despite his being hit thirteen times after shooting down one of twelve attacking enemy aircraft.

Vice Admiral Frederick Mackay Trapnell, USN—Recognized for the development of gear and methods for airplanes to hook on to lighter-than-air aircraft in flight; performed a large amount of hazardous flight testing while at NAS Anacostia and NAS Patuxent River.

Enshrined 1988

Captain Washington I. Chambers, USN—Though not an aviator, he was a strong advocate of naval airpower; the first director of naval aviation; signed the order for the purchase of the navy's first three aircraft.

Jerome C. Hunsaker—Naval constructor; established the first aeronautical engineering course in the United States for the navy at the Massachusetts Institute of Technology in June 1913; made numerous contributions toward the advancement of aeronautical knowledge in the navy; navy's coordinator of research and development.

General Keith B. McCutcheon, USMC—Developer of close-air support in World War II and the Korean conflict; principal advocate for helicopters in the marine corps; oversaw introduction and expansion of helicopter use throughout the marine corps.

Captain David McCampbell, USN—Fighter pilot and air group commander; leading navy ace during World War II, with thirty-four confirmed aerial victories; won the Medal of Honor and Navy Cross in two days during the Battle of Letye Gulf, setting a record by downing nine enemy aircraft during a single action.

Admiral Thomas H. Moorer, USN—PBY Catalina pilot in the defense of the Philippines at the outset of World War II; carrier division commander; Commander, Seventh Fleet; Commander in Chief, U.S. Pacific Fleet; Commander in Chief, Atlantic and NATO's Allied Command Atlantic; two terms as Chief of Naval Operations; two terms as Chairman of the Joint Chiefs of Staff.

Admiral Alfred M. Pride, USN—One of the navy's foremost aviators and test pilots; Chief of the Bureau of Aeronautics; a prime developer of the carrier arresting gear system.

Enshrined 1990

Captain Frank A. Erickson, USCG—The first coast guard helicopter pilot; made the first lifesaving flight ever performed by a helicopter (January 1944); commended for the development of the helicopter rescue hoist and related lifesaving equipment.

Captain Henry C. Mustin, USN—Characterized as the "father of naval aviation" by Adm. William Moffett; devoted his life to the development of naval aviation; commanded naval aviation activities during its first combat action (Vera Cruz, Mexico, in 1914); shaped naval aviation policy as Assistant Director of Naval Aviation, Bureau of Aeronautics.

Admiral James S. Russell, USN—Patrol squadron commander during the World War II Aleutian campaign; carrier division chief of staff; commanding officer of the USS *Coral Sea*; Chief of the Bureau of Aeronautics; cowinner of the Collier Trophy for development of the first carrier-based fighter (F8U Crusader) to fly faster than 1,000 miles per hour; Vice Chief of Naval Operations; Commander in Chief, Allied Forces, Southern Europe.

Rear Admiral Alan B. Shepard, Jr., USN—Fighter pilot; test pilot; astronaut; the first American in space; Chief of NASA's Astronaut Office.

Igor I. Sikorsky—Russian-born aircraft designer; designed the world's first four-engine airplane, used as a bomber during World War I; designed a successful line of flying boats; designed and test-flew the first successful helicopter design; set a world record for helicopter endurance; his company designed a successful line of military helicopters.

George A. Spangenberg—Aeronautical engineer; leading government technical authority for evaluation, selection, and design of naval aircraft weapon systems; Director of Evaluation, Bureau of Aeronautics, then Bureau of Naval Weapons, then Naval Air Systems Command; a primary force in the formulation of navy policy on such programs as the F-111, F-14, and S-3 aircraft.

Enshrined 1992

Lawrence B. Sperry—Pioneer naval aviator and inventor of aeronautical instruments and devices, including the automatic pilot, turn indicator, bank indicator, optical drift sight, improved magnetic compass, the pack parachute, retractable landing gear, and an aerial torpedo; first to install landing lights on aircraft; first to fly a plane tethered to another aircraft; first to transfer fuel in flight; the first civilian to be commissioned an officer by the U.S. Navy Flying Corps.

Lieutenant Commander Edward H. "Butch" O'Hare, USN—Fighter pilot; first navy ace in World War II; won Medal of Honor for single-handedly shooting down five Japanese bombers in defense of the USS *Lexington*; squadron and air group commander; missing in action while pioneering carrier-based night interception near Tarawa.

Rear Admiral William A. Schoech, USN—Naval aviator and aeronautical engineer; Seventh Fleet chief of staff during World War II; commander of a Naval Air Transport Service wing; escort carrier and attack carrier commanding officer; carrier division commander; Commander, Seventh Fleet; Chief of Naval Material.

Admiral Austin Kelvin Doyle, USN—Scouting and fighter pilot; squadron commander; aggressive World War II escort carrier and aircraft carrier commanding officer; introduced jet training to the navy as Commander, Naval Air Training Command; carrier division commander; Chief of Naval Air Training; Commander, Taiwan Defense command.

Vice Admiral Gerald F. Bogan, USN—Fighter squadron commander; test pilot; aircraft carrier executive officer; air station commander; nearly continuous combat command in World War II as aircraft carrier commanding officer, carrier division commander, and task group commander in combat against Japan; premier figure in carrier combat tactics.

Enshrined 1994

Brigadier General Joseph J. Foss—Fighter pilot; Medal of Honor winner; ace with the famed "Cactus Air Force" on Guadalcanal during World War II; squadron commander; leading marine corps ace with twenty-six aerial victories while a marine; brigadier general in the South Dakota Air National Guard; two-term governor of South Dakota; commissioner of the American Football league.

Colonel Gregory "Pappy" Boyington, USMC—Fighter pilot; Medal of Honor winner; ace with six victories with the American Volunteer Group ("Flying Tigers") in China; commander of Marine Fighter Squadron 214 ("Black Sheep"), scoring twenty-two more aerial victories before downing and capture by the Japanese; emerged at the war's end as the marine corps' leading ace.

Captain Ashton Graybiel, MC, USN—Flight surgeon; acknowledged expert in cardiovascular medicine; Director of Research for the Naval School of Aviation Medicine and Research during the formative years of aviation medicine; developed electrocardiographic techniques; experimented with flight disorientation; continued the "Thousand Aviators" study; advanced aeromedical knowledge for naval aviation and the U.S. space program.

Vice Admiral Apollo Soucek, USN—Pioneer test pilot; helped spearhead the advancement of carrier aviation; carrier executive officer during the Solomons campaign during World War II; first commanding officer of the USS *Franklin D. Roosevelt* (CVB 42); carrier division commander during the Korean conflict; Chief of the Bureau of Aeronautics.

Admiral Frederick Michaelis, USN—Fighter pilot; ace with five aerial victories in World War II; aeronautical engineer; developed nuclear weapons tactics; carrier division commander; directed carrier air combat operations against North Vietnam; Commander, Naval Air Force, U.S. Atlantic Fleet; Chief of Naval Material.

Enshrined 1996

Rear Admiral Joseph C. Clifton, USN—Squadron and air group commander; led the first strikes against the Japanese stronghold at Rabaul; credited with two aerial victories; carrier executive officer; commanded an airlift squadron during the Berlin Airlift and a seaplane tender during the Korean War; carrier division commander; Chief of Naval Air Advanced Air Training; Chief of Naval Air Technical Training.

Charles Kaman—Helicopter designer; Chief Aerodynamicist for Hamilton-Standard; founded Kaman Aircraft Corporation; designed first helicopter to perform a loop, first to fly with a gas-turbine engine (HTK), which evolved into the first remotely piloted helicopter; pioneered the intermeshing rotor system and servo-flap technology; produced the HOK/HUK and the long-serving H-2 Seasprite shipboard helicopters.

General Christian F. Schilt, USMC—Early marine corps aviator; served in combat during World War I and in Haiti, the Dominican Republic, and Nicaragua, where he earned the Medal of Honor for dramatic medical evacuation flights under fire; assistant to Gen. Roy Geiger during the Guadalcanal campaign; coordinated air defenses during the Okinawa campaign; commanded the First Marine Air Wing during the Korean War; director of marine corps aviation.

Admiral Forrest P. Sherman, USN—Naval aviation advisor to the Atlantic Conference during World War II; commanded the USS *Wasp* (CV-7); chief of staff to Commander, Air Force, Pacific Fleet; deputy chief of staff to Commander in Chief, Pacific (Adm. Chester Nimitz); Commander Sixth Task Fleet; youngest chief of naval operations ever selected and the first to have spent his entire career in naval aviation.

Vice Admiral James B. Stockdale, USN—Fighter pilot and test pilot; squadron commander; led first American air strikes against North Vietnam; air group commander; awarded Medal of Honor for inspirational leadership during seven-and-one-half years as a prisoner-of-war in North Vietnam; Commander Antisubmarine Warfare Wing, Pacific; president of the Naval War College; candidate for U.S. vice president.

Admiral Maurice F. Weisner, USN—Aircraft carrier navigator; sank an enemy destroyer-escort as a patrol bomber pilot during World War II; patrol squadron commander during the Korean War; commanded two fighter squadrons, an oiler, the aircraft carrier *Coral Sea* (CVA-43); commanded two carrier divisions and the Seventh Fleet during the Vietnam War; Deputy Chief of Naval Operations (Air Warfare); Vice Chief of Naval Operations; Commander in Chief, U.S. Pacific Fleet and U.S. Pacific Command.

L

MEDAL OF HONOR WINNERS

The Medal of Honor is this country's highest award for valor. It originated during the Civil War for those who exhibited courage "above and beyond the call of duty." It was first authorized for the navy and marine corps on 21 December 1861 and for the army and voluntary forces on 12 July 1862.

The medal is awarded in the name of Congress and for this reason is often called the Congressional Medal of Honor. On 20 September 1905, President Theodore Roosevelt ordered the award to be made ceremoniously and the recipient to be in Washington, D.C., for the presentation, which would be made by the president (as commander in chief) or by a representative of the president.

The medal is made in three different designs, one for the sea services (navy, marine corps, and coast guard), one for the army, and one for the air force. The navy medal is bronze, suspended by an anchor from a bright blue ribbon worn about the neck. The ribbon itself contains a cluster of thirteen white stars representing the original thirteen states. The medal itself is a five-pointed star, each ray of which contains sprays of laurel and oak tipped with a trefoil. Minerva, personifying the Union, stands in the center, surrounded by thirty-four stars representing the thirty-four states that existed in 1861. She holds in her left hand an axe bound in staves of wood, the ancient Roman symbol of authority. The shield in her right hand repulses the serpent held by the crouching figure of Discord. On the reverse side of the medal are engraved the recipient's name and the date and place of the act of valor.

The following list of names includes naval aviators, a naval aviation observer, and others whose actions are associated with naval aviation. Some of those listed became part of naval aviation after the action that won their Medals of Honor. Ranks listed are those held at the times of the action.

Antrim, Richard N., Lieutenant, USN—Action in behalf of fellow prisoners while POW, April 1942.

Bauer, Harold W., Lieutenant Colonel, USMC—Air combat, South Pacific, 28 September–3 October 1942 (posthumous).

Bennett, Floyd, Chief Warrant Officer, USN—Pilot on the first flight over the North Pole, 9 May 1926.

Boyington, Gregory, Major, USMC—Air combat, central Solomons Islands, 12 September 1943–3 January 1944.

Byrd, Richard E., Lieutenant Commander, USN—Commander of the first flight over the North Pole, 9 May 1926.

Clausen, Raymond M., Private First Class, USMC—Repeated rescues by helicopter of men under fire, South Vietnam, 30 January 1970.

Commiskey, Henry A., Second Lieutenant, USMC—Led ground attack on strong enemy position, Korea, 20 September 1950.

Corry, William M., Lieutenant Commander, USN—Attempted rescue of pilot from burning aircraft, 2 October 1920 (posthumous).

De Blanc, Jefferson J., Captain, USMC—Air combat off Kolombangara Island, 31 January 1943.

Edson, Merritt A., Colonel, USMC—Led ground combat action in defense of Henderson Field, Guadalcanal, 13–14 September 1942.

Elrod, Henry T., Captain, USMC—Air and ground combat in defense of Wake Island, 8–23 December 1941 (posthumous).

Estocin, Michael J., Lieutenant Commander, USN—Air combat, North Vietnam, 20 and 26 April 1967 (posthumous).

Finn, John W., Chief Petty Officer, USN—Action under fire during attack on NAS Kaneohe Bay, Hawaii, 7 December 1941.

Fleming, Richard E., Captain, USMC—Leader of dive-bombing attack during Battle of Midway, 4–6 June 1942 (posthumous).

Foss, Joseph J., Captain, USMC—Air combat in defense of Guadalcanal, 9 October–19 November 1942.

Galer, Robert E., Major, USMC—Air combat, South Pacific, August–September 1942.

Gary, Donald A., Lieutenant (j.g.), USN—Repeated rescues of trapped men on board the USS *Franklin* (CV 13) following severe combat damage, 19 March 1945.

Gordon, Nathaniel G., Lieutenant, USN—Repeated air rescues of men in the water under fire, Kavieng Harbor, 15 February 1944.

Hall, William E., Lieutenant (j.g.), USN—Determined attacks on enemy carrier, Battle of Coral Sea, 7–8 May 1942.

Hammann, Charles H., Ensign, USNRF—Rescue of fellow pilot under fire during raid on Pola, Austria, 21 August 1918.

Hanson, Robert M., First Lieutenant, USMC—Air combat at Bougainville, 1 November 1943, and at New Britain, 24 June 1942 (posthumous).

Hudner, Thomas J., Jr., Lieutenant (j.g.), USN—Attempted rescue of fellow pilot downed behind enemy lines in Korea, 4 December 1950.

Hutchins, Carlton B., Lieutenant, USN—Remained at controls of aircraft following midair collision to allow crew to escape, 2 February 1938 (posthumous).

Koelsch, John K., Lieutenant (j.g.), USN—Attempted rescue under fire, Korea, 3 July 1951 (posthumous).

Lassen, Clyde E., Lieutenant (j.g.), USN—Night helicopter rescue of two aviators under fire, North Vietnam, 19 June 1968.

McCampbell, David, Commander, USN—Air combat during battles of the Philippine Sea and Leyte Gulf, June and October 1944.

McDonnell, Edward O., Ensign, USN—Established signal station ashore and maintained communications while under fire, Veracruz, Mexico, 21–22 April 1914.

McGunigal, Patrick, Ship's Fitter First Class, USN—Rescued kite balloon pilot entangled underwater, 17 September 1917.

Moffett, William A., Commander, USN—Action in command of a ship at Veracruz, Mexico, 21–22 April 1914.

O'Callahan, Joseph T., Lieutenant Commander, CHC, USN—Inspiration, leadership, and repeated rescues on board the USS *Franklin* (CV 13) following severe combat damage, 19 March 1945.

O'Hare, Edward H., Lieutenant, USN—Air combat in defense of carrier off Rabaul, 20 February 1942.

Ormsbee, Francis E., Jr., Chief Machinist's Mate, USN—Rescued crewman and attempted to rescue pilot in crash of seaplane, Pensacola Bay, Florida, 25 September 1918.

Pless, Stephen W., Captain, USMC—Helicopter rescue of three marines under fire, South Vietnam, 19 August 1967.

Powers, John J., Lieutenant, USN—Determined attacks on enemy ships during Battle of Coral Sea, 4–8 May 1942 (posthumous).

Ricketts, Milton E., Lieutenant, USN—Led damage control party on board the USS *Yorktown* (CV 5) during Battle of Coral Sea, 8 May 1942 (posthumous).

Robinson, Robert G., Gunnery Sergeant, USMC—Air combat as gunner for Lt. Ralph Talbot over Europe, 8 and 14 October 1918.

Schilt, Christian F., First Lieutenant, USMC—Air evacuation of wounded men under fire, Qualili, Nicaragua, 6–8 January 1928.

Smith, John L., Major, USMC—Air combat in defense of Guadalcanal, 21 August–15 September 1942.

Stockdale, James B., Captain, USN—Action in behalf of fellow prisoners while POW, North Vietnam, 4 September 1969.

Swett, James E., First Lieutenant, USMC—Air combat over the Solomon Islands, 7 April 1943.

Talbot, Ralph, Second Lieutenant, USMC—Air combat over Europe, 8 and 14 October 1918.

Van Voorhis, Bruce A., Lieutenant Commander, USN—Determined low-level heavy bomber attack, Solomon Islands, 6 July 1943 (posthumous).

Walsh, Kenneth A., First Lieutenant, USN—Air combat over Vella Lavella, 15 and 30 August 1943.

Congressional Space Medal of Honor

The Congressional Space Medal of Honor was approved by Congress in 1969 for presentation "to any astronaut who in the performance of his duties has distinguished himself by exceptionally meritorious efforts and contributions to the welfare of the nation and of mankind." The following is a list of naval aviators and former naval aviators who have received this award.

Armstrong, Neil A.—Gemini 8 (1966) and Apollo 11 (1969), becoming the first person to walk on Earth's moon.
Conrad, Charles, Jr.—Four space flights from 1965 to 1973, culminating in the first manned Skylab mission.
Glenn, John H., Jr.—Mercury capsule Friendship 7 (1962), becoming the first American to orbit the earth.
Lovell, James A., Jr.—Apollo 13 commander (1970); brought crew safely to Earth following near-disastrous mishap.
Shepard, Alan B., Jr.—Mercury capsule Freedom 7 (1961), becoming the first American in space; Apollo 14 commander, third lunar landing mission (1971).
Young, John W.—Two Gemini and Apollo space flights; commander of the first orbital flight of the Space Shuttle (1981).

NC-4 Congressional Medal

Congress ordered seven of these medals struck in solid gold following the world's first successful transatlantic flight by the navy's Curtiss NC-4 seaplane in May 1919. One medal was presented to each crewman on the NC-4. The seventh medal was presented to the commander of the three-plane flight, whose aircraft was one of two that went down at sea and did not complete the crossing. The recipients are listed below.

Breese, James L., Lieutenant, USN
Hinton, Walter, Lieutenant (j.g.), USN
Read, Albert C., Lieutenant Commander, USN
Rhoads, Eugene S., Chief Machinist's Mate, USN
Rodd, Herbert C., Ensign, USN
Stone, Elmer F., Lieutenant, USCG
Towers, John H., Commander, USN

M

ACES AND MIG KILLERS

In the eighty-year history of aerial combat, the subject of aces and their victories has proven a topic of enduring interest. Navy and marine corps aviators, whether flying from carriers or land bases, occupy a special niche in the history of American aces.

As a matter of policy, the navy and marine corps do not officially acknowledge the "ace" designation, nor do they officially tally aerial victories by individual. The American Fighter Aces Association follows the tradition in requiring five confirmed victories as the minimum standard.

Any "aceologist" recognizes that a flyer's victory score is subject to many variables. Credits-versus-claims is only the starting point for discrepancies. Sometimes aircraft destroyed on the ground are lumped in with aerial victories, or often a higher command issues totals at variance with lower echelons. Some contradictions simply defy explanation. Regardless of the total number of victories, the successful pilot or aircrew is responsible for achieving and maintaining air superiority with his squadron mates.

In the jet era, especially during the Vietnam War and subsequent conflicts, aerial combat has been relatively rare compared with World War II, and only five Americans (three air force and two navy) have won the dis-

Aces and MiG Killers 375

In combat over the Pacific during World War II, Commander David McCampbell became the navy's all-time highest scoring ace, with thirty-four victories over Japanese aircraft. (U.S. Navy)

tinction of "ace" since the Korean War. For that reason, the entire list of known aerial victories by navy and marine corps aircrews during the Vietnam War and subsequent conflicts is presented.

Because many modern fighter aircraft are crewed by a pilot and a radar intercept officer or weapons systems officer, it has become customary to award each crew member with full credit for the victory, rather than the half-credit that is awarded when two aircraft share in a single victory.

As a note of interest, an American Fighter Aces Association study confirmed that the navy's F6F Hellcat fighter of World War II produced more U.S. aces (three hundred) than any other aircraft from any other service.

The following compilation of the naval service's top fighter pilots in each war is intended to update previous lists. Space limitations dictate that the World War II names be limited to those aces generally credited with ten or more victories. In the first column of figures are the commonly accepted victory scores, in this instance taken from R. F. Toliver's 1965 volume, *Fighter Aces*. The second column notes the tallies, where different, from Dr. Frank J. Olynyk, whose exhaustive research is acknowledged as the most authoritative to date. Ranks are those known in each case as the highest attained while active as a combat pilot.

Material for this feature was compiled by J. R. "Bill" Bailey, Dr. Frank J. Olynyk, and Barrett Tillman (while secretary of the American Fighter Aces Association), Robert L. Lawson, John Gresham, and the editor. The list of aerial victories from the Vietnam War, compiled by Robert L. Lawson, is reprinted from the Winter 1983 issue of *The Hook*.

U.S. NAVY

World War I

	Toliver	Olynyk
Lt. David S. Ingalls		6

World War II

	Toliver	Olynyk
Cdr. David McCampbell (MOH)	34	
Lt. Cecil Harris	24	
Lt. Eugene Valencia	23	
Lt. Patrick D. Fleming	19	
Lt. Alexander Vraciu	19	
Lt. Cornelius N. Nooy	19	
Lt. Ira C. Kepford	17	16
Lt. Charles R. Stimpson	17	16

	Toliver	Olynyk
Lt. (j.g.) Douglas Baker	16	16.33
Lt. Arthur R. Hawkins	14	
Lt. Cdr. Elbert S. McCuskey	14	13.5
Lt. John L. Wirth	14	
Lt. Cdr. George Duncan	13.5	
Lt. Cdr. Roger W. Mehle	13.33	5.66
Lt. Daniel A. Carmichael	13	12
Lt. Dan R. Rehm	13	9
Lt. Roy Rushing	13	
Lt. John R. Strane	13	
Lt. Wendell V. Twelves	13	
Lt. Cdr. Clement M. Craig	12	11.75
Lt. Leroy E. Harris	12	9.25
Lt. Cdr. Roger R. Hedrick	12	
Lt. Cdr. William E. Henry	12	9.5
Lt. William J. Masoner	12	
Lt. Cdr. Hamilton McWhorter III	12	
Lt. Cdr. Edward H. O'Hare (MOH)	12	7
Lt. James A. Shirley	12	12.5
Lt. George A. Carr	11.5	
Cdr. Fred E. Bakutis	11	7.5
Cdr. John T. Blackburn	11	
Cdr. William A. Dean	11	
Lt. James B. French	11	
Lt. Philip L. Kirkwood	11	12
Lt. Charles M. Mallory	11	10
Lt. (j.g.) James V. Reber	11	
Lt. Cdr. James F. Rigg	11	
Lt. Donald E. Runyon	11	
Lt. Richard E. Stambook	11	
Lt. Stanley W. Vejtasa	11	10.25
Cdr. Marshall U. Beebe	10.5	
Lt. Russell L. Reiserer	10.5	9
Lt. Armistead B. Smith	10.5	10
Lt. John C. C. Symmes	10.5	11

	Toliver	Olynyk
Lt. Albert O. Vorse	10.5	11.5
Lt. Robert E. Murray	10.33	
Lt. Robert H. Anderson	10	8
Lt. Carl A. Brown	10	10.5
Lt. Cdr. Thaddeus T. Coleman	10	
Lt. Richard L. Cormier	10	8
Lt. Harris E. Mitchell	10	
Lt. T. Hamil Reidy	10	
Lt. Arthur Singer	10	
Lt. John M. Smith	10	
Lt. James S. Swope	10	9.66

Korean Conflict

Lt. Guy P. Bordelon	5

Vietnam War

Lt. Randall Cunningham	5*
Lt. (j.g.) Willie Driscoll (RIO)	5*

* These 5 victories were scored together.

U.S. Marine Corps

World War II

Maj. Joseph J. Foss (MOH)	26
1st Lt. Robert M. Hanson (MOH)	25
Maj. Gregory Boyington (MOH)	22 (+3.5 with AVG)
Capt. Kenneth A. Walsh (MOH)	21
Capt. Donald N. Aldrich	20
Maj. John L. Smith (MOH)	19
Maj. Marion E. Carl	18.5
Capt. Wilbur J. Thomas	18.5

	Toliver	*Olynyk*
Capt. James E. Swett (MOH)	16	15.5
Capt. Harold L. Spears	15	
Maj. Kenneth D. Frazier	14.5	13.5
Capt. Edward O. Shaw	14.5	
Maj. Archie G. Donahue	14	
Maj. James N. Cupp	13	12
Maj. Robert E. Galer (MOH)	13	14
1st Lt. William P. Marontate	13	
Maj. Loren D. Everton	12	
Capt. Harold E. Segal	12	
2d Lt. Eugene A. Trowbridge	12	6
Capt. William N. Snider	11.5	
Capt Philip C. DeLong	11.17 (+2 in Korea)	
Lt. Col. Harold W. Bauer (MOH)	11	10
Capt. Donald H. Sapp	11	10
Capt. Jack E. Conger	10	
Maj. Herbert H. Long	10	

Korean Conflict

Maj. John F. Bolt	6 (+6 in World War II)

AVG = American Volunteer Group (Flying Tigers)
MOH = Medal of Honor winner
RIO = Radar Intercept Officer

Vietnam "MiG Killers"

The following is an unofficial listing of all confirmed and possible aerial victories scored by navy and marine corps aircrews during the Vietnam War. Probables are indicated by a (P) following the type of aircraft believed to be downed. The list was prepared from several official and unofficial sources. Wherever possible, the data has been confirmed by official sources, including many of the aircrews involved.

Date	Time	Mission	A/C	BuNo	Aircrew	Squadron	Modex	Call Sign	CV	CVW	Weapon	Location	Kill
9 Apr. 1965	0840	BarCap	F-4B	151403	Lt. (jg) Terence M. Murphy-KIA Ens. Ronald J. Fegan-KIA	VF-96	NG 602	Showtime	CVA-61	CVW-9	AIM-7	1820/10830	MiG-17 (P)*
Remarks: *ChiCom; High altitude engagement; 602 MIA MiG guns?; Enemy reports downed by friendly
17 June 1965	1030	BarCap	F-4B	151488	Cdr. Louis Page 'Lou' Lt. John C. Smith, Jr.	VF-21	NE 101	Sundown	CVA-41	CVW-2	AIM-7	2008/10515	MiG-17
17 June 1965	1030	BarCap	F-4B	152219	Lt. Jack E.D. Batson, Jr. 'Dave' Lt. Cdr. Robert B. Doremus	VF-21	NE 102	Sundown	CVA-41	CVW-2	AIM-7	2008/10515	MiG-17
20 June 1965	1835	ResCap	A-1H	137523	Lt. Charlie Hartman	VA-25	NE 573	Canasta	CVA-41	CVW-2	20mm	2010/10525	MiG-17
Remarks: 1/2 kill
20 June 1965	1835	ResCap	A-1H	139768	Lt. Clinton B. Johnson 'Clint'	VA-25	NE 577	Canasta	CVA-41	CVW-2	20mm	2010/10525	MiG-17
Remarks: 1/2 kill
6 Oct. 1965	1040	BarCap	F4-B	150634	Lt. Cdr. Dan MacIntyre Lt. (jg) Alan Johnson	VF-151	NL 107	Switch Box	CVA-43	CVW-15	AIM-7D		MiG-17 (P)*
Remarks: *Confirmed, not released
12 June 1966	1446	TarCap	F-8E	150924	Cdr. Harold L. Marr 'Hal'	VF-211	NP	Nickel	CVA-19	CVW-21	AIM-9D	2120/10630	MiG-17
12 June 1966	1450	TarCap	F-8E	150924	Cdr. Harold L. Marr 'Hal'	VF-211	NP	Nickel	CVA-19	CVW-21	AIM-9D	2120/10620	MiG-17 (P)
21 June 1966	1530	Photo/SAR	F-8E	150924	Lt. (jg) Phillip V. Vampatella 'Phil'	VF-211	NP 104	Nickel	CVA-19	CVW-21	AIM-9D	2133/10637	MiG-17D
21 June 1966	1535	ResCap	F-8E	150867	Lt. Eugene J. Chancy 'Gene'	VF-211	NP 101	Nickel	CVA-19	CVW-21	AIM-9D	2133/10637	MiG-17
13 July 1966	1102	TarCap	F4-B	151500	Lt. William M. McGuigan 'Squeaky' Lt. (jg) Robert M. Fowler	VF-161	NL 216	Rock River	CVA-64	CVW-15	AIM-9D	2041/10555	MiG-17
9 Oct. 1966	0945	TarCap	F-8E	149159	Cdr. Richard M. Bellinger 'Dick'*	VF-162	AH 210	Superheat	CVA-34	CVW-16	AIM-9	2132/10548	MiG-21
Remarks: *Deceased

Date	Time	Mission	A/C	BuNo	Aircrew	Squadron	Modex	Call Sign	CV	CVW	Weapon	Location	Kill
09 Oct. 1966	1013	ResCap	A-1H	137543	Lt. (jg) William T. Patton	VA-176	AK 409	Papoose	CVS-11	CVW-10	20mm	2015/10522	MiG-17
20 Dec. 1966	1832	Intercept	F-4B	153022	Lt. H. Dennis Wisely 'Denny' Lt. (jg) David L. Jordan	VF-114	NH 215	Linfield	CVA-63	CVW-11	AIM-7E	1927/10558	An 2
20 Dec. 1966	1841	Intercept	F-4B	153019	Lt. David McCrea 'Barrel' Ens. David Nichols	VF-213	NH 110	Black Lion	CVA-63	CVW-11	AIM-7E	1927/10558	An 2
24 Apr. 1967		TarCap	F-4B	153000	Lt. Charles E. Southwick 'Ev' Ens. James W. Laing	VF-114	NH 210	Linfield	CVA-63	CVW-11	AIM-9B	2123/10616	MiG-17
Remarks: A/C lost this date; possible AAA													
24 Apr. 1967	1645	TarCap	F-4B	153037	Lt. H. Dennis Wisely 'Denny' Lt. (jg) Gareth L. Anderson	VF-114	NH 00	Linfield	CVA-63	CVW-11	AIM-9D	2123/10616	MiG-17
1 May 1967	1244	Flak Supp	A-4C	148609	Lt. Cdr. Theodore R. Swartz 'Ted'	VA-76	NP 685	Sun Glass	CVA-31	CVW-21	Zuni	2121/10620	MiG-17
1 May 1967	1245	TarCap	F-8E	150303	Lt. Cdr. Marshall O. Wright 'Moe'	VF-211	NP 104	Nickel	CVA-31	CVW-21	AIM-9D	2126/10628	MiG-17
19 May 1967	1525	TarCap	F-8E	150348	Cdr. Paul H. Speer	VF-211	NP 101	Nickel	CVA-31	CVW-21	AIM-9D	2050/10540	MiG-17
19 May 1967	1525	TarCap	F-8E	150661	Lt. (jg) Joseph M. Shea	VF-211	NP	Nickel	CVA-31	CVW-21	AIM-9D*	2050/10540	MiG-17
Remarks: *'Herded' MiG with 20mm for position													
19 May 1967	1525	Flak Supp	F-8C	146981	Lt. Cdr. Bobby C. Lee	VF-24	NP 4xx	Page Boy	CVA-31	CVW-21	AIM-9D	2050/10540	MiG-17
19 May 1967	1525	TarCap	F-8C	147029	Lt. Phillip R. Wood	VF-24	NP 405	Page Boy	CVA-31	CVW-21	AIM-9D	2050/10540	MiG-17
21 July 1967	0830	TarCap	F-8C	147018	Lt. Cdr. Marion H. Isaacks 'Red'	VF-24	NP 442	Page Boy	CVA-31	CVW-21	AIM-9D	2103/10619	MiG-17
21 July 1967	0830	TarCap	F-8C	146998	Lt. (jg) Phil Dempewolf	VF-24	NP 4xx	Page Boy	CVA-31	CVW-21	AIM-9	2103/10619	MiG-17 (P)
21 July 1967	0830	TarCap	F-8C	146992	Lt. Cdr. Robert L. Kirkwood	VF-24	NP 424	Page Boy	CVA-31	CVW-21	AIM-9/ 20mm	2103/10619	MiG-17
21 July 1967	0830	Escort	F-8E	150859	Lt. Cdr. Ray G. Hubbard 'Tim'	VF-211	NP 1xx	Nickel	CVA-31	CVW-21	20mm/ Zuni	2118/10612	MiG-17D
10 Aug. 1967	1232	TarCap	F-4B	152247	Lt. Guy H. Freeborn Lt. (jg) Robert J. Elliot	VF-142	NK 202	Dakota	CVA-64	CVW-14	AIM-9	2038/10540	MiG-21
10 Aug. 1967	1232	TarCap	F-4B	150431	Lt. Cdr. Robert C. Davis Lt. Cdr. Gayle O. Elie 'Swede'	VF-142	NK 2xx	Dakota	CVA-64	CVW-14	AIM-9	2038/10540	MiG-21

Date	Time	Mission	A/C	BuNo	Aircrew	Squadron	Modex	Call Sign	CV	CVW	Weapon	Location	Kill
26 Oct. 1967	1300	MiGCap	F-4B	149411	Lt. (jg) Robert P. Hickey, Jr. Lt. (jg) Jeremy G. Morris 'Jerry'	VF-143	NK 1xx	Taproom	CVA-64	CVW-14	AIM-7	2045/10556	MiG-21
30 Oct. 1967	1245	MiGCap	F-4B	150629	Lt. Cdr. Eugene P. Lund 'Gino' Lt. (jg) James R. Borst, 'Bif'*	VF-142	NK 203	Dakota	CVA-64	CVW-14	AIM-7E	2110/10700	MiG-17

Remarks: A/C lost same day, own missile *Deceased

Date	Time	Mission	A/C	BuNo	Aircrew	Squadron	Modex	Call Sign	CV	CVW	Weapon	Location	Kill
14 Dec. 1967	1740	TarCap	F-8E	150879	Lt. Richard E. Wyman 'Dick'	VF-162	AH 204	Superheat	CVA-34	CVW-16	AIM-9D	2045/10605	MiG-17
9 May 1968			F-4B	153036	Maj. John P. Hefferman, USAF 'Jack' Lt. (jg) Frank A. Schumacher	VF-96	NG 1xx	Showtime	CVN-65	CVW-9	AIM-7E		MiG-21 (P)*

Remarks: *Confirmed, not released

Date	Time	Mission	A/C	BuNo	Aircrew	Squadron	Modex	Call Sign	CV	CVW	Weapon	Location	Kill
26 June 1968	1810	MiGCap	F-8H	148710	Cdr. Lowell R. Meyers 'Moose'	VF-51	NL 116	Screaming Eagle	CVA-31	CVW-15	AIM-9	1855/10516	MiG-21
9 July 1968	0850	Escort	F-8E	150926	Lt. Cdr. John B. Nichols III	VF-191	NM 107	Feed Bag	CVA-14	CVW-19	AIM-9/20mm	1835/10530	MiG-17
10 July 1968	1600	MiGCap	F-4J	155553	Lt. Roy Cash, Jr. Lt. Joseph E. Kain, Jr.	VF-33	AE 212	Rootbeer	CVA-66	CVW-6	AIM-9	1845/10520	MiG-21
29 July 1968	1132	MiGCap	F-8E	150349	Cdr. Guy Cane	VF-53	NF 203	Firefighter	CVA-31	CVW-5	AIM-9	1856/10528	MiG-17
1 Aug. 1968	1340	MiGCap	F-8H	147916	Lt. Norman K. McCoy	VF-51	NF 102	Screaming Eagle	CVA-31	CVW-5	AIM-9	1726/10612	MiG-21
19 Sept. 1968	1055	MiGCap	F-8C	146961	Lt. Anthony J. Nargi 'Tony'	VF-111	AK 103	Old Nick	CVS-11	CVW-10	AIM-9	1854/10521	MiG-21
28 Mar. 1970			F-4J	155875	Lt. Jerome E. Beaulier 'Jerry' Lt. Steven J. Barkley	VF-142	NK 201	Dakota	CVA-64	CVW-14	AIM-9		MiG-21
19 Jan. 1972	1358	TarCap	F-4J	157267	Lt. Randall H. Cunningham 'Yank' Lt. (jg) William P. Driscoll 'Willie'	VF-96	NG 112	Showtime	CVA-64	CVW-9	AIM-9	1903/10517	MiG-21
6 Mar. 1972	1325	ForCap	F-4B	153019	Lt. Garry L. Weigand 'Greyhound' Lt. (jg) William C. Freckelton 'Farkle'	VF-111	NL 201	Old Nick	CVA-43	CVW-15	AIM-9	1856/10503	MiG-17
6 May 1972	1410	TarCap	F-4B	150456	Lt. Cdr. Jerry B. Houston 'Devil' Lt. Kevin T. Moore	VF-51	NL 100	Screaming Eagle	CVA-43	CVW-15	AIM-9	1946/10530	MiG-17
6 May 1972	1825	MiGCap	F-4J	157249	Lt. Robert G. Hughes 'Bob'* Lt. (jg) Adolph J. Cruz 'Joe'	VF-114	NH 206	Linfield	CVA-63	CVW-11	AIM-9	2018/10538	MiG-21

Remarks: *killed midair VF-126/121 A-4/F-4

Date	Time	Mission	A/C	BuNo	Aircrew	Squadron	Modex	Call Sign	CV	CVW	Weapon	Location	Kill
6 May 1972	1825	MiGCap	F-4J	157245	Lt. Cdr. Kenneth W. Pettigrew 'Viper' Lt. (jg) Michael J. McCabe 'Mike'	VF-114	NH 201	Linfield	CVA-63	CVW-11	AIM-9	2018/10538	MiG-21
8 May 1972	1005	MiGCap	F-4J	157267	Lt. Randall H. Cunningham 'Duke' Lt. (jg) William P. Driscoll 'Irish'	VF-96	NG 112	Showtime	CVA-64	CVW-9	AIM-9	2106/10521	MiG-17
10 May 1972	0958	TarCap	F-4J	157269	Lt. Curt Dose Lt. Cdr. James McDevitt	VF-92	NG 211	Silver Kite	CVA-64	CVW-9	AIM-9	2127/10620	MiG-21F
10 May 1972	1400	TarCap	F-4J	155769	Lt. Michael J. Connelly 'Matt' Lt. Thomas J.J. Blonski	VF-96	NG 106	Showtime	CVA-64	CVW-9	AIM-9	2057/10620	MiG-17
10 May 1972	1400	TarCap	F-4J	155769	Lt. Michael J. Connelly Lt. Thomas J.J. Blonski	VF-96	NG 106	Showtime	CVA-64	CVW-9	AIM-9	2057/10620	MiG-17
10 May 1972	1400	MiGCap	F-4B	151398	Lt. Kenneth L. Cannon 'Ragin Cajun' Lt. Roy A. Morris, Jr. 'Bud'	VF-51	NL 111	Screaming Eagle	CVA-43	CVW-15	AIM-9	2053/10559	MiG-17
10 May 1972	1400	TarCap	F-4J	155749	Lt. Steven C. Shoemaker 'Steve' Lt. (jg) Keith V. Crenshaw	VF-96	NG 111	Showtime	CVA-64	CVW-9	AIM-9	2057/10620	MiG-17
10 May 1972	1401	Flak Supp	F-4J	155800	Lt. Randall H. Cunningham Lt. (jg) William P. Driscoll	VF-96	NG 100	Showtime	CVA-64	CVW-9	AIM-9	2055/10623	MiG-17
10 May 1972	1403	Flak Supp	F-4J	155800	Lt. Randall H. Cunningham Lt. (jg) William P. Driscoll	VF-96	NG 100	Showtime	CVA-64	CVW-9	AIM-9	2054/10620	MiG-17
10 May 1972	1408	Flak Supp	F-4J	155800	Lt. Randall H. Cunningham Lt. (jg) William P. Driscoll	VF-96	NG 100	Showtime	CVA-64	CVW-9	AIM-9	2053/10622	MiG-17
Remarks: A/C lost same day; SAM; crashed 2019/10640													
18 May 1972	1730	MiGCap	F-4B	153068	Lt. Henry A. Bartholomay 'Bart' Lt. Oran R. Brown	VF-161	NF 110	Rock River	CVA-41	CVW-5	AIM-9	2110/10630	MiG-19
18 May 1972	1730	MiGCap	F-4B	153915	Lt. Patrick E. Arwood 'Pat' Lt. James M. Bell 'Mike'	VF-161	NF 105	Rock River	CVA-41	CVW-5	AIM-9G	2110/10630	MiG-19
23 May 1972	1755	MiGCap	F-4B	153020	Lt. Cdr. Ronald E. McKeown 'Mugs' Lt. John C. Ensch 'Jack'	VF-161	NF 100	Rock River	CVA-41	CVW-5	AIM-9	2125/10615	MiG-17

Date	Time	Mission	A/C	BuNo	Aircrew	Squadron	Modex	Call Sign	CV	CVW	Weapon	Location	Kill
23 May 1972	1755	MiGCap	F-4B	153020	Lt. Cdr. Ronald E. McKeown Lt. John C. Ensch	VF-161	NF 100	Rock River	CVA-41	CVW-5	AIM-9	2125/10615	MiG-17
11 June 1972	1045	MiGCap	F-4B	149473	Cdr. Foster S. Teague 'Tooter' Lt. Ralph M. Howell	VF-51	NL 114	Screaming Eagle	CVA-43	CVW-15	AIM-9	2032/10555	MiG-17
11 June 1972	1045	MiGCap	F-4B	149457	Lt. Winston W. Copeland 'Mad Dog' Lt. Donald R. Bouchoux 'Don'	VF-51	NL 113	Screaming Eagle	CVA-43	CVW-15	AIM-9	2032/10555	MiG-17
21 June 1972	1215	MiGCap	F-4J	157293	Cdr. Samuel C. Flynn, Jr. 'Sam' Lt. William H. John 'Bill'	VF-31	AC 101	Bandwagon	CVA-60	CVW-3	AIM-9	2125/10644	MiG-21
10 Aug. 1972	2019	MiGCap	F-4J	157299	Lt. Cdr. Robert E. Tucker, Jr. 'Gene' Lt. (jg) Stanley B. Edens 'Bruce'	VF-103	AC 296	Clubleaf	CVA-60	CVW-3	AIM-7E	1930/10530	MiG-21J
11 Sept. 1972	1802	MiGCap	F-4J	155526	Maj. Lee T. Lasseter 'Bear'* Capt. John D. Cummings 'Li'l John'*	VMFA-333	AJ 201	Shamrock	CVA-66	CVW-8	AIM-9G	2113/10549	MiG-21
Remarks: A/C lost this date; SAM *Deceased												
28 Dec. 1972	1225	MiGCap	F-4J	155846	Lt. (jg) Scott H. Davis Lt. (jg) Geoffrey H. Ulrich 'Jeff'	VF-142	NK 214	Dakota	CVN-65	CVW-14	AIM-9	2057/10553	MiG-21
12 Jan. 1973	1332	BarCap	F-4B	153045	Lt. Victor T. Kovaleski 'Vic' Lt. (jg) James A. Wise	VF-161	NF 102	Rock River	CVA-41	CVW-5	AIM-9	2027/10713	MiG-17
		Escort	F-4D	667709	Capt. Doyle Baker, USMC 1st Lt. John D. Ryan, Jr., USAF	13 TFS	OC	Gambit 03			AIM-4D		MiG-17
Remarks: Exchange duty 432 TRW; Kill: 17 Dec. 1967; Location: Route Package 6A												
		WX Reece	F-4E	670239	Capt. Lawrence G. Richard, USMC Lt. Cdr. Michael J. Ettel, USN*	58 TFS	ZF	Dodge 01			AIM-7		MiG-21
Remarks: Exchange duty 432 TRW; Kill: 12 Aug. 1972; *Died VF-43 A-4, Oceana, 1974												

Post-Vietnam Victories

Since the end of the Vietnam War, navy aircrews have shot down seven hostile aircraft (six jet fighters and one helicopter) in two incidents with Libyan forces and during the 1991 Persian Gulf War. These victories are listed below.

Date	Aircraft	BuNo	Aircrew	Squadron	Modex	CV	CVW	Weapon	Kill
Libyan Incidents									
19 Aug. 1981	F-14A	160403	Cdr. Henry M. Kleeman / Lt. David Venlet	VF-41	AJ 102	*Nimitz*	8	AIM-9	Su-22
19 Aug. 1981	F-14A	160390	Lt. Larry Musczynski / Lt. (jg) Jim Anderson	VF-41	AJ 107	*Nimitz*	8	AIM-9	Su-22
4 Jan. 1989	F-14A	159437	Lt. Herman C. Cook / Cdr. Steven P. Collins	VF-32	AC 202	*John F. Kennedy*	3	AIM-7	MiG-23
4 Jan. 1989	F-14A	159610	Cdr. Joseph B. Connelly / Cdr. Leo F. Enright	VF-32	AC 207	*John F. Kennedy*	3	AIM-7/9	MiG-23
Persian Gulf War									
17 Jan. 1991	F/A-18C	163508	Lt. Cdr. Mark Fox	VFA-81	AA 401	*Saratoga*	17	AIM-7/9	MiG-21
17 Jan. 1991	F/A-18C	163502	Lt. Nick Mongillo	VFA-81	AA 410	*Saratoga*	17	AIM-9	MiG-21
6 Feb. 1991	F-14A	162603	Lt. Stuart Broce / Cdr. Ron McElraft	VF-1	NE 103	*Ranger*	2	AIM-9	MI-8

N

Naval Aviation Associations and Museums

Associations

The Ancient Order of the Pterodactyl

The Ancient Order of the Pterodactyl is dedicated to the promotion of camaraderie among past and present coast guard aviators and their supporters, support for coast guard aviation and its goals, and recognition of coast guard aviation history. Membership is open to all who are serving or who have served honorably under flight orders in coast guard aviation, including those exchange pilots of other military services and foreign governments. This association publishes a newsletter, the *Pterogram*, about three times per year for its members. Address: P.O. Box 9917, Mobile, Alabama 36691.

Association of Aviation Ordnancemen

The Association of Aviation Ordnancemen is a professional and fraternal association for past and present aviation ordnancemen. Address: Frank Thill, 1103 Myra Avenue, Chula Vista, California 91911.

Association of Naval Aviation, Inc. (ANA)

The Association of Naval Aviation (ANA) is a nonprofit, tax-exempt professional, educational, and fraternal society of naval aviation, whose main purpose is to educate the public and national leaders on the vital roles of navy, marine corps, and coast guard aviation as key elements in the national defense structure. ANA promotes public discourse on the key current issues impacting naval aviation through published writing, symposia, speeches, and discussions with various interest groups. ANA also seeks to foster the strong pride, esprit de corps, and fraternal bonds which exist among those associated with naval aviation. ANA publishes a quarterly magazine, *Wings of Gold,* and has many local squadrons (chapters) throughout the United States and overseas. An annual convention is held each spring. Membership is open to all military personnel and civilians interested in supporting naval aviation. Address: 5205 Leesburg Pike, Suite 200, Falls Church, Virginia 22041-3863. Phone: (703) 998-7733, (800) 666-9ANA, Fax: (703) 671-6052.

Aviation Boatswain's Mate Association

The Aviation Boatswain's Mate Association is a professional and fraternal organization for past and present aviation boatswain's mates. The association's symposium provides a forum to identify problems and recommend solutions to naval aviation safety and flight deck operations. Address: Bill Sowers, 2240 Wild Oak Crescent, Virginia Beach, Virginia 23456.

The Early and Pioneer Naval Aviators Association (Golden Eagles)

The Golden Eagles are dedicated to preserving the bonds of the past and fostering a pioneer spirit among present and future naval aviators. Membership is by invitation only and is made up of leading figures from naval aviation. The organization is strictly limited to two hundred members. An annual convention is held each spring. Address: Admiral E. L. Feightner, USN (Ret), 2009 North 14th Street, Arlington, Virginia 22201-2514. Phone: (703) 527-3065.

Naval Aviation Museum Foundation, Inc. (NAMF)

The Naval Aviation Museum Foundation (NAMF) is a charitable educational foundation dedicated to supporting the National Museum of Naval Aviation in preserving the history and heritage of navy, marine corps, and coast guard aviation. NAMF raises funds for the museum's development, operates a library in the museum, publishes *Foundation* (a naval aviation history magazine), and the newsletter *Flyby* jointly with the museum; and annually co-sponsors, with the U.S. Naval Institute, the Naval Aviation Symposium. Membership is open to all military personnel and civilians. Address: P.O. Box 33104, 1750 Radford Boulevard, NAS Pensacola, Florida 32508-3104. Phone: (800) 327-5002, (904) 453-2389, Fax: (904) 457-3032.

Naval Helicopter Association (NHA)

The Naval Helicopter Association (NHA) is a nonprofit professional organization whose purpose is to promote recognition for and enhance the prestige of the U.S. naval vertical flight community. NHA is dedicated to promoting the use of vertical lift aircraft in the navy, marine corps, and coast guard, and in keeping its members informed of new developments and accomplishments in rotary-wing aviation. NHA publishes a quarterly journal, *Rotor Review*. A convention is held annually, and membership is open to military personnel and civilians. Address: P.O. Box 180460, Coronado, California 92178-0460. Phone: (619) 435-7139.

Marine Corps Aviation Association (MCAA)

The Marine Corps Aviation Association (MCAA) is a nonprofit organization dedicated to perpetuating the spirit and comradeship of marine corps aviation, fostering professional excellence, and recognizing noteworthy achievements. Several local squadrons are organized around the United States, and a convention is held annually. MCAA publishes a quarterly newsletter, *The Yellow Sheet*. Address: P.O. Box 296, Quantico, Virginia 22134. Phone: (800) 336-0291, (703) 640-6161, DSN 278-2854, Fax: (703) 640-0823.

The Silver Eagles Association, Inc. (SEA)

The Silver Eagles Association (SEA) is dedicated to fellowship among former enlisted naval aviation pilots and perpetuation of the prominent role they played in the development and progress of naval aviation. SEA publishes a newsletter, *The Scuttlebutt,* five times a year. Membership is open to all former enlisted pilots of the navy, marine corps, and coast guard. Nine wings (chapters) are organized around the United States, and a convention is held annually. Address: P.O. Box 4111, Pensacola, Florida 32507-0111. Phone: (904) 438-9093.

The Tailhook Association

The Tailhook Association is a nonprofit corporation dedicated to fostering, encouraging, studying, and developing support for the aircraft carrier, sea-based aircraft (both fixed-wing and rotary-wing), and aircrew of the United States of America, and to educate the public in their appropriate role in the national defense structure. The Tailhook Association publishes a quarterly journal, *The Hook.* Regular membership is open to those who have made a carrier arrested landing as a crew member; associate membership is open to all military personnel and civilians interested in supporting the goals of the Tailhook Association. Address: 9696 Businesspark Avenue, San Diego, California 92131-1643. Phone: (619) 689-9223 or (800) 322-HOOK.

The U.S. Naval Institute

Though not an aviation-specific organization, the U.S. Naval Institute is a professional organization for the sea services which devotes considerable attention to issues involving naval aviation. It sponsors several professional seminars and symposia each year and publishes two magazines that often feature naval aviation: *Proceedings,* a professional journal, and *Naval History.* Its publishing house, Naval Institute Press, publishes many books on naval aviation. Address: 118 Maryland Avenue, Annapolis, Maryland 21402. Phone: (410) 268-6110.

VP International Association

Headquartered at Greenwood Canadian Forces Base in Nova Scotia, VP International is a professional organization for maritime patrol flyers of all nations. Many of its members are U.S. Navy active and retired VP personnel. Membership requires two thousand hours in maritime patrol aircraft. The association publishes a professional journal, *Maritime Patrol*. Address: 14 Wing, CFB Greenwood, Nova Scotia, Canada B0P 1N0. Phone: (902) 765-5447.

Museums

Many museums throughout the United States have naval aircraft in their collections. The museums with the larger collections of naval aircraft are listed below. In addition, many naval aircraft are on display on bases and other locations. NAS Oceana, Virginia; NAS Cecil Field, Florida; NAS Jacksonville, Florida; and NAS Miramar, California, each have a significant number of aircraft on display near their gates.

The Cunningham Air Museum

To be located on MCAS Cherry Point, North Carolina, this museum is expected to be in operation in 1997. It will have a collection of aircraft types flown by the marine corps. Construction is being funded through the A. A. Cunningham Air Museum Foundation, 207 West Main Street, Havelock, North Carolina 28532. Phone: (919) 447-0573.

The Intrepid *Museum*

Located in New York City, this museum features the *Intrepid* (CVS 11), an *Essex*-class carrier and veteran of World War II and the Vietnam War. A large number of naval aircraft are displayed on her deck. The LPH *Guadalcanal* is scheduled to be added to the museum. Open during the summer 10:00 AM–5:00 PM Monday through Saturday and 10:00 AM–6:00 PM on Sunday; after Labor Day it is closed Monday and Tuesday. Address: The *Intrepid* Museum, Pier 86, West 46th Street and 12th Avenue, New York, New York 10036. Phone: (212) 245-0072.

The *Intrepid* (ex-CVS 11), berthed at New York City, is one of three *Essex*-class aircraft carriers that now serve as aviation museums. (via *Naval Aviation News*)

The Marine Corps Air-Ground Museum

Located on MCB Quantico, Virginia, this marine corps museum houses a large collection of aircraft and combat vehicles that served the marine corps. Open from 1 April until the Thanksgiving holiday, 10:00 AM–5:00 PM Tuesday through Saturday and 12:00 Noon–5:00 PM Sunday. Address: MCAG Museum, MCB Quantico, Virginia 22134. Phone: (703) 784-2606.

The MCAS El Toro Command Museum

Located on MCAS El Toro in Santa Ana, California, this young museum run by the MCAS El Toro Historical Foundation includes a large collection of aircraft types once flown by the marine corps. The museum is scheduled to move to Miramar, California, upon closure of El Toro. Open 10:00 AM–4:00 PM Wednesday through Sunday. Address: Command Museum, MCAS El Toro Historical Foundation, MCAS El Toro, Santa Ana, California 92709. Phone: (714) 559-6795.

The Naval Air Test and Evaluation Museum

Located by the main gate at NAS Patuxent River, Maryland, this navy museum exhibits naval aircraft and artifacts that emphasize the contributions to naval aviation of the test center at Patuxent River. Open Fridays and Saturdays 11:00 AM–4:00 PM and Sundays 12:00 Noon–5:00 PM. Phone: (301) 863-7418.

The National Air and Space Museum

Located at the corner of Independence Avenue and 6th Street in Washington, D.C., as part of the Smithsonian Institution, the National Air and Space Museum includes the Sea-Air Hall exhibit devoted to naval aviation, and displays other naval aircraft through rotating exhibits. (Many historic naval aircraft are housed at the museum's Silver Hill annex awaiting display or under restoration; tours of this facility can be arranged by prior appointment.) Open 10:00 AM–6:30 PM daily. Address: NASM, The Smithsonian Institution, Washington, D.C. 20560.

The National Museum of Naval Aviation

Located on NAS Pensacola, Florida, this navy museum is the official museum of U.S. naval aviation. It is one of the three largest aviation museums in the world and displays the world's largest collection of historic naval aircraft and naval aviation artifacts, including the NC-4 flying boat. Administered under the auspices of Commander Naval Air Training Command, this museum is also the owner of many naval aircraft on display in other museums. The museum includes the Emil Buehler Naval Aviation Library and receives the bulk of its support from the Naval Aviation Museum Foundation. Open 9:00 AM–5:00 PM daily except on the Thanksgiving, Christmas, and New Year's holidays. Address: 1750 Radford Boulevard, NAS Pensacola, Florida 32508. Phone: (904) 452-3604.

The National Museum of Naval Aviation in Pensacola, Florida, houses the world's largest museum collection of naval aircraft (Emil Buehler Naval Aviation Library)

The New England Air Museum

Located at Windsor Locks, Connecticut, the museum includes several naval aircraft among its collection. Open 10:00 AM–5:00 PM daily. Address: Bradley International Airport, Windsor Locks, Connecticut 06096. Phone: (203) 623-3305.

The Patriots Point Naval and Maritime Museum

Located near Charleston, South Carolina, this museum features several ships, the centerpiece of which is the USS *Yorktown* (CVS 10), an *Essex*-class veteran of World War II and the Vietnam War. Naval aircraft are displayed on her deck, and among the 107 exhibits are the Test Pilot Hall of Honor and the Carrier Aviation Hall of Fame. Open 9:00

AM–9:00 PM daily. Address: 40 Patriots Point Road, Mount Pleasant, South Carolina 29464. Phone: (803) 884-2727.

The Pima Air and Space Museum

Located near Davis-Monthan AFB in Tucson, Arizona, this museum holds a large collection of aircraft, including many naval types, mostly post-World War II types drawn from the Aerospace Maintenance and Regeneration Center (AMARC). (Of note, AMARC also displays aircraft for public viewing on a part of the facility.) Open 9:00 AM–5:00 PM daily except for the Thanksgiving and Christmas holidays. Address: 6000 East Valencia Road, Tucson, Arizona 85706. Phone: (520) 574-9658.

The San Diego Aerospace Museum

Located in Balboa Park in San Diego, California, this museum's aircraft collection includes many naval types. Open 10:00 AM–6:00 PM daily Memorial Day through Labor Day, and 10:00 AM–4:30 PM the rest of the year. Address: 2001 Pan American Plaza (Balboa Park), San Diego, California 92101. Phone: (619) 234-8291.

The USS Lexington *Museum*

Located at Corpus Christi, Texas, this young museum is housed on board the USS *Lexington* (AVT 16), an *Essex*-class World War II veteran that long served as the navy's training carrier. Naval aircraft are displayed on her deck. Open 9:00 AM–8:00 PM daily. Address: 2914 Shoreline Boulevard, Corpus Christi, Texas 78402. Phone: (512) 888-4873.

O

Naval Aviation Periodicals

There are several periodicals devoted exclusively to naval aviation published by the navy and private associations. Others devote considerable attention to naval aviation. In addition, many reunion associations specific to particular units or aircraft publish newsletters. Listed below are several publications that are generally available.

Airborne Log—A magazine published periodically by Lockheed Aeronautical Systems Company, 86 South Cobb Drive, Marietta, Georgia 30063-0244. Contains news and features for the VP, VQ, and VS communities. Distributed to selected naval aviation units and is available upon request.

Approach/Mech—An internal magazine published bimonthly by the Naval Safety Center, 375 A Street, NAS Norfolk, Virginia 23511-4399, a combination of the former *Approach* and *Mech* magazines. Deals with flight and maintenance safety, including many first-person accounts. Distributed without charge to naval aviation units and is available to subscribers from the Superintendent of Documents, Government Printing Office, 710 North Capitol Street NW, Washington, D.C. 20402.

Flightlines—An internal newsletter published periodically by Coast Guard Headquarters, 2100 2nd Street S.W., Washington, D.C. 20593. Contains safety articles and other information of primary interest to coast guard aviation. Distributed without charge to coast guard aviation activities.

Flyby—A newsletter published quarterly jointly by the National Museum of Naval Aviation and the Naval Aviation Museum Foundation, Inc., P.O. Box 33104, 1750 Radford Boulevard, Suite B, NAS Pensacola, Florida 32508-3104. Contains news and announcements on the activities of the National Museum of Naval Aviation and the Naval Aviation Museum Foundation. Available with membership in the Naval Aviation Museum Foundation.

Foundation—A magazine published semiannually by the Naval Aviation Museum Foundation, Inc., P.O. Box 33104, 1750 Radford Boulevard, Suite B, NAS Pensacola, Florida 32508-5402. Contains articles on naval aviation history. Available with membership in the Naval Aviation Museum Foundation.

The Hook—A professional journal published quarterly by the Tailhook Association, 9696 Businesspark Avenue, San Diego, California 92131-1643. Contains articles on past and present carrier operations and the current activities of carrier air wings. Available with membership in the Tailhook Association and also by subscription.

Marine Corps Gazette—A professional journal published by the Marine Corps Association, Box 1775, Quantico, Virginia 22134. Contains news, features, and commentary on issues affecting the marine corps, including naval aviation. Available with membership in the Marine Corps Association and also by subscription.

Maritime Patrol—A magazine published biannually by VP International Association, 14 Wing, CFB Greenwood, Nova Scotia, Canada BPO 1NO. Contains news, features, and historical articles on maritime patrol aviation worldwide. Available with membership in VP International.

Naval Aviation News—An internal magazine published bimonthly by the Naval Historical Center for the Chief of Naval Operations, Building 157-1, Washington Navy Yard, 901 M Street SE, Washington, D.C. 20375-5059. Contains policy, news, features, and historical articles of interest to naval aviation personnel at all levels. Distributed without charge to navy, marine corps, and coast guard aviation units, and is available to subscribers from the Superintendent of Documents, Government Printing Office, 710 North Capitol Street NW, Washington, D.C. 20402.

Naval History—A magazine published bimonthly by the U.S. Naval Institute, 118 Maryland Avenue, Annapolis, Maryland 21402. Contains articles on naval history, including naval aviation. Available by subscription.

Proceedings—A professional journal published monthly by the U.S. Naval Institute, 118 Maryland Avenue, Annapolis, Maryland 21402. Contains articles and essays on naval topics, including many on naval aviation. Available with membership in the U.S. Naval Institute, or by subscription.

Rotor Review—A magazine published quarterly by the Naval Helicopter Association, P.O. Box 180460, Coronado, California 92178-0460. Contains news, features, and historical articles of interest to the naval helicopter community. Available with membership in the Naval Helicopter Association.

Sea Power—A magazine published monthly by the Navy League of the United States, 2300 Wilson Boulevard, Arlington, Virginia 22201-3308. Contains news, features, and background articles on issues of interest to the naval services, including naval aviation. Available with membership in the Navy League and also by subscription.

Wings of Gold—A magazine published quarterly by the Association of Naval Aviation, Inc., Suite 200, 5205 Leesburg Pike, Falls Church, Virginia 22014-3863. Contains a wide range of news and feature articles on naval aviation and association activities. Available with membership in the association and also by subscription.

The Yellow Sheet—A newsletter published quarterly by the Marine Corps Aviation Association, P.O. Box 296, Quantico, Virginia 22134. Contains articles and information on marine corps aviation and association activities. Available with membership in the association.

P

SUGGESTED READING AND REFERENCE

Naval aviation and naval aircraft are popular subjects with professionals, historians, modelers, and the public alike. Hundreds of books and monographs on naval aviation subjects (in whole or in part) have been published, as well as thousands of magazine articles, too numerous to list here. Listed below are a few of the finest and most comprehensive nonfiction books written on U.S. naval aviation, most of which are works on naval aircraft and naval aviation history.

Cressman, Robert J., Steve Ewing, et al. *"A Glorious Page in Our History": The Battle of Midway, 4–6 June 1942.* Missoula, Mont.: Pictorial Histories Publishing Co., 1990. 226 pages. An excellent account of U.S. naval aviation's finest hour, the Battle of Midway, which turned the tide in the Pacific in World War II.

Donald, David, and Jon Lake, eds. *U.S. Navy and Marine Corps Air Power Directory.* London: Aerospace Publishing Ltd., 1992. 232 pages. A well-illustrated comprehensive reference of naval aviation organization, stations, aircraft, and weapons. An updated edition is forthcoming.

Elliott, Maj. John M., USMC (Ret.). *The Official Monogram U.S. Navy & Marine Corps Aircraft Color Guide.* Vol. 1, 1911–1939. Boylston, Mass.: Monogram Aviation Publications, 1987. 193 pages.

―――. *The Official Monogram U.S. Navy and Marine Corps Aircraft Color Guide.* Vol. 2, 1940–1949. Sturbridge, Mass.: Monogram Aviation Publications, 1989. 193 pages.

―――. *The Official Monogram U.S. Navy and Marine Corps Aircraft Color Guide.* Vol. 3, 1950–1959. Sturbridge, Mass.: Monogram Aviation Publications, 1991. 194 pages.

―――. *The Official Monogram U.S. Navy and Marine Corps Aircraft Color Guide.* Vol. 4, 1960–1993. Sturbridge, Mass.: Monogram Aviation Publications, 1993. 203 pages. These four lavishly illustrated volumes detail the history of markings and paint schemes used on U.S. naval aircraft.

Francillon, Rene J. *Tonkin Gulf Yacht Club: U.S. Carrier Operations off Vietnam.* Annapolis, Md.: Naval Institute Press, 1988. 214 pages. An exhaustive reference work on carrier operations during the Vietnam War, combined with a monograph account of operations of the USS *Coral Sea* (CVA 43) in that war.

Grossnick, Roy A. *Dictionary of American Naval Aviation Squadrons.* Vol. 1: *The History of VA/VAH/VAK/VAL/VAP/VFA Squadrons.* Washington, D.C.: U.S. Government Printing Office, 1995. 562 pages. The first of a series of encyclopedic works on naval aviation squadrons, including their history, aircraft type, deployments, commanding officers, and awards. Also available on CD-ROM.

Grossnick, Roy A., ed. *Kite Balloons to Air Ships: The Navy's Lighter-than-Air Experience.* Washington, D.C.: U.S. Government Printing Office, 1986. 79 pages.

Hallion, Richard P. *The Naval Air War in Korea.* Baltimore: Nautical & Aviation Publishing Co. of America, 1986. 244 pages. This is the only comprehensive English-language work on naval aviation in the Korean conflict; meticulously researched and documented.

Knott, Capt. Richard C. *The American Flying Boat: An Illustrated History.* Annapolis, Md.: Naval Institute Press, 1979. 262 pages. A fine history of American flying boats, mostly in naval service, written by a former patrol seaplane pilot.

―――. *A Heritage of Wings: A History of Aviation in the U.S. Navy.* A forthcoming comprehensive history of U.S. naval aviation to be published by the Naval Institute Press.

Larkins, William T. *U.S. Navy Aircraft, 1921–1941* and *U.S. Marine Corps Aircraft, 1914–1959.* Combined reprint of both volumes; New York:

Orion Books, 1988. 391 and 203 pages, respectively. Classic illustrated works of aircraft types, markings, and organization of the period.

Lawson, Robert L., ed. *The History of US Naval Air Power.* New York: The Military Press, 1985. 256 pages. This superbly illustrated general history of U.S. naval aviation from its beginnings through the early 1980s is one of the finest books ever produced on this subject.

Mersky, Peter B. *U.S. Marine Corps Aviation: 1912 to the Present.* Annapolis, Md.: The Nautical & Aviation Publishing Company of America, 1983. 310 pages. Although somewhat dated now, this remains a good history of Marine Corps aviation.

Mersky, Peter B., and Norman Polmar. *The Naval Air War in Vietnam.* 2d ed. Baltimore: Nautical & Aviation Publishing Co. of America, 1986. 226 pages. A concise account of naval aviation in the Vietnam War.

Nichols, Cdr. John B., USN (Ret.), and Barrett Tillman. *On Yankee Station: The Naval War over Vietnam.* Annapolis, Md.: Naval Institute Press, 1987. 175 pages. A frank account of the navy carrier air war over Vietnam, woven with first-person experiences of one of the authors, a fighter pilot in that war.

Pearcy, Arthur. *U.S. Coast Guard Aircraft since 1916.* Shrewsbury, England: Airlife, 1991. 330 pages. A thorough reference work on coast guard aircraft types.

Polmar, Norman. *Aircraft Carriers.* Garden City, N.Y.: Doubleday, 1969. 788 pages. Although dated, this remains the finest general history of the aircraft carrier in print.

———. *The Naval Institute Guide to the Ships and Aircraft of the U.S. Fleet.* 16th ed. Annapolis, Md.: Naval Institute Press, 1996. 639 pages. The standard reference, periodically updated, on U.S. naval ships and aircraft, with comprehensive sections on naval aviation organization and equipment.

Rausa, Capt. Rosario, USNR. *Gold Wings, Blue Sea: A Naval Aviator's Story.* Annapolis, Md.: Naval Institute Press, 1980. 200 pages. A first-person account of a navy attack pilot that captures the essence of life as a naval aviator.

Reynolds, Clark G. *The Fast Carriers: The Forging of an Air Navy.* Huntington, N.Y.: R. E. Krieger, 1978. 502 pages. A reprint of a classic work on the development of carrier aviation and its impact on naval history.

Sherrod, Robert. *History of Marine Corps Aviation in World War II.* Washington, D.C.: Combat Forces Press, 1952. 496 pages. A comprehensive history of marine corps aviation in World War II, written by an acclaimed war correspondent assisted by a team of marine historians. This book has been reprinted in recent years.

Swanborough, Gordon, and Peter M. Bowers. *United States Navy Aircraft since 1911.* 3d ed. Annapolis, Md.: Naval Institute Press, 1990. 612 pages. The standard reference work on all aircraft operated by the navy, marine corps, and coast guard.

Turnbull, Archibald D., and Clifford C. Lord. *History of United States Naval Aviation.* New Haven: Yale University Press, 1949. 345 pages. A detailed, comprehensive history of the development of U.S. naval aviation up to World War II.

Turpin, Capt. Anthony, USNR, and Cdr. Richard Shipman, USNR, eds. *Wings at the Ready: Seventy-five Years of the Naval Reserve.* Annapolis, Md.: Naval Institute Press, 1991. 193 pages. An illustrated commemorative history of the naval air reserve.

Van Vleet, Clarke, and William J. Armstrong. *United States Naval Aviation, 1910–1980.* Washington, D.C.: U.S. Government Printing Office, 1981. 547 pages. An official chronology of U.S. naval aviation through 1980, with numerous appendixes. An edition updated through 1995, prepared by the Naval Aviation History Office, is scheduled for publication in 1997 and will be available on CD-ROM.

Wooldridge, E. T., ed. *Into the Jet Age: Conflict and Change in Naval Aviation, 1945–1975.* Annapolis, Md.: Naval Institute Press, 1995. 336 pages. A collection of the reminiscences of distinguished naval aviators who brought naval aviation and the aircraft carrier into the jet age.

Q
NAVAL AVIATION ACRONYMS, ABBREVIATIONS, AND TERMS

A/A   Angle of attack
AAA   Antiaircraft artillery
AAED   Airborne active expendable decoy
AAM   Air-to-air missile
AATC   Amphibious air traffic control
AAW   Antiair warfare
AAWC   Antiair warfare commander
ABDR   Aircraft battle damage repair
ABF   Advanced bomb family
ABFC   Advanced base functional component
A/C   Aircraft
ACDUTRA   Active duty for training
ACE   Air combat element
ACEVAL   Air combat evaluation
ACINT   Acoustic intelligence
ACIP   Aviation career incentive pay (flight pay)
ACLS   Automatic carrier landing system
ACM   Air combat maneuvering
ACMR   Air combat maneuver range

ACO Airborne communications officer
ADIZ Air defense identification zone
ADR Aircraft damage repair
ADS Active dipping sonar
ADVCAP Advanced capability
AEDO Aerospace Engineering Duty Officer
AEW Airborne early warning
AGL Above ground level
AGM Aircraft ground mishap
AI Air intercept; artificial intelligence
AIC Air intercept controller
AICUZ Air installation compatibility use zone
AIM Air intercept missile
AIMD Aircraft Intermediate Maintenance Department
AIMVAL Air intercept missile evaluation
AIO Air Intelligence Officer
Air boss Carrier air officer
AIRS Aircraft inventory reporting system
AIS Acoustic intercept system
ALF Auxiliary landing field
ALSS Aircraft life support system
ALT Altitude
AMB Aircraft Mishap Board
AMCM Airborne mine countermeasures
AMDO Aeronautical Maintenance Duty Officer
AMDS Aircraft maintenance data system
AMO Aircraft Maintenance Officer
AMRAAM Advanced medium-range air-to-air missile
AMRR Aircraft material readiness report
AMSL Above mean sea level
ANA Association of Naval Aviation
Ancient Albatross (Enlisted) The coast guard enlisted aircrewman serving on active duty with the earliest graduation date from an aviation technical school
Ancient Albatross (Officer) The coast guard aviator serving on active duty with the earliest desigation date
AOA Angle of attack

AOC   Aviation Officer Candidate
AOCP   Aviation officer continuation pay
AOM   All officers meeting
APAM   Antipersonnel attack munition
APC   Approach power compensator
APM   All pilots meeting
APU   Auxiliary power unit
AREC   Air resources coordinator
ARM   Antiradiation missile
ARS   Aerial refueling store
ASAT   Antisatellite
ASE   Aviation support equipment
ASIP   All-source imagery processor
ASM   Air-to-surface missile
ASMD   Antiship missile defense
ASO   Aviation safety officer; aviation supply office; aviation supply officer
ASPJ   Airborne self-protection jammer
ASR   Air surveillance radar
ASUW   Antisurface warfare
ASUWC   Antisurface warfare commander
ASW   Antisubmarine warfare
ASWC   Antisubmarine warfare commander
ASWEX   Antisubmarine warfare exercise
ATAP   Antitank, antipersonnel
ATARS   Advanced tactical air reconnaissance system
ATC   Air traffic control
ATDS   Airborne tactical data system
ATKRON   Attack squadron
ATKWING   Attack wing
ATO   Air transfer officer
Autocat   Communications-relay aircraft
AUW   Advanced underseas weapon
AVB   Aviation logistic support ship
AVCAL   Aviation consolidated allowance list
AVDLR   Aviation depot-level repairable
AVIM   Aviation intermediate-level maintenance

AVT   Aviation training ship
AXBT   Air expendable bathythermograph
BAI   Battlefield air interdiction
BALL   Optical landing aid
BARCAP   Barrier combat air patrol
BDA   Battle damage assessment
BDU   Bomb dummy unit
BFIT   Battle force in-port training
BGPHES   Battle group passive horizon extension system
Bingo   Proceed and land at field specified
Bird farm   Aircraft carrier
BIS   Board of Inspection and Survey
Blackshoe   Surface warfare officer
BLU   Bomb live unit
B/N   Bombardier/navigator
Bolter   Take off following unsuccessful arrestment
Bounce   Touch-and-go landings
BRC   Base recovery course
BRG   Bearing
Brownshoe   Naval aviation officer
Buddy store   Detachable refueling store
BuNo   Bureau Number (aircraft serial number)
BVR   Beyond visual range
C³   Command, control, and communications
C³I   Command, control, communications, and intelligence
CAG   Carrier air wing commander
CAINS   Carrier aircraft inertial navigation system
CANTRAC   Catalog of Navy Training Courses
CAP   Combat air patrol
CAPTOR   Encapsulated torpedo
CARGRU   Carrier group
CARQUAL   Carrier qualification
CAS   Calibrated air speed; close-air support
CASREP   Casualty reporting system
CASS   Command-activated sonar system
Cat   Catapult
CATCC   Carrier air traffic control center

CAVU   Ceiling and visibility unlimited
CBR   Chemical, biological, & radiological warfare
CBU   Cluster bomb unit
CCA   Carrier controlled approach
CDC   Combat direction center (formerly CIC, combat information center)
Centurion   A flyer who has made one hundred carrier landings
CEP   Circular error probable
CGAF   Coast guard air facility
CGAS   Coast guard air station
CGATC   Coast guard air training center
CH   Channel
CHOP   Change of operational control
CILOP   Conversion in lieu of procurement
CINC   Commander in chief
CINCCENT   Commander in Chief, Central Command
CINCEUR   Commander in Chief, European Command
CINCLANTFLT   Commander in Chief, U.S. Atlantic Fleet
CINCPAC   Commander in Chief, Pacific Command
CINCPACFLT   Commander in Chief, U.S. Pacific Fleet
CINCSOUTH   Commander in Chief, Southern Command
CINCUSACOM   Commander in Chief, U.S. Atlantic Command
CINCUSNAVEUR   Commander, U.S. Naval Forces Europe
CIWS   Close-in weapons system
CLARA   Ball not in sight
Clean   Aerodynamically clean—wheels up, flaps up
CMC   Commandant of the marine corps
CNATECHTRA   Chief of naval air technical training
CNATRA   Chief of naval air training
CNAVRES   Chief of naval reserve
CNET   Chief of naval education and training
CNO   Chief of naval operations
CO   Commanding officer
COD   Carrier on-board delivery
COEA   Cost and operational effectiveness analysis
COMATKWING   Commander attack wing
COMCARAEWWING   Commander carrier airborne early warning wing

COMCARAIRWING   Commander carrier air wing
COMCARGRU   Commander carrier group
COMCRUDESGRU   Commander cruiser destroyer group
COMCVWR   Commander reserve carrier air wing
COMFAIR   Commander fleet air (followed by location)
COMFITWING   Commander fighter wing
COMFLELOGSUPWING   Commander fleet logistics support wing
COMHELTACWING   Commander helicopter tactical wing
COMHELWINGRES   Commander helicopter wing reserve
COMHSLWING   Commander helicopter antisubmarine light wing
COMHSWING   Commander helicopter antisubmarine wing
COMINT   Communications intelligence
COMNAVAIRESFOR   Commander naval air reserve force
COMNAVAIRLANT   Commander Naval Air Force, U.S. Atlantic Fleet
COMNAVAIRPAC   Commander Naval Air Force, U.S. Pacific Fleet
COMNAVAIRSYSCOM   Commander naval air systems command
COMOPTEVFOR   Commander operational test and evaluation force
COMPATWING(S)   Commander patrol wing(s)
COMRESPATWING   Commander reserve patrol wing
COMSAT   Communications satellite
COMSEACONWING   Commander sea control wing
COMSEC   Communications security
COMSECONDFLT   Commander, U.S. Second Fleet
COMSEVENTHFLT   Commander, U.S. Seventh Fleet
COMSIXTHFLT   Commander, U.S. Sixth Fleet
COMSTRIKFIGHTWING   Commander strike fighter wing
COMTHIRDFLT   Commander, U.S. Third Fleet
COMVAQWING   Commander electronic combat wing
CONUS   Continental United States
Corral   Aircraft parking area on a carrier
CPH   Cost per hour
CQ   Carrier qualification
Crunch   A deck-handling mishap involving damage to an aircraft
CSAR   Combat search and rescue
CSP   Contingency support package
CSR   Crew-seat ratio
CTF   Commander Task Force
CV   Multipurpose aircraft carrier

CVBG Aircraft carrier battle group
CVIC Aircraft carrier intelligence center
CVN Multipurpose aircraft carrier (nuclear-powered)
CVW Carrier air wing
CVWR Reserve carrier air wing
CWC Composite warfare commander
DACM Defensive air combat maneuvering
DACT Dissimilar air combat training
DAIR Direct altitude indicator read-out
DAS Direct air support
DECM Deceptive electronic countermeasures
Delta Hold and conserve fuel signal
Det Detachment
DICASS Directional command-activated sonar system
DIFAR Directional frequency analysis and ranging
DIFDEN Duty in a flying status not involving flying
DIFOPS Duty in a flying status involving operational or training flights
Dirty Aerodynamically dirty—wheels down, flaps down
DME Distance-measuring equipment
DOD Department of Defense
DON Department of the Navy
Down Aircraft in a nonflying status
DPRO Defense plant representative office
DST Destructor (a type of mine)
Dud An aircraft, manned and ready for flight, which is unable to be launched
EAF Expeditionary airfield
EAT Expected approach time
ECCM Electronic counter countermeasures
ECM Electronic countermeasures
ECMO Electronic countermeasures officer
EHF Extremely high frequency
ELF Extremely low frequency
ELINT Electronic intelligence
EMCOM Emission control
EMI Electromagnetic interference

EMP   Electromagnetic pulse
EMSP   Enhanced modular signal processor
EO   Electro-optical
EOD   Explosive ordnance disposal
ESLATS   Executive strike leader attack training syllabus
ESM   Electronic surveillance measures
ETA   Estimated time of arrival
ETD   Estimated time of departure
ETE   Estimated time enroute
EVAL   Electronic warfare tactical evaluator
EW   Electronic warfare
EWAC   Electronic warfare aircraft commander
EWC   Electronic warfare coordinator
EWOP   Electronic warfare operator
EXCAP   Expanded capability
FAA   Federal Aviation Administration
FAC   Forward air controller
FACSFAC   Fleet air control and surveillance facility
FAD   Fleet air defense; force activity designator
FAE   Fuel-air explosive
FAF   Final approach fix
FAM   Familiarization
FAMMO   Full ammunition
FCLP   Field carrier landing practice
FDR/FA   Flight data recorder/fault analyzer
FE   Flight engineer
FEBA   Forward edge of battle area
Feet dry   Report made by a flyer crossing a coastline heading inland
FFAR   Folding-fin aircraft rocket
FHP   Flying hour program
FISP   Fly-in support package
FIST   Fleet imagery support terminal
FITCOMPRON   Fighter composite squadron
FITWEPSCOL   Naval Fighter Weapons School (Topgun)
FITWING   Fighter wing
FL   Flight level
FLDO   Flying limited duty officer

FLE Fatigue life extension
FLECOMPRON Fleet composite squadron
FLELOGSUPRON Fleet logistics support squadron
FLIP Flight information publication
FLIR Forward-looking infrared camera
FLOLS Fresnel lens optical landing system
FLTSAT Fleet satellite
FLTSATCOM Fleet satellite communications
Fly One Forward area of a carrier flight deck
Fly Three Aft area of a carrier flight deck
Fly Two Midships area of a carrier flight deck
FM Flight mishap
FMC Full mission capable
FMF Fleet Marine Force
FMFLANT Fleet Marine Force, U.S. Atlantic Fleet
FMFPAC Fleet Marine Force, U.S. Pacific Fleet
FMS Foreign military sales
FNAEB Field naval aviator evaluation board
FOB Forward operating base
FOD Foreign object damage
FORCAP Force combat air patrol
FOSP Follow-on support package
Foul deck A condition in which the carrier landing area is not ready to land aircraft
FPM Feet per minute
FRAMP Fleet replacement aviation maintenance personnel
FRM Flight-related mishap
FRS Fleet readiness squadron
FSD Full-scale development
FSR Flight surgeon's report
FY Fiscal year
Gaggle A group of aircraft flying together
GAU Aircraft gun unit
GBU Guided bomb unit
GCA Ground-controlled approach
GCU Guidance control unit
GFE Government-furnished equipment

Golden Helix   The naval aviator serving on active duty in the navy, marine corps, or coast guard with the earliest date of designation as a naval helicopter pilot
GPB   General-purpose bomb
GPETE   General-purpose electronic test equipment
GPS   Global Positioning System
GPWS   Ground proximity warning system
Grape   Purple-shirted aviation boatswain's mate (Fuel)
Gray Eagle   The naval aviator on active duty with the earliest designation date
Gray Owl   The naval flight officer serving on active duty with the earliest designation date
Gripe   A fault in aircraft status; an "up" gripe still allows safe flight; a "down" gripe must be fixed before further flight
GS   Ground speed
GSE   Ground-support equipment
HAC   Helicopter aircraft commander
HALE   High altitude-low endurance
HARM   High-speed antiradiation missile
HC   Helicopter combat support squadron
HCS   Helicopter combat support squadron special
HDC   Helicopter direction control
HEC   Helicopter element coordinator
HEED   Helicopter emergency escape device
HEELS   Helicopter emergency egress lighting system
HEL   High-energy laser
HELO   Helicopter
HERO   Hazard of electronic radiation to ordnance
HF   High frequency
HFAJ   High-frequency antijam
HFDF   High-frequency direction-finding
HFE   Human factors engineering
HLS   Helicopter landing system
HM   Helicopter mine countermeasures squadron
HMH   Marine heavy helicopter squadron
HMLA   Marine helicopter light-attack squadron
HMM   Marine medium helicopter squadron

HMT   Marine helicopter training squadron
HMX   Marine helicopter squadron (development and executive transport)
HOMS   Hellfire optimized missile system
HOTAS   Hands-on throttle and stick
HQMC   Headquarters Marine Corps
HR   Hazard report
HS   Helicopter antisubmarine squadron
HSL   Helicopter antisubmarine squadron light
HSLWING   Helicopter antisubmarine light wing
HSWING   Helicopter antisubmarine wing
HT   Helicopter training squadron
HUD   Heads-up display
Huffer   Aircraft engine start support equipment
HULTEC   Hull-to-emitter correlation
IADS   Integrated air-defense system
IAF   Initial approach fix
IAM   Inertially aided munitions
IAS   Indicated air speed
ICAO   International Civil Aviation Organization
ICAP   Improved capability
ICLS   Instrument carrier landing system
ICS   Internal communications system
IFARS   Individual flight activity reporting system
IFF   Identification friend or foe
IFR   In-flight refueling
IFT   In-flight technician
IIR   Imaging infrared
ILS   Instrument landing system/integrated logistics support
IMA   Intermediate maintenance activities
IMC   Instrument meteorological conditions
IMINT   Imagery intelligence
INMARSAT   International maritime satellite
INS   Inertial navigation system
INSURV   Inspection and survey
INVG   Integrated night vision goggles
IOC   Initial operational capability
IP   Instructor pilot; initial point

IPADS   Improved processor and display system
IRDS   Infrared detection set
IRR   Individual ready reserve
IRST   Infrared search and track
ISAR   Inverse synthetic aperture radar
JAST   Joint attack strike technology
JATO   Jet-assisted takeoff
JBD   Jet blast deflector
JCN   Job-control number
JCS   Joint Chiefs of Staff
JINTACCS   Joint interoperability of tactical communications and control systems
JTF   Joint Task force
JTIDS   Joint Tactical Information Distribution System
KIAS   Knots indicated air speed
Kilo   Aircraft report indicating mission readiness
LAMPS   Light airborne multipurpose system
LANTFLT   U.S. Atlantic Fleet
LASER   Light amplification by stimulated emission of radiation
LAU   Launcher unit
LCS   Low-cost sonobuoy
LDG   Landing
LDGP   Laser-designated general purpose
LDO   Limited duty officer
LF   Low frequency
LFA   Low frequency active
LGB   Laser-guided bomb
LGTR   Laser-guided training dummy
LHA   Amphibious assault ship (general-purpose)
LHD   Amphibious assault ship (multipurpose)
LLD   Light landing device
LLLTV   Low-light level television
LO   Low observable
LOC   Line of communication
LOE   Level of effort
LOFAR   Low-frequency analysis and ranging
LORAN   Long-range aid to navigation
LOS   Line of sight

LOX Liquid oxygen
LPH Amphibious assault ship (helicopter)
LRD Laser-ranging device
LSE Landing signal enlisted
LSO Landing signal officer
LST Laser spot tracker
LTA Lighter-than-air
MACG Marine air control group
MACS Marine air control squadron
MAD Magnetic anomaly detection
MAG Marine aircraft group
MAGTF Marine air-ground task force
MALS Marine aviation logistics squadron
MALSE Marine aviation logistics support element
MARTD Marine air reserve training detachment
MASS Marine air support squadron
MATSG Marine air training support group
MAW Marine aircraft wing
MAWTS Marine aviation weapons and tactics squadron
MAYDAY International aircraft distress signal
MC Mission commander; mission control; mission capable
MCAF Marine corps air facility
MCALF Marine corps auxiliary landing field
MCAS Marine corps air station
MCATD Marine corps air training detachment
MCM Mine countermeasures
Meatball Red light image in the Fresnel lens landing system
MEB Marine expeditionary brigade
MEDEVAC Medical evacuation
MEF Marine expeditionary force
MER Multiple ejector rack
MEU Marine expeditionary unit
MFD Multi-format display
MIJI Meaconing, intrusion, jamming, interference
MILSTRIP Military standard requisition and issue procedure
MIM Maintenance instruction manual
MIR Mishap investigative report

MLSF   Mobile logistics support force ships
MOA   Military operating area
MOCC   Mobile operations command center
MOD   Modification
MOVLAS   Manually operated visual landing system
MPA   Maritime patrol aircraft
MR   Mishap report
MRT   Maximum rated thrust
MSL   Mean sea level
MSR   Mobile sea range
MTACS   Marine tactical air command squadron
MTBF   Mean time between failures
MTIP   Maintenance Training Improvement Program
MWCS   Marine wing communications squadron
MWSG   Marine wing support group
MWSS   Marine wing support squadron
NA   Naval aviator
NAC   Naval aircrewman
NACES   Navy aircrew common ejection seat
NADEP   Naval aviation depot
NAESU   Naval Air Engineering Support Unit
NAF   Naval air facility
NALC   Naval aviation logistics center
NALCOMIS   Naval aviation logistics command management information system
NAMP   Naval Aviation Maintenance Program
NAMPSOP   Naval Aviation Maintenance Program Standard Operating Procedures
NAMRL   Naval Aviation Medical Research Laboratory
NAMSO   Naval Aviation Maintenance Support Office
NAMTRAGRU   Naval air maintenance training group
NAMTRAGRUDET   Naval air maintenance training group detachment
NAO   Naval aviation observer
NAOMI   Naval Aerospace Operational Medical Institute
NAR   Naval air reserve
NAS   Naval air station

NASA National Aeronautics and Space Administration
NASC Naval Air Systems Command
NATOPS Naval air training and operating procedures standardization
NATSF Naval Air Technical Services Facility
NATTC Naval Air Technical Training Center
NAVAIR Naval Air Systems Command
NAVFAC Naval facility
NAVREPS Naval representatives to Federal Aviation Administration
NAVSTA Naval station
NAVSTKWARCEN Naval Strike Warfare Center
NAWC Naval Air Warfare Center
NAWC–AD Naval Air Warfare Center-Aircraft Division
NAWC–WD Naval Air Warfare Center-Weapons Division
NAWS Naval Air Weapons Station
NDB Nuclear depth bomb
NEC Naval enlisted classification
NFO Naval flight officer
NFWS Naval Fighter Weapons School (Topgun)
NMAC Near midair collision
NMCM Not mission capable–maintenance
NMCS Not mission-capable–supply
NOAA National Oceanic and Atmospheric Administration
NOBC Naval officer billet code
NOTAM Notice to airmen
NRL–FSD Naval Research Laboratory Flight Support Detachment
NSWC Naval Strike Warfare Center
NTDS Navy tactical data system
Nugget New, inexperienced aviator
NVG Night vision goggles
NWP Naval warfare publication
NWS Naval weapons station
OAB Outer air battle
OFT Operational flight trainer (simulator)
OINC Officer in charge
OJN Over-water jet navigation
OLF Outlying landing field
O&MN Operations and maintenance budget (navy)

OOD   Officer of the deck
OPCON   Operational control
OPEVAL   Operational evaluation
OPLAN   Operations plan
OPNAV   Office of the Chief of Naval Operations
OPSEC   Operations security
OPSO   Operations officer
OPTAR   Operating target (funding)
OPTEVFOR   Operational Test and Evaluation Force
ORE   Operational readiness evaluation
OSAP   Ocean surveillance air patrol
OTC   Officer in tactical command
OTCIXS   Officer in tactical command information exchange system
OTH   Over-the-horizon
OTH-T   Over-the-horizon targeting
PAA   Programmed aircraft authorization
PACFLT   U.S. Pacific Fleet
PAR   Precision approach radar
PATRON   Patrol squadron
PATWING   Patrol wing
PAX   Passenger
PC   Plane commander
PD   Probability of detection
PGM   Precision-guided munitions
PIM   Position and intended movement
PLAT   Pilot landing-aid television
PM   Periodic maintenance or preventative maintenance
PMA   Program manager (air)
PMC   Passengers/mail/cargo; partial mission-capable
PMCF   Post-maintenance check flight
PMCM   Partial mission capable–maintenance
PMCS   Partial mission capable–supply
PMRF   Pacific Missile Range Facility
POSIT   Position
PPC   Patrol plane commander
PQS   Personnel qualification standard
Prang   Crash

Pri-fly Primary flight control (aircraft carrier control tower)
PTR Pilot training rate
QA Quality assurance
QEC Quick engine change
RAC Risk assessment code
RADAR Radio detection and ranging
RADHAZ Radiation hazard
RAM Radar absorptive material
RAST Recovery Assist, Securing, and Traversing System
RAT Ram-air turbine
RATACC Radar air traffic control center
RCS Radar cross-section
R&D Research and development
RDT&E Research, development, test, and evaluation
Ready deck Flight deck is ready to recover aircraft
Recce Reconnaissance
Recon Reconnaissance
Respot To reposition aircraft on a carrier deck preparatory to flight operations
RF Radio frequency
RFF Ready for ferry
RFI Ready for issue
RIO Radar intercept officer
ROE Rules of engagement
RON Remain overnight
RPM Revolutions per minute
RPV Remotely piloted vehicle
RRR Rapid runway repair
RVL Rolling vertical landing (V/STOL)
RVTO Rolling vertical takeoff (V/STOL)
RWR Radar warning receiver
RWY Runway
SAM Surface-to-air missile
SAMSON Strike-fighter decoy
Sand blower Low-level mission
SAR Search and rescue; synthetic aperture radar
SASP Single advanced acoustic processor

SATCOM Satellite communications
SDLM Standard depot-level maintenance
SDO Squadron duty officer
SE Support equipment
SEAD Suppression of enemy air defenses
SECNAV Secretary of the navy
SENSO Sensor operator
SERE Survival, evasion, resistance, and escape
SEVAL Senior electronic warfare tactical evaluator
SF Standard form
SIGINT Signals intelligence
Silver Falcon The earliest designated naval aviator or naval flight officer of the ready reserve actively participating in a drilling status
Silver Hawk The marine corps aviator serving on active duty whose designation date precedes that of any other marine corps aviator
SITREP Situation report
SLAM Stand-off land-attack missile
SLAR Side-looking airborne radar
SLATS Strike Leader Attack Training Syllabus
SLCM Surface-launched cruise missile
SLEP Service life extension program
SNDL Standard Navy Distribution List
Sonobuoy Air-droppable floating sound sensor
SOP Standard operating procedure
SQMD Squadron manpower document
SSM Surface-to-surface missile
STOL Short takeoff and landing
STOVL Short takeoff, vertical landing
SUPO Supply officer
SUS Sound underwater signal
SWIP Systems Weapon Integration Program
SYSCOM Systems command
TACAIR Tactical aircraft
TACAMO "Take charge and move out" strategic communications system
TACAN Tactical air navigation system
TACCO Tactical coordinator

TACGRU Tactical air control group
TACINTEL Tactical intelligence
TACMEMO Tactical memorandum
TACNAV Tactical navigation
TACRON Tactical air control squadron
TACTS Tactical aircrew combat training system
TAD Temporary additional duty
TALD Tactical air-launched decoy
TAMPS Tactical Air Mission Planning System
TAR Training and administration of reserves
TARCAP Target combat air patrol
TARPS Tactical air reconnaissance pod system
TAS True air speed
TAT Turn-around time
TD Technical directive
TDY Temporary duty
TECHEVAL Technical evaluation
TEMADD Temporary additional duty
TEMDU Temporary duty
TER Triple ejection rack
TERPES Tactical electronic reconnaissance processing and evaluation system
TFCC Tactical flag command center
Tilley Carrier deck crash crane
TINS Tactical inertial navigation system
TIT Turbine inlet temperature
TJS Tactical jamming system
TN Tactical navigation
T/O Takeoff
TOT Time on target
TOW Tube-launched, optically sighted, wire-guided missile
TRACOM Training command
TRAM Target recognition and attack multisensor
Trap Successful carrier arrestment
TRARON Training squadron
TRAWING Training air wing
TRE Tactical receive equipment

Acronyms, Abbreviations, and Terms   421

TRNGO   Training officer
TSC   Tactical support center
UAV   Unmanned aerial vehicle
UHF   Ultra-high frequency
UIC   Unit identification code
UNCLAS   Unclassified
UNK   Unknown
VA   Attack squadron
VAQ   Tactical electronic warfare squadron
VAST   Versatile avionics shop test
VAW   Carrier airborne early-warning squadron
VC   Fleet composite squadron
VERTREP   Vertical replenishment
VF   Fighter squadron
VFA   Strike fighter squadron
VFC   Fighter composite squadron
VFR   Visual flight rules
VHF   Very high frequency
VLAD   Vertical linear array DIFAR
VLO   Very low observable
VMA   Marine attack squadron
VMAQ   Marine tactical electronic warfare squadron
VMAT   Marine attack training squadron
VMC   Visual meteorological conditions
VMFA   Marine fighter attack squadron
VMFA(AW)   Marine all-weather fighter attack squadron
VMFAT   Marine fighter attack training squadron
VMFT   Marine fighter training squadron
VMGR   Marine aerial refueler/transport squadron
VMGRT   Marine aerial refueler/transport training squadron
VOD   Vertical on-board delivery
VOR   Visual omni range
VP   Patrol squadron
VPU   Patrol special projects unit
VQ   Fleet air reconnaissance squadron, or strategic communications squadron
VR   Fleet logistics support squadron

VRC Fleet logistics support squadron (COD)
VS Sea control squadron
V/STOL Vertical/short takeoff and landing
VT Training squadron
VTOL Vertical takeoff and landing
VX Air test and evaluation squadron
VXE Antarctic development squadron
W&B Weight and balance
WC Work center
WOD Wind over deck
WSIP Weapon system improvement program
WST Weapons system trainer (simulator)
WX Weather
X Experimental
XMIT Transmit
XO Executive officer
Yellow sheet Aircraft flight record
ZIP-LIP Communications minimized
ZT Time zone
Zulu Universal Coordinated Time

INDEX

Abraham Lincoln, USS (CVN 72), 48, 160, 163, 328
ACDUTRA, 266, 268–69, 272
aces and aerial victories, 6, 32, 41, 374–85
Achille Lauro incident, 47
aerographer's mate (AG), 187, 201–2, 213
aeronautical engineer, 19
aerospace engineering duty officers (AEDO): as astronauts, 116; career path of, 121; command opportunities for, 113; designator, 108, 113, 115; evolution of, 112–13; program, 112–14, 130; as test pilots, 227–28
Aerospace Maintenance and Regeneration Center (AMARC), 394
aerospace maintenance duty officers (AMDO): career path of, 122; designator, 108, 114; evolution of, 114; program, 114–15; reserve, 271
aerospace medicine, 240–58
Aerospace Research Pilot School, U.S. Air Force, 130, 132
Agana, NAS, 331

airborne early warning wing, 144–45
Airborne Log, 395
air combat element, 286–87
Air Command and Staff College, 129
aircraft carriers, 158–86; antisubmarine, 160; ASW module, 124; characteristics, 162; combat direction center, 124; in crisis response, 164–66; deployment pattern, 186; deployment preparation, 185; description of, 158–59, 162; development of, 159–60, 164, 166; electronic warfare module, 125; as flagship, 184–85; naval reserve force, 161 nuclear-powered, 161, 183; organization of, 166–68; postcommand tours in, 128; restricted availability, 185; rotation of, 185–86; as symbol of power, 166; vulnerability of, 164
aircraft carriers, command of: authority to command, 166–67; commanding officer, 155, 166–67, 170, 182, 184–85; Morrow Board, 166; path to command, 182–84

aircraft carriers, flight operations of, 171–82; ACLS, 182; angled deck, 159, 179; arresting gear, 179–80, 184; barricade, 181; catapult officer, 174, 176–77, catapults, 159, 162, 172, 174–75, 178; elevators, 159, 162; flight deck, 159, 162; flight deck control; 173; flight deck jerseys, 171–72; foreign object damage, 171, 173; Fresnel lens, 177–78; ground support equipment, 168; jet blast deflectors, 159; landing, 56; landing aids, 182; launch procedures, 171–76; MOVLAS, 177; plane guard, 171, 174; recovery procedures, 176–82; "starboard delta," 171–72

aircraft carriers, organization of: AIMD, 168; Air Boss, 168; Air Department, 168, 184, 196; air officer, 168; air traffic control center, 176; departments, 167; executive officer, 167; "mini-boss," 168

aircraft designation system, 316–18

Aircraft Intermediate Maintenance Department (AIMD), 115, 167–68, 201, 207

aircraft maintenanceman (AF), 118, 200–201

Aircraft Mishap Board (AMB), 233, 243

aircraft types, fixed wing: A-1 (AD) Skyraider, 32–33, 36–37, 40, 380–81; A-3 (A3D) Skywarrior, 35, 37, 98; A-4 (A4D) Skyhawk, 35, 45, 60, 66–69, 71, 316, 334, 338, 353, 383; A-5 Vigilante, 40, 46; A-6 (A2F) Intruder, 35, 40–41, 44, 46–49, 52, 98, 144–45, 281, 291, 318–19, 333, 338; A-7 Corsair II, 40–41, 46–47, 49–50, 52, 98; A-12, 48; AJ Savage, 31; AV-8 Harrier, 44, 46, 69, 286, 292, 295, 323, 341; B-29 Superfortress, 279; B-52 Stratofortress, 42; Boeing 737, 47; C-2 Greyhound, 40, 60–62, 73–75, 98, 104, 170, 319, 334, 337; C-4, 308, 326, 352; C-18, 325; C-24, 325; C-9 Skytrain II, 264, 293, 319, 337; C-12 Huron, 98, 190, 293, 318–19, 337; C-20 Gulfstream II/III, 293, 308, 320, 352; C-130 Hercules, 46, 74–75, 264, 288, 295, 301–2, 304, 307, 309, 320, 337–38, 342, 351–54; C-135, 156, 325; DH-4, 277; E-2 Hawkeye, 40, 47, 60–62, 73–75, 80–81, 85, 89, 98, 112, 124, 170, 301, 309, 320, 333; E-6 Mercury, 48, 60–62, 74–75, 78, 98, 103, 320, 337; EA-6B Prowler, 40, 42, 47, 49, 69, 78–79, 289, 292, 295, 318–19, 333, 341; F/A-18 Hornet, 46–47, 49–50, 53, 69, 80, 84, 88, 90, 98, 112, 170, 175, 177, 204, 225, 232, 265, 283, 290, 292–93, 295, 321, 333, 335–36, 338, 341–42, 353, 385; FH Phantom, 31; F2H Banshee, 32; F3D Skyknight, 33; F3H Demon, 35; F4D Skyray, 35; F4F/FM Wildcat, 20, 22, 25, 278; F-4 (F4H) Phantom II, 40, 46, 291, 325–26, 353, 380–84; F4U Corsair, 28, 31, 32, 278, 280; F-5 Tiger II, 292, 320, 342; F6F Hellcat, 20, 25–26, 28, 31, 32, 353, 376; F7U Cutlass, 35; F8F Bearcat, 31, 353; F-8 (F8U) Crusader, 38, 40, 46, 281, 380–84; F9F Panther/Cougar, 32, 34, 35, 353; F11F Tiger, 35, 353; F-14 Tomcat, 43, 46–50, 53, 69, 80, 90, 97–98, 156, 170, 178–79, 189, 192, 205, 212, 226, 260, 316, 321, 334–35, 338, 385; F-86 Sabre, 326; F-111, 47; FJ Fury, 31, 35; G-8, 301, 308, 326, 352; Hawk, 69; HS-2L, 276; J4F Widgeon, 298; Loening OL-5, 297–98; MiG-17 Fresco, 380–84; MiG-19 Farmer, 383, MiG-21 Fishbed, 50, 380–84; MiG-23 Flogger, 47, 385; Mustang, 20; N-9, 276; Curtiss NC, 297, 373, 392; OV-10 Bronco, 39, 291; P-2 (P2V) Neptune, 31, 39; P-3 (P3V) Orion, 39–40, 43–44, 46, 48–49, 74, 78, 98–99, 101, 124, 126, 188, 194, 212, 222, 269, 318, 321, 336–38; P4M Mercator, 31; P-5 (P5M) Marlin, 39; PBJ Mitchell, 24; PBM Mariner, 31; PBY Catalina, 14, 16–17, 23, 298; PB2Y Coronado 23; PB4Y (P4Y) Liberator/Privateer, 21, 23–24, 29, 33; PC-9 Mark II (JPATS), 62–64; PV Ventura/Harpoon, 21, 23; R-6, 276; R4D Skytrain, 37; S-2 (S2F) Tracker, 36, 75; S-3 Viking, 44, 46–47, 53, 69, 78, 79, 98, 105, 124, 170, 180, 321, 337–38; SB2C Helldiver, 25, 31; SBD Dauntless, 20, 24–25, 278, 318; Sopwith Camel, 8; Spitfire, 20; SU-22 Fitter, 46, 385;

T-1 Jayhawk, 60, 74–75, 78–80; T-2 Buckeye, 60, 64, 66, 69, 71, 74, 74, 79–80, 321, 338; T-34 Turbomentor, 59–64, 74–75, 77–78, 119, 342; T-37, 59–61, 63–64, 72, 74–75, 321, 334, 335, 338; T-38 Talon, 326; T-39 Sabreliner, 60, 78–80, 293, 321, 337–38; T-43, 60, 78–79; T-44 Pegasus, 60, 72–74, 323, 338; T-45 Goshawk, 54, 60, 63–64, 66, 69–72, 323, 338; TBF/TBM Avenger, 20, 22, 24–25, 25, 31; Triad, 2; U-1 Otter, 326; U-6 Beaver, 326; U-21 Ute, 326; U-16 Albatross, 301; U-25 Falcon, 301–2, 307, 323, 351–52; U-38, 308, 326, 352; V-22 Osprey, 54, 323; Vought UO-4, 297; X-26, 326; X-31, 326
aircraft types, rotary wing. *See* helicopter types
aircrewmen, 192–94, 200, 213, 300, 314
aircrew survival equipmentman (PR), 81, 212–13, 310
air facilities, naval, list of, 349
airfields, hosting naval aviation, 349–50
Air Force, U.S.: Air Education and Training Command, 60; fleet replacement training, 96; joint training with, 59, 72, 74, 77–79; SERE, 82. *See also* squadrons, Air Force
airships. *See* LTA aircraft
air stations, Coast Guard, 304–5, 351–52
air stations, Marine Corps, 291, 350
air stations, naval, 128, 346–50
air traffic controller (AC), 118, 187, 198–99, 213
Air War College, 129
air warfare director. *See* director, air warfare
air weapons stations, naval, 225, 266, 336, 338, 350
Akagi, Japanese carrier, 17
Akron, USS (ZRS 4), 11
Alameda, NAS, 339, 348
alcohol, 252
Aleutians, 17, 23
America, flying boat, 3
America, USS (CV 66), 43, 47, 49–50, 159, 161, 327
amphibious assault ships (LHA, LHD, LPH), 279

Ancient Order of the Pterodactyl, 386
anymouse, 234–35
Approach/Mech, 234–35, 395
Armed Forces Staff College, 125, 130
Armstrong, Neil A., 37, 358, 373
Army Command and General Staff College, 129
Army War College, 130
Association of Aviation Ordnancemen, 386
Association of Naval Aviation, 387, 397
associations, naval aviation, 386–90
astronauts, naval, 116–17, 130, 356
Atlanta, NAS, 267, 333, 337, 340, 348
Atlantic Command, U.S., 148
Atsugi, NAF, 143, 148, 332–35, 337, 349
attack wings, 144–45
auxiliary landing fields, 348
aviation administrationman (AZ), 211, 213
aviation boatswain's mate (AB), 118, 174, 183–84, 196–98, 213; aircraft handling (ABH), 191, 196–98; fuels (ABF), 191, 196–97; launching and recovery equipment (ABE), 191, 196–97
Aviation Career Incentive Pay (ACIP), 132–33
Aviation Continuation Pay (ACP), 133–34
aviation duty officer (ADO), 48, 108–10
aviation electrician's mate (AE), 118, 200, 213, 309
aviation electronics technician (AT), 118, 187, 192–93, 208, 213, 309
aviation experimental psychologist, 81, 242–43
aviation machinist's mate (AD), 118, 188–89, 199–200, 213, 309
Aviation Maintenance Officers Course, Senior, 115
Aviation Maintenance Officers School, 114
aviation medical safety officer, 243
aviation medicine schools, 241
Aviation Officer Continuation Pay (AOCP), 133
aviation optometrist, 242–43
aviation ordnanceman (AO), 118, 206–7, 213
Aviation Ordnance Officer Career Course, 118–19
aviation physiologist, 81, 242–43, 246

Aviation Preflight Indoctrination (API), 57–59, 77
Aviation Repair and Supply Center, Coast Guard, 306
Aviation Safety Command Course, 234
aviation safety officer, 105, 234–35
Aviation Safety Officer Course, 234, 243
aviation storekeeper (AK), 202–3, 213
aviation structural mechanic (AM), 118, 187, 203–6, 213; Coast Guard, 309–10; hydraulics (AMH), 203–5; safety equipment (AME), 203–4; structures (AMS), 203–5
aviation supply officer (ASO), 115, 271, 315
aviation support equipment technician (AS), 118, 206–8, 213
Aviation Technical Training Center, Coast Guard, 305–6, 310
Aviation Training Center, Coast Guard, 304–5
aviation warfare systems operators (AW), 118, 209–11, 213, 270; Coast Guard, 310; and mandatory NEC, 194; as rescue swimmers, 195–96
aviator, naval, 56; as astronaut, 116–17; career pattern of, 119–20; and carrier command, 166–67; definition of, 108–9; designator, 107–8; and transfer to AEDO, 113
avionics technician (AV), 118, 200, 208–9

Barbers Point, NAS, 143, 336, 348
Barking Sands, PMRF, 350
Base Closure and Realignment Commission, 218, 224
Basic Naval Aviation Officer School (BNAO), 111
Bataan, USS (LHD 5), 329
battle force, 153–54
battle groups, carrier, 142, 153–54, 163, 168, 183–84; commander of, 147, 154–55, 170, 184–85; as instruments of policy, 186
Beaufort, MCAS, 341–42, 350
Belleau Wood, USS (LHA 3), 328
Bellinger, Patrick N. L., 3, 361
Bennett, Floyd, 10, 361, 370
Billingsley, W. D., 346

Birmingham, USS (CL 2), 2–3
Bismarck Sea, USS (CVE 95), 28
Block Island, USS (CVE 21), 22
blood donation, 256
Blue Angels (Naval Flight Demonstration Squadron), 242, 353–55
Bogan, Gerald F., 366
Bogue Field, MCALF, 350
Bolt, John F., 33, 379
bombing, 5–6, 10, 16–17, 25, 34
Bon Homme Richard, USS (LHD 6), 329
Bordelon, Guy B., 32, 378
Boxer, USS (CV 21), 32
Boxer, USS (LHD 4), 329
Boyington, Gregory "Pappy," 366, 370, 377
Brand, Vance D., 358
Brunswick, NAS, 144, 188, 336–37, 348
Bunker Hill, USS (CV 13), 29
Bureau of Aeronautics, 10, 110, 215–16, 229, 262
Bureau of Medicine, 245–47
Bureau of Ordnance, 215–16
Bush, George, 49, 54
Byrd, Richard E., 10, 360, 370

Cactus Air Force, 22
caffeine, 253
Cambodia, fall of, 42
Camp Pendleton, MCAS, 98, 295, 340–41, 350
Carl, Marion E., 362–63
Carl Vinson, USS (CVN 70), 46, 160, 328
Carrier Airborne Early Warning Weapons School, 157
carrier air wings, 53, 128, 143, 149–50, 185; commander ("CAG"), 146–47, 154–55, 170–71; composition of, 170; deputy commander, 147; described, 168–69; list of, 148; reserve, 146, 168, 262–66
carrier group, 124, 151, 153, 184; chief of staff, 154; commander, 154, 185
carrier qualification, 65–66, 69, 71, 74, 109
Carrier Striking Force, Commander, 151
catapult, aircraft, 3. *See also* aircraft carriers
Cecil Field, NAS, 98, 144, 265, 295, 335, 337, 341, 348, 390
Center for Naval Tactical Warfare, 155, 157
Central Command, U.S., 149, 152–53
chain of command: administrative,

Index   427

137–38, 284–91; joint, 138; operational, 147–48, 151, 153
Chambers, Washington Irving, 2, 346, 364
Chase Field, NAS, 147
Cherry Point, MCAS, 295, 341–42, 350, 390
Chevalier, Godfrey De C., 8, 361
Chief of Naval Air Training, 141, 146
Chief of Naval Operations (CNO), 138, 214, 217, 237–38, 262, 396; Office of (OPNAV), 138–39, 215, 343; vice chief, 139
chief warrant officer (CWO), 108, 117–18
China Lake, NAWS, 225, 338, 350
Chitose, Japanese carrier, 27
Chiyoda, Japanese carrier, 27
Chu Lai, Vietnam, 280
Civil Aeronautics Administration, 346
class-desk officers, 220
Clifton, Joseph C., 367
close air support, 10, 283, 292; in Korea, 32, 279; in Nicaragua, 276; in Okinawa, 279; in the Philippines, 278; in Vietnam, 281
Coast Guard, missions of, 300–303
Coast Guard aviation: area commander, 303–4; aviators, 56, 308; Chief, 303; Direct Commission Aviator Program, 56, 302, 308; enlisted ratings, 309; force reductions, 302; history of, 14, 296–302; organization of, 303–6; naval aviation pilots, 188; naval flight officers, 308–9; Officer Candidate School, 56–57, 308; rescue swimmers, 310
coffee, 253
College of Naval Warfare, 129
command, squadron, 59, 96, 99–100, 122, 147, 235, 239; by NFOs, 111; screen, 127; tour, 127–28
Command and Staff College, Marine Corps, 129
Commander, Naval Air Force, U.S. Atlantic Fleet, 138, 141
Commander, Naval Air Force, U.S. Pacific Fleet, 138, 141
Commander, Naval Air Reserve, 263, 265
Commander, Naval Shore Activities, U.S. Atlantic Fleet, 141
Commander, Operational Test and Evaluation Force, 141

commanders, types of, 141, 143
Competency Aligned Organization (CAO), 218, 224
Composite Warfare Commander, 155
Conrad, Charles, Jr., 358, 373
Constellation, USS (CV 64) 38, 159, 161, 327
Coral Sea, Battle of the, 16
Coral Sea, USS (CV 43), 43, 48
Corpus Christi, NAS, 59–60, 72–74, 147, 338, 349
Crippen, Robert L., 358
cruiser-destroyer group, 124, 153, 155, 184
cryptanalysis, 16
cryptologic officers, 108; as NAOs, 112
Cunningham, Alfred A., 3–4, 275–76, 360
Cunningham, Randall, 41, 54, 378
Cunningham Air Museum, 390
Curtiss, Glenn H., 2–3, 6, 346, 361

Dallas, NAS, 341
Davis-Monthan AFB, 394
Davison, F. Trubee, 261
D-day, 20
decompression, 241
Defense Language Institute, 130
Defense Management Review, 217
defense plant representative (DPRO), 114
Defense Systems and Management College, 115
Denton, Jeremiah, 54
Department Head Screen Board, Aviation, 126
designators, naval aviation, 107–8
Diego Garcia, NAF, 349
director, air warfare (N88), 139–40, 215, 235, 284; adviser in strike warfare, 140; special assistant for publications and operational records (N88H), 85
Doolittle, James H. "Jimmy," 16
Doyle, Austin K., 366
Driscoll, William "Willie," 45, 378
Dwight D. Eisenhower, USS (CVN 69), 43, 49, 160, 328

Early and Pioneer Naval Aviators Association (Golden Eagles), 387
Eastern Solomons, Battle of the, 22
Edwards AFB, 132

El Centro, NAF, 68, 349, 355
Electronic Combat Weapons School, 157
electronic combat wing, 145
Ellyson, Theodore G. "Spuds," 2, 361
El Toro, MCAS, 98, 285, 295, 340, 342, 350, 391–92
Ely, Eugene B., 2, 360
Emil Buehler Naval Aviation Library, 392
engineering duty officers (EDOs), as astronauts, 116
enlisted aviation warfare specialist (EAWS), 195, 213
enlisted personnel: in Blue Angels, 355; Coast Guard, 309–10; contributions of, to flight operations, 187–88; as naval aviation pilots, 188, 192; and nonaviation ratings, 191; rate training and, 189–91; ratings mergers, 191; and strike in ratings, 189–90; supervision of, 191
Enterprise, USS (CV 6), 15–17, 22–23, 25, 28–29
Enterprise, USS (CVN 65), 35, 39, 47, 160, 327
Erickson, Frank A., 364
Essex, USS (CV 9), 19, 25, 32, 36, 159–60, 390–91, 394
Essex, USS (LHD 2), 329
European Command, U.S., 148
executive officer: of aircraft carrier, 167; of squadron, 127–28
exploration, 10, 31, 37
Exxon Valdez incident, 302
eye care, 253–54

Fairchild AFB, 82
Fallon, NAS, 157, 336, 340
fear, 248
Field Flight Evaluation Board, 243
Field Naval Aviator Evaluation Board, 243
fighter wing, 144–45
First Aeronautical Detachment, 5
First Aviation Force, 276
First Aviation Squadron, 276
fitness, physical, 55, 57, 193, 195, 248–50
fitness reports, 121, 134
Flately, James H., Jr., 362
fleet air commanders, 141–43, 153
Fleet Logistic Support Wing, 266

Fleet Readiness Squadron (FRS), 79–81, 96, 119–20, 126–27, 146, 232; command of, 96, 99, 128; instructors, 96, 123; and training of enlisted personnel, 190, 193, 200, 206, 208, 210
Fleet Replacement Aviation Maintenance Training Program (FRAMP), 96, 190, 199–200
Fleet, U.S. Atlantic, 87, 96, 138, 143–45, 148, 151, 298, 343
Fleet, U.S. Pacific, 14, 89, 96, 138, 145, 148, 151, 343
fleets, numbered: Second, 138, 151–52; Third, 138, 151–53; Fifth, 138, 151–52, 185; Sixth, 31, 138, 148, 151–53, 185; Seventh, 31, 138, 151–53, 185
flight engineer, 187, 193–94, 200, 206
Flightlines, 396
flight lunches, food poisoning in, 250
flight officer, naval (NFO), 56; and AEDO transfer, 113; as airborne communications officer, 78; as astronaut, 116–17; career pattern of, 119–28; and carrier command, 166–67; Coast Guard, 308–9; designator, 107–8; as electronic evaluator, 78; evolution of, 110–11; as flight test crew, 227–28; as navigator, 78; as radar intercept officer (RIO), 80; and squadron command, 111; as tactical coordinator, 78; training of, 77–81; as weapons and sensors officer (WSO), 80
flight surgeons, 81, 115, 147, 233, 240–47; as astronauts, 356, 358; as aviation medicine specialists, 242; in Blue Angels, 355; relations with, 244; as residents in aerospace medicine, 242; role of, 243–44; Special Board of, 247; training program for, 241–42
Flyby, 388, 396
flying boats, 3, 11, 21, 31, 33–34, 36, 40
flying limited duty officer (FLDO), 48, 56–57, 108, 117
Folmar, Jesse, 33
Forrestal, USS (CV 59, AVT 59), 31, 35, 39, 50, 159
Fort Benning, 81
Fort Myers, 1
Fort Worth, NAS, 266–67, 334, 337, 342, 349

Foss, Joseph J., 366, 371, 377
Foundation, 388, 396
Franklin, USS (CV 13), 29
Franklin D. Roosevelt, USS (CVA 42), 39
Futenma, MCAS, 285, 340, 342, 350

Garn, Jake, 54
Garrett, H. Lawrence, 54
Geiger, Roy M., 361
George Washington, USS (CVN 73), 50, 160, 162, 328, 344
Gibson, Robert "Hoot," 358
Glenn, John H., 37, 54, 280, 357, 373
Glenview, NAS, 263
Grampaw Pettibone, 235
Graybiel, Ashton, 367
Great Depression, 12
Grumman, Leroy R., 362
Guadalcanal, USS (LPH 7), 47, 390
Guadalcanal campaign, 22–24
Guam, USS (LPH 9), 46, 328
Guantanamo Bay, NS, 350

Haiphong Harbor, mining of, 41
Hall of Fame, Carrier Aviation, 393
Hall of Honor, Naval Aviation, 359–68
Hall of Honor, Test Pilot, 393
Halsey, William F. "Bull," 16, 30, 363
Hammann, Charles H., 6, 371
Harkin, Tom, 54
Harry S. Truman, USS (CVN 75), 50, 160, 328
Hawaii, MCB, 285, 351
hazardous duty, 247–48
heat injury, 257
Heinemann, Edward H., 363
helicopter antisubmarine wing, 144–45
helicopter antisubmarine wing light, 144–45
Helicopter Landing Trainer (HLT), 76
helicopter types: H-1 Iroquois (Huey), 39, 41, 98, 284, 293, 295, 318, 323, 340–41; H-1 Sea Cobra/ Super Cobra, 41, 46–47, 293–95, 318, 324, 338, 340–41; H-2 Seasprite, 41, 44, 98, 270, 272, 324, 329, 332; H-3 Sea King, 41, 46, 48, 97, 293, 301, 318, 324, 331–32, 334, 338, 340; H-6 Cayuse, 326; H-34 (HSS) Seabat, 36; H-46 Sea Knight, 41, 46, 86, 97, 283, 293, 295, 324, 329, 331, 340–41; H-53 Sea Stallion/ Super Stallion/Sea Dragon, 41–42, 45– 48, 97, 283, 288, 293, 295, 324, 331, 332, 339–41; H-57 Sea Ranger, 60, 72325, 333; H-58 Kiowa, 326; H-60 Seahawk/Jayhawk/ Blackhawk, 46, 48, 52, 87–88, 97, 152, 170, 307, 325, 329, 331–32, 338, 340, 351– 52; H-65 Dolphin, 307, 309, 325; Mi-8 Hip, 385
Helicopter Wing Reserve, 266
Henderson Field, 22–23
high-frequency direction finder, 22
Hinton, Walter, 7
Hiroshima, atomic bombing of, 30
Hiryu, Japanese carrier, 17
Hiyo, Japanese carrier, 26
Ho Chi Minh Trail, 41
Hook, The, 389, 396
Hornet, USS (CV 8), 16–17, 22–23
Hunsaker, Jerome C., 364
hunter-killer escort carrier groups, 22
hyperventilation, 241, 254–56
hypoxia, 241, 254–56

Identification Friend-or-Foe (IFF), 26
Inchon, USS (LPH 12, MCS 12), 328–29
Independence, USS (CV 62), 46, 49, 159, 161, 327
Independence, USS (CVL 22), 19, 25, 28
Industrial College of the Armed Forces, 130
Ingalls, David S., 6, 363, 376
instructor: astronaut, 117; flight, 61, 124, 146; NATOPS, 123; reserve, 268
Integrated Program Teams, 218, 224
intelligence officer, 108, 119; as NAOs, 111–12
Intrepid, USS (CVS 11), 390–91
Intrepid Museum, 390–91
Iwakuni, MCAS, 350
Iwo Jima, Battle of, 27
Iwo Jima, USS (LPH 2), 279, 328

Jacksonville, NAS, 97–98, 144, 195, 332, 336–37, 344, 349, 390
John C. Stennis, USS (CVN 74), 50, 160, 328
John F. Kennedy, USS (CV 67), 43, 46, 48–50, 65, 159, 161, 265, 328

430 Index

Johnson, Lyndon, 38
Joint Attack Strike Technology, 53–54
Joint Military Intelligence College, 123, 130
Joint Primary Aircraft Training System (JPATS), 54, 62–64

Kadena, NAF, 349
Kaga, Japanese carrier, 17
Kaman, Charles, 367
kamikaze, 27–29
Kaneohe Bay, MCAF, 336, 339–41, 350–51
Keesler AFB, 202
Keflavik, NAS, 349
Kerwin, Joseph P., 358
Key West, NAS, 349
Khe Sanh, Vietnam, 282
Kingsville, NAS, 60, 64, 66, 71, 147, 338
Kitty Hawk, USS (CV 63), 35, 37, 51, 159, 175, 327

landing signal officer (LSO), 69, 102, 147, 159, 172, 176–81
Langley, USS (CV 1), 8, 15
Lehman, John, 54
Leigh light, 22
Lemoore, NAS, 98, 145, 148, 295, 335, 349
Lexington, USS (CV 2), 9, 15–16
Lexington, USS (CV 16, AVT 16), 43, 50, 394
Leyte Gulf, Battle of, 26
liberty engine, 4
lighter-than-air craft. *See* LTA aircraft
limited duty officer (LDO), 114, 118; designator, 108, 117; and paths of advancement, 118; program, 117. *See also* flying limited duty officer
Liscome Bay, USS (CVE 56), 25
Little Rock AFB, 98
Logistic Support Activities, 218, 228
Long Island, USS (AVG 1, CVE 1), 19
Los Angeles, USS (ZR 3), 11
Lovell, James A., 357, 373
low-pressure chamber, 246, 255
LTA aircraft, 4, 11–12, 21, 31, 36, 86

MacDiarmid, Donald B., 363
Macon, USS (ZRS 5), 12
Maddox, USS (DD 731), 38
maintenance check pilot, 123

Maintenance Training Improvement Program, 195
Marianas, Battle of the, 27
Marine Aeronautic Company, 275; First, 276
Marine air control groups, 286–87
Marine aircraft groups, 286–87
Marine aircraft wing aviation support element, 285
Marine aircraft wings, 281, 284–85, 287, 293
Marine air-ground task force, 287
Marine Corps, Headquarters, 284, 289
Marine Corps Air-Ground Museum, 391
Marine Corps aviation: aerial navigators, 295; air-ground team, 283; air reserve, 277, 279; Aviation Observer School, 112; carrier operations, 277–79, 281, 284; commandant, 214; deputy chief of staff for aviation, 140, 284; helicopter development, 36, 279; history of, 3, 10, 275–83; replacement training squadrons, 96, 295; restructuring, 284
Marine Corps Association, 396
Marine Corps Aviation Association, 388, 397
Marine Corps Gazette, 396
Marine expeditionary force, 287
Marine wing support groups, 286–87
Maritime Patrol, 390, 396
markings, aircraft, 343–45
Martin, Glenn L., 361
Mayaguez incident, 42–43
Mayport, NS, 97, 332, 350
McCain, John S., 27
McCampbell, David M., 364, 371, 375–76
McCandless, Bruce, 44, 358
McCutcheon, Keith B., 364
McEntee, William, 1
medals, 358, 369–73
Medical Service Corps, 242
medication, 250–51
Melca, Leonard M., 297
Memphis, NAS, 190, 198–99, 200, 204, 206–8, 210–11, 213
Meridian, NAS, 59, 64–65, 67, 147, 190, 203, 338, 349
Michaelis, Frederick, 367
midshipmen, 188

Midway, Battle of, 16–17
Midway, USS (CV 41), 31, 35, 43, 49–50, 159–60
Mildenhall, NAF, 349
mines, 3, 41–42, 45
Miramar, NAS, 98–145, 148, 285, 334–35, 341–42, 349, 390
Misawa, NAF, 349
mishaps, 230, 232–34, 236
missiles, air-to-air, 35, 43
mission commander, 123, 126
Mississippi, USS (BB 23), 3
Mitscher, Marc A., 25, 361–62
Moffett, William A., 10, 12, 110, 262, 360, 371
Moffett Field, 265, 332, 336, 349
Moorer, Thomas H., 364
Musashi, Japanese battleship, 26
museums, naval aviation, 390–94
Mustin, Henry C., 3, 10, 365

Nagasaki, atomic bombing of, 30
Naples, NSA, 142, 350
Nassau, USS (LHA 4), 329
National Aeronautics and Space Administration (NASA), 116, 356
National Air and Space Museum, 392
National Museum of Naval Aviation, 359–60, 392–93, 396
National War College, 130
NATOPS, 96, 105, 112, 235–39, 249; Advisory Group, 237; coordinator, 237–39; evaluator, 238; instructor, 123, 239; manuals, 236–37; model manager, 238; officer, 105
Naval Academy, U.S., 2, 13, 56–57, 123, 275, 346
Naval Aeronautics, Office of, 3
Naval Aerospace and Operational Medicine Institute (NAOMI), 241–42, 247
Naval Aircraft Factory, 11
Naval Aircrew Candidate School, 193, 210
Naval Air Intelligence Officers Course, 119
Naval Air Maintenance Training Group, 199–200
Naval Air Pacific Repair Activity, 228
Naval Air Reserve: affiliation, 268–69; air combat adversary role, 265; augment activities, 267–68; electronic warfare training, 265; force-level reductions, 265; history of, 13, 30, 260–65, 268; number of squadrons, 84, 267; organic airlift, 264; organization, 265–67; promotion, 273; reserve force squadrons, 270–71; retirement, 273; total force concept, 274; training and pay, 271–73
Naval Air Reserve, Commander, 263, 265
Naval Air Reserve Command, 263
Naval Air Reserve Training Command, 262
Naval Air Systems Command, 113–14, 215, 222–23, 225, 228–29; comptroller, 219, 225; deputy commander for acquisition and operations, 219; headquarters, 218–19; history of, 215–18; reserve units, 268
Naval Air Technical Services Facility, 228
Naval Air Test and Evaluation Museum, 392
Naval Air Training Command, 56, 59, 77, 81, 117, 124, 262, 295, 392, 343
Naval Air Warfare Center, 113, 130, 133, 218–19, 223, 225–28; Aircraft Division, 198, 225–27; Weapons Division, 225, 227
naval aviation, history of: during Berlin crisis (1961), 36, 263; between world wars, 10–14; in Bosnia, 54; in Cold War, 35–36, 43–48; during Cuban missile crisis, 37; drug interdiction and, 48; early developments in, 1–2; and first aircraft purchase, 2; and first combat (Mexico), 3; and first naval aviator, 2; and first shipboard landing, 2; and first takeoff from ship, 2; and first transatlantic crossing, 6; and force-level reductions, 48–49, 52; in Grenada, 46, 164; during Iran hostage crisis, 46; in Iran-Iraq War, 47; in Korean War, 32–35, 164, 262; in Lebanon, 46, 164; during Libyan crises, 46–47, 164; in 1950s, 23; in Persian Gulf War, 48–51, 142, 153, 164, 264; and post–Gulf War crises, 51–52; and postwar demobilization, 30; procurement problems and, 48–49; during *Pueblo* crisis, 41; in Six-Day War, 41; in Vietnam War, 37–43; in World War I, 4–6; in World War II, 14–30

Naval Aviation Acquisition Operation Council, 219
naval aviation cadet (NAVCAD), 53, 56
Naval Aviation Depots (NADEPs), 114, 218–19, 222–24
Naval Aviation Engineering Service Unit, 228
Naval Aviation Maintenance Office, 228
Naval Aviation Museum Foundation, 388, 396
Naval Aviation News, 235, 396
naval aviation pilots (NAPs), 188
Naval Aviation Schools Command, 57, 77, 118
Naval Aviation Science and Technology Office, 221
Naval Aviation Supply Office, 215, 219, 221, 229
Naval Aviation Systems Team, 214–15, 229
Naval Command and Staff College, 129
Naval Deficiency Act, 296
Naval Doctrine Command, 155
Naval Enlisted Classification Codes (NECs), 191–92, 194, 200, 206, 208
Naval European Rework and Repair Activity, 228
Naval Fighter Weapons School (Topgun), 157
Naval Helicopter Association, 397
Naval Historical Center, 85, 235, 396
Naval History, 389, 397
Naval Institute, U.S., 359, 388–89, 397; *Proceedings,* 389, 397
Naval Medical School, 241
naval militia, 260–61; First Yale Unit, 261
Naval Ordnance Missile Test Station, 227
Naval Postgraduate School, 105, 115, 123, 129, 131, 234
Naval Reserve, Chief of, 263, 265
Naval Reserve Flying Corps, 261–62
Naval Reserve Officers Training Corps (NROTC), 56–57, 123
Naval Safety Center, 234, 237
Naval Space Command, 117
Naval Strike Warfare Center, 157
Naval Surface Reserve Force Command, 263
Naval Technical Training Center Corry Field, 79
Naval Training Systems Division, 225, 227
Naval War College, 127, 129
Navy Department, 260
Navy League of the United States, 397
Navy–Marine Corps Intelligence Training Center, 119
New England Air Museum, 393
New Orleans, NAS, 267, 335–37, 349
New Orleans, USS (LPH 11), 328
New River, MCAS, 97, 112, 295, 339–41, 350
Nimitz, Chester W., 16
Nimitz, USS (CVN 68), 43, 46, 160–62, 174, 328
Nixon, Richard, 41
Norfolk, NAS, 60, 75, 80, 97–98, 141, 144, 234, 265, 331–34, 337, 340, 349
North Atlantic Treaty Organization (NATO), 151, 153, 283
North Carolina, USS (ACR 12), 3
North Island, NAS, 97–98, 141, 145, 195, 266, 331, 337–38, 349

observer, naval aviation (NAO), 110–12, 313
Oceana, NAS, 98, 144, 148, 295, 333–34, 336, 349, 390
oceanographic officers, 108, 116; as NAOs, 112
Officer Candidate School, 56–57, 123
O'Hare, Edward H. "Butch," 15, 366, 372, 377
Oil Pollution Act, 302
Okinawa, Battle of, 29
Ommaney Bay, USS (CVE 79), 27
Operation Earnest Will, 47
Operation El Dorado Canyon, 47
Operation Endsweep, 42
Operation Frequent Wind, 42
Operation High Jump, 31
Operation Linebacker I, 41
Operation Linebacker II, 42, 164
Operation Market Time, 39
Operation Prairie Fire, 47
Operation Rolling Thunder, 38, 41, 164
OPNAV. *See* Chief of Naval Operations
Oriskany, USS (CVA 34), 38
Osborn, Robert, 231, 235
outlying landing fields, 348

Pacific Command, U.S., 148
parachutist, naval, 81, 213; wings, 314–15
Patriots Point Naval and Maritime Museum, 393
patrol wings, 128, 143–46
Patuxent River, NAS, 222, 225–26, 338, 339
Pearl Harbor, 14
Peleliu, USS (LHA 5), 329
Pennsylvania, USS (ACR 4), 2
Pensacola, NAS, 60, 74, 76–78, 111, 118–19, 147, 190, 198–200, 203–4, 206–8, 210–13, 241, 296, 338, 392
periodicals, naval aviation, 395–97
Philippines campaign, 27
Philippine Sea, USS (CV 47), 31–32, 36
photographer's mate (PH), 211–13
physical examination, flight, 241, 243–47
Pima Air and Space Museum, 394
Pirie, Robert B., 363
plane captain, 187, 189, 192, 200, 204
Point Mugu, NAWS, 225–26, 331, 336, 338, 350
Pride, Alfred M., 364
Princeton, USS (CVA 37), 32
Princeton, USS (CVL 23), 26
prisoners of war (POWs), 42
procuring contract officer, 225
program executive officer (PEO), 215, 217–18, 225, 228
program manager (PMA), 217, 221, 228
program manager, assistant: for engineering, 220; for logistics, 221
Pterogram, 386

Quantico, MCAF, 340, 350; MCB, 391

radar, 22, 36
Radford, Arthur W., 362
Randolph AFB, 60, 78–79, 308
Ranger, USS (CV 4), 12, 14, 19, 20
Ranger, USS (CV 61), 49–50, 159, 263
Read, Albert C., 7, 361, 373
Ready Reserve, 269–70
Reese AFB, 59–61, 74
refugees, Vietnamese, rescue of, 43
remotely-piloted vehicles (RPVs), 50, 89
Rennel Island, Battle of, 23
rescue swimmers, 195–96; badge, 213; Coast Guard, 310; required of AWs, 195–99, 210
Retired Reserve, 270
retro-rockets, 21
Richardson, Holden C., 361
Robinson, Robert G., 6, 363
Rodgers, John, 2, 11
Ronald Reagan, USS (CVN 76), 50, 160, 328
Roosevelt, Franklin, 14, 298
Roosevelt, Theodore, 369
Roosevelt Roads, NS, 142, 334, 350
Rosendahl, Charles E., 362
Rota, NS, 350
Rotor Review, 387, 397
Russell, James S., 365
Ryujo, Japanese carrier, 22

Sable, USS (IX 81), 18
safety, aviation, 230–36
Safety Program, Naval Aviation, 232
St. Lo, USS (CVE 63), 27
Saipan, USS (LHA 2), 328
Samuel B. Roberts, USS (FFG 58), 47
San Diego Aerospace Museum, 394
Santa Cruz, Battle of, 23
Saratoga, USS (CV 3), 9, 15, 22, 25, 28
Saratoga, USS (CV 60), 43, 47, 49–50, 159
Schilt, Christian F., 366–67, 372
Schoech, William A., 366
scuba policy, 258
Scuttlebutt, The, 389
Sea-based Weapons and Advanced Tactics School, 157
sea control wing, 144–45
seaplanes, 4, 10, 12
Sea Power, 397
Selected Air Reservist, 270
Selected Reserve, 270
selection boards, 134–36
SERE, 82
Shenandoah, USS (ZR 1), 11
Shepard, Alan B., Jr., 37, 356, 365, 373
Sherman, Forrest P., 368
Shokaku, Japanese carrier, 23, 26
Short Airfield for Tactical Support (SATS), 280
Sigonella, NAS, 331, 349
Sikorsky, Igor I., 365

Silver Eagles Association, 389
Sims, William S., 11
Skyhook, Project, 31
Smith, Edward C., 298
Soryu, Japanese carrier, 17
Soucek, Apollo, 367
South Weymouth, NAS, 267, 349
space, naval aviation in, 54, 116–17, 356–58
spacecraft: Apollo, 357–58, 373; Gemini, 357, 373; Mercury, 356–57, 373; *Mir,* 358; Skylab, 358, 373; Space Shuttle, 356, 358, 373
Spangenberg, George A., 365
Special Operations Command, U.S., 149
Sperry, Lawrence B., 365
squadron, 83–106; commanding officer, 99–100, 104, 127–28; command master chief, 106; designations, 86–95; executive officer, 99–100, 127–28; lineage, 84–85; nicknames, 85; numbers, 84; traditions, 85; watch organization, 106
squadron departments: administrative, 100, 122, 150; command services, 100; maintenance, 102–4, 122, 150; operations, 100, 102, 122, 150; safety, 104–5, 122, 150, 234; training, 102, 150
squadrons, Air Force, 59; 35th FTS, 59–61, 72, 75; 52nd FTS, 60, 74; 562nd FTS, 60, 78
squadrons, Coast Guard, 298–99
squadron types, Marine Corps: H&HS, 291; HMA, 95; HML, 95; HMLA, 287–88, 340; HMH, 288, 339; HMM, 288, 340; HMT, 97–98, 288, 295, 341; HMX, 288, 341; MACS, 286; MALS, 287; MASS, 286; MTACS, 286; MWCS, 287; MWSS, 287; SOES, 289, 291; SOMS, 289, 291; VMA, 290, 341; VMAQ, 290, 341; VMAT, 290, 295, 341; VMFA, 266, 290–91, 293, 341–42; VMFA(AW), 290–91, 342; VMFAT, 98, 291, 295, 342; VMFT, 291, 342; VMGR, 291, 342; VMGRT, 291, 295, 342
squadron types, Navy: HAL, 95; HC, 86, 91, 97–98, 195, 266, 331; HCS, 91, 266–67, 331; HM, 87, 91, 97–98, 332; HS, 87, 91, 97, 195, 266, 332, 345; HSL, 87–89, 91, 97–98, 266, 332; HT, 87, 92, 333; TACRON, 95; VA, 92, 98, 333, 345, 380–81; VAQ, 88, 92, 98, 170, 265–66, 333, 345; VAK, 95; VAW, 60, 75, 80–81, 88, 98, 170, 266, 333–34, 345; VC, 49, 89, 92, 334; VF, 46, 48, 50, 87, 89–90, 93, 98, 170, 266, 334–35, 345, 380–85; VFA, 50, 87, 90, 93, 98, 170, 266, 335, 345, 385; VFC, 93, 266–67, 336; VFP, 95; VP, 89, 93, 98–99, 128, 144, 261, 266, 269, 336, 395; VPU, 94, 336; VQ, 94, 98, 101, 103, 170, 336–37, 345, 395; VR, 94, 98, 266–67, 337; VRC, 94, 98, 104, 170, 337, 345; VRF, 95; VS, 94, 98, 105, 170, 337–38, 345, 395; VT, 59–60, 64–66, 72, 74–75, 77–81, 87, 95, 98, 111, 119, 338; VX, 89, 95, 130, 141, 338; VXE, 95, 338; VXN, 95;
stand-off land attack missile (SLAM), 49
Stewart Field, 342
Stockdale, James B., 54, 368, 372
Stone, Elmer F., 7, 296–97, 362, 373
Strategic Command, U.S., 149
strategic communication wing, 145
strike fighter wing, 144–45
submarines: detection of, 3–6, 19–21; and sonobuoys, 21; U-boats, 4, 14, 22, 36
Sugden, Charles E., 296
surface warfare officers: as astronauts, 116; as battle group commanders, 184–85
Sweet, George C., 1

T-45 Training System (T45TS), 69–72
Tactical Air Command Center (TACC), 287
tactical air-launched decoy (TALD), 49
Tactical Air Reconnaissance Pod System (TARPS), 212
Taiho, Japanese carrier, 26
Tailhook Association, 389, 396
Talbot, Ralph, 6, 372
TAR (training and administration of reserves), 107, 114, 262–63, 271
Tarawa, USS (LHA 1), 46
task force: commanders, 143; examples of, 153; TF 24, 298; TF 84, 144
Taylor, David W., 6
Test and Evaluation Master Plan, 219
Test Pilot School, British Empire, 130, 132
Test Pilot School, U.S. Naval, 113, 130–31

Thach, John S., 362
Theodore Roosevelt, USS (CVN 71), 46, 160, 178, 328
Ticonderoga, USS (CVA 14), 38
Tinker AFB, 98, 143, 145, 337
tobacco, 252
Tonkin Gulf incident, 38
Topgun, 157
Top Level School, Marine Corps, 130
torpedo, 10, 16–17, 25; acoustic, 22
tours of duty: department head tour, 125–27; "disassociated" sea tour, 124, 133; first sea tour, 119–23; first shore tour, 123; major command tours, 128; postcommand tours, 128; second sea tour, 124–25; squadron command tour, 127–28
Towers, John H., 2–3, 7, 360, 373
training, fleet readiness, 96–98
training, undergraduate flight, 56–77; air combat maneuver, 66, 68; entry requirements, 56–57; formation flying, 64, 66–67, 71, 76; instruments, 64, 66–67, 72, 74–76; mission planning, 68; pipelines, 59; syllabi, 64; weapons, 68
training air wings, 59–60, 143, 146–47
training devices: crew positional, 146; interactive computers, 63, 71, 74, 77; Radio Instrument Orientation Trainer, 77; simulators, 58, 63–64, 69, 74, 97, 116, 146; Training and Integration System, 72; weapon systems trainers, 146
training pipelines, aviator: E-2/C-2, 60, 62, 73–74; E-6, 60–62, 74; helicopter, 60–62, 72, 75–77; maritime, 60–62, 72–74; primary, 59–63; strike, 59–60, 62, 64–68, 71
training pipelines, NFO: primary, 60, 77; intermediate tactical, 60, 78; advanced ATDS, 60, 78, 80; advanced strike, 60, 78–79; advanced strike/fighter, 60, 78–80; maritime navigator, 60, 78
Trapnell, Frederick M., 363–64
Treasury Department, 296–97, 300
Truman, Harry, 32
Tustin, MCAS, 98, 295, 339–41, 350

Versailles Treaty, 8, 11
vertigo, 256
Vietnam, South, fall of, 42
Vietnam War, 37–43, 263, 281–82, 301
visual acuity, 245
Von Paulson, Carl C., 297
VP International Association, 390, 396

warfare qualification, 123
warrant officer, chief. *See* chief warrant officer
Washington, NAF, 336–37, 349
Wasp, USS (CV 7), 14, 19, 23
Wasp, USS (LHD 1), 46, 329
Weisner, Maurice F. "Mickey," 368
Weitz, Paul, 358
Whidbey Island, NAS, 98, 143, 145, 157, 295, 333, 336–37
White, Henry C., 298
Whiting, Kenneth, 5, 362
Whiting Field, NAS, 59–60, 62, 76, 147, 242, 333, 338
Wilbur, Ted, 235
Willow Grove, NAS, 267, 336–37, 339
wings (insignia), 311–15
wings, functional, 143–44
Wings of Gold, 387, 397
Wolverine, USS (IX 64), 18
women in naval aviation, 18–19, 45, 53
Works Progress Administration, 346
World War I, 3–6, 164, 260–62, 275–76, 297
World War II, 14–30, 159, 164, 262, 277–79, 297–300
Wright brothers, 1–2

Yamamoto, Isoroku, 17
Yamato, Japanese battleship, 29
Yellow Sheet, The, 388, 397
Yorktown, USS (CV 5), 15–17
Yorktown, USS (CVS 10), 393
Young, John W., 358, 373
Yuma, MCAS, 287, 341, 350

Zuiho, Japanese carrier, 23, 27
Zuikaku, Japanese carrier, 27

About the Editor

Lt. Cdr. Richard R. Burgess, USN (Ret.), was a P-3C patrol plane navigator, tactical coordinator, and mission commander with Patrol Squadrons 9 and 45, deploying several times to operating sites in the Atlantic, Pacific, and Mediterranean. He also served on the USS *George Washington* (CVN 73) during its first deployment and on the staff of Commander, Carrier Group 4. A graduate of Auburn University, he was commissioned in 1975 and was designated a naval flight officer the following year.

He earned a master's degree in strategic intelligence at the Defense Intelligence College and spent three years as an analyst of Soviet submarine operations with the Defense Intelligence Agency. He was editor of *Naval Aviation News* magazine from 1989 to 1993. The father of six children and stepfather of three, he lives in Virginia Beach with his wife, Eleanor.

The Naval Institute Press is the book-publishing arm of the U.S. Naval Institute, a private, nonprofit society for sea service professionals and others who share an interest in naval and maritime affairs. Established in 1973 at the U.S. Naval Academy in Annapolis, Maryland, where its offices remain today, the Naval Institute has more than 85,000 members worldwide.

Members of the Naval Institute receive the influential monthy magazine *Proceedings* and discounts on fine nautical prints, ship and aircraft photos, and subscriptions to the bimonthly *Naval History* magazine. They also have access to the transcripts of the Institute's Oral History Program and get discounted admission to any of the Institute-sponsored seminars offered around the country.

The Naval Institute's book-publishing program, begun in 1898 with basic guides to naval practices, has broadened its scope in recent years to include books of more general interest. Now the Naval Institute Press publishes about 100 titles each year, ranging from how-to books on boating and navigation to battle histories, biographies, ship and aircraft guides, and novels. Institute members receive discounts of 20 to 50 percent on the Press's nearly 600 books in print.

Full-time students are eligible for special half-price membership rates. Life memberships are also available.

For a free catalog describing Naval Institute Press books currently available, and for further information about U.S. Naval Institute membership, please write to:

Membership & Communications Department
U.S. Naval Institute
118 Maryland Avenue
Annapolis, Maryland 21402-5035
Telephone: (800) 233-8764
Fax: (410) 269-7940